men of the earth

An Indian couple eating, painted by John White
in the late sixteenth century. Thomas Hariot wrote of
the Indians: "They are verye sober in their eating
and trinkinge, and consequently verye longe lived
because they doe not oppress nature. . . . I would to God
we would followe their exemple."

Theire sitting at meate.

men of the earth

An Introduction to World Prehistory

"The Lord created man of the earth,
and turned him into it again."

Ecclesiasticus 17:1

Brian M. Fagan

University of California, Santa Barbara

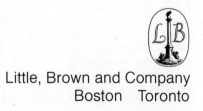

Little, Brown and Company
Boston   Toronto

Library of Congress Catalog Card No. 73-21223

First Printing

Published simultaneously in Canada
by Little, Brown & Company (Canada) Limited

Printed in the United States of America

credits

Cover: Sixteenth-century painting by John White of Indians fishing. Copyright the British Museum.

The sources for the text figures appear below, except for those given with the illustrations. Much of the art that was drawn for this book is the work of Richard H. Sanderson; some illustrations are by Graphics Group Inc. The author thanks the publishers, photographers, and illustrators for granting permission to use their material. The figures without specified credits have been drawn especially for this book.

Frontispiece: Copyright the British Museum.

Chapter 1: 1.2 Redrawn from Colin Renfrew, "New Configurations in Old World Prehistory," *World Archaeology,* 1970, 2,2. *1.3* From Sir Mortimer Wheeler with permission of the Society of Antiquaries of London. *1.4* From *Invitation to Archeology* by James Deetz. Copyright © 1967 by James Deetz. Reprinted by permission of Doubleday & Company, Inc.

Chapter 4: 4.1 and *4.4* Adapted from *Glacial and Quaternary Geology* by R. F. Flint. Copyright © 1971 by John Wiley and Sons. Reprinted by permission of John Wiley & Sons, Inc., the author, and *(4.4)* Dr. Julius Büdel. *4.2* Redrawn from K. P. Oakley, *Frameworks for Dating Fossil Man,* Weidenfeld & Nicolson, Ltd. *4.3* Redrawn from Karl Butzer, *Environment and Archaeology,* Aldine Publishing Company. *4.5* Based on Ian Cornwall, *Ice Ages,* figure 31 (London, John Baker, A. & C. Black, Ltd.; New York, Humanities Press, Inc.).

Chapter 5: 5.2a Adapted and *5.3* Reprinted with permission of Macmillan Publishing Co., Inc., from *The Ascent of Man* by David Pilbeam. Copyright © 1972 by David Pilbeam. *5.5* By Jay H. Matternes; *5.8* J. Desmond Clark; *5.9a,b,* and *c* After Lowell

So many people have criticized and worked over this book that I cannot hope to expose them for what they are — unmerciful critics. All I can do is dedicate *Men of the Earth* to them with deep gratitude, and also to

> Jacquie and Ralph, with love
> Bob and Merle, the best neighbors in the world
> Freda, Milton, and Woody who bullied, encouraged,
>   and entertained
> Rochelle who took everything apart
> Phyllis who typed
> and Brazen Beasts everywhere.

"Canst thou draw out leviathan with an hook?" — Job 41:1

to the reader

Men of the Earth represents an attempt to write a straightforward account of human history from the origins of man up to the beginnings of literate civilization. This book assumes that the reader has not previously studied archaeology. Technical terms have been kept to a minimum and are defined in parentheses where they first occur. Definitions of commonly used technical terms appear in the glossary at the back of the book.

Anyone who takes on a task having the magnitude of a world prehistory must make several difficult decisions. One such decision was to gloss over many heated archaeological controversies and sometimes to give only one side of an academic argument. But each chapter has notes — also at the back of the book — that are designed to lead you into the more technical literature and the morass of agreement and disagreement that characterizes world prehistory.

The structure of *Men of the Earth* is comparatively straightforward. Part One deals with general principles of archaeology, theoretical views of the past, the Pleistocene, and the theory of evolution. The remainder of the book is devoted to the story of human prehistory. Each major section is preceded by an essay outlining some features of various stages of prehistory and discussing, where appropriate, the major theories that seek to explain how events such as the origins of cities occurred. I would advise you to pay close attention to the tables, which put cultural names, sites, dates, and other subdivisions of prehistory into a framework. The tables in Chapter 4 are particularly important as you progress through Parts Two and Three. Key dates and terms appear in the margins to give you a sense of chronological direction throughout the text. Your attention is also directed to the note about radiocarbon dates that starts Chapter 13 on page 202.

Dates quoted in this prehistory are generally stated in years "before present" (B.P.) for dates earlier than 20,000 years ago. More recent dates, later than 19,999 years ago, are quoted in A.D./B.C. terms and related to the death of Christ, as is normal practice. The date of 20,000 as a change-over point is arbitrary. Dates near 20,000 are handled in such a way as to be most logically understood either B.P. or A.D./B.C. being used as circumstances warrant.

For readers interested in calibrating radiocarbon dates, we have added a simplified calibration table, compiled from a detailed paper on the subject published while this book was being set (Table 13.2, page 212).

All measurements are given in both metric and nonmetric units. Metric equivalents are used as the primary unit except in the case of miles/kilometers. More readers conceive of long distances in miles, so it seemed logical to use them first.

to the instructor

Reactions of fellow archaeologists to the news that I was writing a world prehistory have ranged from ones of enthusiasm to the view that I was crazy. Indeed, sometimes I have wished that the book had never been started. Difficult decisions had to be made and challenging problems had to be resolved — all of which are less pressing in the classroom, where more flexibility in presentation is possible. To place the book into a pedagogical context, a summary of the necessary decisions follows.

One immediate problem was the deluge of archaeological literature. An enormous and seemingly never-ending flood of books and periodicals has gushed across my desk. Pleistocene geochronology alone has changed radically in the past few years. The new calibrated radiocarbon chronologies have caused major adjustments in thinking about world prehistory. Cultural process and the advent of systems approaches have begun to alter traditional views of prehistory. Above all, reliable field data from hitherto unexplored areas of the world are changing many ideas about such basics as the origins of agriculture.

Men of the Earth is as up-to-date as possible. I have probably missed some critical references and misled readers with some wrong information, but I hope that instructors will update this account from their specialized knowledge. One major realization from this project has been how difficult it is to keep current with the literature, even within my own field of archaeology. Soon it will be a full-time job to keep up with the progress of archaeology: truly the days of the specialist are upon us.

The question of geographical imbalance has always been in the back of my mind. Inevitably, courses reflect the instructor's own catholic interests and depth of knowledge. A book on world prehistory cannot. The tendency is to look at prehistory in ethnocentric terms, from a

European or an American perspective in most instances. This view seems patently wrong in a time of ardent internationalism. I have tried to give "equal time" to all parts of the world, although paucity of material has sometimes forced me back into well-trodden stamping grounds. I am bound to be accused of missing key sites or areas. To such castigations I can only plead *mea culpa* and the limitations of space and cost.

This book was designed to give a coherent story of world prehistory, a conscious decision on my part. Everyone who works with beginning students has to balance strict scientific accuracy and terminological precision against the dangers of misinformation and overstatement. I have tried to avoid a catalog and have deliberately erred on the side of overstatement. After all, the objective in a first course is to introduce the student to a fascinating and complex subject. The overstatement is more likely to be remembered and to stick in his mind. It can always be qualified at a more advanced level, leaving the complexities of academic debate to more specialized syntheses and to advanced courses. The important truth that students should learn early in the game is that science deals not with absolute truth, but with successive approximations to the truth. Half a truth is better than no truth at all.

The final issue concerns theoretical orientation. Here anyone rash enough to tackle a world prehistory balances on the horns of a delicately poised and sharp-pointed dilemma. I have decided not to case this book within the framework of a tightly structured theoretical position. My reasons are pragmatic. Nearly everyone who teaches archaeology has a theoretical bias that comes across in his courses. Most instructors prefer to choose their course content in the context of this bias and to impose their own theoretical cast on the basic material.

The issue of general laws of cultural process is being intensely debated. An intensive search for such laws is in progress. Some argue that general laws are essential to any account of world prehistory; others disagree, maintaining that world prehistory is too complex a subject to permit general laws or a theoretical context that is all-embracing. Furthermore, they argue, such laws as have been drafted are so generalized as to be virtually platitudinous.

I believe that the individual instructor should have the option to structure his prehistory course within the framework of general laws and whatever theoretical position he chooses to maintain. For this reason, I have written *Men of the Earth* without an overwhelming theoretical framework. If there is a pervasive theme, it is the gradual progress of mankind as a member of the world ecological community. Both the ecological approach and systems models offer exciting possibilities for the future study of culture process.

Finally, I would like to thank the eight reviewers who read the draft of the book. Some of their comments were rude, which was good for the manuscript. Others were polite, which was good for my morale. But they were always constructive and helpful, which made the constant process of compromise possible. Without their help this book would never have been completed.

contents

men of the earth

"We are concerned here with methodical digging for systematic information, not with the upturning of earth in a hunt for the bones of saints and giants or the armory of heroes, or just plainly for treasure."
Sir Mortimer Wheeler

I
prehistory

1

archaeology

the antiquity of man

Man has long been curious about his ultimate origins, and his curiosity has been manifested in legend, in folklore, and through systematic inquiry. Archaeological research is nothing new. During the sixth century B.C., King Nabonidus of Babylon dug under his palace in search of his ancestors. Ancient Chinese and Classical writers speculated about the ages of stone, copper, and iron through which man had passed on his long way to civilization. The Greeks lived in a small Mediterranean world surrounded by prehistoric tribes. They were aware of the diversity of mankind, of the strange customs and exotic art objects made by barbarian peoples on the fringes of their known world.

550 B.C.

A.D. 52

During the Middle Ages the dogma of the Christian church dominated Western thinking, and men were comfortable with the story of man's creation as set out in the first chapter of Genesis. "Time we may comprehend," wrote antiquary Sir Thomas Browne in A.D. 1539, "It's but six days elder than ourselves." In 1650 the celebrated Archbishop Ussher of Armagh, Northern Ireland, used the complicated genealogies in the Bible and proclaimed that the world was created in 4004 B.C. Dr. Lightfoot of Oxford went even further and dated the Creation to 9:00 A.M., October 23, 4004 B.C. Before the Creation stretched the vast eternity of God: man's beginning was labeled, cataloged, and fully accepted.[1]*

A.D. 1650

As early as the thirteenth century, the European world had become aware of the Mongols through the travels of Marco Polo and the conquests of Genghis Khan. Later, maritime discoveries simply added to the bewildering diversity of mankind. The sixteenth and seventeenth centuries brought a quickening of interest in maritime voyaging and exploration. Hardy mariners from the Atlantic seaboards of western Europe ventured far southward toward the tip of Africa and to the New World in search of China. Expeditions returned with gold and other valuable raw materials, occasionally bringing back an Indian or an African as an example of the strange peoples living "exotic" lives in faraway countries. "How falls it out that the nations of the world, coming all of one father, Noe, doe varie so much from one another, both in bodie and minde?" asked Renaissance writer Du Bartas.[2]

A.D. 1650 and later

Seventeenth- and eighteenth-century philosophers were fascinated by the American Indian and the South Sea islanders. The concept of the "noble savage" became fashionable. The life of primitive peoples was painted as a desirable Adam-and-Eve-like existence. Others spoke of Western civilization as if it were the highpoint of mankind's achievement, a level of culture to which all men aspired. Seventeenth-century scholars became fascinated with the earlier history of their own countries. Had "noble savages" lived in Europe before known history began with the Romans? Soon wealthy gentlemen were digging into ancient Egyptian tombs, Greek temples, well-known prehistoric monuments such as Stonehenge in England, and Roman earthworks looking for the past. They found a mass of prehistoric artifacts, many of them comparable to the strange artifacts brought back from Africa and America by merchant adventurers. By the mid-sixteenth century all sorts of speculations were circulating about the nature of the people whose lives were marked only by conspicuous monuments. "They were, I suppose, two or three degrees less savage than the Americans," wrote British antiquarian John Aubrey about the ancient Britons in the 1660s.

A.D. 1659–1670

The tools of prehistoric man were familiar sights in private collections and museums three hundred years ago, including crudely flaked stone axes found in river gravels and plowed fields all through Europe. Such stones were dismissed by many scientists as "thunderbolts." But Indian stone tools were so similar to many "thunderbolts" that some archaeologists changed their minds and recognized the flaked stones as the tools of very primitive men. Today we know the "thunderbolts" were stone axes made over 100,000 years ago.

A.D. 1700

In 1715, a stone ax was found with the bones of an elephant in gravel beds under the City of London. Other axes were found in the same levels of river gravels and lake beds as the bones of such extinct animals as the saber-toothed tiger and the long-tusked elephant. The finds sparked considerable speculation. How could it be, people asked, that man had lived in the same world as long as extinct animals that had not lived in Europe for thousands of years? Had man lived in another world before Ussher's date of 4004 B.C., a world overwhelmed by Noah's flood? Did not these finds conflict with the Biblical story of the Creation? There

A.D. 1715

seemed to be no time for all of prehistory to fit into the six thousand years between the Creation and A.D. 1800.

A ferocious academic debate began between theologians and the scientists. In 1859 it moved into a new phase with the widespread acceptance of the notion that man had an enormously long history, one that extended back many thousands of years before 4004 B.C.[3] The new philosophy resulted from a number of scientific developments. Geologists William Smith and Sir Charles Lyell showed that the earth had been formed by processes of deposition, erosion, and other natural geological phenomena. Earlier scholars thought the world was formed by a series of catastrophic floods that had successively terminated life in time for the creation of a new order as stated in the Bible. Noah's flood was regarded as the last of these inundations. Biologist Charles Darwin's theory of evolution by natural selection allowed scientists to envision a process of continual evolution of man resulting from an origin among his ancient ape relatives. French archaeologist Jacques Boucher de Perthes provided evidence that man had lived at the same time as certain extinct animals, when he discovered hundreds of stone axes and animal bones in the gravels of the Somme Valley in northern France.

A.D. 1859

anthropology, archaeology, and history

The nineteenth-century world was one in which human frontiers expanded rapidly and interest in the past flourished. Napoleon's expedition to the Nile in 1798 introduced many people to the fascinating world of ancient Egypt. The settlement of the American West revealed new and exciting horizons in the New World. European kings supported scientific expeditions to uncover the ruins of Mesoamerica. British imperialism reigned in the Near East and India, and British and French diplomats set out to dig in the abandoned mound villages of the Near East in search of the origins of agriculture and of ancient civilizations mentioned in the Bible.[4] Sir Richard Burton, David Livingstone, and other dedicated travelers penetrated deep into Africa and revealed a fascinating kaleidoscope of black tribes who had a long but unknown history. The mysterious Orient was explored by both European and American merchants as the isolation of China and Japan began to melt away in the face of Western technology and aggressive military adventures. The incredible diversity of man was fully revealed to Western eyes for the first time.

A.D. 1798

Anthropology, often defined as "the study of man," came into its own in the mid-nineteenth century as scholars began to study the exotic peoples found by the explorers.[5] Early anthropologists speculated on the progress and degeneration of man, trying to discover why some people had developed more complex societies while others had remained hunters or peasant farmers living a precarious existence under a constant threat of famine.

The effect of Victorian imperialism was the erection of artificial boundaries transcending long-established cultural, linguistic, and racial boundaries. Prehistoric peoples were abruptly forced into an industrial, literate, and aggressive civilization. A watered-down and often tawdry version of Western culture was transplanted to wide areas of Africa and Asia, where, in this century, for the first time many prehistoric societies have emerged into the domain of written history. The postwar years have seen the emergence of many new nations, often situated in areas where written records and history books began with the advent of nineteenth-century explorers, missionaries, and, later, colonial rule.

Our own intellectual curiosity about our origins has been transformed among many of the world's nations and ethnic minorities into an impelling search for historical traditions long submerged by colonial rulers or alien historical educational systems. While many societies may feel little identity with the earliest ape-men, they do look back closer in time, at least as far as the origins of their own traditional cultures, little modified from prehistoric times until the nineteenth century. In contrast, many readers will undoubtedly think of archaeology as a journey into nostalgia for a simpler and less complicated past when the pressures of twentieth-century life and instant communication were less compelling.

human culture

Both anthropologists and archaeologists study "culture," the latter concentrating on extinct cultures. But what exactly is culture? Scholars have produced all sorts of definitions. Culture is a distinctively human attribute, defined many years ago by anthropologists Clyde Kluckhohn and William Kelly as "historically created designs for living, explicit and implicit, rational and irrational, and non-rational, which exist at any given time as potential guides for the behavior of man."[6]

We all live within a culture, be it middle-class American, Greek, Bushman, and so on. Our own culture places much emphasis on the automobile and the television set. The Bushmen rely on the bow and arrow for their livelihood. We all live in a world whose social customs are culturally determined. All cultures are made up of human behavior and its results; they consist of a complex and constantly interacting set of variables.

Human culture is never static, always adjusting to both internal and external change, whether environmental, technological, or societal. It has increased in complexity since the first appearance of men on this planet.

The first humans had few artifacts, a rudimentary communication system, and a simple economy. Compare their culture with that of the Egyptian Pharaoh Tutankhamun, for example, and it is obvious that human cultures have developed great complexities. The story of human history is to a large degree the history of the development of human cultures and of cultural evolution through time.

Archaeologists study human cultures by working with the tangible remains of human activity, with the tools, food residues, and other finds preserved in archaeological sites. Less tangible aspects of human culture such as social customs or rules of social descent are almost impossible to reconstruct from archaeological data, except under a few carefully controlled circumstances.

From time to time we shall refer to archaeological groupings, for example, the "Acheulian" culture or the "Magdalenian" culture. Such "technocomplexes" and "culture-groups" are part of an archaeologist's regular vocabulary. They consist of the material remains of human culture preserved at a given point in space and time at several sites, concrete expressions of the common social traditions that bind together a culture. In other words, when we speak of the Magdalenian culture, we refer to the archaeological culture that represents a prehistoric social system, defined in a context of time and space, that has come down to us in the form of tools or other durable objects. The term "Magdalenian" is quite arbitrary, derived in this case from the cave site, La Madeleine, France, where the tools of the culture were first discovered.

The geographical extent or content of any archaeological culture is also defined somewhat arbitrarily, but as precisely as possible, so that the use of an archaeological term has an exact implication for other scholars. Much of the archaeological data summarized in this book consists of carefully compiled chronological sequences of archaeological cultures often extending over thousands of years of prehistoric time.

archaeology and the archaeologist

Archaeologists have become familiar figures on television screens and in the pages of popular periodicals. To most people, archaeology is synonymous with excavation, digging for the past. Although the stereotyped, almost *New Yorker* image of the bearded or pith-helmeted digger is rapidly passing into history, excavation is often regarded as a form of informal treasure hunt in search of statues, gold, and rich graves. Although many digs do yield spectacular finds, archaeology has moved a long way from being merely a search for valuable objects. Archaeology has developed both as a branch of historical enquiry and as part of anthropology. It has become a sophisticated field of research, pursued with a battery of technical aids and scientific methods. Today's archaeologist uses computers and slide rules as well as detailed theoretical models and hypotheses, rigorously tested by data obtained in meticulous excavations and from detailed study of the resulting finds in his laboratory.[7] We now seek information about lifeways, cultural processes, and human adaptations in prehistoric times.

team research

Fortunately, the archaeologist can rely on the assistance of scholars from other disciplines, too. Botanists and zoologists can identify seeds and bone fragments from ancient living sites, throwing light on prehistoric diets. Geologists study the lake beds, gravels, and caves in which many tools from the early millennia of human history are found. Paleontologists and paleobotanists, specialists in the evolution of mammals and plants, study the bones of extinct animals and the pollens of long-vanished plants. They help reconstruct ancient climates, which have fluctuated greatly through man's long history. Chemists and physicists have developed radioactive methods of dating, based on volcanic rocks and organic substances such as bone and charcoal found in archaeological sites. These techniques have produced a rough chronological framework for human history that extends back over two million years. Much data on human evolution and the physical characteristics of early humans are furnished by physical anthropologists, who study the skeletal remains of prehistoric man.

Then, too, the archaeologist relies on the findings of historians and cultural anthropologists for assistance. Early documentary records of the deeds of kings and of political events aid excavations in the Nile Valley and the Near East. Historians can help explain Indian responses to white expansion in the Midwest, where long-established cultural traditions were abandoned as the newcomers scattered the older inhabitants of the country. These changes are revealed in archaeological sites by sharp differences in pottery styles or settlement patterns.

Many human societies have no written history, but the anthropologist with his notebooks, photographs, and tape recorders can provide a wealth of data from contemporary society. Information on house designs, economic practices, and the like is a potential source of analogy with prehistoric sites of the same basic type in the same area. Analogical techniques, which antiquarians and historians have used for centuries, have been developed to a fine art by the twentieth-century archaeologist. Modern archaeology is truly a multidisciplinary team effort, depending on the work of scientists from many fields of inquiry. In the course of one afternoon, an excavator may call on a glass expert, an authority on sea shells, an earthworm specialist, and a soil scientist. Each has his piece to contribute to the archaeological jigsaw.

the archaeological record

The archaeologist's work has been likened to that of a detective, who pieces together events from numerous fragmentary clues. British archaeologist Stuart Piggott has described archaeology as the "science of rubbish.[8] His choice of words is apt, for we seek to find out about prehistoric man from the traces of his activities that he has left behind him. These traces come in many forms: as giant pyramids or earth mounds; as pottery fragments or beads; as broken animal bones or seeds, the remains of meals eaten long ago; or in the form of burials and the grave furniture found with them.

The amount we can find out about the past is severely limited by soil conditions. Stone and baked clay are some of the most lasting substances from the past, surviving under almost all conditions. Wood, bone, leather, and metals are much less durable and only occasionally remain for the archaeologist to find. Arctic conditions have been known to freeze whole sites, preserving highly perishable items such as wooden tools or, in Siberia, the complete carcasses of extinct mammoths.[9] The waterlogged bogs of Denmark have preserved the corpses of long-dead human sacrifices, and wooden tools survive well under similar conditions. Everyone has heard of the remarkable tomb of the Egyptian Pharaoh Tutankhamun ("King Tut"), whose astonishing treasure survived almost intact in the dry climate of the Nile Valley for over three thousand years.[10]

But most archaeological sites are found under conditions in which only a few durable finds survive. Reconstructing the past from the finds in them is a real jigsaw puzzle, like that posed by American archaeologist James Deetz:

Take a glass coffee pot, a set of rosary beads, a wedding ring, a fishing pole complete with reel, a jewelry box, a pair of skis, an eight ball from a pool table, a crystal chandelier, a magnifying glass, a harmonica, and a vacuum tube and break them to pieces with a hammer. Bury them for three centuries, and then dig them up and present them to a literate citizen of Peking. Could he tell you the function of the objects which these fragments represent?[11]

The data from survey and excavation constitute the "archaeological record."

time

Early scholars had a brief time scale into which they fitted the story of mankind. The world began with Adam and ended with Western civilization. Today's archaeologist looks back over a long panorama of human events, a landscape dotted with archaeological sites, human fossils, and major developments in human endeavor. We now realize that man has a long ancestry that extends back over two million years into the past. Many laymen also share this new perspective of our past, at a time when we are reaching out into space in search of new worlds. But still the same questions are asked of archaeologists at a busy excavation or in a museum. "How old is it?" "How do you know the age?"

At the end of the eighteenth century, geologists first began to realize that the earth's rocks were stratified in successive layers, one formed after another. The advantages of stratigraphy were soon grasped in archaeological sites, and stratigraphy is now one of the fundamental cornerstones of time measurement in archaeology.[12] The successive occupation layers of any archaeological site are carefully excavated one by one with a proper eye for their vertical position one above the other. The "law of superposition" allows that the lowest occupation level on a site is older than those accumulated on top of it. These older layers are known to have been occupied before the later ones, but, in the absence of additional information, there is no way to tell how much earlier in years the lower levels are than the later ones (Figure 1.1).

Early nineteenth-century archaeologists in Denmark built up a "Three-Age" system for classifying the past, which is still used today. This relative chronology envisaged a three-part subdivision of prehistoric time into a Stone Age, Bronze Age, and Iron Age, technological stages when man used only tools of those materials. This broad classificatory scheme was widely adopted in the Old World, and the notion of a Stone Age has passed into popular usage. The Three-Age system did not take root in the Americas, largely because the pre-Columbian Indians made little use of metals.[13]

How do we date the past in years? Numerous "chronometric" dating techniques have been tried over the years, but only a few have survived the test of continual use (Table 1.1).

The potassium-argon method can be used to date geological strata and the earliest millennia of human history up to about half a million years ago. One can calculate the age of cooled volcanic rocks like basalt or volcanic ash with the potassium-argon technique by measuring the ratio of potassium 40 (K40) to gas argon (A40) in the rock. Radioactive K40 decays at a fixed rate to form A40. In a given sample of cooled volcanic

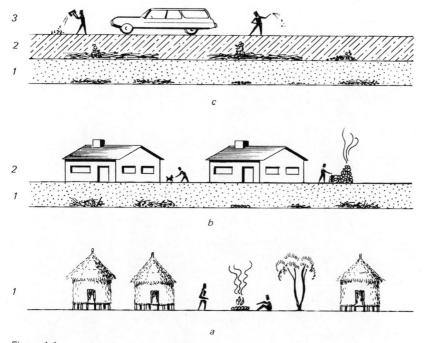

Figure 1.1
Superposition and stratigraphy. The schematic diagram shows:

a. A farming village built on virgin subsoil. After a period, the village is abandoned and the huts fall into disrepair. Their ruins are covered by accumulating soil and vegetation.

b. After an interval, a second village is built on the same site, with different architectural styles. This, in turn, is abandoned. The houses collapse into piles of rubble and are covered by accumulating soil.

c. Twentieth-century man parks his car on top of both village sites and drops litter and coins which, when uncovered, reveal to the archaeologist that the top layer is modern.

An archaeologist digging this site would find that the modern layer is underlain by two prehistoric occupation levels, that square houses were in use in the upper of the two, which is thus the later (law of superposition), and that round huts are stratigraphically earlier than square ones at this locality. Therefore, village 1 is earlier than village 2, but when either was occupied or how many years separate village 1 from 2 cannot be known without further data.

rock, the ratio of $K40$ to $A40$ can be measured accurately with a spectrometer and then used to calculate the approximate age. Fortunately, many early human settlements are found in volcanic areas like East Africa. Volcanic rock layers covering human campsites have been dated by the potassium-argon method. The technique has been most useful for dating the origins of man, but it suffers from the disadvantage of being

Table 1.1
Dating methods in prehistory.

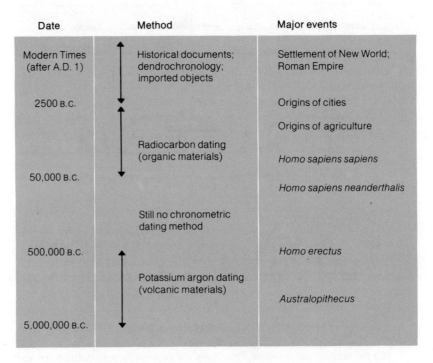

Date	Method	Major events
Modern Times (after A.D. 1)	Historical documents; dendrochronology; imported objects	Settlement of New World; Roman Empire
2500 B.C.		Origins of cities
		Origins of agriculture
	Radiocarbon dating (organic materials)	*Homo sapiens sapiens*
50,000 B.C.		*Homo sapiens neanderthalis*
	Still no chronometric dating method	
500,000 B.C.		*Homo erectus*
	Potassium argon dating (volcanic materials)	*Australopithecus*
5,000,000 B.C.		

The following conventions have been used in the tables throughout the book:

—————— A continuous line means that the chronology is firmly established.

– – – – – A broken line means the chronology is doubtful.

——————▶ A line terminating in an arrow means the time span continues beyond the arrow.

——————⊣ A line terminating with a horizontal bar means the limit of chronology is firmly established.

—————– – – A line ending with dashes means the limit of chronology is still doubtful.

?Escale   A question mark beside the name of a site means its date is not firmly established.

(Torralba) Site names appear in parentheses.

comparatively inaccurate, for each date has a large statistical margin of error.

The radiocarbon dating method, developed by physicists J. R. Arnold and W. F. Libby in 1949, is based on the fact that living organisms build

Table 1.2
The accuracy of radiocarbon dates shown by an example.

Sample radiocarbon date = 3,621 ± 180 years (plus or minus factor)
1 standard deviation = 3,441 to 3,801 years
  With 1 deviation, chances are 2 out of 3 that the date span is correct.

2 standard deviations = 3,261 to 3,981 years
  With 2 deviations, chances are 19/20 that the date span is correct.

---

up their own organic matter by photosynthesis and by using atmospheric carbon dioxide. The amount of radiocarbon present in the organism is equal to that in the atmosphere. When the organism dies, the radiocarbon (C14) atoms begin to disintegrate at a known rate. Thus it is possible to calculate the age of an organic object by measuring the amount of C14 left in the sample. The initial quantity of radiocarbon in a particular sample is low, so the limit of detectability is soon reached. Samples more than 50,000 to 60,000 years old contain insufficient quantities of C14 for measurement.

Radiocarbon dating is most effective for sites dating between 50,000 and 2,000 years before the present (B.P.). Dates can be taken from many types of organic material, including charcoal, shell, wood, or hair. When a date is received from a radiocarbon dating laboratory it bears a statistical plus or minus factor, the significance of which is explained in Table 1.2 and Figure 1.2. Most dates given in this book are derived from radiocarbon dated samples and should be recognized for what they are — statistical approximations.[14]

Radiocarbon dating was originally hailed as the solution to the archaeologists' dating problems. Later research has shown this enthusiasm to be a little optimistic.[15] Unfortunately, the rate of carbon 14 production in the atmosphere has fluctuated considerably owing both to changes in the strength of the earth's magnetic field and to alterations in the level of solar activity. By working with tree-ring chronologies obtained from the California bristlecone pine, several radiocarbon laboratories have produced correction curves for radiocarbon dates between about 1500 B.C. and the earliest pine tree dates of about 6000 B.C. Calibrated dates have not yet come into wide use because of the provisional nature of the calibration tables, but standardized correction charts are likely to alter the world's radiocarbon chronologies very radically within the next decade. (See Table 13.2, page 212.)

More recent millennia can be dated by other means, too. Writing first began about 3000 B.C. in Mesopotamia, and for thousands of years non-

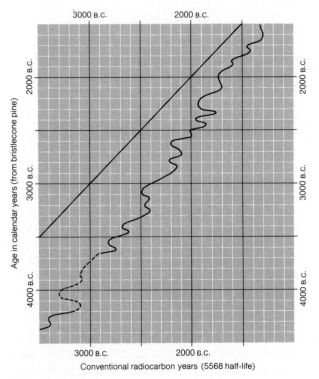

Figure 1.2
A calibration chart for the conversion of radiocarbon dates into calendar dates, using tree-ring data from the bristlecone pine.

literate peoples traded with literate townsmen and merchants. Distinctive objects such as china bowls, glass jugs and beads, and coins were widely distributed over enormous distances, far from their original centers of manufacture. These items often have short, and known, periods of manufacture and can be used to provide accurate dates for prehistoric sites.

One of the most accurate archaeological chronologies of all comes from the southwestern United States. Many years ago Dr. A. E. Douglass developed a dating method using the annual growth rings of trees as a basis for dating the wooden house beams of prehistoric houses in desert Arizona. In areas of markedly seasonal rainfall, each tree ring represents a year's growth. The rings can be counted and joined together in long sequences from different trees and correlated with fragmentary beams from Indian pueblos to as far back as the first century B.C., when the first wooden house frames were constructed in this area, and back even further with trees alone. Unfortunately "dendrochronology" can only be used in areas such as the Southwest where there is marked seasonal rainfall and regular growth of annual tree rings.

Many dating methods have been devised in recent years, most of them still experimental and limited in application. The reader is referred to the technical literature for details of such methods as thermoluminescence and archaeomagnetism.[16] Table 1.1 shows the chronological brackets covered by each of the major dating methods described here. But, despite over a century of experimentation, a major segment of human prehistory, from about 500,000 years to 50,000 years ago, remains undated. Although potassium-argon techniques can be used to date the earliest millennia of prehistoric time, the margins of error for the early samples are so large that the readings for a site even a quarter of a million years old are quite meaningless. By using large dating samples it is possible to overlap with carbon 14 dates of about 60,000 years B.P. But the accuracy of the isotopic measurements of argon will need to be improved before the gap can be bridged satisfactorily.

finding and digging

The archaeological site is the starting point of most inquiry into the past; indeed, an excavation has become the symbol of the archaeologist. Sites themselves come in all sizes and shapes. The pyramid of Cheops in Egypt is an archaeological site. So is colonial Williamsburg, Virginia, skillfully reconstructed by archaeological excavations in recent years.[17] Olduvai Gorge, Tanzania, is one of the most famous sites in the world, for it contains some of the earliest human settlements ever discovered. The city of Anyang in China is a center of Shang civilization which has been completely uncovered by excavation. The scope of archaeology extends from the earliest campsites of the first apemen to buildings built and abandoned during the Industrial Revolution or even later.[18]

Given this great diversity of archaeological sites, it is hardly surprising that scholars have developed numerous techniques for finding the past. Many large sites such as the Indian mounds at Cahokia, Illinois, are easily found, but others can only be discovered by deliberate reconnaissance in the field. Archaeologists look for the accidental exposure of prehistoric sites by water or wind erosion, earthquake action, or other natural means. Rabbits and other burrowing animals may bring bones or stone tools to the surface in caves and other localities favored by man for shelter, water supplies, and other reasons. Farmers plow up thousands of prehistoric objects. Road-making and urban development involve massive earthmoving and destruction of the past. As a result of the greed of treasure hunters and collectors, as well as the impetuousness of nine-

teenth-century excavators, many of the world's most important archaeological sites have been despoiled.

The destruction of sites has reached crisis proportions in the United
States, a crisis brought about by greatly increased rates of federal and
private land development, the activities of pothunters and treasure
seekers, and the ruthless commercial exploitation of Indian sites by pro-
fessional dealers. We are rapidly reaching a point where large segments
of American prehistory will remain blanks forever because the critical
evidence for them has been indiscriminately destroyed by the ignorant.
Archaeologists are responding to the crisis with appeals for more financial
support, close looks at enforcement legislation, and, above all, systematic
attempts to educate the public about the importance of archaeology.[19] A
similar but perhaps less critical situation exists in parts of Europe.

The last century has seen the development of an impressive battery
of scientific techniques for the excavation of archaeological sites. These
are based on the premise that digging up a site destroys it and that the
archaeologist's primary responsibility is to record a site for posterity as
he digs it up. Earthworks, agricultural field systems, and other conspicuous prehistoric sites have been plotted from the air using aerial photog-
raphy and an overhead view as a means of finding the past.[20] Since 1945,
scientific methods have been refined by the systematic use of sampling
techniques as well as the development of highly accurate recording
methods essential to such complicated sites as caves and the remains of
historical buildings buried under modern cities.[21] Most modern archaeologists make a distinction between area or horizontal excavation, where
the objective is to uncover large areas of ground in search of houses or
village layouts, and vertical excavation on a more limited scale designed
to uncover stratigraphical information or a sequence of occupation layers
on a small scale (Figure 1.3).

Much of our knowledge of the earliest men and of prehistoric hunters
and gatherers is obtained from the excavation of abandoned living sites.
Lakeside camps or convenient rock overhangs were favored by hunters
who needed protection from predators and the weather in addition to
abundant water supplies and ready access to herds of game and vegetable
foods. Olduvai Gorge in Tanzania is famous for its prehistoric settlements, small lakeside campsites occupied by early men for a few days
or weeks before they moved on elsewhere in their constant search for
game, vegetable foods, and fish.[22]

Fortunately for archaeologists, discarded food bones and tools were
abandoned where they were dropped. Crude windbreaks were left to be
burned down by the next bushfire or blown away by the wind. In the
case of Olduvai, the gently rising waters of a prehistoric lake slowly

covered the living floors and preserved them for posterity with the tools lying where they were dropped. Other hunters lived by the banks of large rivers. Their tools are found in profusion in river gravels that were subsequently jumbled and resorted by floodwater, which left a confused mass of tools rather than undisturbed living floors for the archaeologist to uncover.[23]

Caves already occupied over half a million years ago were reoccupied again and again as man returned to favored localities. Many natural caves and rock-shelters contain deep occupation deposits that can carefully be removed by meticulous excavation with dental pick, trowel, and brush. Thus the sequence of occupation layers can be uncovered virtually undisturbed from the time of abandonment.[24]

Farmers tend to live in larger settlements than hunters, for they are tied to their herds and gardens and move less often. Higher population densities and more permanent settlements have left more conspicuous archaeological sites from the later millennia of human history. In the Near East and many parts of the New World, farming sites were reoccupied again and again over periods of several thousand years; resulting in the formation of deep mounds of refuse, house foundations, and other occupation debris. These "tells" require large-scale excavation and extensive earthmoving if anything is to be understood about the layout of towns and settlements. Excavation is much easier with one-level open sites that merely require careful horizontal excavation to uncover houses and other features.

Prehistoric burials are found that date from about 70,000 years ago. It is hardly surprising that a great deal of archaeological knowledge is based on excavations in burial mounds, cemeteries, and graves. Skeletons and their accompanying grave goods tend to give us a rather one-sided view of the past, that concerned with funerary rites. Some of the most famous prehistoric burials are those of the royal kings deposited at Ur of the Chaldees in Mesopotamia during the second millennium B.C. (Chapter 18),[25] as well as the graves of Shang chiefs in China where royal kings were accompanied by their charioteers and many retainers (Chapter 21).[26] The mounds of Pazyryk in Siberia are another celebrated instance of spectacular burial customs (Chapter 20),[27] where important chiefs were buried with their chariots and steeds, the latter wearing elaborate harness trappings preserved by ice that formed when water entered the tombs and froze.

The diversity of archaeological sites is such that it is impossible to cover all of them here, for the peoples described in this book have been uncovered by using almost every technique of excavation known to science, from blasting with dynamite to digging with needles.

Figure 1.3

Vertical and horizontal excavations at Maiden Castle, Dorset, England. Although archaeologists excavate in many different ways and sometimes use sampling techniques, there is a basic distinction between vertical (a) and horizontal (b) types of
excavation.

a. A vertical excavation shows the use of a narrow trench to cut through successive
   layers of an earth rampart. Notice that only a small portion of the layers in the
   trench walls has been exposed by the vertical cutting. The objective of this excavation was to obtain information on the sequence of layers on the outer edge of the
   earthwork and in the ditch which originally lay on its exterior side. To obtain such
   information, only a narrow trench was needed to record layers, the finds from them,
   and the dating evidence.

b. *In contrast, this excavation consists of a grid of square trenches laid out with intervals of unexcavated soil between them. The grid method is designed to expose large segments of ground on a site so that buildings and even layouts of entire settlements can be traced over much larger areas than those uncovered in a vertical excavation. Horizontal excavation is widely used when budget considerations are of little concern and the archaeologist is looking for settlement patterns. This photograph shows a classic example of horizontal excavation, carried out at Maiden Castle in 1938.*

studying the finds

Finds made in archaeological sites come under many categories. They may include the fragmentary bones from game hunted by prehistoric man or from domesticated animals. Vegetable foods such as edible nuts and cultivated crops are sometimes found in archaeological sites where preservation conditions are favorable. Pottery, stone implements, iron artifacts, and, occasionally, bone and wooden tools all serve to build up a picture of man's technical achievements. Archaeologists have developed elaborate classification systems and sophisticated analytic techniques for classifying and comparing human artifacts.[28] They use collections of stone tools, pottery, or other artifacts like swords and brooches as a basis for studying human culture and its development. Whatever the classificatory techniques used, however, the final objective of the laboratory analysis of bones, pottery, and other material remains is the study of prehistoric culture and of cultural change in the past.

Archaeological information consists, as we have said, of a wide array of distinctive objects, some of them food residues, others tools, all of them the result of different human behaviors. We classify them into arbitrary groups either on the basis of their shape or design or by their use, the latter a difficult process (Figure 1.4). We fit them together to form a picture of a human culture, really making a catalog of tools and activities.

The Sears, Roebuck catalog provides an admirable example of an inventory of modern American culture. The multitude of human artifacts in it can be clustered into distinctive groups, such as clothing, ornaments, and knives. Archaeologists go through a similar exercise with their finds, calling all the objects from a single, sealed occupation level an "assemblage" of artifacts.

To take our analogy a little further, compare the Sears catalog for 1970 with that for 1920. There are a lot of radical differences in the two assemblages. A comparison of the two would enable you to build up quite different pictures of two societies separated by fifty years of cultural development. The workings of archaeological research are concerned with comparing one assemblage of artifacts with assemblages from different layers in the same site or other sites near or far away from the original find spot. Our record of human activity consists of innumerable classified and cataloged archaeological finds whose relationships one with another, either individually or as a group, determine much of the story of human culture that follows on these pages.

explanation and interpretation

Archaeology involves much more than merely induction and inference from the archaeological record, for our ultimate aim is to *explain* the past rather than simply to describe it. Archaeology has three objectives: reconstructing culture history, reconstructing past lifeways, and studying cultural processes.[29] Until recently, most archaeologists concentrated on basic descriptions of human culture, rather than on studies of cultural change and the relationships between different human societies.

In part, their concern with explanation has developed at the same time that advanced quantitative methods were introduced to aid in sorting and evaluating archaeological evidence.[30] New theoretical models have been constructed. Archaeologists have sought to explain *why* as much as *how*. Why, for example, did early man rely on vegetable foods for much of his diet? How did man first begin farming in the Near East? Why did the Mayan empire of Mesoamerica collapse so suddenly? A multitude

Figure 1.4

Inference from an artifact. The Chumash Indian parching tray from Southern California provides an example of the inferences that can be made from an archaeological find. We can examine these under different headings:

Function: *The flat round shape of the tray is determined by its function, for such trays were used to roast seeds by tossing them with embers in the tray. The function of a tray normally cannot be inferred from its shape, but identical modern versions have been found that are used for parching. Thus, we employ the technique of analogy to infer the archaeological find had the same function.*

Context: *The archaeological context of the tray is defined in terms of site, level, square, etc.; its relationship to other features, such as houses, also is recorded. Unless this information is known, the tray is merely an isolated specimen devoid of a cultural context or even a date. Context cannot be inferred from an artifact alone.*

Construction and materials: *The tray was made of reed, its red-brown color determined by the reed, known from modern observations to be the best material available. The steplike decoration on the tray was dictated by sewing and weaving techniques of basketry. The diamond patterns were probably added as a personal touch by the craftsman who made it. The shape and the decoration of the tray are repeated in many others that have been found and are evidently part of a well-established Chumash basketry tradition. More information concerning construction and materials can be obtained about an artifact than in any other category of inference.*

Behavior: *The parching tray reveals something about the cooking techniques of the Chumash, but again only by using analogy.*

Clearly, the range of inferences that can be made from archaeological finds alone is rather limited, especially when the find has no context in a site.

of large and small explanations of the past are being sought by new research methods. Human culture was constantly changing throughout prehistory, but identification and exploration of the changes present a far from easy task. Today, many archaeologists seek to apply the theoretical concepts of anthropology to archaeological evidence in attempts to arrive at general laws of cultural progress. Others are primarily concerned with the history of culture, viewing each society as a unique phenomenon. Let us now look at some theories of the past.

2

theories of prehistory: looking at the past

A frantic pace of archaeological digging in the eighteenth century provided an enormous mass of new information about the prehistoric past, far more than had been available to earlier antiquarians. But there was no means of classifying the diverse finds into any formal framework. "Everything which has come down to us from heathendom is wrapped in a thick fog," complained Danish scholar Rasmus Nyerup in 1806.

A few years later another Dane, Christian Jurgensen Thomsen, rearranged the collections of the National Museum in Copenhagen in a new way. He divided the tools and weapons in the museum into three broad periods of prehistory: a Stone Age when metals were unknown, a Bronze Age, and an Iron Age.[1]* Thomsen's strictly technological classification of prehistory was soon widely accepted, its chronological validity having been proved by excavations in Denmark and elsewhere in Europe (Table 2.1).

In 1838 Danish zoologist Sven Nilsson developed an economic model for the past in which he argued for four stages of human development: a *savage* stage when man was a hunter, *herdsman* and *agriculturalist* stages, and a fourth phase, *civilization*, which had man using writing and coinage.[2] Nilsson's economic model was developed from both archaeological data and anthropological observations.

Still another Dane, J. J. A. Worsaae, recognized that Thomsen's Three Ages were a technological framework for prehistoric times with a wide application in Europe. But Worsaae wondered what this model meant

* See pages 380–381 for notes to Chapter 2.

in terms of human history. How did man acquire bronze weapons? Did one people invent metal tools and then spread their innovation to other parts of the world? Or did metallurgy come into being in many different areas?[3] Worsaae raised one of the dominant concerns of nineteenth- and early twentieth-century archaeology: Did culture change result from *diffusion, migration,* or *independent invention*? Did great migrations of tribes and warriors carry new ideas throughout the world? Alternatively, did ideas diffuse by trade or word of mouth in the hands of a few people? Or did such major innovations as agriculture or metallurgy develop in several areas of the world quite independently?

the progress of man

Both Nilsson's and Thomsen's schemes implied a universal scheme of human economic and technological development everywhere, a popular notion at a time when *The Origin of Species* was taking the scientific world by storm. The doctrine of social evolution had been propounded long before Darwin came on the scene. Such an eminent social scientist as Herbert Spencer viewed human prehistory as a logical extension of bio-

Table 2.1
Some classification schemes for prehistoric times used in the nineteenth century compared with a technological scheme widely used in the Old World today.

Commonly used today	C.J. Thomsen	Sven Nilsson	Edward Tylor
IRON AGE	IRON AGE	CIVILIZATION HERDSMAN AND AGRICULTURALIST	CIVILIZATION
BRONZE AGE	BRONZE AGE	HERDSMAN AND AGRICULTURALIST	BARBARISM
Neolithic[a] (or "New Stone Age")		HERDSMAN AND AGRICULTURALIST	BARBARISM
STONE AGE Mesolithic[a] Paleolithic (or "Old Stone Age") { Upper Paleolithic Middle Paleolithic Lower Paleolithic	STONE AGE	SAVAGE	SAVAGERY

[a]The terms "Mesolithic" and "Neolithic," though outdated, are sometimes found in the literature.

logical evolution.[4] The decades following the publication of *The Origin of Species* were ones in which evolution held a strong grip on academic minds. Edward Tylor was one anthropologist with evolutionary leanings who had a profound influence on early archaeology. He was an avid supporter of the notion of human progress: "The knowledge of man's course of life from the remote past to the present will guide us in our duty of leaving the world better than we found it." Tylor argued that the civilized institutions of Western civilizations had their origins in those of ruder peoples.[5]

In general terms, Tylor was an evolutionist. He accepted the broad three stages of human culture, labeled Savagery, Barbarism, and Civilization. He even said that the institutions of man were as distinctly stratified as the earth upon which he lived; and he thought that similar human nature caused a uniform succession from savagery to civilization all over the world. For all his evolutionism, however, Tylor still favored the diffusion of some human traits and was prepared to accept this process as a major contributor to human history.

diffusionists

Diffusion had been recognized as a process of cultural change by Worsaae and other nineteenth-century archaeologists. Oscar Montelius, another Scandinavian scholar, studied the development of various tools or weapons from prehistoric sites in Europe, constructed regional sequences of them, and built complicated chains of interlinking tool types from the Near East to the Atlantic coast.[6] It was assumed that most inventions had spread from Egypt and Mesopotamia and come into use later in outlying areas of Europe.

During the 1890s American anthropologist Franz Boas refined a diffusionist approach to human culture and did so in the context of his research into folk tales. His purpose was to arrive at history, for he wanted to test evolutionary theories by seeing if folk tales and other cultural traits exhibited the patterns of growth attributed to them by evolutionists. The diffusionist method allowed him to arrive at historical accounts of cultural phenomena even in the absence of written documents. Considerable amounts of historical data could be gleaned by tracing the spread of culture traits over given regions. Boas soon rejected evolutionism altogether and substituted the laws of evolution with those of diffusionism. Evolution had cultures developing or progressing along predictable lines toward greater complexity and sophistication. Diffusionism would have cultures developing very largely by receiving new traits from the outside and then modifying them to bring them into conformity with the existing culture. Both the methods of diffusionism and the view of history associated with it dominated American anthropology from the early 1900s until about 1930, when new approaches surfaced.

Grafton Elliot Smith, an anatomist and amateur archaeologist, was one of the foremost diffusionists of half a century ago.[7] Smith served in Cairo for awhile, where he studied ancient Egyptian skulls and the techniques of mummification. Smith and his disciples, principally W. J. Perry, were captivated by Egypt's ancient greatness. When they looked up from their skulls, they had a vision of a great and ancient mariner folk, the People of the Sun, who arose in Lower Egypt and spread over the earth in search of gold, precious stones, and shells. They brought their archaic civilization with them, one where the arts of stone architecture, sun worship, agriculture, irrigation, and metallurgy were paramount, as well as warfare and the prevalence of social classes. Such institutions were conceived but once, it was claimed, in wise and ancient Egypt, to spread inexorably not only in Europe and Asia but also in the Pacific, Mexico, and Peru. Elliot Smith's flamboyant view of human history became popular among laymen largely on account of its simplicity.

Diffusionism was nothing new in Smith's day, for many early prehistorians were attracted by simplistic notions of the past. One has only to review some of both the early and present-day literature on the peopling of America to be aware of its pervasive influence on archaeological thinking. Though few people still regard the Ethiopians as serious candidates for the honor of being the first Americans, diffusionist theories still surface in archaeological circles: for example, Thor Heyerdahl's *Kon-Tiki* and *Ra* expeditions, both attempts to bolster diffusionist hypotheses (Chapters 15 and 22).

The tremendous explosion of new archaeological data in this century has militated against simplistic explanations of human achievement. Fortunately, some scholars had a mind for detailed research and challenged the extreme theories of earlier decades with a thoroughness that set prehistory on a new footing.

boas and childe

One such scholar was Franz Boas (1858–1942), an anthropologist of German birth who emigrated to the United States and received an appointment at Columbia University, which he held all his life. He dominated American anthropology until his death in 1942.[8]

Boas attacked those who sought to compare primitive societies in general terms. He helped establish anthropology as an exact science, applying scientific methods to the collection and classification of data. He instilled respect for the notion that data should not be subordinated to a priori theoretical schemes. For example, he recorded folktales with extreme care in their original native languages with interlineal translations into English, to avoid bringing any distortion into his account. Similarly, he and his students collected an incredible amount of data on designs drawn on pots, woven on basketry, and executed on other materials. Their objective was to trace diffusion and hence history, but always with a regard for supplying hard data with as little distortion as possible. They attempted to seek explanations of the past from meticulous study of individual artifacts or customs. Archaeology became a source of information against which one checked historical reconstructions produced by historians, as well as history in its own right.

V. Gordon Childe (1892–1957) was another scholar who had a profound effect on New World and Old World archaeology. His life's work was the study of prehistoric European civilization, a task that involved him in the identification, classification, and chronological ordering of a multitude of sites and archaeological finds.[9]

Gordon Childe had a love for the eastern Mediterranean and Near East. He thought of European prehistory in terms of the East. All the higher arts, including civilization, had come from what he called the Most Ancient Near East. Human history went through developmental stages, presaged by major revolutions, such as an "Urban Revolution," which implied revolutionary changes in the human condition. He built up his story of the past by means of complicated cultural sequences within limited geographical areas and compared them with those from neighboring regions, allowing cultural evolution an important place in European prehistory. He was able to combine evidences of diffusion into an evolutionist framework, producing a form of "modified diffusionism."

Childe published a series of eloquent books with wide popular appeal, of which *What Happened in History* (1942) is a typical example. His basic aim was to distill from archaeological remains "a preliterate substitute for conventional history with cultures instead of statesmen as actors and migrations instead of battles."[10] He drew together approaches to the past from various schools, particularly the Marxists, convinced that he had much to learn from man's rational, intelligent progress from his earliest development. Childe's methodology continues to influence European, Asian, and American archaeologists, although his notions of "cultures" and "developmental stages" are slowly being replaced by more sophisticated models based on huge data banks of basic archaeological information (Chapter 17).

ecology and explanation

Gordon Childe and many of his contemporaries were not overly concerned with prehistoric ecology. But as early as the 1930s, American anthropologist Julian Steward was beginning to articulate and develop the modern view that ecological factors are crucial to an understanding of the past. Steward viewed human cultures as adaptations to the subsistence and ecological requirements of a local region. His view was in sharp contrast to the conventional pre-World War I approach that built up human cultures through the accumulation of culture traits through diffusion and not as responses to ecological factors. Englishman Grahame Clark was among the first to study the relationships between prehistoric man and his environment. He excavated the famous Stone Age hunting camp at Star Carr in England and placed it in an ecological context.[11] Clark's work had its roots in earlier research by other fieldworkers, such as Sir Cyril Fox who had mapped prehistoric sites against geographical information in his classic *Personality of Britain*.[12] Some American archaeologists moved away from the classification of tools toward the study of cultural change in the past, viewing millennia of prehistory against the background of the complex and ever-changing environment. Unfortunately, a few more enthusiastic scholars began to think of environment as the dominating factor in cultural change. The result has been a school of "environmental determinists," whose work reflects a preoccupation with simplistic views of human adaptations.[13] Some of the most sophisticated research is now in ecological areas, as archaeologists increasingly concern themselves with ever-changing cultures and environments.

Most archaeologists are now as much concerned with the question of "why" in archaeology as they are with "how," the latter being the traditional goal of many scholars of previous generations. Computers, systems models, and other sophisticated research tools are transforming our knowledge of the past.[14] So much archaeological data are available that we can see that an extreme diffusionist view of the origins of civilization not only is overly simplistic but is no explanation at all.

Radiocarbon chronologies have shown that agriculture began more or less simultaneously in Asia and the Near East. Cities arose first in the Near East about 5,000 years ago. The Pre-Columbian inhabitants of the New World and the Chinese also assumed most of the apparatus of urban civilization, but each with its distinctive style. Prehistoric societies in many parts of the world have progressed toward urban civilization, taking advantage of geographical, ecological, and cultural opportunities to develop new economic strategies and new social structures.

Few archaeologists would now challenge the view that man must be a balanced part of nature if he is to continue to survive. In a recent, highly fascinating, and provocative essay on human ecology Richard A. Watson and Patty Jo Watson have written a series of syntheses of human "ways of life," each of them a way in which man interacts with the physical environment to satisfy the basic animal requirements of protection, nourishment, and reproduction.[15] The Watsons' descriptions are abstractions, sobering in that they show how man cannot be successful in the end if his methods of utilizing the physical environment to satisfy his ends disrupt the ecological community in which he is the dominant animal. Ecological balance is essential to our protection, nutrition, and reproduction and is the ultimate relationship mankind must maintain with nature. Our narrative of world prehistory is a story of human progress told within a framework of biological and cultural evolution, as well as of increasingly complex interactions with the physical environment leading to the alarming ecological imbalances of today. (At this point, readers familiar with the principles of evolutionary theory should go ahead to Chapter 4.)

3

understanding evolution

A basic understanding of the mechanisms of evolution is essential to any examination of world prehistory. Biological evolution has played a major role in shaping our destiny, for the evolution of culture has gone hand in hand with the evolution of man. So a brief summary of evolutionary principles is appropriate here.

"As many more individuals of each species are born than can possibly survive, and as consequently there is a frequently recurring struggle for existence, it follows that any being, if it vary however slightly in any manner profitable to itself ... will have a better chance of surviving, and thus be naturally selected.... This ... I have called Natural Selection, or the Survival of the Fittest."[1]* Over a century ago the great biologist Charles Darwin described the basic mechanisms of evolution in his work, *The Origin of Species.* The doctrine of evolution itself was nothing new. Many scientists before Darwin, including Lamarck, Buffon, and even Darwin's own grandfather, had recognized that animals and plants had not remained unaltered through time but were continuously changing. They intimated that all organisms, including man, were modified descendants of previously existing forms of life. But Darwin removed evolution from the domains of pure speculation by showing how evolution occurs.

As early as 1837 he had started a series of notebooks on the changes in species. Then, a year later, he read Thomas Henry Malthus's famous *Essay on the Principle of Population,* first published in 1798. Darwin immediately realized that he was on the track of an idea of the greatest importance. Malthus had argued realistically that man's reproductive capacity far exceeds the available food supply. In other words, men compete one with another for the necessities of life. Competition causes famine, war, and all sorts of misery. Similar competition occurs among all living organisms. Darwin wondered if new forms had in part occurred as a result of the "struggle for existence," in which well-adapted individuals survive and the ill-adjusted are eliminated.

The theory of evolution implied that the accumulation of favorable variations over long periods of time must result in the emergence of new species and the extinction of old ones. This was heresy in early Victorian England, for the account of the Creation in Genesis was sacrosanct, that all the creatures on earth had sprung into being at the same moment, some 6,000 years ago. Darwin himself was a devout Christian who began only gradually to doubt the biblical account of the Creation. So he delayed publication of his ideas for twenty years. Then in 1858, he received a draft of an essay by Alfred Russel Wallace, who had reached similar conclusions. A month later Darwin and Wallace presented a joint paper on their work to the Linnaean Society. A year afterward Darwin published what he called a "Modest Abstract" of his voluminous notes in a single book, *The Origin of Species*. This monumental volume was greeted initially with both effusive praise and vicious criticism, as scientists and churchmen took sides over the issue of the Creation. But gradually the echoes of controversy died away as Darwin's revolutionary theories were bolstered by more and more field observations.[2]

The theory of evolution and the findings of geologists had a profound effect on research into human origins. Archaeologists could now envisage a vast and open-ended period of time before the present in which man had developed into a literate and sophisticated being. Then there was the implication that man had descended from the apes, his direct ancestors. No other tenet of evolution caused as much furore as the implication that man had ape-like ancestors. Cartoonists lampooned the idea; clerics were horrified. Even Darwin himself was cautious. "Light," he remarked in *The Origin of Species*, "will be thrown on the origin of man and his history."[3]

natural selection

Darwin's explanation of evolution was based on the principle of natural selection.[4] He observed that all living things tend to increase their numbers at a prolific rate. A single salmon, for example, may deposit 28 million eggs in one season. Darwin's second and logical observation was that no one organism swarms uncontrollably over the earth. In fact, the population of any living creature remains relatively constant over long periods of time. If we accept these observations as valid, we can conclude that not all individuals in a single generation can survive. In other words, nature is a constant "survival of the fit." Darwin also observed that individuals in a population are not alike but differ in various features. He concluded that individuals endowed with the most favorable variations would have the best chance of survival and of passing on their favorable characteristics to their descendants. Of course, Darwin also argued that the unfit do not proliferate, for nature selects against those who are not suited to given conditions of existence. Natural selection serves both as a conservative force pruning out aberrant forms and as a positive force that allows the fit to reproduce, the obvious and fundamental condition to survival.

heredity

While Charles Darwin was aware that evolution is inseparably tied to the mechanisms of inheritance, he was at a loss to explain how given traits were passed from parent to offspring. The theory of evolution was incomplete without the answers to two questions: Why do living things vary and how do the variations occur? What rules govern the handing down of traits from one generation to the next? Unfortunately, Darwin was unaware of the publications of an Austrian monk, Gregor Johann Mendel. In 1866 Mendel demonstrated the fundamental laws of inheritance, using the common garden pea as the basis for comprehensive breeding experiments under controlled conditions.[5] No one read Mendel's papers until 1900, long after Darwin's death.

Mendel investigated inheritance by breeding many successive generations of the common garden pea in his monastery garden. Instead of studying every feature of each pea plant, Mendel concentrated on seven easily compared pairs of characteristics of the pea, including the form of the ripe seed (round or wrinkled), the color, and the position of flower. He cross-fertilized smooth and wrinkled lines of peas. He found that the first-generation offspring were smooth, while the hybrid offspring when crossed with each other produced both wrinkled and smooth peas in a proportion of 3 to 1. In subsequent hybridizations the characteristics of smoothness and wrinkling were recombined in all possible ways. Mendel surmised that each male sex cell and egg-producing organ from a pea plant contained certain factors (now known as genes) that determined the development of the plant's offspring. He then formulated a series of biological laws that underlay his findings. First, he stated that heredity is transmitted by a large number of independent, inheritable units. Second, when each parent contributes the same kind of gene, a constant characteristic is produced in the children. A hybrid results from two different kinds, which will again separate when the hybrid forms its own reproductive cells. Third, the hereditary units are unaffected by their long association with others and emerge from any union as distinct units again. Any given generation is descended from only a small fraction of the previous one. The genes transmitted by the most successful individuals in reproduction will predominate in the next generation. As a result of unequal reproductive capacities in individuals with different hereditary constitutions, the genetic characteristics of a population become altered with each successive generation. The composition of a population can never remain constant, for evolution is ultimately the changes in the genetic composition of a population with the passage of each generation.

chromosomes and cells

While Charles Darwin had given all of the hundreds of thousands of animal and plant species a common ancestry and Gregor Mendel had provided laws governing the descent of species, the hereditary units that account for all the differences were not explained until this century. The chromosome, a tiny thread-like structure in the nucleus of the living cell, was eventually identified as the container for Mendel's hereditary units or genes. As egg or sperm cells divided (meiosis), the chromosomes in them divided in half, so that half of each chromosome pair went into each cell, the full complement of chromosomes being reestablished at fertilization of an egg by sperm. Early researches on chromosomes showed that inheritance operated through the transmission of self-producing matter, but that genes combined or interacted to produce their effects within the gene complex of an organism.

The chemistry of the gene was imperfectly understood until the materials from which chromosomes were made had been analyzed. Chromosomes were found to be made up of combinations of deoxyribonucleic acid (better known as DNA), ribonucleic acid (RNA), and various proteins. DNA was found to be the raw material of heredity, for it was capable of producing complete copies of itself when injected into a cell. The materials that make up DNA are not capable of building billions of new forms. Such creative diversity comes from its structure, a spiral with two coils linked by four interlocking chemical subunits. The sequence in which these units are arranged determines heredity, a sequence with an almost infinite number of possible orders. These variations in the molecular structure of DNA affect the hereditary control effect of genes over cell growth. When the variations are sufficiently stable to be inherited in the genes of the offspring, then a mutation occurs.

gene pools

All the genes possessed by a population constitute its gene pool, the reservoir of genetic materials available to the population for the inheritance of the next generation. Cell division processes within male and female tend to transmit the gene pool to succeeding generations relatively unchanged. If there is random mating within a large population and if there are no mutations, the gene pool within the population will remain constant from one generation to the next. Genetic equilibrium will be maintained and no evolution will occur. Both mutation and natural selection are important agents to upset equilibrium, as are, to a lesser extent, both genetic drift and mixture of population — the four forces of evolution.

Natural selection was described by Charles Darwin as being constantly at work "daily and hourly scrutinising, throughout the world, the slightest variations; rejecting those that are bad, preserving, and adding up all that are good." Inheritable variations are affected by the environment in which the population lives. If some individuals carrying new genes survive and reproduce, new genes are added to the gene pool, and the characteristics of the population are altered to that extent. If, however, the environment affects the survival of the new genes and they fail to reproduce, then the gene pool is unaltered. It follows that if the new individuals with the new genes and the traits resulting from them survive with greater frequency, the frequency of the new genes in the population will increase from generation to generation. Natural selection is the way in which environmental factors act on genetic variation to produce variant individuals who, if they reproduce most frequently, are the best adapted to an environment. Obviously, the gene carriers who are most responsive to the environment in terms of their reproductive capabilities will be those who survive. Thus the population becomes better adapted to its environment.

mutation

An inheritable change in the structure of a gene is known as a mutation. Mutations occur in single genes at a low but constant rate, generally thought to be an uncontrollable chance phenomenon. Since the number of genes in the human body is enormous, the mutability of the organism as a whole is obviously much higher. Most gene mutations are changes for the worse, which is hardly surprising since normal genes represent the most favorable mutations accumulated over long periods of time.

Lethal mutations, which kill their holders, have no evolutionary consequences, for the individual has no chance to reproduce. Nonlethal forms of mutation can be established if their possessors outbreed their competitors (natural selection) and by chance interbreed for the most part among themselves but occasionally with sister populations (genetic drift). Only a very small proportion of the many mutations that occur and are positive rather than lethal have the necessary qualities to change the physical character of a population very rapidly in a stable environment.

Whether or not a given mutation has a selective advantage depends on the environment or the ecological niche with which the population has to contend. Environments are constantly changing, which in turn means that the selective effect on the gene pools of all the populations inhabiting these environments also alters. Environmental change is thus just as important a part of evolution as genetic change. But an environment is a biological as well as a geological phenomenon. Every change in plant or animal life is in itself an environmental change that affects everything else in the environment. Thus there is a feedback effect that produces environmental changes for other organisms in the same ecosystem. The cumulative effects of organic changes through time have resulted in more and more rapid evolutionary rates as one geological era has succeeded another. The fastest rate was during the Pleistocene times, the Age of Man.

genetic drift

An isolated human population may undergo genetic changes (evolution) as a result of chance rather than natural selection. American geneticist Sewall Wright demonstrated that a small group of people who move to new hunting grounds and subsequently become isolated from their ancestral groups can undergo alterations in their genetic character simply by the law of chance rather than by mutation. The distribution of genes is such that quite by chance any given trait may occur with unusual rarity in the breakaway population. Isolation and intermarriage allow this occurrence to remain at an unusually low level, with a resultant considerable difference between the original population and the offshoot group. It also follows that further splinter groups from the original band of outcasts may also display random variations that may eliminate the particular trait altogether. If the process of genetic drift is carried through several breakaways and many short generations, major changes in human populations could occur. Genetic drift was an important process during Stone Age times when the world's population was much smaller than today's. Now the jetliner has increased genetic contact between groups to the extent that genetic drift is less significant.

adaptive radiation

Food supplies, shelter, and space are among the resources that govern the capacity of a population of organisms to increase. An organism has an unlimited ability to multiply, but the available supply of resources in a given environment is limited. When populations rise to the extent that resources are inadequate, one can expect some individuals to explore new environments where competition for resources is low. This tendency of individuals to exploit new opportunities can result in the emergence of new species from an ancestral stock. If colonization of previously unexploited habitats is successful, then a rich array of new species can result, each better fitted to survive and reproduce under the new conditions as opposed to the old. The spreading of populations into different environments, accompanied by divergent adaptive changes of emigrant populations, is known as "adaptive radiation."

The evolution of the primates has proceeded through a complex evolutionary line, with man and nonhuman primates branching off from a common ancestral species during the more recent geological eras. Speciation has occurred frequently, whenever two or more groups from an original population have become isolated from one another. In adapting to their separate environments they have gone through sufficiently major genetic modifications so that their genetic modules are incapable of interacting on one another. The result is differential evolution through adaptive radiation. A species consists of a population whose members are capable of interbreeding between themselves but are incapable of doing so with members of other populations or do not regularly do so. The peopling of the world and the population explosion among mankind has resulted in large part from the evolution of new species of men who have themselves spread from their homelands into progressively more varied environments that have accelerated their diversity and development.

The primates underwent adaptive radiation when they first arose during the Cenozoic, about 75 million years ago. Most of their distinctive characteristics evolved as specializations for a tree-living way of life. The primates have evolved along differentiated and branching lines that cover such widely differing animals as the tree shrew, lemur, gorilla, and chimpanzee, to say nothing of man, the most advanced primate, primarily on account of his superior locomotion skills and enlarged brain. Man's successful adaptation to the world's environments has been the result of his superior intelligence, gradually acquired in the course of evolution.

race

Modern man is certainly different from his predecessors, who are described in Chapters 5 to 7. It is important to realize that there have been different kinds of men. Adaptive radiation has led to a family of men (known as Hominidae) of which modern man, *Homo sapiens* (man the wise), is only one member and the sole survivor.[6]

Different populations of mankind exist throughout the world and can, and do, interbreed successfully. For over a century physical anthropologists have been trying to classify human races, the term "race" implying a geographically defined cluster of local populations. But attempts at classification, while showing that race, culture, and language vary independently, are almost always man-made combinations of different phenomena. Often these consist of a small selection of the enormous number of variations occurring in human beings. Such racial classifications not only are arbitrary but also do not explain human variation.[7]

The term "race" has limited application at best, although it is sometimes applied to linguistic or cultural groups with few distinctive biological attributes. The boundaries of human races, if they can be delimited at all, are at best blurred and constantly shifting. Migrations, intermarriage, and, in recent centuries, colonial settlement have radically altered the distributions of mankind. The distinguishing characteristics of any major groupings of mankind have been blurred by intermixing so that each consists of a multitude of diverse genotypes. In truth, the whole world today is a single large neighborhood, for contemporary man lives in a single reproductive community.

4

the pleistocene

Man and his environment are inextricably linked, to the extent that no one can hope to understand human culture or cultural evolution without understanding the world's natural environment as well. Major changes in climate during the past two million years have helped determine where man lived, his diet, and the distribution of population.

For most of geological time, the world's climate was warmer and more homogeneous than it is today. As early as the Miocene (Table 4.1), widespread uplift of land and mountain formation began, which continued through the Pliocene into later time.[1]* Temperatures were lowered on the new highlands, and glaciers formed on the high ground in the highest latitudes. For a long time glaciers and their accompanying ice sheets were confined mainly to highlands in high latitudes, but in more recent times huge ice sheets have spread repeatedly over middle latitudes in the northern hemisphere (Figure 4.1). Spreading alternated with shrinking, with the periods of extensive ice sheets being called "glacial" ages, interrupted by "interglacials" when warmer climates returned. The duration of each glacial or interglacial was variable (Table 4.2), and the details of many earlier glacials still remain uncertain. Much of human history has unfolded against a backdrop of glacial advances and retreats during the Pleistocene epoch, an arbitrarily defined segment of geological time.[2]

The Pleistocene period perhaps covers some 3 million years of geological time out of the 4 billion years or more of the earth's history. Plant life and animal life have been in existence for about half a billion years, but man first appears between 2.5 and 5 million years ago. Although his origins may extend back into the Pliocene, the Age of Man is truly the Pleistocene, one of the most remarkable periods in the earth's history.

* See pages 381–382 for notes to Chapter 4.

Table 4.1
  Geological epochs, from over 60 million years ago.

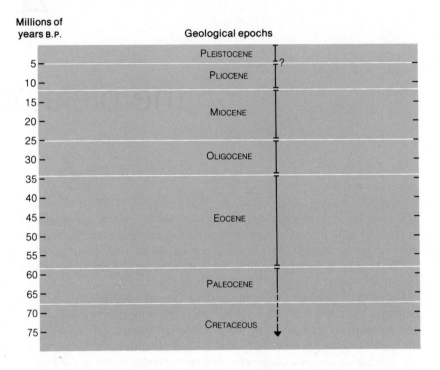

The glacial ages of the Pleistocene mainly affected higher latitudes. Ice sheets covered up to three times more land area than they do today. In what are now more tropical latitudes, less conspicuous and highly complex climatic shifts took place. Climatic zones shifted, depending on the extent of arctic zones. The dry Sahara supported some grassland vegeta-

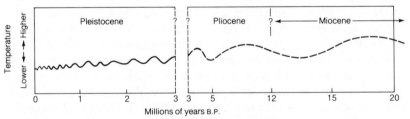

Figure 4.1
  A curve demonstrating long-term temperature changes on earth since the Late Mio-cene. The dotted line through the right half of the diagram indicates a lack of data. The left half shows that the general trend is toward cooler temperatures with fluctuations. The scale of years changes at 3 million years.

Table 4.2
Geological events, climatic changes, and chronology during the Pleistocene (highly simplified), with approximate dates given.[a]

Temperature (Lower → Higher) / Climate	Dating method	Date (B.P.)	Periods	Epochs	European Mammal Ages	European Glacials/Interglacials	North American Glacials/Interglacials	Prehistory
Present climate	C14 dating	10,000	QUATERNARY	HOLOCENE	HOLOCENE	HOLOCENE	HOLOCENE	Cities, Agriculture / Settlement of New World / Hunters and gatherers
	Indirect dating	75,000		PLEISTOCENE	UPPER PLEISTOCENE	WEICHSEL	WISCONSIN	*Homo sapiens*
		?130,000				*Eem*	SANGAMON	
		?200,000			MIDDLE PLEISTOCENE	SAALE	ILLINOIAN	
		?400,000				*HOLSTEIN*	*YARMOUTH*	*Homo erectus*
		?850,000			LOWER PLEISTOCENE (*Villafranchian*)	ELSTER	KANSAN	
Uncertain climatic sequence	Potassium argon dating	?5,000,000	TERTIARY	PLIO-CENE		Uncertain sequence of geological events	Uncertain sequence of geological events	Early hominids and *Australopithecus africanus*

[a]Data are from Flint, 1971 — the chronology of earlier glacial periods is controversial. Flint's terminology has been adopted for this book, and for simplicity and clarity northern European terms are used for the entire Old World. The Alpine glaciations are no longer used for other than local correlations.

tion during colder spells; the Mediterranean became a temperate sea. Snow lines were sometimes lowered on tropical mountain ranges; rain forests expanded and contracted, depending on the abundance of rainfall. The world's sea levels fluctuated between periods of colder and warmer climate. The vast ice sheets locked up enormous amounts of the earth's water, lowering sea levels far below their present levels. Land bridges were formed as the continental shelf emerged from the ocean that now covers it. Britain was joined to France. Many of Southeast Asia's islands were part of the mainland. Siberia and Alaska had a vast land connection. When the ice sheets melted, sea levels rose and flooded many habitats that had been the homes of hunters and gatherers and vast herds of game.

The Pleistocene was a period of great diversity in world climates, one in which regional climatic zones were formed or altered with almost bewildering rapidity. Perhaps the role of glaciations and ice sheets in prehistory has been exaggerated, even if they periodically closed off large areas of the world to human settlement. The minor shifts in local climate patterns in more southern latitudes, in annual rainfall or vegetational cover, were of great significance to hunters and gatherers who depended on the environment for food, water supplies, and shelter.

the great ice age

In 1839, the great geologist Sir Charles Lyell named the Pleistocene ("most recent") strata of northern Europe, using their fossil mollusk content as a basis for his nomenclature. At about that time a young Swiss scientist, Louis Agassiz, proposed that Europe had been covered by vast ice sheets during a "great ice period."[3] Agassiz and other geologists soon recognized that the ice sheets on the slopes of the Alps had left layers of glacial debris called "drifts," which were identical to similar geological deposits found over wide areas of northern Europe and in the United States. The acclaim given to Agassiz's work soon led to the mapping of glacial deposits in Europe and the New World. Geologists subdivided the Pleistocene into various alternating phases of warm and cold climates. In 1874, Scottish geologist James Geikie wrote *The Great Ice Age*,[4] a classic work on Pleistocene glaciation, in which he proposed six glacial subdivisions within the Pleistocene, each of them being a period of intense arctic cold.

Then two Austrian geologists, A. Penck and E. Brückner, studied glacial drifts and gravels in four northern Alpine river valleys and modified Geikie's six stages down to four major Pleistocene glacial advances: Gunz, Mindel, Riss, and Würm, named after Alpine valleys.[5] Great ice sheets flowed southward from Scandinavia and the northern parts of the New

World, covering parts of Denmark and northern Germany as well as the northern parts of the midwestern United States (Figure 4.2). The Alpine glaciers extended into much lower altitudes than they do today. Arctic mammals such as the mammoth, reindeer, and Arctic fox roamed European plains.

Penck's and Brückner's Pleistocene glacial periods were separated from each other by prolonged interglacials, when sea levels rose and the world enjoyed a period of warmer and often drier climate (Table 4.2). When the longest interglacial was at its height, such animals as the hippopotamus were living in the Somme, Thames, and other European rivers. The glaciations themselves were not all unrelenting cold, for considerable changes in temperature occurred as the ice sheets advanced and retreated. During the height of the Weichsel (last) glaciation, the mean annual temperature may have been 10° to 15° C lower than today's value, while it may have been 2° to 3° C higher during interglacials. These figures are gross generalizations based on inadequate evidence.

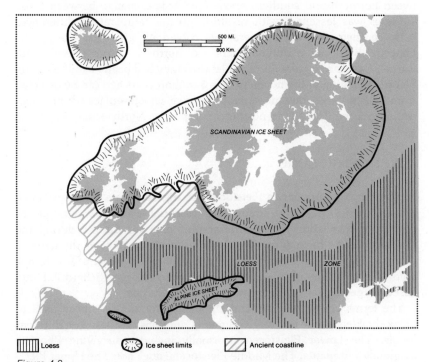

Figure 4.2
The maximum extent of the European ice sheets during the Weichsel glaciation. Notice the greater land surface and smaller sea areas. (After Oakley.)

Penck's and Brückner's four major glacial advances were accepted as a basic framework for Pleistocene glaciation for many years. But their four glaciations in fact represent only a small and very late function of the earth's glacial history, which began over 10 million years ago. So, to form a background for the human cultures described in this book, we must describe a generalized framework of Pleistocene climatic changes. The major events are shown in Table 4.2, and we recommend that you study this carefully as you read on.

the beginnings of the pleistocene

34,000,000– 12,000,000 B.P.

The Pleistocene epoch is now calculated to be some 2 to 3 million years long, although the exact beginning date remains uncertain.[6] For some 85 million years, until about 10 million years ago, the world had enjoyed a prolonged period of warm climate. The Oligocene and Miocene epochs saw the formation of great mountain chains such as the Alps and the Himalayas. Landmasses were uplifted; there was less communication between northern and southern areas. Free heat exchange between those latitudes was lessened, with resulting greater temperature differences between them. Marine temperatures cooled off gradually during the Pliocene. By about 3 million years ago, northern latitudes, while still warmer than today, were much cooler than they had been 70 million years before. A cooling of the northern seas 3 million years ago can be detected from finds of temperate, northern molluscks, which replace warmer species, in marine deposits in northern Europe and North America.

12,000,000– ?5,000,000 B.P.

lower pleistocene

Any attempt to summarize Pleistocene stratigraphy in a few pages is an act of temerity, but some summary is essential. Table 4.2 gives an approximate correlation of the stratigraphic data for Europe during the Pleistocene. We have added North America at the right of the table to give the glacial background to the first human settlement. The terminology used is that advocated by Pleistocene geologist Richard F. Flint,[7] based on geological stratigraphy in northern Europe.

The terms Lower, Middle, and Upper Pleistocene have been used to break the Pleistocene into large segments, subdivisions based on different fossils. The Lower Pleistocene normally includes surviving Pliocene mammals and plants. The Middle Pleistocene does not. The Upper Pleistocene contains more northern mammals than the Middle Pleistocene.

?5,000,000 B.P.

The earliest portion of the Pleistocene is named the Villafranchian, after a series of early fossil-bearing beds from southern Europe (Table 4.2). The French deposits contain many Pliocene animal fossils as well as wild horses, cattle, elephants, and camels, all of which appear for the first time in the Pleistocene. Fossil pollen grains from Villafranchian lake beds in southern France belong to both cool- and warm-loving species, as if spells of cooler climate were separating long periods of warmer weather.[8] Other Lower Pleistocene fossil beds are known from Africa, where early hominids hunted both large mammals and smaller animals. But the Lower Pleistocene is still a virtual blank climatically, a time when early man first began toolmaking and the lakeside camps at Olduvai Gorge were in use (Chapter 5). It seems unlikely that the climatic changes of the early Lower Pleistocene were as drastic as those of later millennia.

middle pleistocene

The three most recent glaciations of northern Europe were named after three German rivers, the Elster, the Saale, and the Weichsel:[9] Elster glacial deposits covered much of central Britain, the Low Countries, and central Europe as far east as the Ural Mountains. With the Alpine ice extending northward and local glaciers on the Pyrenees and the Caucasus, much of Europe between latitudes 40° and 50°N was arctic plains country, with severe winters on the shores of the Mediterranean. The Kansan glaciation in North America was equivalent to the Elster and extended southward from three ice caps near the 60th parallel in Canada. Its southern limits were Seattle, St. Louis, and New York. At the height of the Elster, some 32 percent of the world's landmasses were covered with ice, and sea levels sank about 197 meters (650 ft.) below their present heights.

Elster
500,000 B.P.

The succeeding interglacial, sometimes called the Holstein, or Great Interglacial, lasted from about 400,000 years, to some 200,000 years ago. The climate was temperate, at times milder than today in northern latitudes (Figure 4.3). It was during the Great Interglacial that human settlement of temperate latitudes took hold in earnest, as small bands of hunters exploited the rich game populations of European river valleys.[10]

Holstein
?400,000–
200,000 B.P.

The Saale glacial began about 200,000 years ago, a glacial period that coincided with the Illinoian in North America. In places the Saale was fully as intense as the Elster, with an arctic climate persisting over much of the neighboring parts of Europe, marked by extensive deposits of wind-blown dust. The Saale did not last as long as the Elster, giving way to the Last Interglacial, or Eem, about 130,000 years ago, a period of more temperate climate that was much shorter than the Holstein, lasting only about 60,000 years. The bones of large mammals like the elephant have been found in many Eem deposits in central Europe. Temperatures at

Saale
?200,000–
130,000 B.P.

Eem
?130,000–
75,000 B.P.

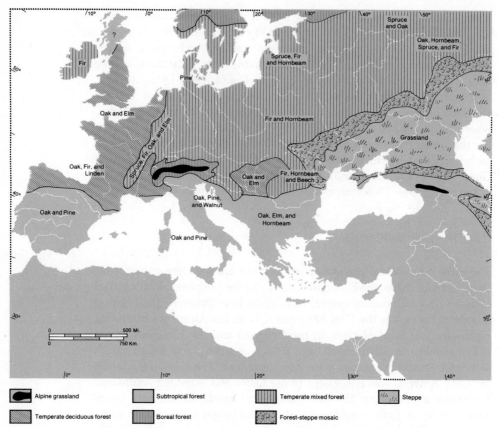

Figure 4.3
Generalized distribution of vegetation in Europe during the height of the Holstein interglacial. (After Butzer.)

the height of the interglacial may have been comparable to those of recent times.

upper pleistocene

Weichsel 75,000–10,000 B.P.

The Weichsel glaciation (or Wisconsin, in North America) formed the last great Pleistocene ice sheet in Europe. About 70,000 years ago the climate cooled off rapidly as tundra vegetation replaced forests in central Europe (Figure 4.4). By about 50,000 years ago the sea level was over 106 meters (350 ft.) below its present height.

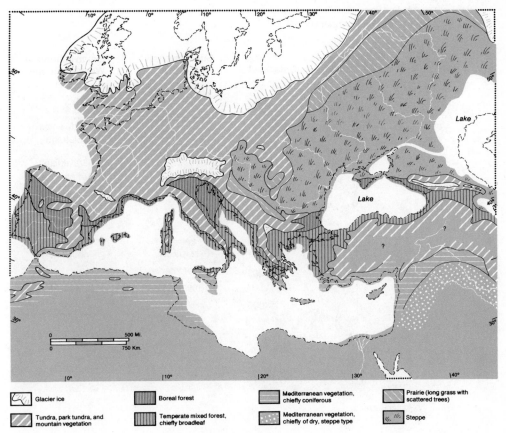

Figure 4.4
Generalized distribution of vegetation in Europe at the height of the Weichsel glaciation. (After Büdel.)

The Weichsel glaciation has been divided into three broad phases by
geologists (Table 4.3).[11] An initial cold period, lasting some 30,000 years
from 70,000 B.P., was followed by a slightly warmer interval that ended
in 30,000 B.P. The late Weichsel was an intensely cold phase dating from
within the last 30,000 years, but by 10,000 to 11,000 B.P. the ice sheets
had begun to retreat for the last time. Arctic cold continued to hinder
human settlement in extreme eastern Europe and Siberia until the end
of the Weichsel (Chapter 9). Man first crossed the Bering Straits at a
time of low sea level during the last glaciation and settled in North
America (Chapter 11) (Figure 4.5).

Table 4.3
The Weichsel glaciation.[a]

Temperature ← Lower Higher →	Date (B.P.)	Subdivisions of Weichsel	Human cultures in Western Europe
		POSTGLACIAL	
	10,000–	LATE GLACIAL	Magdalenian
	20,000–	UPPER PLENIGLACIAL	Solutrean
			Gravettian
	30,000–		Aurignacian
		PAUDORF or MAIN WEICHSEL INTERSTADIAL	Chatelperronian
	40,000–		
	50,000–	LOWER PLENIGLACIAL	Mousterian
	60,000–	warmer interval	
		warmer interval	
	70,000–		
		EEM	INTERGLACIAL

Present climate

[a]After Butzer.

the last ten thousand years

8000 B.C.   The end of the Pleistocene is normally taken to coincide with the final retreat of the ice sheets into the Scandinavian and Alpine mountains and arctic North America. We are said to live in Holocene or "Recent Times." Many scientists prefer to think of us as still living in the Pleistocene, for they have great difficulty defining the boundary between Pleistocene and Holocene.

The shrinking of the Weichsel ice sheets was accompanied by a rapid rise in world sea levels to modern heights. The North Sea was flooded, 6000 B.C.   and Britain was separated from the Continent about 6000 B.C.[12] The Bering Land Bridge was covered. Considerable climatic and environmental changes have taken place since the spread of forests into temperate Europe at the end of the Weichsel glaciation some 8000 years B.C. (Table

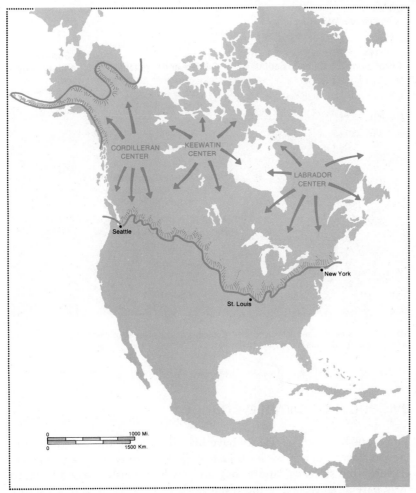

Figure 4.5
The maximum extent of Pleistocene glaciation in North America. The arrows show the direction of ice flow from the three ice sheet centers. (After Cornwall.)

4.4). The warmest climate was during the Atlantic period, about 6,000 years ago, when summers were warmer and winters milder. Warmer, more cloudy, and moister climates have persisted since a little before the Christian era to the present day.

4000 B.C.

Modern Times

Most of the major achievements of human history have taken place since the beginning of the Weichsel glaciation, and the majority of them within the comparatively temperate millennia of Postglacial times.

Table 4.4
Climatic oscillations in Europe.[a]

C14 Chronology	Climatic period	Climate and vegetation	European archaeology
A.D. 1	Sub-Atlantic	More beech forests (colder and wetter)	HISTORIC
600 B.C. –			IRON AGE
2000 B.C. –	Sub-boreal	More pine forests (warm, dry)	BRONZE AGE
3000 B.C. –			AGRICULTURE
4000 B.C. –	Atlantic	Oak, elm, lime, and elder forests, or mixed oak forests (warm, moist)	
5800 B.C. –			HUNTING AND GATHERING
	Boreal	Hazel and oak forests on increase (rather dry)	
7000 B.C. –			
	Pre-boreal	Pine and beech forests (cool, with rising temperatures)	
8300 B.C. –			
	Late Glacial	Arctic tundra (cold)	

[a]Although this table is based only on northern European data, it gives some idea of climatic variations over the past 10,000 years in one part of the world.

evidence for climatic change

Numerous branches of science have helped build up the varied story of the Pleistocene epoch we have just outlined. Botany, zoology, geomorphology (the study of landforms), and nuclear physics have all played their part in constructing the framework of Pleistocene geological and climatic events. Unlike earlier geological epochs, the Pleistocene is unique in that man lived and hunted over much of the terrain covered by ice sheets or arctic steppe during the more temperate interglacials. Thus the remains of hunting camps and butchery sites, stone tools, and split mammal bones are sometimes found in lake beds and other geological deposits that can be dated by geologists and fitted directly into the complex sequence of Pleistocene climatic events.

The chronology of the Pleistocene is based to a great extent on sequences of such locally based phenomena as river gravels, glacial deposits, estuary and lake beds, and wind-blown sands, supported by detailed studies of former landscapes.[13] The bones of large and small mammals have been used to subdivide the period.

During Pleistocene times, climatic change caused the repeated displacement of plants and animals from their original habitats.[14] When a glacial began, the trend was for plants and animals to move to lower altitudes and warmer latitudes. Populations of animals spread slowly toward more hospitable areas. The result was a mixing with populations already living in the new areas, creating new communities with new combinations of organisms. This repeated mixing surely affected the directions of evolution in many animal forms. No one knows exactly how many species of mammals emerged during the Pleistocene, although Björn Kurtén has estimated that no less than 113 of the mammal species now living in Europe and adjacent Asia have appeared during the last 3 million years.

Stone Age man killed a wide variety of animals for food. Broken mammal bones are found in river gravels or in campsites and other settlements. Early man often preyed on now-extinct animals, whose carcasses sometimes sank into lake mud or washed into river backwaters, where their skeletons were buried for archaeologists to find thousands of years later. The fossils of long-extinct elephants and other mammals have been used as a means of building up a sophisticated chronological framework for the Pleistocene. The evolution of certain large mammals has proceeded rapidly during the past 4 million years. Elephants, for example, changed radically during each glacial and interglacial period. It is possible to date Lower and Middle Pleistocene sites within very broad limits merely by examining elephant teeth; each species of these gregarious beasts has a different tooth pattern that serves to distinguish it from earlier and later forms.[15] The teeth can also reflect diets of grass or leaves and thus help in reconstructing vegetation zones.

*"The art of fabricating arms, of preparing aliments,
of procuring the utensils requisite for this preparation,
of preserving these aliments as provision against the seasons
in which it was impossible to procure a fresh supply
of them — these arts, confined to the most simple wants,
were the first fruits of a continued union, and
the first features that distinguished human society from
the society observable in many species of beasts."*
Marquis de Condorcet

II
hunters
and gatherers

Part Two begins with a chapter on the origins of man. This essay is multidisciplinary in nature and attempts to place the latest archaeological discoveries in a behavioral context. The chapter is separated from Chapter 6 by a short Retrospect, a summary statement on the earliest hominids. This leads to an account of *Homo erectus* and his culture, which in turn is followed by another Retrospect, a quotation on "Elemental Man."

The emergence of modern man, a controversial subject, is treated in Chapter 7. The remaining chapters of Part Two deal with advanced hunter-gatherers in various parts of the world. These chapters are separated from the chapter on *Homo sapiens* by a brief essay on the complexity of hunting and gathering, which sets the stage for the remainder of Part Two.

Both the Retrospects and the statement on hunter-gatherers are designed to give you a brief respite from the flow of detailed narrative. You may prefer to read these statements in advance of the chapters themselves.

5

the origins of man

A century ago the great Victorian zoologist Thomas Huxley eloquently made the point: "The question of questions for mankind, the problem which underlies all others, and is more deeply interesting than any other — is the ascertainment of the place which man occupies in nature and of his relations to the universe of things."[1]* Huxley was an intellectual giant in an age of staggering advances in science, a product of the exciting decades when scientists first accepted the concept of a high antiquity for man and the basic principles of evolution. In 1859, Charles Darwin had cautiously remarked in *The Origin of Species:* "Light will be thrown on the origin of man and his history." Other scientists, among them Huxley who was nicknamed "Darwin's Bulldog," soon fully and publicly explored the implications of evolutionism for man's ancestry. Many of them believed that man was more closely related to such apes as the chimpanzee and the gorilla than to the monkeys (Table 5.1).

the search for human origins

Today, most biologists believe that the many points of similarity in behavior and physical characteristics between man and his closest primate relatives, the chimpanzee and the gorilla, can be explained in terms of identical characteristics in each group inherited from a common ancestor millions of years ago.[2] Differences between man and the apes can thus be recognized as having evolved since each had begun his own separate development from a common ancestor.

More than ten decades of intensive research into man's origins have resulted in considerable controversy among experts both on the details

* See pages 382–384 for notes to Chapter 5.

Table 5.1
Man's development: 10 million to 10,000 years.

Date (B.P.)	Technology[a]	Economy[a]	Brain changes[a]	Body changes[a]
10,000–	Bows and arrows	Food production		
20,000–				
	Art			
40,000–	Blade technology	Specialized hunting and gathering	Modern brain	Modern man
	Mounted tools		Modern speech	
	"Prepared-core" technology			
200,000–				Reduction of facial skeleton ("snout" and "muzzle")
	Fire in use		Pre-modern speech	
500,000–	Hand axes	Big game hunting	Rapid brain expansion	
2,000,000–				
	Stone toolmaking	Hunting and gathering	Reorganization of brain and slow size expansion	Bipedalism is perfected — change in forelimbs
				Bipedalism begins (?)
10,000,000–				

[a] The developments on this table appeared at the period indicated by their placement. They are assumed to continue until being either replaced or refined.

of human evolution and over the extent of the chasm that exists between man and his closest primate relatives. Ever since the discovery of the skull of Neanderthal man in Germany in 1856, archaeologists and human paleontologists have searched for traces of human fossils.[3] The first bones of an earlier human than Neanderthal man, *Homo erectus*, were found by Eugene Dubois in Java in 1891. His discoveries were followed by the dramatic finding of *Homo erectus* at Choukoutien, China, in 1927.[4] A few years before, a young anatomist, Raymond Dart, described the first skull of *Australopithecus,* the "Southern Ape," from Taung in South Africa. Dart's find is now recognized as an early ape-man.[5]

The last twenty years have seen many new discoveries of fossil hominids (hominid — family of mammals represented by man). L. S. B. and Mary Leakey have spent over thirty years excavating at Olduvai Gorge, Tanzania, where they have found the bones of early hominids, the remains of their living floors, and evidence of toolmaking potassium-argon-dated back to at least 1.75 million years ago.[6] In recent years archaeologists have worked with success in southern Ethiopia and around Lake Rudolf in Kenya, finding fossil remains of *Australopithecus,* and perhaps *Homo,* dating back at least 5 million years.[7]

Major advances in human genetics and blood-group research have produced much evidence of relevance to human origins. Scientists have realized that we can learn much about early man from studies of both human and primate behavior, especially when we attempt to hypothesize about the ways in which man became "human." Pleistocene geology has become a highly sophisticated field of research. Physicists have developed radiometric dating methods that have extended the chronology of man's origins from a modest million years ago back at least three times further. A multidisciplinary approach to the origins of man is transforming the knowledge of our ancestry.[8]

Despite all this research, however, a small though increasing number of fossils represent our total knowledge of early man — in the case of the Australopithecines, for example, the remains of perhaps 200 individuals. Too few fossils have led to bad taxonomies, great controversies, and wide disagreements. New species of hominids have been created on the basis of single, fragmentary skulls. The anatomists have failed to agree on research methods that could lead to agreement on the significance of the fossils found in the past century.[9]

theories of human origins

Huxley also spelled out his view of the divergences between man and apes: "the structural differences which separate man from the gorilla and chimpanzee are not so great as those which separate the gorilla from the lower apes." These words appear in his classic book *Man's Place in Nature,* a series of essays in which he explored the implications of evolutionary theory for human origins. Huxley had little to go on, for the only fossil skull he could study was Neanderthal man, discovered seven years before. So he made a detailed comparison of the anatomies of man and the apes. Their basic anatomy is so strikingly similar that everyone feels some form of identity with the chimpanzee when one sees him in a zoo or performing on a stage. But Huxley realized there was a gap between chimpanzees and humans, a gap that was a measure of divergent evolution from a common ancestor. The question is, when did man separate from the nonhuman primates? Experts disagree violently when asked this question. There are at least four theories on the origins of the human line, which are summarized in Figure 5.1.

Scheme A

The first school hypothesizes that humans separated into a distinct family before the origins of the monkeys and apes about 40 million years ago. Proponents of this theory argue that a small, nocturnal insect-eater named the tarsier is more closely related to man than any other living primate.[10] But it is unlikely that human ancestry passed through a stage that would be identified as a tarsier, although the fossil evidence is still very limited.

Scheme B

A second group of paleontologists consider that apes and men separated from a common stock in the Oligocene or the Early Miocene era, about 20–30 million years ago (Figure 5.2).[11] This theory is widely accepted, allows for an ape-like ancestry for man only to the extent that an early unspecialized ape may have been ancestral to both man and apes. Unfortunately, the fossil record before the early Pleistocene is very incomplete, although a number of fossils have been advanced as possible candidates.

ramapithecus

One possible claimant for man's ape-like ancestor is a little-known fossil primate named *Ramapithecus* (*Rama*, a Hindu god; *pithecus,* from *ape*), a dozen specimens of whom have been found in Africa and India. *Ramapithecus* first came to light in 1932 at Haritalyangar in the Siwalik Hills, some 200 miles (322 km.) north of New Delhi in India. The late Miocene deposits in which the fragmentary jaws and teeth were found are estimated to date to some 12–15 million years ago, but the chronology is highly uncertain. A jaw of *Ramapithecus* was subsequently found at Fort Ternan in Kenya. This specimen was potassium-argon-dated to about 14 million years. This *Ramapithecus* is later than the date of 20–30 million years proposed for the separation of man and apes by supporters of the second theory.

As early as 1934 George Lewis, the discoverer of the Indian fossils, was claiming that *Ramapithecus* was the earliest known hominid.[12] Unfortunately, we have only jaws and teeth to go on, so it is difficult to assess how close this early primate lies to the origin of man's lineage among the apes. The jaws are smaller than those of the Australopithecines of the Lower Pleistocene, but the muscle attachments for chewing appear

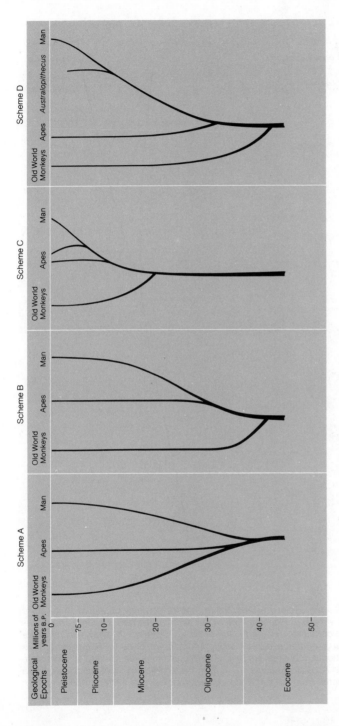

Figure 5.1

Four highly simplified versions of human evolution, three of which (A–C) are described in the text and identified in the page margins. Richard Leakey's provisional scheme (D) is based on his recent discovery of "Skull 1470" in East Rudolf, Kenya. Few details of this important find were available when this text was being written, so the significance of Skull 1470 could not be assessed in this book. But Richard Leakey believes that his new discovery is evidence for the contemporaneity of Homo and Australopithecus some three million years ago, and that the Australopithecines became extinct, whereas Skull 1470 and its contemporaries were in the direct line of human evolution. Only future discoveries will substantiate Leakey's theory or cause it to be rejected. See also Figure 5.2.

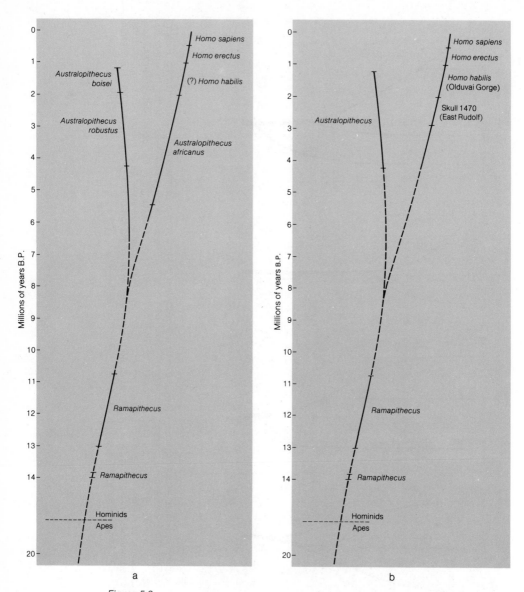

Figure 5.2

Two views of human evolution. Diagram (a) shows a widely accepted view, corre-
sponding to Scheme B in Figure 5.1 with the names of the fossils added. The broken
lines indicate uncertainties, owing to lack of fossils. Diagram (b) shows Richard Leakey's latest view of human evolution, taking into account Skull 1470. Leakey believes
that Australopithecus robustus is a male Australopithecine, and Australopithecus africanus, a female Australopithecine. (Diagram a after Pilbeam, with modification; diagram b constructed from table in National Geographic, June 1973, p. 829.)

better developed than those of apes. The snout is reduced, and the teeth are smaller than those normally found in apes. In particular, the canines are small, in contrast to those of the baboon, for example. Such teeth are used by modern apes for defense and in the quest of food. If *Ramapithecus* did not use his teeth for these purposes, he must have had other ways to protect himself and survive in the intensely competitive environment in which he lived, surrounded by many species of apes and predators. The absence of canines meant that *Ramapithecus* may have made greater use of his hands both in feeding himself and in defense.

Many physical anthropologists believe that *Ramapithecus* is an early human, citing the similarities of his jaws and teeth to those of *Australopithecus* and later fossil men. *Ramapithecus* may have walked upright and used his hands more than an ape. But the limb bones we have are too incomplete to give a definite answer. Those who believe that *Ramapithecus* was a hominid argue that the human family separated from the apes and left the forest before *Ramapithecus* lived in Africa and Asia during the Late Miocene and Early Pliocene.[13]

molecular biology and human evolution

A third view of human origins has been proposed by some researchers in molecular biology, who argue that man separated from the apes as recently as 5 million years ago (Figure 5.1), a radically different approach to human evolution. Two biochemists, Vincent Sarich and Allan Wilson, believe that albumin protein substances found in blood in primates has evolved at a constant rate.[14] Thus the difference between the albumins of any pair of primates can be used to calculate the time that has elapsed since they separated one from another. Sarich and Wilson have shown that apes and men are closer than monkeys and humans. Thus, they argue, apes and men have a more recent common ancestry. They estimate that apes and Old World monkeys diverged about 23 million years ago, the gibbon and man only about 12 million years ago, and that the chimpanzee, gorilla, and man last shared a common ancestor 4–5 million years ago. Unfortunately, the apparent separation of apes and humans is so recent that statistically reliable numbers of differences have not yet accumulated. Early hominids found in East Africa date back at least 5 million years, and the molecular data make a separation of more than 10 million years ago almost impossible.

One possible explanation for the biochemical similarities between apes and man may be that they live longer than other primates.[15] Thus, the random changes in albumin and other elements may take longer to accu-

Scheme C

mulate in man, since they appear during the maturation of sex cells. So there will be less difference between animals with long generation times than between those with shorter ones.

The biochemists' short chronology conflicts with the longer time scale for the separation of man and apes proposed by paleontologists. The basic objection to the longer time scale is simply the lack of fossil evidence belonging to the time between *Ramapithecus* some 14 million years ago and the Australopithecines, the earliest of whom flourished around 5 million years before the present. Unfortunately, fossil-bearing deposits dating to this time period are rare and are little studied.

Scheme D   Richard Leakey, son of the late L. S. B. Leakey, has proposed another scheme of human evolution, based on his discovery of a new skull, known as "1470," from the East Rudolf area. Unfortunately, details of the new skull were sketchy at the time of going to press. But Leakey considers that man and the Australopithecines were contemporaries about three million years ago. He also regards the robust and gracile Australopithecines described below as male and female versions of the same animal. Only future discoveries will lead to widespread acceptance of Leakey's hypothesis.

We do know that the Pliocene era was one of great geological upheaval, when major earth movements and fracturing of the earth's crust caused considerable adjustments in primate environments. Landmasses became more isolated from one another, as areas of desert, especially in the Near East, became more extensive, separating primate populations in Asia from those on the African continent. The great African Rift Valley was formed during the Pliocene, an area where many of the most famous early hominid campsites are found.

The African savannah with its islands of residual forests and extensive grassland plains was densely populated by many species of mammal as well as specialized tree dwellers and other primates. Both the chimpanzee and the gorilla evolved in the surviving forests of earlier times. On the savannah plains other primates were flourishing in small bands, probably walking with an upright posture, and, conceivably, making tools as well. Unfortunately, no fossil remains of these creatures have been found so far; thus we do not know when primates first achieved the bipedal posture that is the outstanding physical feature associated with man. If *Ramapithecus* is a hominid, then future discoveries of his hip bones and limbs will show that he walked upright, a posture most suitable for open country. If he is not, then his hip bones will display anatomical features more suited to life in the trees.

Hominids who walked upright probably adapted gradually to a life on the plains. In many ways they were preadapted to life in open country. For example, they were certainly capable of running or walking short distances, could hold themselves erect without any difficulty, and probably carried and used objects for tools and for defense at times. The issue of a long or short chronology for human evolution will probably be resolved on the basis of future discoveries of both *Ramapithecus* finds and other Pliocene fossils. In the meantime, most students of human evolution tend to favor a separation of man from the apes about 20–30 million years ago.

the evolution of behavior

American anthropologist Sherwood L. Washburn has long studied the evolution of man from the perspective of the development of kinds of behavior that first distinguished early human populations from the apes. The processes of natural selection and the resulting adaptations determine reproductive success and the fates of all populations.[16] Modern man has resulted from the success of the behaviors of his ancestors that have evolved over millions of years of human achievement.

Washburn has argued that, given the close relationship between man and the African apes, it is likely that our early ancestors went through a long period of four-footed posture with their hands and feet adapted to grasping. The Old World monkeys still retain primitive quadrupedalism, but as early as Miocene times, the teeth of monkeys and apes were quite different.

The early apes evolved an arboreal adaptation, climbing in trees and feeding off fruit as well as low-growing foods. Adaptations in their anatomy followed, with modifications in the chests, shoulders, elbows, and wrists to allow swinging from branch to branch, climbing, hanging, and reaching out for food, as well as other new behavior patterns. Unfortunately, we lack the fossil bones that would tell us when these changes took place.[17]

An upright posture and two-footed gait are man's most characteristic physical features, which probably stemmed from modified behavior patterns of the early apes. We can obtain an insight into the behavior modifications that took place by taking analogies from modern African ape behavior, for example, that of the chimpanzee, so ably studied by Jane van Lawick-Goodall and familiar to many readers of the *National Geographic*. In contrast to monkeys, chimpanzees use objects for play and display, carry them in their hands, and use sticks to fish for termites. Leaves are used for cleaning the body and sipping water, and the chimpanzees actually improve their sticks slightly with their teeth if need be when searching for termites. Chimpanzees have in fact inherited behavior patterns far closer to man's than to those of any monkey.

Although modern chimpanzees are certainly not man's direct ancestor, careful observation of their behavior gives some clues to the probable conditions under which human origins took place. For example, both the chimpanzee and the gorilla are knuckle-walking apes, a specialized way of moving in which the backs of the fingers are placed on the ground and act as main weight-bearing surfaces (Figure 5.3). Jane van Lawick-Goodall has found that chimpanzees knuckle-walk for long distances, although some 85–90 percent of their food comes from the trees.[18] Knuckle-walking postures are only occasionally used by man — by football linemen and athletes at the starting block, for example.[19] With longer arms, as might have occurred in ancestral hominids, that posture would have been easier to assume.[20] Knuckle-walking may be an intermediate stage between the purely arboreal adaptation of the ape and the human bipedal posture.[21]

The hackneyed usage of "man coming down from the trees" probably had its origins in the almost paranoid reaction to Darwin's *Descent of Man* in 1871. In fact this image is incorrect, for Jane van Lawick-Goodall, George Schaller, and other primatologists have observed that knuckle-walking chimpanzees and gorillas, the closest relatives of man, spend much of their time on the ground. If our ancestors were knuckle-walkers, as seems possible, they, too, were probably on the ground before bipedalism was evolved.

Chimpanzees, as knuckle-walking, object-using apes, have been seen to prey on other primates and small antelopes. The change from knuckle-walking to bipedalism probably resulted from more frequent object use and hunting, which led to a greater use of bipedalism and of the anatomy that made it possible. More object use, the carrying about of one's tools, and more intensive hunting evolved in feedback relationship with bipedalism. The success of the whole behavior pattern led to the evolution of primates with the human attribute of upright posture, as well as the characteristic patterns of hunting and gathering and tool-making that went with it.

Animal behavior specialist George Schaller has argued that it might be more productive to compare hominids with carnivores such as lions or wild dogs who live on the African savannah.[22] Lions, hyenas, and wild dogs hunt in groups and share their food. In so doing they engage in a form of cooperative hunting that has several advantages. They are more successful killers, can prey on larger animals, and, by eating most of the kill at one time, waste less food. A solitary hunter is obliged either to protect the food he does not consume immediately after the kill or to hunt again when he is hungry. Group hunting allows some members of the pride or pack to guard the young while others hunt and bring back food, which is then regurgitated for the rest.

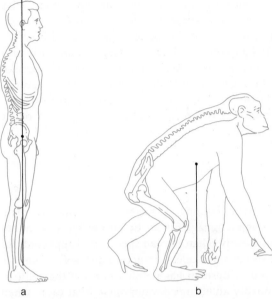

Figure 5.3
Bipedalism versus quadrupedalism.

a. *Human bipedal posture. The center of gravity of the body lies just behind the midpoint of the hip joint and in front of the knee joint, so that both hip and knee are extended when standing, thus conserving energy.*
b. *A knuckle-walking chimpanzee. The body's center of gravity lies in the middle of the area bounded by the legs and arms. When the ape walks bipedally, its center of gravity moves from side to side and up and down. The human center of gravity is displaced much less, making walking much more efficient. (After Zihlman.)*

Cooperation in the chase and the sharing of food are highly beneficial in their effects on social carnivores. Early hominids, too, may have benefited from a growing cooperation in pursuit of game, whose availability was less assured than that of wild vegetable foods in the forest. The social life of carnivores is striking for the diversity and the low degree of dominance among them. Although one sex is dominant over another among lions and hyenas, for example, within each sex there are no hierarchies. Nonhuman primates have a social life structured by hierarchies of dominance, a pattern that has been altered to a radical degree among humans, who, when they began systematic hunting, had to cooperate far more closely with one another than their nonhuman, predominantly vegetarian relatives.

Wolves are highly social carnivores whose habits have been intensively studied in recent years. They are also cooperative hunters who share their food, like the wild dogs. Their facial expressions are constantly changing, each mien having a special meaning, just as it does among humans. Play faces, threats, submissiveness, or a demonstration of friendship are communicated by social animals for whom cooperation is a way of life.[23]

A huge reservoir of firsthand observations on primates and carnivores now exists, from which one can speculate about human origins. Speculation is all very well, even if based on insights from increasingly rigorous field observations, but in the final analysis the story of human origins will have to be written from the fossil record and archaeological evidence from early hominid living floors.

language

Human language is one of the defining characteristics of modern man. It is not clear, however, when language first came into being. We cannot tell from skeletal remains exactly when human speech first appeared, for the detailed relationships between skeletal structure and soft tissue are lost forever. Linguist Philip Lieberman has pointed out that the acquisition of language was probably an abrupt development "that came when the number of calls and cries that could be made with the available vocal mechanism increased to the point where it was more efficient to code features."[24]

Lieberman regards spoken language as a recent development, something that *Australopithecus africanus* and early *Homo* did not possess. The human vocal tract allows vowels such as *a*, *i*, and *u* to be produced. Such vowels are widely found in human languages. The neural and anatomic abilities necessary for such language were developed together, the result of a long evolutionary process that involved changes in anatomical structure through mutation and natural selection to enhance speech communication. Such parallel developments, argue Lieberman and his colleagues, are consistent with the way in which other human abilities evolved. Tool using depends on an upright posture, an opposable thumb, and neural ability. Similarly, vocal communication came about through the presence of enhanced mental ability, which increased the probability of the retention through natural selection of an anatomical mutation that would enhance the phonetic repertoire and the rate of communication. The increased anatomical phonetic ability would in turn increase the retention of mutations enhancing the neural abilities involved in speech encoding, decoding, syntax, and so on.

The early hominids all lack the output mechanisms necessary for the production of speech. Colorado anthropologist Gordon Hewes has suggested that *Australopithecus* probably used a small number of gestures to point out landmarks, foods, water, and basic directions.[25] As time went on and human technology became more complex, more and more gestures were needed until, some 75,000 to 50,000 years ago, selective pressures caused a greater emphasis on spoken language.

The first emergence of language remains a highly controversial issue. Some scholars believe that language developed very early, perhaps as early as Australopithecine times. Others feel that early hominids may not have needed to talk. The real value of language, apart from the stimulation it gives brain development, is that it permits subtle feelings and nuances to be conveyed, which are far beyond the power of grunts or gestures to communicate. But while we may assume that the early hominids needed to communicate more than nonhuman primates, we simply do not know, and may never know, when language began.

australopithecus

Archaeologists have found traces of an early hominid belonging to the genus *Australopithecus* dating back at least 5 million years in East Africa. *Australopithecus* was first identified in 1924 by Raymond Dart, an anatomist at the University of Witwatersrand, among some fossils, including a skull, sent to him by a miner working at a limestone quarry near Taung, South Africa (Figure 5.4). Some months later Dart published his study of the Taung skull and noted that it had small canine teeth.[26] The reduced canines and the position of the skull on the backbone implied both an upright posture and an increasing use of the hands instead of the teeth for defense. Raymond Dart proudly named the Taung baby *Australopithecus africanus* ("the Southern Ape of Africa"), regarding it as a hominid. His report was greeted coolly. Most investigators considered *Australopithecus* to be an ape, more like the chimpanzee or the gorilla than man.

Dr. Robert Broom, a medical doctor and paleontologist, was a prolific discoverer of Australopithecines in the 1930s and 1940s. Broom and John Robinson, his assistant and successor, found the remains of several dozen new Australopithecines, as well as traces of a more robust species, that had the same brain size and posture as the *A. africanus* type. The more robust fossil material was labeled *Australopithecus robustus* to distinguish it from the lighter (gracile) *A. africanus* form.

Australopithecus africanus was probably 107–127 centimeters (42–50 ins.) tall; the females weighing 40–60 pounds (18–27 kg.) were somewhat lighter than the males (Figure 5.5).[27] The posture was fully upright, with the characteristic curvature of the spine that places the trunk over the pelvis for balanced walking. Apes do not have such an anatomical feature, nor are their legs proportionately as long as those of *Australopithecus*. The foot was small, with a well-developed big toe. *Australopithecus*'s appear-

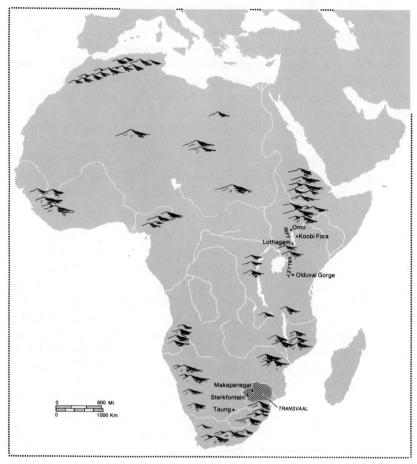

Figure 5.4
Archaeological sites in Africa mentioned in Chapter 5. These sites and a few others represent the worldwide distribution of the earliest hominids.

ance was remarkably human, but with an ape-like snout that was less prominent than an ape's. The canines were small, and the incisors were placed vertically in the jaw in contrast to the outward-sloping incisors of the ape. A flat nose was combined with a well-developed forehead, and the brow ridges were much less prominent than those of his modern tree-living relatives. The brain had an average size of about 450 cubic centimeters, much less than that of a modern human male (1,450 cc) and slightly larger than that of the chimpanzee (400 cc).

Australopithecus robustus was both larger and heavier than the *africanus* forms. The trunk was more barrel-like. The biggest contrasts were in the facial appearance and in the teeth. *Australopithecus robustus* had a low forehead and a prominent bony ridge on the crest of the skull, which supported massive chewing muscles. The brain size was slightly larger than the *A. africanus* form. Unlike *A. africanus*, *A. robustus* had relatively well-developed cheek teeth; his molars were also larger.

Figure 5.5
   Australopithecus africanus. *After extensive research, artist Jay H. Matternes drew this portrait of an* Australopithecus *group.*

Much debate surrounds the relationship between the lighter and the more robust Australopithecine forms. They may have coexisted quite happily in East and South Africa, perhaps competing with each other. But the robust form became extinct some half a million years ago, leaving no direct descendants. It has been argued that *A. robustus* was in fact the male of a single *Australopithecus* species.[28] Alternatively, environmental differences may have caused the robust species to develop differently from the more adaptable *A. africanus,* which made greater use of its new opportunities and bipedal posture.

The southern African Australopithecines from Taung and the Transvaal were originally found without tools or other traces of living activities, cemented in cave earth and associated with large numbers of broken mammal bones, especially baboon skulls. These cemented levels were so hard that they had to be extracted in lumps by blasting, and the bones were extracted from them in the laboratory with hammers, chisels, and chemicals. Animal bones, Australopithecine remains, and stones were jumbled up in the cemented cave earths. No traces of campsites remained in the caves.

The Transvaal sites and the Taung quarry are far from any volcanoes, so the prospects of obtaining potassium-argon dates for their Australopithecine levels are minimal. Only the mammalian bones from the caves give a rough framework for dating most South African Australopithecines to the Lower Pleistocene, between 5,000,000 and 850,000 years ago, although the robust forms may be somewhat later. This dating is, however, highly debatable.

the archaeology of early man

As we said in Chapter 1, man's dependence upon culture for survival is a unique attribute that serves to distinguish him from the nonhuman primates. In his use of more permanent home bases, man is at variance with the modern apes, whose sleeping places leave few tangible remains for archaeologists to find. Man relies on his tools and weapons for survival, defense, and effective adaptation to his environment. Toolmaking may have evolved as a direct result of the adoption of a bipedal posture. The hands were freed for new tasks; manipulatory skills were developed.

Early hominids began to use stone, wood, and bone for their artifacts; they camped by the banks of shallow lakes or waterholes where game congregated and other food resources were available. After a brief stay, the occupants of such a site would move away. The campsite, littered with bones, stone tools and chips, and perhaps crude shelters of brush, would be scattered. Sometimes the tools were covered by the waters of a lake or windblown sand, which softly mantled the tools, preserving them in place for archaeologists to uncover thousands of years later. The brief account of the archaeology of the early hominids that follows is based on the meticulous research work of an international army of scholars from many scientific disciplines.

omo and east rudolf

Many traces of *Australopithecus* and probably another form of more advanced but still little known hominid have been found in the northern parts of Kenya and southern Ethiopia. The oldest Australopithecine so far discovered comes from Lothagam in Kenya, on the western shores of Lake Rudolf. A solitary jaw fragment of a man-ape has been potassium-argon-dated to 5.5 million years. No tools were found with this fossil.

5,000,000 B.P.

Extensive exposures of Late Pliocene and Lower Pleistocene fossil-bearing beds have been found in the Omo Valley on the Kenya-Ethiopia border north of Lake Rudolf. Many extinct mammals, reptiles, and other vertebrates have been recovered from the valley sediments. The teeth and lower jawbones of both gracile and robust Australopithecines as well as possible traces of *Homo* have been found and potassium-argon dated to between 1.8 and 3.7 million years ago. Few stone tools have come from the Omo sediments. Only one campsite has been located where food-bones and tools may possibly be found together when the locality is completely dug.

3,700,000–
1,800,000 B.P.

Lake Rudolf lies in a remote and hot area of northern Kenya, which today supports little more than desert scrub vegetation. In recent years Richard Leakey, son of the excavators of Olduvai Gorge, has been working with a team of scientists on the eastern side of the lake, searching for early hominids. He has located a thousand square miles of Pliocene and Lower Pleistocene fossil-bearing sediments that have already yielded the broken bones of fossil mammals, stone tools, and over forty hominid fragments.[29] The hominids include both Australopithecines and unmistakable specimens of individuals with the more advanced anatomical features assigned to *Homo,* including a so-far undescribed, complete skull. Australopithecines predominate among the East Rudolf hominids, but show considerable anatomical variation within the group.

A major site at Koobi Fora on the shores of the lake has yielded sixty stone tools embedded in volcanic lava, including chopping tools and stone flakes as well as broken animal bones. Potassium-argon tests for the lava with the tools have given an age of 2.61 million $\pm$ 260,000 years for the artifacts, extending the age of human toolmaking back some 850,000

2,610,000 B.P.

years beyond the Olduvai living floors. Scatters of choppers and flakes from other localities, some in association with broken-up animal bones, may turn out to be some of the earliest human kill-sites or home bases in the world.

Australopithecine fossils found elsewhere in the East Rudolf region are thought to be earlier than the Koobi Fora tools — some of the fossil-bearing deposits may date back as far as 4 million years. Research in East Rudolf has hardly begun, and fieldwork is being concentrated on a search for occupation sites where the hominids camped or butchered their prey. The ecologists and geologists have determined that the East Rudolf hominids were living on a swampy floodplain, using scattered tree cover at the edge of small streams for shelter and as a source of fruit.

olduvai gorge

Our present knowledge of the way of life of Lower Pleistocene hominids comes almost entirely from Olduvai Gorge, a spectacular rift in the great Serengeti Plains of northern Tanzania where earth movements have exposed hundreds of meters of lake beds belonging to a long-forgotten Pleistocene lake. The site was first discovered by a German entomologist, Wilhelm Kattwinkel, in 1911. Leakey reconnoitered the Olduvai in 1931 and almost immediately found stone tools on the slopes of the gorge. The Leakeys have excavated there on and off ever since, recovering enormous numbers of stone tools and the bones of over 150 species of extinct mammals, to say nothing of myriads of fish fragments, from the four great series of lake beds that form the walls of the gorge (Table 5.2).[30]

But it was not until 1959 that the first Australopithecine remains of any significance came to light on the living floors that the Leakeys had excavated so carefully. In that year the almost complete skull of a robust Australopithecine came from a living floor in Bed I, the lowest of the four lake-bed series in the gorge (Figure 5.6). Later, a more gracile hominid came from a level slightly lower than that of the original robust skull. Fortunately, fragments of lava came from the Olduvai floors, which could be used for potassium-argon-dating. The living floor upon which the Leakeys' first skull was found has been dated to approximately 1.75 million years ago. The earliest occupation levels at Olduvai date to about 2 million years ago.

1,750,000 B.P.

The more gracile hominid remains from the levels slightly below those of the original robust find consist of parts of the skull of a juvenile, together with a collarbone and some hand bones from at least two individuals. The skull fragments are said to belong to a rather larger-brained hominid than *Australopithecus africanus*, with a dental pattern somewhat

Table 5.2
Highly schematic diagram of Olduvai Gorge, Tanzania, showing chronology and positions of fossils and tools.

Date (B.P.)

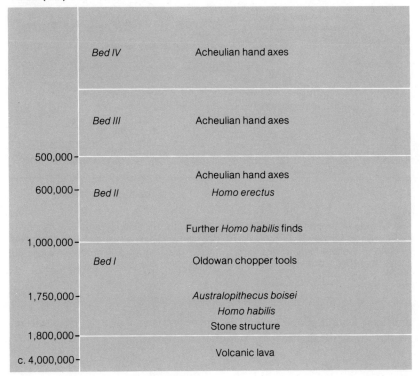

Date (B.P.)	Bed	Fossils and tools
	Bed IV	Acheulian hand axes
	Bed III	Acheulian hand axes
500,000 –		Acheulian hand axes
600,000 –	Bed II	Homo erectus
		Further Homo habilis finds
1,000,000 –	Bed I	Oldowan chopper tools
1,750,000 –		Australopithecus boisei
		Homo habilis
		Stone structure
1,800,000 –		
c. 4,000,000 –		Volcanic lava

similar to that of the gracile Australopithecine. A reconstruction of the hand bones revealed an opposable thumb, an anatomical feature allowing both powerful gripping and the precision manipulation of fine objects. The latter would have permitted the making of complex tools. Intermediate between the hand of modern man and that of the apes, the Olduvai hands display great flexure and muscularity in the finger bones, perhaps attributable to their ancestry among knuckle-walkers.

Other fragments of the gracile hominid have come from the floor where *Australopithecus boisei* was found and from the lower part of Bed II. Leakey and his colleagues named this gracile hominid *Homo habilis*, or "handy man," a new species of the genus *Homo* that was more advanced anatomically and more skillful in toolmaking than *Australopithecus africanus*.[31] Traces of this more advanced hominid may also occur in the Omo Valley

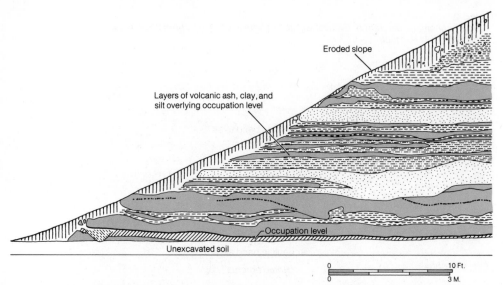

Eroded slope

Layers of volcanic ash, clay, and
silt overlying occupation level

Occupation level

Unexcavated soil

0   10 Ft.
0   3 M.

Figure 5.6
Stratigraphic profile across floor FLK, Bed I, Olduvai Gorge, Tanzania, where the
Leakeys found their first hominid skull. Note the occupation level at the bottom of the
drawing overlaid by horizontal layers of ash, clay, and silt. The eroded slope of the
lake bed (Bed I) appears at left. The trench was dug into this slope.

and East Rudolf. Some scientists consider *Homo habilis* to be a variant
within the Australopithecine population of the time.

living sites

The archaeology at Olduvai is strikingly different from that on other sites
where *Australopithecus* has been found. The Leakeys have unearthed
abandoned living sites (living floors) where the hominids camped, cut
up their food, and perhaps slept. They made stone tools on their camp
floors and may even have made crude shelters. The living floors in the
lowermost bed at Olduvai are literally fossilized human behavior. Tools
and bones on the floors lie in almost exactly the same positions in which
they were dropped by the occupants.

The so-called *Zinjanthropus* floor, for example, is 1,036 meters (1,239
yds.) square.[32] More than 4,000 artifacts and bones have come from the
floor, many concentrated in a working area some 4.7 meters (15 ft.) in
diameter, where shattered bones and rocks are densely crowded into a
small space. Found nearby was another pile of more complete bones that

was separated from the main concentration by a less densely scattered zone. The larger piles may have resulted from efforts at bone-marrow extraction, while the barer, arc-shaped area between these bone heaps and the pile of more complete fragments may have been the site of a crude windbreak of branches, for the arc lies in the path of the prevailing winds today.

One living floor at the very bottom of the gorge yielded not only stone artifacts but also a crude semicircle of stones encircling a slightly depressed area in the floor. This feature has been interpreted as the foundation of a windbreak and dated to about 2,030,000 years ago, perhaps the oldest living structure so far discovered (Figure 5.7).

2,000,000 B.P.

oldowan culture

For many years the Leakeys had found crudely chipped stones in the lake beds at Olduvai, but their makers remained shadowy figures. Similar artifacts came from the *Zinjanthropus* floor in Bed I (Figure 5.8) and

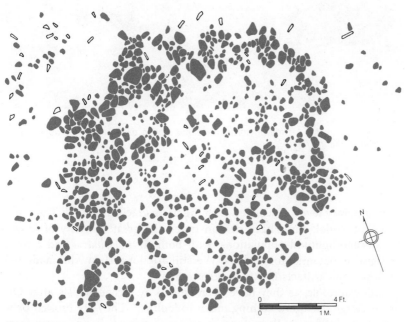

Figure 5.7
The earliest dwelling in the world? A much simplified floor plan of a stone circle on floor DK, Bed I, Olduvai Gorge, Tanzania. Many artifacts and bones are omitted.

Figure 5.8
Living floor in Bed I, Olduvai Gorge, Tanzania, during excavation. Dr. Louis Leakey is standing at the right.

contemporary levels associated with the more gracile hominid. The Omo and East Rudolf finds have demonstrated the great diversity of Lower Pleistocene hominid populations, with both *Australopithecus* and a form of *Homo* as potential toolmakers. We still are not certain who made the earliest stone artifacts in Africa (Figure 5.9).

Oldowan

?2,500,000 B.P.

?500,000 B.P.

Oldowan tools, as they have been named by archaeologists after Olduvai Gorge itself, are nothing much to look at.[33] They are broken pebbles, some little more than stone chunks with a few flakes removed from them. Angular lumps and flakes of lava were selected for making these tools. Some Oldowan tools are so crude that only an expert can tell them from a naturally fractured rock — and the experts often disagree. The Oldowan tools strike one as being extremely practical implements; many of them are so individual in design that they give an impression of being haphazard artifacts, not standardized in the way that later Stone Age tools were. Archaeologists have great difficulty in classifying them, for they do not fall into distinct types (Figure 5.10).

Oldowan tools were probably used for a wide range of activities, including cutting up and skinning animals and preparing vegetable foods. The tools cannot be described as primitive, for many display a sophisticated understanding of the potential uses of stone in toolmaking.

For many years everyone thought that the earliest stone tools would be nothing more than simple split pebbles, so easy to make that they could easily be confused with the "chopping tools" made by such natural phenomena as water action, soil erosion, or stones falling from high cliffs.[34] Although Oldowan stone tools are easily confused with naturally fractured stones when found in river gravels or away from sealed occupation sites, we now know that the Olduvai hominids were skillful stone toolmakers, using intractable lava to make weapons, scrapers, and cutting tools. The tools themselves were probably used for cutting skin too tough for teeth to cut.

the diet of early man

The Olduvai discoveries give us a remarkable insight into the way of life of early hominids who camped by small lakes and lived by both hunting and gathering some 2 million years ago. The campsites at Olduvai were well-established, temporary home bases to which early hominids returned to live, eat, and sleep.

Bed I floors contain the remains of some medium-sized antelope and wild pigs, which were undoubtedly hunted by the inhabitants, but smaller animals predominate. Rodents and fish may have been eaten; gathering and scavenging were probably important activities. British archaeologist Glynn Isaac has described the archaeological study of the Pleistocene diet as "a little like navigating in the vicinity of an iceberg: more than four fifths of what is of interest is not visible."[35] All we suggest at the moment is that, over 2.5 million years ago, at least some hominids were relying on a significant proportion of game meat for their diet.

The African savannah environment is such that hunting was by no means the only easy source of livelihood available to early hominids. The gathering of fruit and vegetable foods in season has traditionally been a major source of human diet in Africa. Anthropologist Richard Lee, who has spent many years studying the !Kung Bushmen of the Kalahari desert,

Figure 5.9

The earliest human stone technology consisted of simple techniques, which are explained here. Stone, of course, was not the only material used by the toolmakers. Unfortunately, no wooden artifacts have survived; bone tools were mainly in the form of flakes or fragments. Some chopping tools from Olduvai Gorge are illustrated in Figure 5.10.

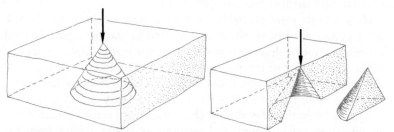

The making of stone tools involves the fracturing of flinty types of rock. When a blow is struck on such a rock, a cone of percussion is formed by shock waves rippling through the stone. A flake is formed (right) when the block (or core) is hit at the edge, and the stone fractures along the edge of the ripple.

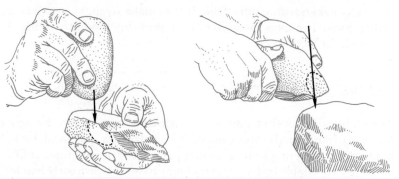

The earliest toolmakers used either a hammerstone (left) or an anvil (right) to remove flakes and make chopping tools. These simple methods remained the fundamental techniques of stoneworking throughout prehistory, although they grew more complex to produce more sophisticated tools for numerous purposes.

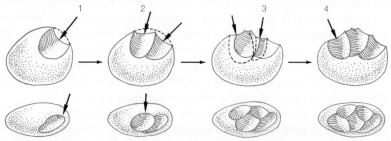

Making a chopping tool. First, sharp blows with a hammerstone or anvil are struck near the natural edge of a pebble to remove flakes. The pebble is then turned over, and more blows are struck on the ridges formed by the scars of the earlier flakes. A chopping tool with a strong, jagged working edge results.

Figure 5.10
Two Oldowan chopping tools (front and side views) made by removing a few flakes from lava lumps to form jagged working edges, indicated by arrows (four-fifths actual size).

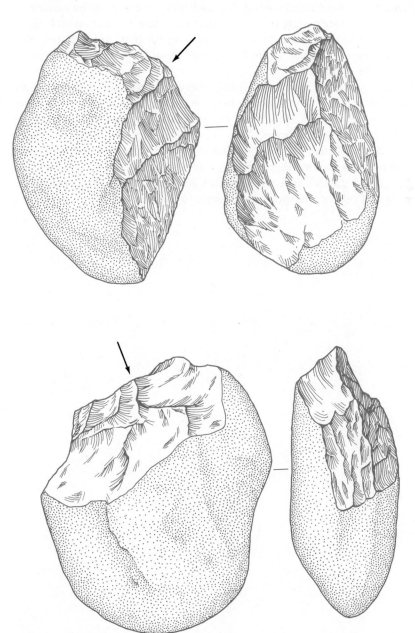

argues that the use of basketry or skin containers to carry vegetable foods and liquids is a basic human invention.[36] The consequences of this innovation in terms of food-sharing, social roles, and the development of home bases were fundamental, for meat does not have to be carried in containers. Once people began to collect vegetable foods from their territory in baskets or skins, they were foraging for food to be shared; this development radically altered hominid social life and the course of human development.

We have raised many tantalizing questions about the origins of man that remain unanswered, largely because we lack both fossils and archaeological information. How many lineages of hominids were there at the beginning of the Pleistocene? Why are the fossils of hominid populations so varied? Because of sexual variation? What behaviors and ecological preferences separated them one from another? How did they make their living? Did they all live on campsites and make tools? The answers to these and related questions must await further research.

retrospect
the earliest humans

We have passed in review over the archaeological evidence for the origins of man and have speculated about the sequence of behavioral events that took place at the beginning of human history. The time has come for a brief retrospect, a look back at man so far.[37]

By about a million and a quarter years ago man had a rather larger brain than the nonhuman primates. Mankind stood upright, with free-swinging arms and opposed thumbs on the hands, which facilitated the manipulation of small objects. Lower Pleistocene hominids lived in small groups of families, each family remaining together both for protection to enable offspring to grow to maturity in safety and for economic reasons during periods of intensive care of the young. Members of the family shared food. The labor of hunting and gathering was divided between them.

Cooperation between individual members of the family extended to cooperation between members of the group as a whole, particularly in the hunt. This is in contrast to the nonhuman primate, who hunts as an individual.

The degree of communication required by such sharing and cooperation was far more systematic and became more intentional. This communication involved both the intention to communicate and the understanding of such a communication by another group member. Instinct had much less of a hold on communication. As the need for cooperative behavior became imperative, the development of language was basically related to cooperative behavior in family and group and was needed for protection, hunting, and the maintenance of a home base within the hunting territory.

Mankind was now using tools made with carefully learned skills. Toolmaking skills were gained by observation, practice, and communication through language, a vehicle for the transmission of knowledge from generation to generation. The pounding of stones one against another and the cutting of wood or bone were skills within the problem-solving capabilities of Lower Pleistocene hominids.

Large hunting territories were now needed, carefully guarded to ensure stable food supplies. Several hundred square miles of thoroughly investigated territory probably supported a population of about one individual to every 5 or 10 square miles (13 or 26 km.). Compared with nonhuman primates, early man needed much more territory to support himself and his chosen preference for meat eating. The more successful the hunting, the more easily meat supplies were available, and further hunting ensued. Improved techniques of hunting and gathering did not necessarily lead to more food and higher population densities. Rather, the greater level of success placed increased demands on the physical environment. Hunting territories became larger and more sparsely populated.

The Australopithecines occupied an ecological niche on the open savannah that was different from that of man's nearest living relatives, the chimpanzee and the gorilla. A new way of life came into being, which eventually came to include toolmaking, new social structures, and ever-increasing intelligence. The success of this way of life led us across the border between "nonhuman" and "human."

6

hand axes and choppers

first discoveries of *homo erectus*

Thirty-one years after the discovery of Neanderthal man in 1856, a young Dutch doctor sailed for an army post in remote Sumatra. Eugene Dubois had accepted his new appointment determined to find the "missing link" between apes and men. He argued that man, being descended from the apes, would have evolved in the tropics far from glaciated areas, and thus he searched in Sumatran caves for traces of early man. Having found nothing of interest, and hearing rumors of an ancient skull discovery in Java, he arranged to be transferred there. Dubois decided to dig in the gravels of the Solo River near Trinil in central Java, where he found fossil animal bones and, in 1891, the skullcap of an ape-like man. The new skull was long and low, with massive brow ridges and an ape-like look. At the same site, the following year he found a complete femur that displayed many human features and belonged to the same creature as the skull.

Three years later Dubois announced his discovery and named his hominid *Pithecanthropus erectus* ("ape-man who walked upright"). We would now classify it as *Homo erectus*. Although he could not date *Pithe-canthropus* accurately, Dubois claimed that he was a morphologically intermediate being between ape and man, with an upright, human posture. A vicious outcry greeted Dubois's announcement. His findings were dismissed with contempt and considered heresy by the church, for many people still refused to believe that man had ape-like ancestors. So the bones were locked away from public view by their finder until twenty-eight years later when the tide of scientific opinion had turned.[1]*

* See pages 384–386 for notes to Chapter 6.

Related finds were announced by Davidson Black, a Canadian anatomist who taught in Peking in the 1920s and was greatly interested in fossils. For centuries the Chinese had been digging fossil bones from caves and pounding them up to make medicines. From 1920 onward, the limestone quarries at Choukoutien hill, some 25 miles (40 km.) from Peking, yielded a steady stream of human teeth. In 1921, Swedish geologist J. G. Anderson and his Austrian associate O. Zdansky were shown Choukoutien and began to dig there. Zdansky found more teeth. So interesting were the finds that Davidson Black persuaded the Rockefeller Foundation to support the work and began an intensive study of a tooth found by Zdansky in 1927. The anatomist was convinced that the tooth was human and announced the discovery of a new genus and species of man, *Sinanthropus pekinensis.* The diggings continued during 1927–1928, and the limestone caves in the hill yielded thousands of fossil animal bones. In 1929 the first complete skull of *Sinanthropus* (Figure 6.1) was found by Chinese archaeologist W. C. P'ei. Subsequent excavations led to the discovery not only of further human remains but also of stone tools, crude bone tools, traces of fire, and bones of deer, sheep, and pigs that Peking man had eaten when he occupied the Choukoutien caves. Plant and vegetable remains came from the deposits, too. The Choukoutien deposits were dated by paleontologists to the Middle Pleistocene and estimated to be half a million years old.[2]

Dutch paleontologist G. H. R. von Koenigswald went to Java in 1936 to check on Dubois's discoveries. He found an older *Pithecanthropus* at Sangiran, to the west of Trinil, as well as other, more modern, skulls at the original site. Franz Weidenreich, who was now working at Choukoutien, and von Koenigswald compared their finds and realized that the Chinese and Javanese skulls differed little more than two races of mankind. They were both obviously human in posture and in general anatomical features, far more so than would be possible for any ape-man or nonhuman primate. *Sinanthropus* and Java skulls were reclassified as *Pithecanthropus,* with the terms *erectus* and *pekinensis* being used to distinguish the finds from the two areas.[3]

In subsequent years *Homo erectus* fossils have come to light in other places. Fragments came from Lant'ien, 600 miles (960 km.) southwest of Peking. A lone jaw similar to other *Homo erectus* examples was found in river sands at Mauer, Germany, in 1907. Another possible find came from Vertesszöllös, Hungary, 30 miles (48 km.) from Budapest. A coastal cave at Sidi Abderrahmane, Morocco, and a quarry at Ternifine in Algeria have also yielded remains of *Homo erectus.* One of the most celebrated finds was a skull found in Bed II at Olduvai Gorge, potassium-argon-dated to some 600,000 years ago. This skull was found in levels that have yielded

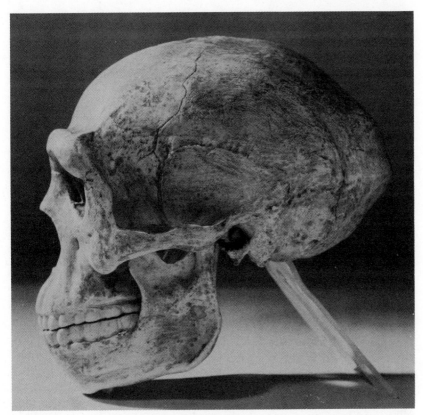

Figure 6.1
A plaster cast of Homo erectus *from Choukoutien.*

tool types quite different from those unearthed in Bed I, which is associated with Australopithecines and *Homo habilis.*

homo erectus

The most striking thing about *Homo erectus* is his wide geographic distribution. In contrast to earlier hominids, who are at present known only from Africa, *Homo erectus* has been found in many extremes of environment, ranging from tropical semiarid savannah in Africa to temperate latitudes in China.

Perhaps as early as 1.3 million years ago, Lower Pleistocene hominids gave birth to the earliest bands of *Homo erectus.* This development may

?1,300,000 B.P.

have occurred in several places at different times. The earliest fossils have been found in the tropics of Africa and Southeast Asia. As the population of *Homo erectus* increased, some bands stayed on in the tropics while others spread out into new areas. Over a prolonged period of time small groups of hunters repeatedly broke away from their relatives and settled a few miles away in new hunting territory. This process was repeated again and again, taking *Homo erectus* northward into temperate latitudes. New cultural and social adaptations were stimulated by the challenges of surviving in new environments. The adaptations may even have speeded up the evolution of the species. Certainly the evolution of new and highly versatile behavior patterns was essential, as were new cultural habits.

Homo erectus had expanded considerably northward by 750,000 years ago, for traces of human settlement in southern France date to the Villafranchian (Table 4.2 and Chapter 6), while the Choukoutien finds belong in the Middle Pleistocene and are estimated to date between some 500,000 and 300,000 years ago.

The skull bones of *Homo erectus* show that the new hominids had a brain capacity averaging between 775 and 1,100cc and showing much variation. It is probable that their vision was excellent and that they were capable of considerable thought processes. The *H. erectus* skull is more rounded than that of earlier hominids; it also has conspicuous brow ridges and a sloping forehead. With a massive jaw, much thicker skull bones, and teeth with cusp patterns somewhat similar to those of *Australopithecus africanus* and modern man, *H. erectus* had limbs and hips fully adapted to an upright posture. He stood about 5 feet high (153 cm.) with hands fully capable of precision gripping and of a wide range of toolmaking activities.[4]

It is in his brain size that *Homo erectus* is a distinctive form of man, capable of far more sophisticated cultural and social activities than earlier hominids. Throughout the millions of years that earlier hominids roamed the African savannah, there were few technological changes in the simple stone choppers they used or alterations in the hunting and gathering quest. But when we encounter *Homo erectus* in the archaeological record, we immediately find a greater diversity both of tool forms and of human activities (Table 6.1).

hand axes

Olduvai Gorge tells us what biological and cultural changes took place as *Homo erectus* appeared for the first time. The first hand axes, the characteristic tools associated with *Homo erectus* throughout much of the Western world, appear in upper Bed II, overlying the chopping tools and

Table 6.1
Sites (in parentheses), cultures, and fossils from Africa, Asia, and Europe during the Middle Pleistocene.

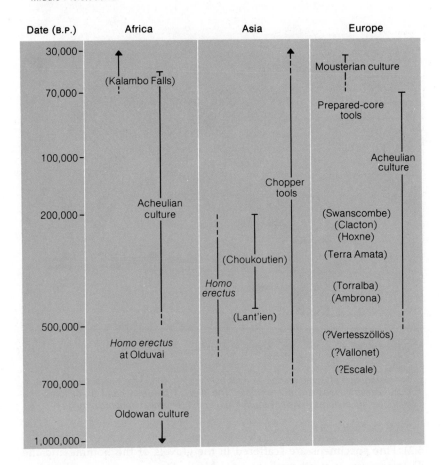

the living floors of earlier hominids found in Bed I and the lower parts of Bed II.[5] For some time, however, earlier tool traditions remained in use alongside hand ax technology. Hand axes are thought to be general-purpose tools; they have short cutting edges and rounded bases, and were probably used for a multitude of purposes, from skinning animals to digging up wild roots. The culture associated with the *Homo erectus* skull at Olduvai is known as the Acheulian, a widespread archaeological "cul-   Acheulian
ture" named after the town of St. Acheul in northern France.

Acheulian hand axes have been found in river gravels, lake beds, and other geological situations over enormous areas of the Old World (Figure

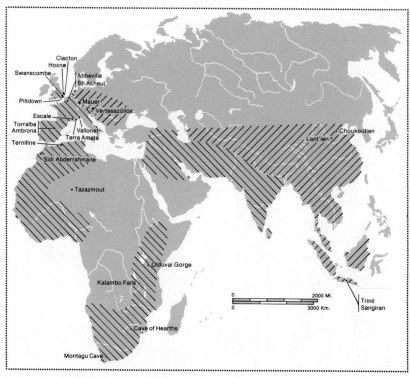

Figure 6.2
The distribution of Homo erectus and his cultures, showing sites mentioned in the text. Culture distributions are approximate. The division between hand ax cultures and chopper tool cultures in Asia is roughly along the Himalayan mountain range.

6.2). Fine specimens are scattered in the gravels of the Somme and the Thames rivers in northern Europe, in North African quarries and ancient Sahara lake beds, and in sub-Saharan Africa from the Nile Valley to the Cape of Good Hope. Acheulian tools are common in some parts of India, as well as in Arabia and the Near East as far as the southern shores of the Caspian Sea. They are rare east of the Rhine and in the Far East, where chopping tools were in common use until comparatively recent times.[6] No one has been able to explain why hand axes have this restricted distribution. Were such multipurpose tools used only in big-game hunting camps? Was their use restricted by the availability of flint and other suitable raw materials? Did environmental conditions affect the hunters' choice of toolkits? We do not know.

The first Acheulian tools at Olduvai are found with choppers and crude flakes of the Oldowan type. In later times a considerable range of flake scraping tools occur, too, some of which were probably used for woodworking. That the ultimate ancestors of Acheulian tools lie within the Oldowan is unquestionable, but the process of technological evolution involved is likely to have occurred in many places. Bed II at Olduvai contains three different types of toolkits, the first of which is of the Oldowan tradition so familiar from Bed I (Figure 5.10). The second, more developed toolkit is thought to have evolved from a chopper tool culture in which simple pointed choppers, rare hand axes, and crude, battered spheroidal tools made their appearance. This stone tool tradition is only slightly more developed than the Oldowan of Bed I. Over a third of the tools from the third toolkit consists of hand axes and cleavers, labeled Acheulian by the discoverers (Figure 6.3). The Acheulian appears suddenly at Olduvai; its tools are made of larger rocks than the smaller choppers characteristic of the Oldowan.[7] The Atlantic coast of Morocco is another area where both Oldowan and Acheulian toolkits occur at the same site. There, again, early Acheulian tools suddenly appear in the early Middle Pleistocene.

In contrast to the Oldowan, which shows virtually no change through its enormously long life, the Acheulian culture shows considerable variation throughout its history. The development of the hand ax and its associated toolkit were ably documented by Mary Leakey at Olduvai, where the earliest Acheulian hand axes are little more than crudely blocked out lumps of lava with jagged edges and rough points (Figure 6.4). Similarly crude hand axes have been found at Abbeville in the Somme Valley of northern France and in the Sahara. The serpentine edges of the early hand axes in Bed II at Olduvai give way to more advanced artifacts in later levels of the gorge. The hand-ax edges become straighter, often flaked with a bone hammer that gave a flatter profile to the ax (Figure 6.3). In contrast to earlier specimens, the bases are carefully rounded and finished. A butchery tool known as a cleaver makes its appearance as a hand ax with a straight and untrimmed cutting edge, often made on a flake (Figure 6.5).

The Acheulian hand ax is, after the Oldowan chopper, the most widespread and longest lived of all human tool forms. The Olduvai Bed II floors have not yet been accurately potassium-argon-dated, but the earliest Acheulian there is estimated to date to some 400,000–600,000 years ago. At the other end of the time scale, the late Acheulian hunting camps at the Kalambo Falls on the border of Tanzania and Zambia in central Africa are estimated to be about 60,000 years old. The Acheulian culture in Africa, if not elsewhere, lasted as long as half a million years.[8]

500,000–
60,000 B.P.

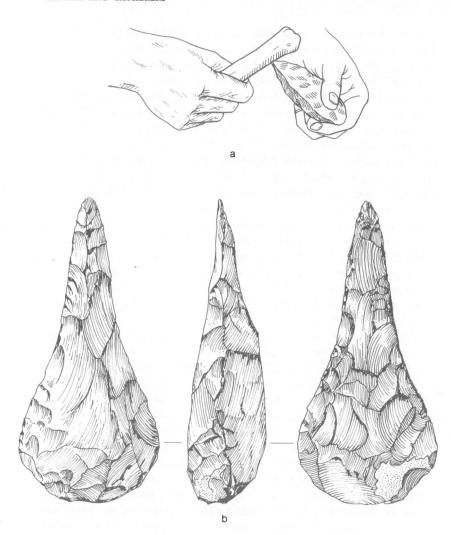

Figure 6.3
Acheulian hand ax technology.

a. Making a hand ax. The earliest hand axes were crudely flaked, pointed objects.
   Their development was a logical extension of the chopping tool, as they had two
   cutting edges instead of one (see Figure 6.4). Simple hammerstone techniques
   were used to manufacture these axes. Later, Acheulian hand ax makers used a
   hammer of wood or bone to finish off their implements. This technique resulted
   in straighter working edges and a finer finish.
b. A finished hand ax (three views) from Swanscombe, England (one-third actual size).
   The Acheulians used wooden tools such as spears and clubs, but few examples
   have been found (see Figure 6.6).

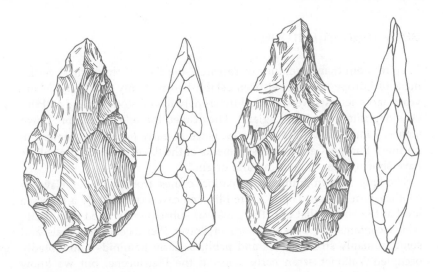

Figure 6.4
Two early hand axes from Olduvai Gorge, Bed II, front and side views (three-quarters actual size). (After Leakey.)

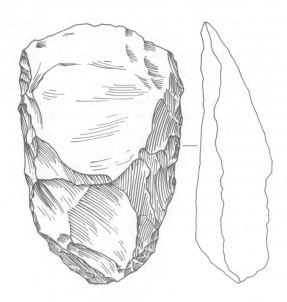

Figure 6.5
A cleaver with a straight cutting edge from Baia Farta, Angola, Africa, front and side views (one-half actual size).

early man in europe

Despite more than a century of research, the date of the earliest settlement of Europe has not yet been established with any reliability. Many years ago scientists were excited by crudely flaked stones found in Pliocene deposits in eastern England. They called these "eoliths," or "dawn stones," and claimed they were evidence of early human settlement in northern Europe. Careful measurements of the flake angles on the eoliths have shown them to be of natural origin.[9]

The first known human occupation comes from Vallonet Cave in southeastern France. There, a late Pliocene cave was filled by a high sea level at the end of that era. The cave was subsequently filled with earth, which contains the broken bones of Lower Pleistocene mammals and some humanly struck flakes and pebbles. Early hominids undoubtedly occupied Vallonet at an early stage in the Pleistocene, but we know nothing of their physical characteristics or economic practices and little of their artifacts.[10]

Another early campsite was discovered by Hungarian geologist M. Pedsi at Vertesszöllös near the Danube in 1963.[11] A series of occupation deposits found in the upper-terrace slopes of the Ataler Valley yielded the remains of mammals ranging in size from bears to dormice. The animals in the collection are species that became extinct in the late Lower Pleistocene and are found with concentrations of stone artifacts and burned bones. The Vertesszöllös stone tools include both choppers and simple scrapers. Parts of a human skull came from the same level as the tools. Human paleontologists believe that the Vertesszöllös skull comes from a more advanced *Homo erectus* than the Olduvai or the Asian populations, who had a larger brain than his relatives'.

300,000 B.P. Europe was widely settled by Acheulian people during the Holstein interglacial some 300,000 years ago. Hand-ax sites abound in western Europe; some of them are described in this section. These sites represent the first widespread settlement of temperate latitudes in the west, for no Lower Pleistocene camps have yet been found in Europe itself, with the possible exception of Vallonet and Vertesszöllös.

the clactonian

Many years ago British archaeologists Hazzledine Warren and Reginald Smith amassed a huge collection of choppers, flakes, and cores from a Middle Pleistocene river system near Clacton, northeast of London.[12] The

Figure 6.6
  Wooden spearhead from Clacton, England, from the Lower Paleolithic (about one-
  eighth actual size).

collections contained no hand axes. But large numbers of simple flakes
had been removed from large cores by a stone hammer. A wooden spearhead, the earliest wooden tool yet found, also came from the site (Figure
6.6). Pollen samples from the peaty deposits of the river system included
oak, pine, alder, and hazel, all temperate forest trees. Botanists compared
the Clacton pollens with pollens found at an Acheulian campsite at Hoxne
in nearby Suffolk and with other grains found in the lower levels of the
great "Middle Terrace" of the Thames at Swanscombe, east of London.
They agreed that all three localities were occupied in the Holstein interglacial.[13]

The Swanscombe quarry, on the southern side of the Thames Valley   ?200,000 B.P.
near London, had been famous for its fine stone hand axes long before
fragments of a fossil skull were discovered with Acheulian hand axes
at the quarry in 1934.[14] But the lower gravel levels at Swanscombe are
littered with flakes and chopper tools of the same type found at Clacton.

These horizons, which contain no hand axes, are overlain by the "Middle Gravels," which have yielded huge quantities of hand axes as well as some skull bones of a hominid "far more like modern man than *Homo erectus*, yet quite distinct from ourselves."[15]

Clactonian ?200,000 B.P.The scatter of English chopper tool sites has been classified under the cultural label "Clactonian," but the only technological links with other prehistoric cultures lie with the chopping tools of Asia and the Oldowan of Africa. The Clactonian sites pose many intriguing questions. Did Acheulian hunters use choppers instead of hand axes when occupying Clactonian sites? Or did man migrate from Africa to Europe more than a million years ago, before he had developed the more sophisticated hand-ax technology characteristic of later millennia? If he did, few durable traces of his tentative occupation of northern latitudes remain for archaeologists to study. Perhaps the first attempt at human settlement in Europe was a failure. In this case, a second, later population of Acheulian hand-ax makers moved into Europe some three or four hundred thousand years later. This settlement was both successful and long-lived. Numerous Acheulian sites have been discovered north of the Mediterranean. They were occupied by hunter-gatherers who either settled in virgin territory or assimilated and wiped out the earliest humans to venture into temperate European regions.

acheulian sites

Although some living floors at Olduvai Gorge have given us an insight into the home bases of Lower Pleistocene man, camping places of the earliest hominids are rare, and our knowledge of their way of life is necessarily incomplete. Many more settlements abandoned by Acheulian people have been found in an undisturbed state. The concentrations of food waste and tools in such campsites have been investigated carefully by teams of archaeologists, providing some vivid perspectives on the activities of their inhabitants.

By late Acheulian times many campsites were being occupied more intensively and for longer periods than before.[16] Others were being used year after year on a seasonal basis, for the concentrations of living debris are far denser than at earlier sites. The refined working edges of the hand axes and cleavers used by the later Acheulians are straighter and were more carefully trimmed (Figure 6.3). Stone spheres, formed by constant pounding of pebbles to achieve a globular shape, are commonly found on later Acheulian floors, and may have been used for preparing vegetable foods and smashing food bones.[17]

terra amata

The Acheulian base camp at Terra Amata in Nice, France, has provided remarkable evidence of shelters built by hunters living on a beach dune on the shores of the Mediterranean. Terra Amata has been dated to the early part of the Holstein interglacial.[18] The climate was temperate but cooler and more arid than today's. The hunters visited Terra Amata for short periods between late spring and early summer over a period of at least eleven years. Wild oxen, stags, elephants, and rhinoceroses, as well as small mammals, were hunted, while seafood also figured in their diet.

?300,000 B.P.

Henry de Lumley, the French archaeologist who dug Terra Amata, recovered the remains of a number of shelters from the settlement. The hunters built oval-shaped huts about 8–15 meters (26–50 ft.) in length and 4–6 meters (13–20 ft.) wide, with an entrance at one end (Figure 6.7). A series of posts about 7 centimeters (3 in.) in diameter formed the walls; their bases were reinforced with lines of stones. The roof was supported by center posts, and a hearth was located in the center of some dwellings. The floors were covered with organic matter, including human feces, ash, and stone tools. Imprints of skins laid on the floors were found in some huts.

butchery sites: ambrona and torralba

Sometimes Acheulian hunters killed a large mammal and camped around the carcass as they cut it up. Butchery sites have been excavated in Africa and Spain, identified by partially dismembered carcasses of hippopotamuses and other large animals. A few large cutting tools and small numbers of flakes were found with the abandoned bones.[19]

The most famous and extensive butchery sites are in the Torralba and Ambrona valleys in Spain, where the dismembered skeletons of large extinct elephants are found with the tools used to cut them up. Torralba lies in a deep valley some hundred miles northeast of Madrid.[20] The Ambrona site was found a mile (1.5 km.) away from Torralba. Some bubbling springs were probably active in the area in Middle Pleistocene times, rendering the deep valley a favored locality for big-game hunters. The Torralba locality produced the remains of at least 30 elephants of an extinct straight-tusked variety, 25 deer, and a few rhinoceroses, wild oxen, and rare carnivores. Pine trees, nurtured by a somewhat colder climate than today's, covered the landscape at the time Torralba was occupied.

Geologist Karl Butzer has dated Ambrona and Torralba to the late Elster glacial, over 400,000 years ago, a period before the Acheulian

?400,000 B.P.

occupations of Swanscombe and the Somme Valley in northern France. F. Clark Howell exposed some 278 square meters (333 sq. yds.) of the Torralba settlement, 28 square meters (33 sq. yds.) of which were covered

Figure 6.7
Reconstructions of houses at Terra Amata, France.

by the remains of the left side of a large elephant. The hindquarters were gone, but the tusks, jaw, and part of the backbone lay on the ground. An area to the southeast of the carcass contained the broken remains of some of the rib cage and the right limbs of the same elephant, as well as traces of fire and skinning tools. The hunters had evidently cut up small parts of the carcass after removing them from the body.

Ambrona yielded two levels of occupation, the lower of which was a kill site where 30–35 elephants had been dismembered. The bones of wild horses were about half as common as the elephants'. Concentrations of broken food bones were found all over the site, but the center of the butchery area contained a concentration of large bones, most of them from a nearly complete old bull elephant. The individual bones had been removed by the hunters, and the skull had been smashed, presumably to get at the brain. Most of the limb bones were missing. In one place a series of elephant bones had been laid in a line, perhaps to form stepping stones in the swamp in which the elephants were dispatched.

The Spanish kill sites were littered with stone tools used for dismembering the hunters' prey. Crude Acheulian hand axes and cleavers were outnumbered by a range of scraping and cutting tools. The stone lumps from which the flakes were made are conspicuously absent at these sites, as if the hunters took their tools with them to the butchery areas. Some pieces of humanly worked wood were found at Torralba, too, some of the oldest wooden artifacts in existence.

kalambo falls

British archaeologist J. Desmond Clark was lucky enough to find a remarkable Acheulian campsite at the Kalambo Falls on the Tanzania-Zambia border. In the early 1950s Clark examined the eroded edges of the Kalambo River immediately upstream from the spectacular falls, 221 meters (726 ft.) high. He found numerous hand axes washing out from the banks.[21] By excavating into the river banks, he was able to uncover a series of Stone Age living floors, some only 10,000 years old and others going back to Acheulian times. The earliest floor occupied the bank of a small stream course that had run into a shallow lake behind the Kalambo Falls. The water table had covered the floor soon after its abandonment, waterlogging and preserving logs, wooden tools, and concentrated masses of vegetal material accumulated by the Acheulians.

The eastern edge of the floor was occupied by a semicircle of carefully placed boulders. They are thought to have formed the foundations of a crude windbreak of branches, for the arc of the stones faces into the prevailing winds. Hand axes, flake tools, cleavers, and stone chippings were scattered elsewhere on the floor, lying in the exact positions where

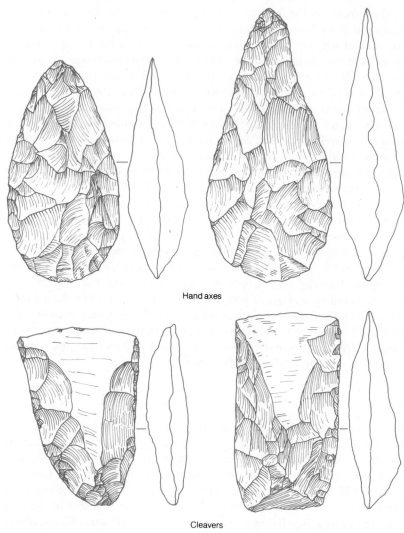

Hand axes

Cleavers

Figure 6.8
Acheulian tools from Kalambo Falls, Zambia, front and side views (one-third actual size).

?60,000 B.P.

they were dropped by their users (Figure 6.8). This living floor, which has been radiocarbon dated to over 60,000 years ago, obviously represents a late survival of Acheulian culture in the hands of a more advanced hominid than *Homo erectus*.

specialized toolkits

Acheulian living floors can reflect activities other than butchery.[22] Picks and woodworking tools are common at some African sites where man lived in a more forested environment and relied more heavily on wild vegetable foods for his diet. Others are workshop sites, such as that at Tazazmout in the Sahara, where spreads of chipping debris lie close to a source of raw material suitable for making stone tools. As an analogy, Australian aborigines are known to have camped close to fine stone outcrops for many generations, trading stone suitable for making axes over enormous distances.

In contrast to Lower Pleistocene living floors, these Middle Pleistocene floors show considerable variation in small-tool shapes from one site or region to another. The variability may reflect the hunters' personal idiosyncracies and divergent economic tasks. The length of time a living site was occupied probably varied considerably, although time estimates and population densities are hard to calculate.

Regular visits to a favored hunting spot over a period of some years may account for the dense concentrations of bones at Torralba and the enormous numbers of hand axes at Swanscombe. Other settlements may have served as temporary camping sites for several bands of hunters from a large area when they congregated at one spot to feast on the results of a communal game drive.

homo erectus in asia

Acheulian hand axes have been found as far east as India, but few traces of these characteristic tools of *Homo erectus* have come to light in the Far East or Southeast Asia. Instead, the earliest hunters made use of crude chopping tools and simple implements made of rough flakes. Early chopping tool sites are to be found in the regions immediately to the south of the Himalayas in India and Pakistan. The crude pebble choppers from these sites have been grouped into a "Soan" culture, which was practiced to the north of the hand-ax areas of central and southern India.

Soan—no dates in years

The chopping tool tradition extends eastward into Burma, Malaysia, Indonesia, and Borneo, where it exhibits local manifestations.[23] It was the work of the first humans to penetrate into Southeast Asia, probably during the Lower Pleistocene. The low sea levels of the Elster glaciation would have allowed widespread colonization of the major islands of Southeast Asia. Most of the chopper tool finds, which come from river

Figure 6.9
*Choukoutien Locality I: a general view
(left), with the excavation grid painted
on the rock face above the site; the
floor of the cave (right).*

gravels, have been classified into various local variants that need not concern us here. Eugene Dubois's finds of *Homo erectus* at Trinil in Java have not been associated directly with chopping tools, but there can be little doubt that choppers were in use in the area.

the first chinese

Most fossil hominids found in Chinese Pleistocene sites are in a highly fragmentary state. Climatic conditions during the Lower Pleistocene were not particularly harsh, but no one has yet found *Australopithecus africanus* on Asian soil. The earliest human fossils come from Kungwangling Lant'ien in Shensi Province of north-central China, are classified as *Homo erectus* and have been dated to before the Mindel glaciation or to a warm phase in it. The Lant'ien hunters were living during a period of mild and fairly dry climate, perhaps during a warm interval in Elster. Some crude stone choppers have been found near the fossil remains. These finds date to the early Middle Pleistocene.[24]

choukoutien

Most of our knowledge of Middle Pleistocene hunters in the Far East comes from Choukoutien sites, which were dug many years ago by P'ei Wen Chung and others, and are being restudied by Chinese scholars, including P'ei.[25] Choukoutien hill contains several limestone caves, sandwiching layers of human and animal debris, but the pertinent data came from Locality I (Figure 6.9).

For long periods the site was occupied by carnivores such as hyenas and bears. But at other times *Homo erectus* took over the cave, until, at the end of the occupation, he was the permanent occupant of Choukoutien. Some sixty species of animals were associated with *Homo erectus*, including the bones of elephants, two kinds of rhinoceroses, bears, horses, camels, deers, and many small rodents. The dismembered carcasses of camels, water buffalo, bison, horses, boars, and mountain sheep were also brought to the cave. The animals from Choukoutien have been assigned to the Holstein interglacial.

Choukoutien
450,000–
200,000 B.P.

Some Choukoutien levels are rich in human tools made mostly from quartzite. Chopping tools with jagged edges were roughly chipped from coarse rocks (Figure 6.10). But most of the stone tools were little more than crude flakes, struck from stone cores and used without further

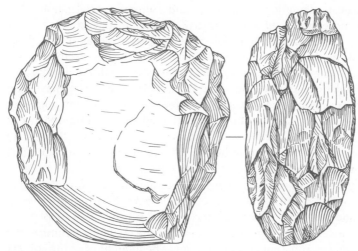

Figure 6.10
  A crude chopping tool from Choukoutien, China, front and side views (one-half actual size). (After Movius.)

shaping. A few rough scraping tools or knives were made, as were some simple bone points and clubs. Traces of fires abound at Choukoutien, some of the earliest evidence for the controlled use of fire ever found.

The simple choppers of the first Asians resemble the Oldowan tools of the first Africans. Such similarities can be explained as merely the logical result of simply flaking a pebble to produce a jagged working edge. But did toolmaking originate in Africa and then spread eastward with early bands of more adaptable hominids than Lower Pleistocene hunters? Or did man begin to manufacture artifacts quite independently in Asia before the Middle Pleistocene? We have remarked on the lack of Australopithecine remains in Asia, but that does not mean that earlier hominids did not live there. Future archaeologists may be able to tell us whether toolmaking was invented in more than one place as we learn more from new discoveries.

man the hunter

There is a sameness about the tools of *Homo erectus* that is both depressing and remarkable. Acheulian hand axes from as far apart as Olduvai Gorge, the Thames Valley, and the Indian peninsula are basically similar in shape — the same is true of many other large and small artifacts possessed by *Homo erectus*. Most surviving Acheulian tools are made of stone and give us an extremely limited view of subsistence activities, ecological adaptations, or diet. It is quite possible that different Acheulian bands had ecological adaptations and social and cultural specializations that varied far more than their surviving artifacts would suggest.

University of California archaeologist Glynn Isaac has approached the problem of the similarity of Acheulian sites from the perspective of ethnographic analogy.[26] The hand-ax makers lived in small bands, and like sparse populations of modern hunter-gatherers, many may have had meaningful groupings no larger than a few families. In such societies today, male culture may retain a distinctive adaptive continuity that is centered on a limited territory.[27] The women, on the other hand, may be more mobile, moving into other bands or returning to their original locality, providing a mechanism both for diffusion of cultural and technological innovations and for their reinforcement in the place of origin. Such a system of cultural transmission would tend to be highly resistant to major innovation and change, preserving basically effective adaptations over large areas for long periods of time. In the Acheulian culture, the long millennia of apparent equilibrium must be thought of in the context of the more rudimentary brain and economic adaptations of *Homo erectus*.

Big-game hunting was a major source of food for *Homo erectus.* In Africa, for example, the dry savannahs that were his environment were not as abundant in vegetable foods as the forests where the chimpanzee and gorilla flourished. But enormous herds of mammals roamed the plains, until the arrival of the nineteenth-century explorer with his rifle. *H. erectus* could hunt aged, crippled, or young animals and tackle mature animals and larger beasts, perhaps on a cooperative basis as do wild dogs or wolves today.

The Torralba elephants were buried in clays, which must have been treacherous marsh for the heavy Middle Pleistocene beasts. Hunters could watch the valley floors where the elephants roamed. At a strategic moment, they would drive the unsuspecting beasts into the swamps by lighting grass fires and shouting. The elephants could then be killed and butchered at leisure. (Cooperative hunts of this type were common in Africa until the 1920s.)[28] Perhaps it is no coincidence that F. Clark Howell found scatters of charcoal over wide areas of the Torralba site, possible evidence of fiery game drives.

The gathering of wild vegetable foods such as nuts, berries, and seeds was undoubtedly an important activity, although next to nothing survives in archaeological sites. Hunting was probably more important in temperate latitudes, where vegetable foods are scarce for part of the year. Within their territory the hunters knew the habits of every animal and the characteristics of many edible vegetable foods and medicinal plants; they were familiar with their country's inconspicuous landmarks and strategic features. In the same way, today's villagers in the Upper Amazon basin know the carrying capacities of different soil types and the economic potential of most trees, grasses, and shrubs within their gardens and personal territory. Only now with the coming of urbanization and increased specialization in economic activities have we divorced ourselves from our intimate relationship with our surrounding environment.

Fire, too, had a major impact on human history. Early man must have been familiar with the hungry flames of brush fires caused by lightning or volcanic eruptions. Grass fires destroy old vegetation, and game grazes happily on the green shoots that spring up through the blackened soil a few weeks later. Hunters also observed herds of game fleeing from massive brush fires. Thus a familiarity with natural fires may have led *Homo erectus* to keep fires alive for his own use, kindling wood from a brushfire or flames from a seepage of natural gas. As man moved into less hospitable environments, he had a constant need for fire, both to keep him warm at night and to protect him from nocturnal predators. The flames gave him light, helped him with game drives, and enabled him to work long after dark.[29]

Fire appears earliest in colder climates. The hunters of Ambrona, Choukoutien, Terra Amata, and Torralba had fire. Hearths appear at Escale Cave in southern France at the end of the Lower Pleistocene. The earliest cave occupations in Europe seem to coincide with the use of fire. Peking man used fire. Choukoutien Cave has yielded traces of hearths lit there since the earliest occupation of the site. The warmer, subtropical climate of Africa may not have necessitated fire, and it appears there much later. No hearths have been found at Olduvai Gorge, but the Acheulians of the Kalambo Falls were sitting round camp fires and using large logs as firewood 60,000 years ago. Once fire was available, hunting bands were able to survive comfortably outside the normal range of many nonhuman primates.

The Acheulians lived in ecological balance with their natural environments, without affecting them more than did any other large mammal.[30] They were successful hunters who, despite their improved technology and social organization, were in no way the dominant members of their ecological communities. Human solutions to environmental problems did not as yet disrupt the ecological balance, for mankind was only one of many elements in the biological environment.

retrospect
homo erectus

We cannot do better than quote from the Watsons' essay on what they call "Elemental Man," for they summarize the salient points touched on in this chapter admirably:

"Elemental man is a very successful member of his ecological community, but he is not necessarily its dominant member. Despite his improved social and tool techniques, he usually does not disturb the ecological balance. Although he has improved techniques of food procurement, he may have less overall effect on the physical environment than the nonhuman primate because he develops tastes for only certain foods and does not exploit every possible food source. Man's social organization provides a cultural way of arranging separate groups so that each will have access to enough of the kinds of food it prefers. Since men desire meat, they must have large hunting territories. And since, in searching out only certain foods, they pass over many others that are edible, elemental men do not increase in population to the limits of the possible food supply but only to the limits of the preferred food supply. This is true for almost all other animals as well. However, the distinction is an important one to make for man because it is not until he learns to produce — not just to hunt and to gather in the wild — his preferred food supply, and to increase this production greatly, that human beings begin to increase greatly in population. Because of their specialized food interests, protohumans, elemental men, and advanced hunters and gatherers . . . can be supported in successively smaller numbers in a given area than can nonhuman primates. Improved techniques in food procurement do not necessarily lead to greatly increased supplies of food and thus to an increased population. No particular social structure is necessarily related to the simple technology described above, but if language and tools together with a preference for meat do lead to cooperative hunting, which is a reasonable assumption, the result will be an extended range and a small population . . .

"Economic success for the nonhuman primate is individual. Each nonhuman primate collects and consumes his own food. Among protohumans, the economic unit is the family. In the elemental human group it is clear that even the extended family is not necessarily the economic unit. The economic success of elemental man depends upon the cooperative activity of every individual and family within the group; the economic unit is thus the group, and the success of the elemental human way of life is group success. The amount of property owned by individuals and by groups is minimal; and, as a result, men on the elemental level get along better with one another, in families, and in groups than do any other primates, including men whose ways of life are outlined in the following chapters."[31]

7

homo sapiens

The later stages of the Pleistocene epoch saw several major cultural innovations that both preceded and accompanied a major expansion of human populations into northern latitudes and the New World as well as Australia. At the same time, new major centers of human settlement developed in Eurasia, where standards of toolmaking improved rapidly and population densities climbed in some areas.[1]*

more advanced hominids

The earliest human fossils to show more advanced anatomical features than *Homo erectus* at Choukoutien have been found in England and Germany. The Swanscombe site in the lower Thames Valley, which was mentioned in Chapter 6, is a gravel pit that has yielded tens of thousands of perfectly made Acheulian hand axes in the past fifty years.[2] In addition, the back and sides of a human skull have been recovered from Swanscombe (Figure 7.1). They belong to a more advanced hominid than the Chinese *Homo erectus;* the brain size is nearly as large as that of modern man. Unfortunately, the face of the Swanscombe skull is missing, but the roughly contemporary Steinheim cranium from Germany preserves much of the facial structure of an individual similar to the English specimen. The chewing apparatus of the Steinheim fossil is still more massive than that of modern man, while the skull bears pronounced brow ridges, though less extreme than those possessed by earlier *Homo erectus* in China and Indonesia.[3]

200,000 B.P.

Both fossils are without lower jaws, and some debate surrounds their

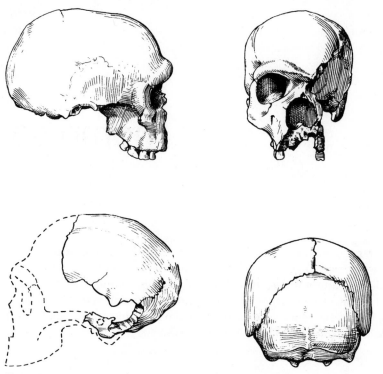

Figure 7.1
   The Steinheim (top) and Swanscombe (bottom) skulls (one-fourth actual size). The
   Swanscombe skull is shown with a tentative reconstruction of the missing parts.

classification. Steinheim and Swanscombe are thought by Bernard
Campbell to be classifiable as *Homo sapiens*, being far more like ourselves
than *Homo erectus* but quite distinct from modern man. Their brain capacity was larger than that of *Homo erectus*, yet they retain fairly massive
chewing muscles and more pronounced brow ridges than are found in
modern man. The status of the Steinheim and Swanscombe finds has
been hotly debated, for in truth too few finds have so far been made
to date the first appearance of *Homo sapiens* with any accuracy.

The fact that both skulls come from Europe does not necessarily mean
that early *Homo sapiens* evolved in northern latitudes alone. No human
fossils dating to around 100,000 years ago have yet been recovered in
Africa or Asia. When they are discovered we may then learn whether
populations with the physical attributes of Steinheim and Swanscombe
lived in southern latitudes. The most likely theory is that *Homo sapiens*
evolved over a wide area of Africa, Europe, and Asia.

The Swanscombe skull was found among abundant traces of toolmaking activity. Pointed hand axes of the Acheulian type abound in the Swanscombe Middle Gravels (Figure 6.3). They display fine workmanship but are hardly the tools of a radically new population of technological innovators. The way of life of the new hominids seems to have been similar to that of *Homo erectus,* an economy based on hunting and gathering.

middle paleolithic

european neanderthals

The discovery of a primitive-looking skull in a cave near Neanderthal, Germany, in 1856 caused a sensation. Expert opinion was sharply divided. Some anatomists dismissed the find as the bones of a pathological idiot or a dead Napoleonic soldier. Others, like Professor Hermann Schaaffhausen, considered the remains to belong to a "barbarous and savage race." "They may be regarded as the most ancient memorial of the early inhabitants of Europe," he wrote.[4] Victorian scientists were struck by the dissimilarities between the Neanderthal skull and that of modern man. The century since the first Neanderthal skull was found has seen the discovery of substantial numbers of Neanderthal individuals, most of them from western Europe, as well as contemporary human fossils from the Near East, Africa, and Asia. Neanderthal man is now recognized as *Homo sapiens neanderthalensis,* a subspecies of *Homo sapiens.*

Most of our anatomical knowledge about Neanderthal people comes from deliberate burials found in the lower levels of large rock-shelters and caves in southwestern France. Their anatomical features are well known. The skull is lower and flatter than that of modern humans. But the Neanderthal brain was almost larger than modern ones. Prominent brow ridges extend over the eye sockets; there is no chin. Neanderthal man stood just over 153 centimeters (5 ft.) high, and his forearms were relatively short compared to modern man's. Until very recently, some anatomists thought that Neanderthal man had walked with a crouched posture, largely because the most authoritative studies had been made on an aged and arthritic individual found at La Chapelle-aux-Saints in France. We now know that the Neanderthalers walked fully upright and as nimbly as modern man.[5]

Neanderthalers first appeared during the Eem interglacial, but they were not widespread. (The evidence is highly uncertain.) Large Neanderthal sites have been found in French caverns, especially in the Dordogne

?100,000 B.P.

Table 7.1
Middle Paleolithic cultures in Africa, Asia, and Europe.

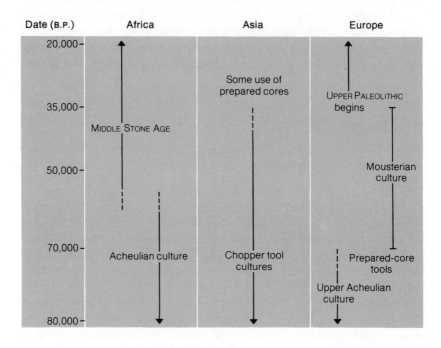

area, where deep river valleys and vast limestone cliffs offered abundant shelter for hunters during the Weichsel glaciation. See Table 7.1. One site is the cave of Le Moustier near Les Eyzies. (The characteristic Neanderthal toolkit is named Mousterian after this settlement.)[6] Open sites are also found at Saltzgitter Lebenstedt in western Germany, where a group of hunters settled about 55,000 years ago.[7] Lebenstedt was found to have been occupied for a few weeks during several summer seasons by a band of up to 50 people. They lived on reindeer, mammoth, and rhinoceros — all tundra forms — as well as some birds, in a locality near the northern margins of the arctic tree limit.

The Neanderthal skeletons found in French caves look like anatomical anachronisms, with massive brow ridges and squat bodies (Figure 7.2). This "classic" variety of Neanderthal is confined to western Europe and is more noticeably different from *Homo sapiens* than contemporary populations found elsewhere in the world, especially around the shores of the Mediterranean and in Asia (Figure 7.3).

Mousterian
Middle Paleo-
lithic (see
Table 7.1)

70,000–
35,000 B.P.

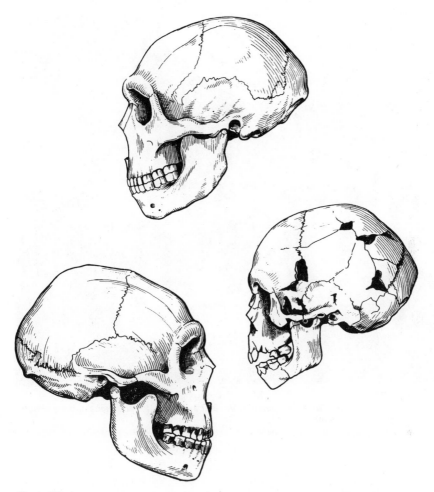

Figure 7.2
A "classic" Neanderthal skull found in Monte Circeo, Italy (top). Two Middle Paleolithic skulls, one from Shanidar, Iraq (bottom left) and the other of a child from Teshik-Tash, USSR.

mousterian cultural patterns

The Mousterian culture of the European Neanderthalers is thought to have developed out of the late Acheulian. Multipurpose tools were made by new stoneworking techniques, based on the careful preparation of flint cores before the flakes used for spearheads and scrapers were removed

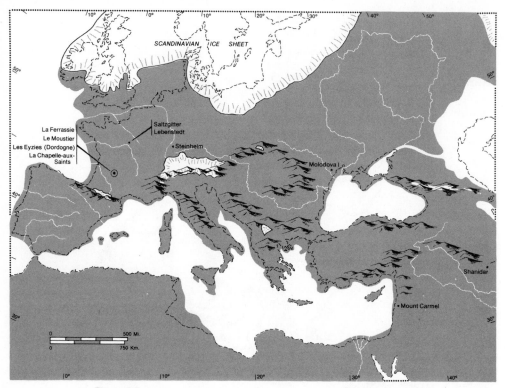

Figure 7.3
Middle Paleolithic sites mentioned in the text in relation to mountains and ice sheets.
Teshik-Tash is omitted.

from them (Figure 7.4). The so-called Levallois technique, named after a suburb of Paris, was used to remove carefully preshaped flakes, perhaps for spearheads, from a single core that was then discarded.[8] This technique had been used by the Acheulians, too. A "disc core" technique was used to remove many flakes of more or less the same size from a single core, which was used until no further flakes could be removed from it. The Levallois and disc techniques were combined with a variety of finishing methods to produce a series of flake tools for specialized purposes.

Points and scraping tools are among the most famous Mousterian artifacts. The edges of both points and scrapers were sharpened with fine trimming, produced by small, step-like trimmings on the edge of the implement (Figure 7.5). These artifacts, which enjoy enormous and almost universal distribution in Middle Paleolithic sites, were used in the chase, for woodworking, and in the preparation of skins.

The French sites have yielded a great diversity of Mousterian artifacts and toolkits. Some levels include hand axes, others notched flakes perhaps used for stripping up meat for drying (flake, Figure 7.5). Some subdivisions of Mousterian culture have been identified on the basis of the prevalence of particular tool types. They may be the surviving toolkits of different tribal bands who had distinct toolmaking traditions derived from earlier cultures. American archaeologists Lewis and Sally Binford, after making a statistical study of the toolkits from multilevel Mousterian cave sites,[9] concluded that the different proportions of tools merely reflect distinct activities such as toolmaking, hunting, butchering, or gathering carried out on the same site at different times.

In the earlier part of the Weichsel glaciation, the Mousterian culture extended from Spain in the west to Uzbekistan, and perhaps beyond, in the east. The northernmost sites occur in Britain, and Mousterian settlements are found on the North African coast. Mousterian is the earliest well-documented human occupation in European Russia, where both cave and open sites were occupied.[10] One of the latter, Molodova I, yielded traces of an oval arrangement of mammoth bones, thought by the excavator to have been used as weights for a skin tent. The hunters concentrated heavily on large mammals such as the mammoth and the bison.

hunting and gathering

Mousterian tools represent some degree of specialization in skin and meat preparation. There seem to have been few innovations in hunting methods, for spears, clubs, and perhaps bola stones remained the weapons of the chase. Middle Paleolithic man was an efficient hunter who was not afraid to tackle large mammoths as well as reindeer and wild horses; he also caught birds and fish. Some Mousterian hunters migrated to the northern tundra in the summer months.[11] In contrast, the rockshelter dwellers of southwestern France occupied their home bases the year round. Both settlement patterns probably reflect localized adaptations to the arctic climate of western Europe.

For many thousands of years the European Neanderthalers were successful in their arctic environment, opening up the arctic tundra for human settlement for the first time. But between 40,000 and 35,000 years ago they were abruptly displaced by anatomically modern men with a more advanced culture.

Figure 7.4
Middle Paleolithic technology — producing a Levallois flake.

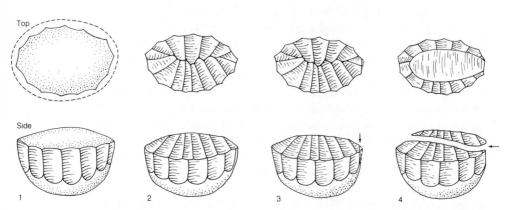

The making of a Levallois core: (1) the edges of a suitable stone are trimmed; (2) then the top surface is trimmed; (3) a striking platform is made, the point where the flake will originate, by trimming to form a straight edge on the side; (4) a flake is struck from the core, and the flake removed. Prepared cores like this one were designed to enable the toolmaker to strike off large flakes of predetermined size.

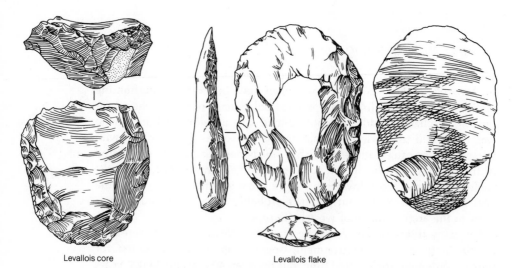

Levallois core

Levallois flake

A Levallois core from the Thames Valley, England, together with a flake from a similar core, show views of the end-product (a large flake) and the by-product (a core) of the above process (one-third actual size).

Figure 7.5
Middle Paleolithic stone technology: composite tools and typical artifacts. Little is known about Middle Paleolithic bone technology or the manufacture of wooden tools.

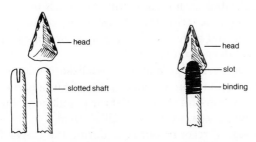

The development of "composite tools," artifacts consisting of several parts joined together to form an effective weapon. Middle Paleolithic hunters made the stone-tipped spear by attaching a pointed stone head to a wooden handle to form this projectile. The head probably fitted into a slot in the wooden shaft and was affixed to it with resin or beeswax; a binding was added to the end of the shaft.

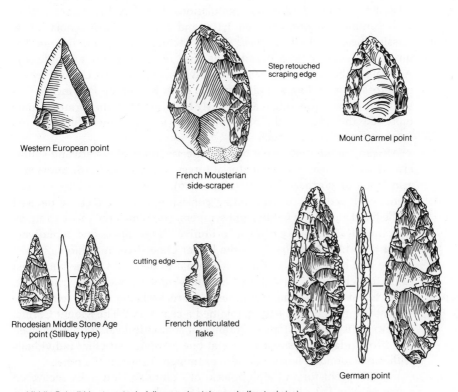

Middle Paleolithic stone tools (all approximately one-half actual size).

african and asian hunter-gatherers

Regional specialization in human cultures is much more marked in the Middle Paleolithic. The technological uniformity of the world was interrupted as hunters and gatherers adapted to environments as extreme as arctic tundra and dense rain forest.

By some 100,000 years ago a more specialized *Homo sapiens* stock was spread widely over the more southern parts of Europe, Asia, and Africa. Considerable variations are shown by these populations, but brow ridges and a sizable jaw are characteristic of all of them.

The archaeological record from Asia during the Upper Pleistocene is poorly dated. Eleven skullcaps and two limb bones, the former broken open at the base, came from Upper Pleistocene beds at Ngandong (Solo), Indonesia. The site cannot be dated accurately.[12] Some crude flake tools and bone tools may be related to these finds. The skeletal material has generated considerable discussion, for the Solo individuals are clearly related to earlier *Homo erectus* populations, but they had larger brains, with volumes ranging between 1,100 and 1,200 cc. Most scholars now classify the Solo skulls as *Homo sapiens,* including them in a lineage that ultimately evolved into populations that resembled, for example, the Australian aborigines. Chinese sites have yielded several Upper Pleistocene fossils, including a skull from Ma'pa in Kwantung Province.[13] This skull has heavy brow ridges and a fairly high forehead, the former shaped more like the ridges of the Solo specimens. Other Chinese finds are too fragmentary to tell us much.

African hunters settled not only on the savannah of eastern and southern Africa but also in the equatorial forest and in the desertic and semiarid lands of northeast Africa (Figure 7.6). New woodworking toolkits were developed in forested country, consisting of crude picks to be used in the hand and many lightweight scrapers. Fossil materials are extremely rare, the latest discovery being a "primitive" *Homo sapiens* find, tentatively dated to c. 130,000 years, from the Lower Omo River in Ethiopia.[14]

The first Middle Paleolithic fossil burial to be found in the Near East came to light in the et-Tabun Cave at Mount Carmel, Israel, in 1932. Later, ten skeletons came from the Skhul rock-shelter nearby, where the Mount Carmel hunters had maintained a cemetery.[15] The Mount Carmel skeletons display an astonishing range of anatomical variation, with massive brow ridges and squat stature at one extreme and taller individuals with more rounded heads and less prominent brows at the other.

35,000–
40,000 B.P.

In 1957, prehistorian Ralph Solecki of Columbia University recovered seven Middle Paleolithic burials from Shanidar Cave in Iraq. Three of them had been victims of a rockfall.[16] The anatomical features of the

?45,000–
70,000 B.P.

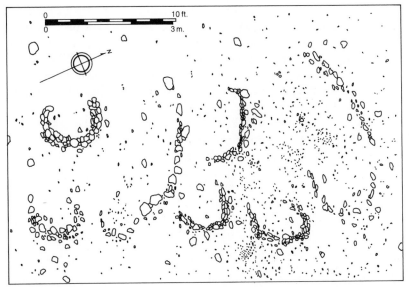

Figure 7.6
A middle Stone Age campsite from the Orange River, South Africa. The plan shows concentrations of boulders and the position of waste from stoneworking activities, the latter shown by small dots surrounding the boulder concentrations.

Shanidar individuals are in some cases more "modern" than those of their European, African, or Asian contemporaries, although the distributions are not very clear.

religion and ritual

Middle Paleolithic man was still a hunter and a gatherer. The world population remained small. The pace of cultural change was slow, but life was more complex than ever before. We find the first signs of religious awareness, of a preoccupation with life hereafter. The Neanderthals buried their dead in shallow pits associated with Mousterian occupation levels of French caves. One rock-shelter, La Ferrassie near Les Eyzies, has yielded the remains of two adult Neanderthals and four children buried close to one another in a single campsite.[17] The Skhul cemetery and Shanidar skeletons were deliberately buried, as was the arthritic individual at La Chapelle-aux-Saints, France. A band of Siberian mountain-goat hunters lived at Teshik-Tash in the western foothills of the Himalayas. They buried one of their children in a shallow pit, surrounding the boy's body with six pairs of wild goat horns.[18]

Some ceremonial concern for the dead was combined with religious beliefs. Concentrations of bear bones found in caves have been inferred to be traces of cult activities, and evidence for cannibalism and animal rituals have come from European caves — signs of man's intellectual exercise and greater consciousness of the subtleties of the world. We find in Neanderthal man and his culture the first roots of our own complicated beliefs, societies, and religious sense. Mankind was nearly as modern as we are today, ready for the rapid explosion of technological and economic advance that characterized the next 30,000 years of history.

the complexity
of hunter-gatherers

The many hunting and gathering societies described in Chapters 8 to 11 differ from earlier hunters in their more complex toolkits and sophisticated food-getting techniques. But their hunting and gathering way of life placed limitations on their abilities to manipulate their effect on the physical environment.

Earlier hominids had already solved the problems of survival through group cooperation and sharing. Now hunters began to stabilize their food supplies through more specialized hunting of one or two species of the larger mammals, through intensive gathering of selected vegetable foods, and through fishing activities. The intellectual demands on the hunters intensified, for a detailed knowledge of plant and animal life was necessary to a far greater extent than in earlier times.

Herds of gregarious mammals move to new grazing grounds at certain seasons. Wild fruits come into season for short periods of time. Stands of wild grass seeds can be picked at well-defined seasons. Salmon runs provide a ready food supply for short periods of time. The food quest had to be carefully timed, so that food resources could be exploited to their fullest advantage, with such factors as food storage and the siting of home bases an increasingly important consideration.

Mankind had earlier lived in ecological balance with his natural environment. Like other mammals he did not disturb this balance, for his numbers were strictly controlled by available food supplies. Later hunters were able to exercise a far greater effect on their environments, for they had become the dominant animals in their ecological communities. As the most successful predators in their communities, they were able to eliminate competition from other predators by hunting them as well. The hunting band dominated the animal community. Its activities determined to some degree the makeup of the animal and vegetable communities in its territory.

For the first time the hunter was having a definite, altering effect on his environment. This effect is apparent to those who are doing the influencing as their hunting methods become more effective, sophisticated, and often highly specialized. From specialized hunting, with its frequent dependence on individual herds of game and perhaps deliberate protection of young and breeding females, and intensive gathering of wild grasses, it is a comparatively short step to deliberate herding of animals and systematic planting of vegetable foods.

The toolkits of the hunter and gatherer underwent great change during the Weichsel glaciation and afterward. More specialized implements of the chase came into use, for example, the bow and arrow and the spear tipped with a stone point mounted on a wooden staff with a binding and a haft. The harpoon, a barbed point attached to a spear handle with a cord and mounted in the end of it, was an effective weapon against large mammals, for the dangling handle prevented easy flight. The spearthrower (see Figure 8.6) increased the arm length of the hunter and allowed the spear itself to be thrown farther and harder.

Composite tools came into use. Soon small stone barbs and scrapers were mounted in wood and in bone handles to form highly effective specialized artifacts for hunting or food preparation. Probably the most important technological innovation was the invention of the bow and arrow, a hunting weapon that, like the blow tube, can direct human energy in a very accurate dimension over longer distances than the manually propelled spear.

Many more materials were employed in toolmaking. Cords and natural adhesives like beeswax were used for mounting tools. Bone and antler were employed more intensively for composite tools as well as in their own right. Skins, horn, hair, and other by-products from the hunters' prey were used for housing and clothes, for lighting, and for coloring. Skins were sewn together with threads; weaving and plaiting were probably employed for the first time. Flexible sewn materials make tents a viable possibility, a far more effective form of shelter than the crude and chilly windbreak of grass or branches. Skin boats for the pursuit of large sea mammals and deep-sea fish are an innovation resulting from sewing, too.

More specialized hunting and gathering means that larger hunting territories are needed to support the population, for the available resources in any territory are not necessarily exploited to the full, merely those food sources that are favored by the hunters. They will fall back on other resources only in times of need. The result is more territorial need and greater competition for resources. Warfare may result as two groups compete for the same limited resources. Under these circumstances group cooperation becomes a vital part of survival, leading to complex rituals such as initiation rites designed to increase group cohesion.

The first human artistic expressions appeared during the Weichsel glaciation, not only in western Europe but also in Australia and in other parts of the world. Art is a logical development among people who had begun to appreciate the advantages of using all kinds of raw materials to fulfill a multitude of needs. The paintings, engravings, and sculpture executed by prehistoric hunters had meaning to the artists who made them. They conveyed a message, the significance of which is usually not apparent to the twentieth-century archaeologist. Art was a logical extension of other technological and creative achievements among the hunter-gatherers.

The hunter-gatherers were by now conscious that they exercised some influence on their environment, but they did this through the use of tools, and only to the extent that they were seeking game or vegetable foods. They were not intent on a systematic modification of the environment, a trend that began with the beginnings of food production as opposed to hunting and gathering.

8

the upper paleolithic:
hunters in western europe

For 50,000 years the Mousterian culture flourished over an enormous area of the Old World. Then, a little before 35,000 years ago, new hunting cultures appeared, with radically new toolkits, the work of anatomically modern men of the *Homo sapiens* type. Around 40,000 years ago, there seems to have been a general trend throughout the Old World in the Middle Pleistocene toward large-brained descendants of *Homo erectus* populations that had lived earlier in the same areas. Some of these "archaic" men were replaced, like the western European Neanderthals. Others in China, Southeast Asia, and eastern Europe may have evolved into modern types by phyletic change and hybridization, hybridizations from original populations that were more modern in aspect.[1]*

The search for ancestors of modern man has centered for many years on the Near East, where a series of Neanderthal-like skeletons were found at Mount Carmel. The burials at Skhul and et-Tabun yielded skulls of more modern appearance, with moderately developed brow ridges and well-rounded skullcaps; the faces are tucked in under the craniums. These are some of the changes that must be accounted for in tracing the origins of modern man, for they serve to distinguish us from more archaic *Homo sapiens*. Donald Brothwell, a British physical anthropologist, has gone so far as to hypothesize that modern man developed in an area bounded by East Africa, Arabia, western Asia, and India.[2] There is no evidence to support his theory, even if it is probable that over 50,000 years ago human populations within this vast area did evolve in the direction of modern man. Similar changes may have taken place elsewhere, too.

* See pages 387–388 for notes to Chapter 8.

The legend of the Garden of Eden is long-lived, and the notion of a single origin for modern man in the Near East, with subsequent migrations of aggressive populations of hunting bands having advanced technology, is also attractive. A migration theory to explain the sudden appearance of new toolkits and modern man in western Europe and other parts of the world has long been popular in archaeological circles.[3] How else, argue its supporters, could one explain the sudden disappearance of Neanderthal populations in Europe? Furthermore, the Mount Carmel burials provide evidence that human populations were evolving in the direction of modern man.

Another school thinks in terms of independent and parallel evolution in different parts of the world. They concede that modern man evolved in the Near East, but they are certain that the same process occurred in Europe, Africa, and perhaps the Far East. Unfortunately, this hypothesis, like the migration theory, is supported by insufficient field evidence. The origins of modern man still remain a mystery despite a quickening pace of discovery.

technological change

There was a sharp biological and technological break throughout Europe immediately before or during the Paudorf interstadial. A similarly radical technological jump is not necessarily found elsewhere in the world. Conversely, the biological change did not necessarily coincide with technological innovation.

The technological changes involved the development of specialized tools for the chase, for bone working and woodworking, and for a host of other activities. New tools were made using distinctive bone and stoneworking techniques.[4] The development of new toolkits may have taken place in several areas, but is well documented in the Near East.

Some of the most complete sequences of Stone Age culture known come from great caves and rock-shelters, such as et-Tabun, Mugharet-el-Wad, and Shanidar, which were visited almost continually by hunting bands from Mousterian times over 70,000 years ago up to the very threshold of modern times. The Mousterian levels contain tens of thousands of carefully retouched points and side scrapers as well as the bones of large deer and wild cattle. These layers are overlain by further occupation levels containing radically different toolkits. In these, the blanks for stone tools were long, parallel-sided blades, which were removed from cylindrical flint cores by using a punch and a hammerstone (Figure 8.1). Some blades were up to 15.2 centimeters (6 in.) long; the tools made from them greatly varied, many of them designed for specific tasks and, in later millennia, mounted in handles. Earlier Stone Age artifacts had more general uses than the specialized toolkits produced by modern man. The Upper Paleolithic is the term given to the new phase of the Stone Age that began with modern man.

By 40,000 years ago the technological diversity of the Old World was such that we must break down our study of the world into geographical areas, documenting the prehistory of hunter-gatherers region by region. A logical starting point is the Upper Paleolithic cultures of central and western Europe, for the area was a major focus of human settlement during the late Weichsel. There has been a tendency to regard the Upper Paleolithic cultures of western Europe as representative of the whole world at this time. Nothing, of course, could be further from the truth, for other distinctive and sophisticated hunting cultures were developing in Asia, Africa, and arctic regions.

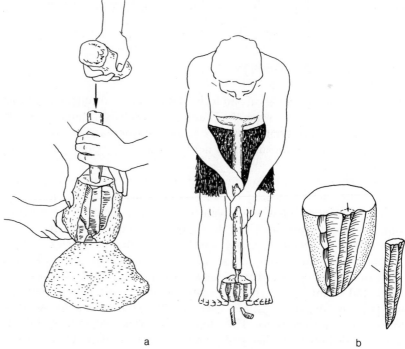

a   b

Figure 8.1
   Upper Paleolithic stone technology was based on the blade technique, which is illustrated here. For stone tools and bone tools, see Figures 8.3 and 8.7.

   a. Two methods of striking off blades from a cylindrical core, with a hand or a chest punch.
   b. A core and a blade from it. The dotted line and arrow show the point where the next blade will be struck off from the core.

the discovery of the upper paleolithic: lartet and christy

A classical area for the study of the Upper Paleolithic is western Europe, where excavations in caves, rock-shelters, and open campsites have uncovered traces of some of the most elaborate hunting cultures ever enjoyed by man. The study began when a French magistrate and amateur fossil hunter, Edward Lartet (1801–1871), heard of the discovery of seventeen human skeletons in a cave at Aurignac in the Haute Garonne in west-central France.[5] Convinced of the antiquity of the engraved bones, flints, and bones of extinct animals found with the skeletons, themselves later buried in a Christian cemetery nearby, he began to explore other caves in the Pyrenees. Soon he turned his attention to Les Eyzies, Dordogne, digging at such rock-shelters as Laugerie Haute, Gorge d'Enfer, La Madeleine, and Le Moustier, now almost household words in world prehistory (Figure 8.2). The energetic magistrate was fortunate to be joined by Henry Christy, a wealthy English banker with a passion for archaeology.

Lartet, Christy, and a small army of amateur prehistorians dug deeply into the French landscape and uncovered Upper Paleolithic man. *Reliquiae Aquitanicae* was Lartet and Christy's great monograph on the French caves, a landmark of prehistory published in 1875.[6] The authors provided a framework for classifying a whole series of Stone Age hunting cultures whose diet was based on such extinct Pleistocene mammals as mammoths, reindeer, and wild oxen. Then five skeletons of the hunters themselves were found in the Cro-Magnon rock-shelter near Les Eyzies in 1868 during some railroad construction work. The skeletons were modern in appearance, belonging to robust, tall people with small faces, high-domed foreheads, and few of the primitive features of the Neanderthalers. Soon archaeologists were referring to "Cro-Magnon man" as a distinct race of *Homo sapiens.*

Edward Lartet's framework for classifying Upper Paleolithic man began with a period when cave bears and mammoths were hunted by the inhabitants of Le Moustier. His other sites belonged in the "Age of Reindeer," a period when the hunters produced a wider range of stone and bone tools than ever before and engraved beautiful patterns and animal designs on antler and bone.

French prehistorian Gabriel de Mortillet (1821–1898) soon reinterpreted Lartet's Reindeer Age in archaeological terms using stone and bone tools as the basis for the classification of French hunting cultures. He grouped Lartet's finds at Le Moustier into the "Moustierian," then divided the Reindeer Age into three epochs — Aurignac, Solutré, and La Made-

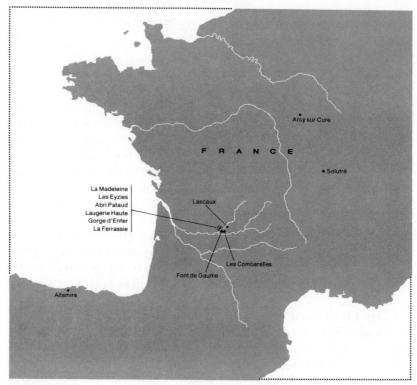

Figure 8.2
Upper Paleolithic sites in southwestern France.

leine, after famous sites where the characteristic tools of each epoch were first found. De Mortillet's scheme has been much modified in the century or so since he published it in his great textbook *Le Préhistorique* in 1883, but the names he employed are still in use (Table 8.1).[7]

the cultural sequence

Western Europe is one of the most intensively excavated areas of the world, but many gaps remain in our knowledge of the Upper Paleolithic. The sequence of hunting cultures in Table 8.1 is in fact far more complex than the simple catalog of names suggests, so it is worth making a few general points first.

The hunting techniques of the Upper Paleolithic were still comparable to those of earlier times.[8] Spears, harpoons, clubs, throwing sticks, and

Table 8.1
French Middle and Upper Paleolithic cultures classified according to various authorities.

Lartet (1875)	De Mortillet (1883)	Commonly used today	Upper / Middle Paleolithic
	La Madeleine	Magdalenian	UPPER PALEOLITHIC
Age of Reindeer	Solutré	Solutrean	
	Aurignac	Gravettian Aurignacian Chatelperronian	
Age of Cave Bear	Mousterian (Le Moustier)	Mousterian	MIDDLE PALEOLITHIC

spearthrowers were used in conjunction with game drives and, probably, snaring to catch a wide variety of game. Fishing was carried out with lines and, later, harpoons, and bottom fish could be trapped in shallow pools during periods of low water.

The reindeer was the most important meat source in western Europe, being replaced by the mammoth in eastern Europe.[9] In Spain, where game herds were less abundant, the meat supply was more diversified. The settlement pattern was determined by the hunting specialization. Those who followed migrating reindeer changed their settlements with the seasons. Abundant game herds did not always migrate, however, and their hunters were able to live in semipermanent settlements. Both caves and open sites were occupied by hunters who had learned to live successfully in tundra, forest, and open steppe country where abundant food supplies were available.

The earliest Upper Paleolithic horizons in French caves immediately overlie Mousterian levels.[10] A transition period is followed by a complete submergence of Mousterian tool types. New toolkits based on blade technology came into fashion, dominated by small penknife blades with delicately curved backs, scrapers, and "burins" (blades with chisel ends used for grooving bone and wood) (Figure 8.3). These early "Chatelperronian" hunters (Table 8.2), named after the site of Chatelperron where they were first found, have left traces of their activities in many caves, where scattered hearths, often fueled by bone rather than wood, overlie Mousterian horizons.

Mousterian

Chatelperronian
35,000 B.P.

Figure 8.3
Upper Paleolithic stone tools.

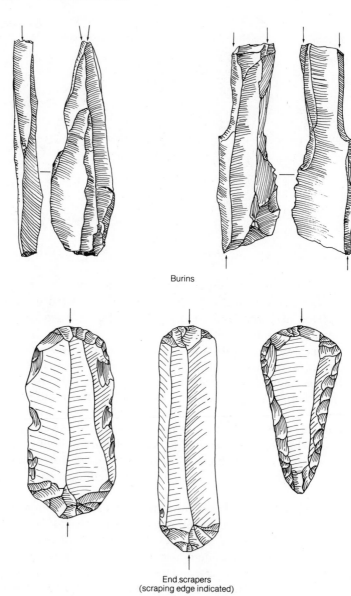

Burins

End scrapers
(scraping edge indicated)

Burins and scrapers, made from blades, are typical artifacts of all stages of Upper Paleolithic times. Burins were used for grooving wood, bone, and particularly antlers, which were made into spears and harpoon points. The chisel ends of burins were formed by taking an oblique or longitudinal flake off the end of a blade. Arrows indicate the chisel ends. Burins were also used to engrave figures. End scrapers were employed on bone and wood. Scraping edges are indicated by arrows.

Chatelperronian

Backed points
(backs indicated)

Aurignacian

Steep scraper
(scraping edge indicated)

Split-base bone point
(split used for mounting)

Blades with sharpened edges or notches

Gravettian

Backed points
(backs indicated; points were probably mounted in a handle or shaft)

Typical Chatelperronian, Aurignacian, and Gravettian tools. Upper Paleolithic technology was based to a great extent on composite tools, of which the stone elements were only a part. Some blade tools were used by themselves, however, for the blade offered a convenient and standardized way of making large numbers of fairly specialized artifacts. Note that the examples shown are typical forms and are associated with other artifacts not illustrated here. *(Two-thirds actual size.)*

Table 8.2

Upper Paleolithic cultures in western Europe with the cultures shown as a line stratigraphic sequence.[a]

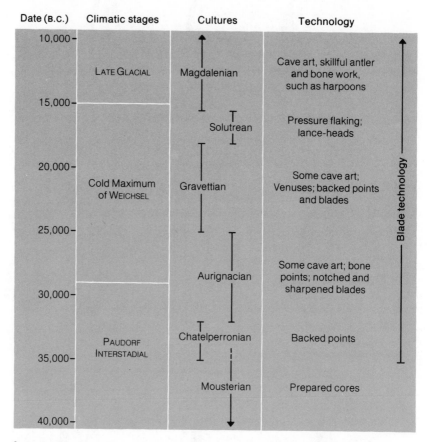

Date (B.C.)	Climatic stages	Cultures	Technology
10,000 –	LATE GLACIAL	Magdalenian	Cave art, skillful antler and bone work, such as harpoons
15,000 –		Solutrean	Pressure flaking; lance-heads
20,000 –	Cold Maximum of WEICHSEL	Gravettian	Some cave art; Venuses; backed points and blades
25,000 –		Aurignacian	Some cave art; bone points; notched and sharpened blades
30,000 –			
	PAUDORF INTERSTADIAL	Chatelperronian	Backed points
35,000 –		Mousterian	Prepared cores
40,000 –			

Blade technology

[a]In reality, there were many overlaps and blendings of cultural traditions that cannot be reflected in a simple table.

Aurignacian 32,000 B.P.

Chatelperronian occupation levels are thin and often transitory, but those of the Aurignacian people (a culture named after the cave of Aurignac) are much deeper. Aurignacian sites are clustered in deep valleys, in shelters which are well protected from wind and cold. Some of the most thoroughly investigated Aurignacian occupation layers come from the Abri Pataud shelter near Les Eyzies, which was meticulously excavated by Harvard prehistorian Hallam L. Movius over many years. Abri Pataud contains 9 meters (30 ft.) of Aurignacian and later occupation.

Thick horizons of hearths, traces of possible huts, and the first signs of bone engraving came from its Aurignacian horizons.

Aurignacian toolkits do not contain the penknife blades found in Chatelperronian layers. There was a greater dependence on bone tools, especially bone points with flattened cross-sections and split bases for mounting on a staff. Notched and sharpened blades were probably used for woodworking (see Figure 8.3b).

Collections of stone and bone tools which have been called "Aurignacian" have been found in central Europe and the Balkans. Conceivably, the Aurignacian was an alien culture from central Europe, which introduced new toolkits and ideas to the west, but this hypothesis is debated.

The succeeding "Gravettian" tradition reached the height of its vigor some 25,000 years ago. Again, backed blades are the dominant tool types, and the specialized scrapers and burins of the Aurignacian have vanished. The Gravettian is well represented at Abri Pataud where a row of hearths extends 9 meters (30 ft.) along the shelter, possibly associated with traces of a long house. Gravettian sculpture and cave art, especially the latter, are abundant and highly characteristic, being found at many sites.

Gravettian
25,000 B.P.

The most famous Gravettian art objects are a series of stone, female figurines with pendulous breasts and grossly exaggerated sexual characteristics (Figure 8.4).[11] Such figures are thought to be fertility symbols, although other explanations have been advanced. Female figurines occur

Figure 8.4
Venus figurine from Willendorf, Germany (photograph of a cast).

from Russia in the east to the Dordogne in the west. Gravettian cave art is both lively and distinctive, and is best depicted at such famous sites as Pair-non-Pair and Lascaux in France.[12]

Lascaux was discovered in 1940 by four schoolboys when their dog vanished down a hole. The cave lies on the left bank of the Vézère River near Montignac. The most famous wall paintings are in the Great Hall of the Bulls, so named after four immense wild bulls. These animals are drawn in thick, black lines, with some filling in of detail. Horses, deer, a small bear, and a strange, unicornlike beast are depicted with the bulls. Many have elongated necks and thick bodies, stylistic characteristics of Aurignacian and Gravettian paintings. Black, brown, red, and yellow are skillfully used to highlight details of the animals.

About 20,000 years ago a short-lived and remarkable hunting culture developed in France. The Solutreans were skillful flintworkers, whose material culture and economy were virtually identical to those of other Upper Paleolithic cultures, with one major exception.[13] They made magnificent pressure-flaked lanceheads (Figure 8.5). The technique of shaping the flint blades by directional pressure applied with a small billet of wood or antler held in the palm of the hand resulted in flat lanceheads with

Solutrean 18,000 B.C.

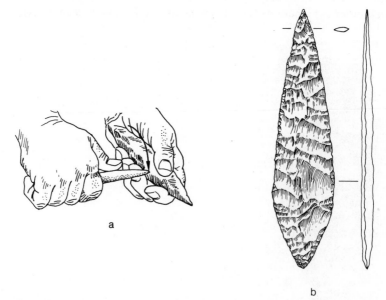

a

b

Figure 8.5
The stoneworking technique of pressure flaking (a), and a product of this technique (b), a Solutrean lancehead (one-half actual size).

regular cross-sections. Beautiful parallel-sided flake scars adorn both surfaces of the laurel leaf points. The tips of the lanceheads were carefully tapered; many of them are so delicate that they can hardly have been used for warfare or the chase.

Some 17,000 years ago, we begin to reach the zenith of the Upper Paleolithic with the evolution of the Magdalenian culture. First identified at the rock-shelter of La Madeleine near Les Eyzies, the Magdalenian hunters achieved a higher density of population in selected parts of western Europe than any of their predecessors.[14] Groups of rock-shelters occupied by these people are stretched out at the base of cliffs along large rivers like the Dordogne and the Vézère. Some Magdalenians also lived in open hunting camps on riverbanks. They hunted arctic animals such as the reindeer and the mammoth, as well as wild horses, bison, and many small mammals like the beaver. Salmon bones are found in the deposits of Magdalenian rock-shelters, too.

Magdalenian 15,000 B.C.

Magdalenian toolkits were more diverse than those of other Upper Paleolithic peoples. Their flintwork was less skillful, except for burins and scrapers used in carving and preparing bones and antlers. The artifacts made of the latter materials were often beautiful: spear points with forked and beveled bases, harpoons, needles, thong softeners, and spearthrowers, which were often decorated with engravings (Figure 8.6). As long ago as 1907, Abbé Henri Breuil, the great French prehistorian, subdivided the Magdalenian into six distinct stages, a classification that was based on flint tools, bone artifacts, and rock art.[15] His six groupings have stood the test of time, although they have been much elaborated.

The greatest variety of bone artifacts comes from the second half of the Magdalenian, when perhaps far greater use was made of wooden tools, too. The diversity of artifacts and game animals increased as the climate began to warm up after the extreme cold of earlier millennia. Salmon, birds, and other smaller game abounded in the more favorable climate. Food supplies were assured; populations of hunters increased. Open campsites were used as extensively as caves. A varied technology and more sophisticated culture at the end of the glaciation gave man increased mastery over the rich environment of western France.

The Magdalenians are most famous for their beautiful rock art, paintings and engravings found deep in the caves of northern Spain and southwestern France (Figure 8.7).[16] One famous site is the cave of Altamira, where the painters left fine renderings of bison in red and black, skillfully painted and engraved on natural bulges on the cave roof to give an impression of relief (Figure 8.8). Friezes and jumbled paintings depict large game animals; white hand impressions, dots, and signs hint at ritualistic activities. The motives of Magdalenian art are thought to be

Figure 8.6
  Magdalenian stone and bone tools. These samples show the proliferation of bone and antler artifacts and the decoration on some of them (various scales).

"Parrot beak" burin
with inclined chisel edge

Stone tools — more irregular than those from earlier millennia

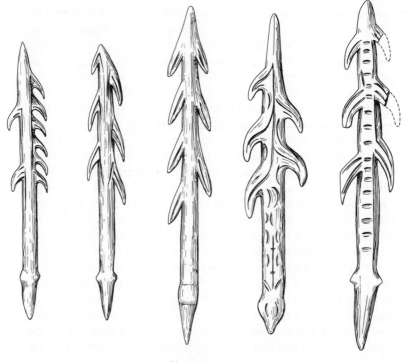

Harpoons

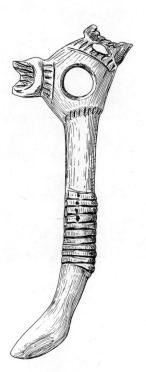

Thong straightener

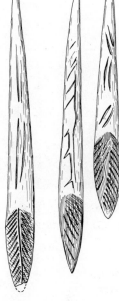

Bone points with forked or beveled bases for mounting

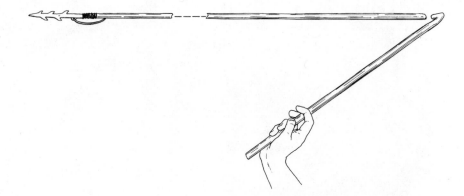

Spearthrower (a hypothetical drawing of one in use)

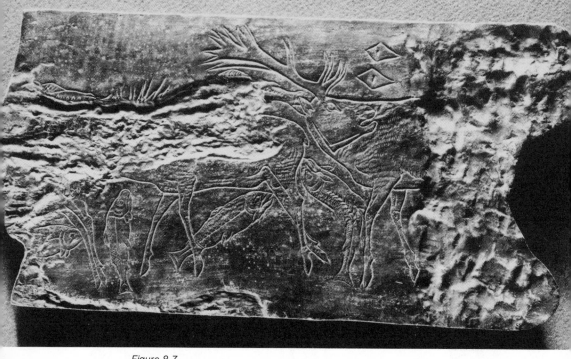

Figure 8.7
  Reindeer licking his flank — a detail of an engraving executed by a Magdalenian craftsman (photograph of a cast).

Figure 8.8
  A bison in a polychrome cave painting at Altamira, Spain.

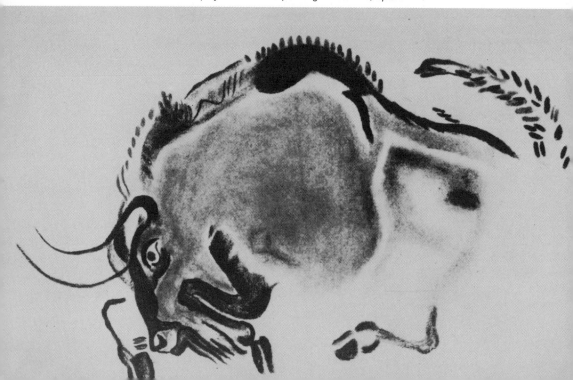

partly religious and to be tied to the continued prosperity of the hunt. But vigorous controversy surrounds this and other theories of Paleolithic art.

The Magdalenian culture was adapted toward arctic animals and a cold climate, so much so that early investigators compared it to that of the Eskimo.[17] It petered out some 12,000 years ago at the end of the Weichsel glaciation. The great herds of reindeer, horses, and bison retreated north or vanished forever, replaced by smaller and more agile forest game. The latest layers in Magdalenian caves are thinner and more poverty-stricken; art dies out, leaving only a few painted pebbles as symbols of a passing era.

10,000 B.C.

European man turned toward lakeside dwelling, placing greater emphasis on fishing and fowling than ever before. Toolkits became more specialized, based on a stone technology oriented toward producing small arrowbarbs, rather than complete hunting weapons. The bow and arrow, introduced to northern latitudes near the end of the Weichsel, is a far more effective weapon against game on the wing than the traditional spear of earlier millennia.

9

hunters
in northern latitudes

The tempo of cultural development has accelerated so dramatically since the emergence of *Homo sapiens* that we are almost dizzy from the twentieth century's frenzied penchant for change. Yet it is only in the past thousand years that Western man has become truly aware of the diversity of mankind. A fascinated audience of urban Europeans marveled at an exotic world peopled by all manner of hunters, fishers, and farmers. Chinese and Muslim literature abounded with tales of the exotic too: "The country of Po-pa-li is in the southwestern sea. [The people] do not eat any of the fine grains, but eat only meat. They often stick a needle into the veins of cattle and draw blood which they drink raw, mixed with milk." Thus did Chinese scholar Tuan Ch'êng-shih describe the pastoralists of Somalia in northeast Africa in A.D. 863.[1]*

We have passed in brief review over the pervasive homogeneity of the Lower and Middle Pleistocene world, when, despite severe technological limitations, hand-ax makers and chopping tool users spread widely over diverse ecological zones, ranging from arctic cold to tropical savannah. The emergence of *Homo sapiens* sees a radical change in the world order, for a far greater diversity of hunting populations began to exploit hunting territories never inhabited in earlier times. During the Elster glaciation some 40,000 years ago, bands of hunters began to exploit the western Russian plains, while the Siberian tundra and the Far East were widely settled by *Homo sapiens* during the final glacial retreat. Japan was already occupied during the late Pleistocene; Australia, perhaps over

* See pages 388–389 for notes to Chapter 9.

30,000 years ago (Table 9.1). The New World, too, was settled by bands of late Pleistocene hunters at least 25,000 years ago.

Many thousands of years have passed since hunting peoples first populated this planet. Most of them have been superseded, assimilated, or driven to extinction by later, food-producing peoples or by the rapacious inroads of modern explorers or colonists. In 15,000 B.C., all human populations were hunters and gatherers. Several thousand years later, farmers had begun to cultivate wild cereals or root crops in parts of the Americas, the Near and Far East, and Southeast Asia. Urban civilizations were flourishing in Mesopotamia by 3000 B.C., while agricultural states were burgeoning in Asia and the New World.

Ethnographer George Murdock has estimated that perhaps only 15 percent of the world's landmasses were peopled by hunter-gatherers by the late fifteenth century A.D. when Columbus voyaged to the New World.[2] The Eskimo and related groups still enjoyed a sophisticated maritime hunting and fishing economy in northern latitudes, as did some Siberian groups. North American Indians relied on hunting and gathering in the northern woodlands and desert West, as did the Fuegans of the

Table 9.1
Late Pleistocene hunters in northern latitudes.

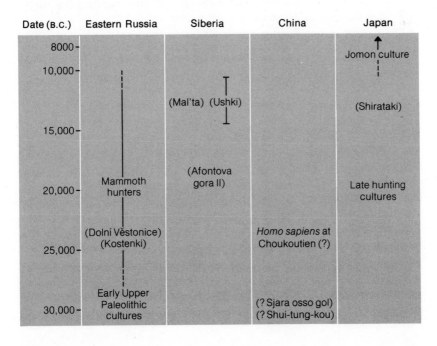

Date (B.C.)	Eastern Russia	Siberia	China	Japan
8000				Jomon culture
10,000				
		(Mal'ta) (Ushki)		(Shirataki)
15,000				
20,000	Mammoth hunters	(Afontova gora II)		Late hunting cultures
25,000	(Dolní Věstonice) (Kostenki)		*Homo sapiens* at Choukoutien (?)	
30,000	Early Upper Paleolithic cultures		(? Sjara osso gol) (? Shui-tung-kou)	

extreme south of the New World. Bushmen and Pygmies hunted in remote corners of Africa. The Australian aborigines continued as hunters and gatherers into modern times. By the nineteenth century, over 80 percent of the world's population were pastoralists or soil cultivators.

In Chapters 9, 10, and 11 we trace the peopling of the world by hunting peoples, some of whom still exist as our oldest surviving links with human prehistory. We begin the story with the more northern latitudes.

mammoth hunters in eastern europe

The undulating plains of western Russia and central Europe show only sparse human occupation before the Upper Paleolithic (Figure 9.1). Open landscapes fostered strong, icy winds during glacial periods. No rocky cliffs formed convenient rock-shelters or cozy caves for hunters to use for their settlements. The inhabitants of the plains had to create artificial dwellings, using their own tools and available raw materials to provide both warmth and shelter.

Although some Mousterians had braved the windy plains, the first extensive settlement is thought to have begun over 25,000 years ago when more advanced hunters began exploiting the arctic fauna of the steppe. The archaeology of the plains has been difficult to piece together, for the hunters lived in temporary camps that do not yield the long sequences of human occupation found in French caves.

?40,000 B.P.

The Kostenki and Borshevo villages lie on the west bank of the Don River in the western USSR.[3] Elephant bones had been found in the banks of the Don near Kostenki for centuries before archaeologists uncovered a series of hunting camps there. The earliest occupations have yielded hollow-based, triangular points, which have strong Mousterian connections. At least two later occupations feature many blade tools, especially small-backed knives and burins, as well as numerous artifacts of mammoth bone and ivory. These giant beasts formed the staple diet of the hunters, who made much use of their carcasses for other purposes as well.

24,000 B.P.

Some tools made by the mammoth hunters serve to link them with Upper Paleolithic peoples to the west. Backed flint blades are found in the Gravettian culture of France and with hunting peoples on the Don. Needles and thong softeners are common tools, too. Venus cult figurines (see also Figure 8.4) extend from southern Russia into southwestern France. The mammoth hunters reproduced their prey and other creatures by carving them in chalk at Kostenki and in clay elsewhere. Their tools were also decorated with geometric patterns. Cave art has been reported from the southern Ural Mountains, where the deer and the mammoth

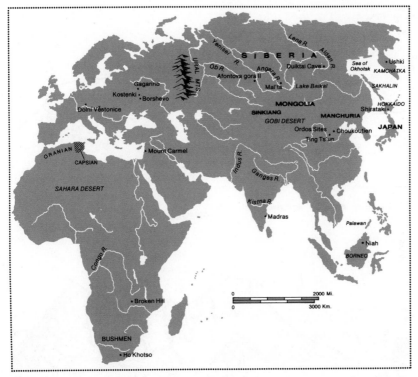

Figure 9.1
Archaeological sites mentioned in Chapters 9 and 10.

were depicted in styles surprisingly reminiscent of those appearing in French caves.

The hunters lived in large, irregular dwellings partially scooped out of the earth, probably roofed with bone or huge mammoth skins (Figure 9.2). Movable bone "poles" probably supported the hides; the edges of the tents were weighted down with huge bones and tusks, which were found lining the hollows at Kostenki and Gagarino in Russia, at Dolní Věstonice in Czechoslovakia, and in other localities.[4] The plans of the houses are so irregular that they can hardly have been built with a rigid timber framework. Some were small, circular structures about 460 centimeters (15 ft.) in diameter, partially dug into the ground. Such dwellings were sometimes built together within the confines of a huge depression, several dozen meters long, with a row of hearths down the center. The hunting bands living within one of these large tented areas must have reached considerable sizes.

We have no means of telling how long the mammoth hunters dwelt

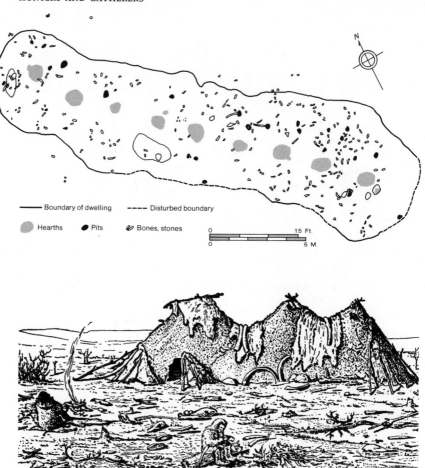

Figure 9.2

The plan of a mammoth hunters' long house (top) from Kostenki IV, USSR and a reconstruction based on finds at Push Kari. This latter example was nearly 12 meters long by 3.7 meters wide (40 ft. by 12 ft.) and stood in a shallow depression.

in their camps, nor whether they were seasonally occupied. The Dolní Věstonice site yielded the remains of over a hundred young mammoths as well as the bones of smaller animals.[5] The plains dwellers' lives were dominated by the mammoth, whose migrations and habits must have determined to a large extent both the movements of the hunters and the size of their bands. At certain times of the year the large beasts undoubtedly moved to new pastures, feeding on young grass in the spring. Cooperative hunting and game drives could have yielded rich hauls of meat and skins.

Mammoths were enormous creatures. We are lucky enough to know much about them from frozen carcasses found in Siberian valleys.[6] The amount of meat that came from one carcass would have been sufficient to support a sizable population of hunters if the meat was dried to preserve it. The bitterly cold winters enabled the hunters to refrigerate fresh meat in ice-block caches, for they must have been familiar with the preservative properties of their arctic environment.

Mammoth skin, bones, sinews, and marrow were valuable for many purposes. Bone was important especially because it provided fuel; burned mammoth bones have come from the Kostenki site and other localities. House frames, "mattocks," pins, needles, and a wide range of small tools were made from the bones of the hunters' prey. Wood was naturally less important in the treeless environment of the steppe. It is hardly surprising to find in this difficult environment such a specialized hunting economy, based on lumbering beasts whose carcasses could support many hungry mouths and fuel fires. The technology of the plains made much use of fire both for warmth and for hardening the tips of spears, as well as in the preparation of flint for pressure flaking. Indeed, fire was a vital element in man's armory as he moved outward to the arctic frontiers of the Paleolithic world.

siberia

The enormous tracts of the Soviet Union to the east of the Ural Mountains form a huge amphitheater that ends on the frontiers of the Arctic.[7] Mountain ranges surround Siberia on all sides except the Arctic North. Remote from the Atlantic and Pacific weather patterns, Siberia is dry country with harsh, cold winters and short, hot summers. Treeless plains, known as tundra, predominate in the far north and extend to the shores of the Arctic Ocean, for precipitation has been too sparse to form the huge ice sheets that covered much of western Europe and North America during the Weichsel glaciation. The plains become covered with coniferous forest in more southern latitudes with their more temperate climate, but large, gregarious mammals can find little to feed on in the sparse undergrowth of the forests. During the Weichsel the tundra probably extended farther south than it does today, and perhaps there was a higher game density for Siberian hunters to prey on.

During much of the Weichsel the regions of Russia, Siberia, and the Far East open to human settlement were limited by local northern glaciers and a vast zone of glacial lake and marsh country to the south of the ice sheets between the Ural Mountains and the Yenisei River. There is meager evidence for Stone Age occupation of Siberia prior to the Weichsel, and traces of human life before the last cold snap of the glaciation are confined to five sites from the more southern parts of Siberia. The tools from these settlements remain imperfectly described. It is only in succeeding millennia that we find traces of more intensive occupation. Most Pleistocene sites in Siberia have been found in large river valleys such as those of the Ob, Yenisei, Angara, and Lena. Many more will undoubtedly be found as archaeological research continues, especially in central and northeastern Siberia, for these parts of the Arctic North were found to be inhabitable even under the severest conditions of the Weichsel glaciation.

Pollen grains have come from riverside sites occupied during the late Weichsel. They reflect an arctic steppe environment, with a low rainfall and harsh winters. The steppe was far from devoid of animal life, for large mammals were able to survive on stunted grasses and other forage that was rarely buried under deep snow. Food was within easy reach to support large herds of game. The hunters preferred reindeer, wild horses, and wild cattle rather than mammoths and other large animals.

The toolkits of these early Siberians were well adapted to hunting under severe conditions. They made less use of blade tools than Upper Paleolithic peoples to the west, relying on crudely made flake tools for many of their scraping implements. Burins were in use for bone working, while wedge-shaped cores were used for making small blades employed as stone barbs or blades in bone tools. Such cores are widespread in extreme northern China, Mongolia, Japan, and restricted parts of North America. Bone awls and needles, pendants, and beads complete the preserved toolkits.

Mal'ta
12,750 B.C.

Probably the most famous Siberian Paleolithic site is Mal'ta, near Irkutsk at the south end of Lake Baikal.[8] Mal'ta has been radiocarbon dated to 14,750 ± 120 years ago. Over 200 reindeer and 7 mammoths were killed by the Paleolithic occupants, who were living, like their western counterparts, in large campsites in partially sunken houses, probably with skin walls and roofs.

The Mal'ta toolkit contained the scrapers and burins so typical of western settlements, as well as some points and scraping tools that are obvious survivals from Mousterian traditions and imply an earlier occupation of the area. A wealth of needles, ornamented bones, and a tusk engraved with a mammoth and some crude female and bird figurines link the Mal'ta people with the hunting traditions of European *Homo sapiens* (Figure 9.3). The Mal'ta animal bones show a mixture of both arctic and plains game, such as the horse. The long-house pattern of the western Russian plains survives here as a similar adaptation to the harsh Siberian climate.

Over fifty Paleolithic sites are known from the Yenisei Valley, the

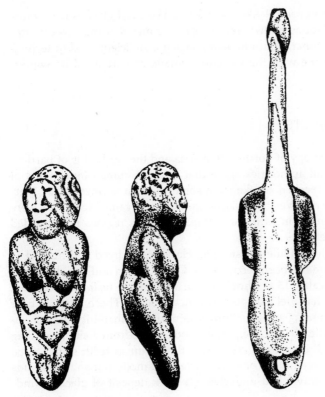

Figure 9.3
Figurines from Mal'ta, Siberia: a bone female figurine (actual size), two views (left); and an ivory bird (two-thirds actual size) (right).

largest being Afontova gora II, recently dated to 20,900 ± 300 years.[9] Large pebble scrapers, sometimes called *skreblo* (a characteristic Siberian artifact), many bone tools, and small-blade artifacts were in use at this locality.

Afontova gora II ?18,900 B.C.

The earliest settlement of Siberia depended, like that of the western plains, on a successful adaptation to the harsh realities of living in the open arctic. A characteristic of plains hunting is the use of a huge territory by small bands of hunters, who range widely in search of their prey, perhaps camping near their kills for a few days before moving on or returning to a favorite place again and again at a certain time of year. The initial settlement of the Siberian corridor may owe its beginnings to the restless wanderings of mammoth hunters who gradually moved eastward into Siberia in pursuit of their favorite quarry. The Mousterian elements in their toolkit may have resulted from contacts with Neanderthal populations in central Asia isolated by Weichsel glaciers from more advanced populations elsewhere. We can surmise that man was unable to inhabit arctic Siberia until he had reached a sufficient level of techno-logical skill to cope with the extreme climatic conditions of its winters and summers.

chinese hunters

The early archaeology of northeastern Asia and the Far East is of particu-lar interest, for all authorities agree that the first human inhabitants of the New World reached Alaska from somewhere in northern Asia. Dur-ing the height of the Weichsel glaciation, extensive game-rich plains were available for hunters in extreme northeast Siberia, regions now flooded by the Bering Sea.

Throughout the Middle Pleistocene, *Homo erectus* lived and hunted in China. His culture has been recovered at Choukoutien and was described in Chapter 6. Locality 15 at Choukoutien, another site near that occupied by *Homo erectus,* has yielded more advanced tools.[10] These artifacts bear more skillful trimming and more purposeful shapes than the crude chop-pers of the Middle Pleistocene. Similar tools came from a site near Ting Ts'un in Shansi Province, together with three human teeth stated to be intermediate between those of *Homo erectus* and modern man.[11] The finds were made in a gravel bed underlying a thick deposit of glacial, wind-blown silt.

This loess was deposited during the height of the Weichsel glaciation, blown southward from arctic regions far to the north of China. Cold and dry winds carried fine dust for hundreds of miles, blanketing northern China with fertile soils of great importance in later millennia. Ting Ts'un was occupied during a warm interval in the glaciation, but only a few traces of human settlement from warmer intervals in the glaciation have been located in the loess country.

Some hunters of small game camped at Shui-tung-kou in the Ordos desert.[12] Others lived at Sjara Osso Gol on the southern borders of the same region in a terrain that contained both small lakes and sand dunes. The bones of elephants, rhinoceroses, deer, horses, wild goats, and os-triches indicate a relatively damp climate and open plains. Flake points and scrapers have been found, as well as tiny blade cores used for making small tools like those of late Pleistocene hunters in the west.

Seven *Homo sapiens* burials were discovered in another cave at the very summit of Choukoutien hill. Bone and horn ornaments accompanied rare stone artifacts. The skeletons were deliberately buried, and were covered with red pigment. Unfortunately, the burials are undated, as are both the Ordos sites, but they are thought to represent the earliest appearance of modern man yet recorded in China.[13]

Between the end of the Pleistocene and the rise of the bronze-using civilizations of central China in the second millennium B.C., human activity is recorded only in scattered finds of stone tools and potsherds at small surface sites scattered throughout the vast desert and grassland regions of Mongolia, Manchuria, and the Ordos. The shifting sands of the Gobi Desert are largely uninhabited today. In earlier times, rains were more abundant, and the Gobi supported a sparse game population. Scatters of microlithic stone tools testify to an abundant hunting population whose camping places were strategically placed near water holes. The small cores and finely trimmed arrowbarbs of the Gobi hunters are found over an enormous area from Manchuria to Sinkiang, their southern limit of distribution lying along the great mountain ranges that separate the Gobi Desert from the Yellow River drainage basin. Although no radiocarbon dates for Gobi sites have been processed, many of the hunting camps belong to the warmer period immediately after the end of the Weichsel glaciation, when the desert supported rich fauna and some standing water.

paleolithic japan

During the height of the Weichsel glaciation, the main Japanese islands were joined not only to one another but also to the Asian mainland at the island of Sakhalin. The islands were apparently settled during the Middle or Upper Pleistocene. For a long time, Japan was an Asian cul-de-sac, with a long continuity of human culture.

About 20,000 years ago a continuous sequence of late Pleistocene hunting cultures evolved, with a technology based on a sophisticated blade technique in obsidian. Burins were commonly used; bifacially worked projectile heads and small tools came into fashion later (Figure 9.4).[14] The island of Hokkaido has yielded many important late Pleistocene sites, especially those found at Shirataki, several of which date back around 15,000 years. 18,000–8000 B.C.

As early as 12,000 years ago many hunter-gatherers had settled by sea and lake shores, relying on shellfish for much of their diet. Mussels, oysters, and fish from both deep and shallow water were obtained, and dugout canoes, remains of which have survived in later sites, were used in this activity. Deer and wild pigs were hunted inland; the weapons were arrows tipped with finely flaked, concave stone heads. Wild vegetable foods were collected. These people lived in circular houses that were partly sunk below ground level and heated with a central fireplace. Jomon 10,500 B.C.

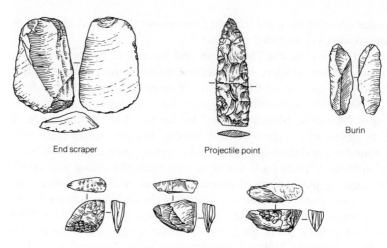

End scraper   Projectile point   Burin

Wedge-shaped bladelet cores

Figure 9.4
Paleolithic implements from Hokkaido, Japan (one-third actual size).

Japanese scholars have grouped sites of this type in the "Jomon" cul-ture. Jomon sites are remarkable for their clay vessels.[15] Elsewhere in the world, pottery is normally associated with an agricultural economy.[16] For most of their long history, however, the Jomon people were hunters and gatherers, although they began to cultivate millet, buckwheat, and beans in later millennia.

hunter-gatherers in northeast asia

The extreme northeastern parts of the Far East offered a variety of envi-ronments to hunter-gatherers. Inhospitable coniferous forest covered more southern latitudes in the interior, giving way to arctic tundra some hundreds of miles below the Arctic Circle. The coasts of the Sea of Okhotsk and the Bering Sea offered rich fishing grounds to those who camped by their shores. The middle Aldan River has yielded Diuktai Cave, where crude scrapers made on pebbles and bifacial stone points are associated with other cultural remains said to resemble early artifacts found on the Japanese islands.[17] Unfortunately, Diuktai is still undated, but it is one of the most eastern Pleistocene settlements yet discovered in Siberia.

14,500–
10,500 B.C.
    An isolated Paleolithic site near Ushki Lake on the Kamchatka Penin-sula has yielded several layers of human occupation, the earliest dating

to the fifteenth millennium B.C., at the very end of the Weichsel glaciation. A later horizon dates to the eleventh millennium; both this and earlier levels have yielded small stone tools.[18]

At the end of the Pleistocene, fishing was an important activity near lakes and seacoasts, as was the hunting of forest animals. The hunters of the tundra presumably still lived off the reindeer; different emphases in hunting and gathering patterns occurred in the various ecological zones. Technology was based on crude stone pebbles and some small-blade artifacts, a toolkit that was already adapted to the forest environment of the Siberian plateau. Thus at the end of the Pleistocene we do not find the rapid transformation of toolkits and hunting practices so characteristic of the coast, where ecological changes were more extreme. We must stress that almost nothing is known of this important period of human history in Siberia, except for indications of a cultural difference between coastal and interior inhabitants.

In the far north, the shores of the Bering Strait were peopled by arctic maritime hunters whose pattern of exploitation of the coastal environment developed in the north at the end of the Pleistocene. This pattern was perpetuated by the rich Eskimo, Aleut, Chukchi, and Koryak hunting cultures which have survived into modern times and extended across the northern latitudes of the New World as far east as Greenland and the Atlantic coast.

10

hunters
in southern latitudes

Many of the world's surviving hunter-gatherers live in tropical environments. Archaeological traces of their activities are abundant and have been the subject of intensive study.[1]*

upper paleolithic cultures
in the mediterranean basin

The Mediterranean basin provided a wealth of hospitable environments for Upper Paleolithic hunters. Deep cave deposits and numerous open sites testify to their activities. In the Near East, the new blade technologies of Upper Paleolithic hunters appear around 35,000 B.C., both at Mount Carmel and at other caves in the Levant.[2] The hunters ate many gazelles; this meat diet provided a staple for thousands of years. The toolkits of the hunters grew smaller as they placed increasing reliance on backed blades and spearheads, many of them mounted in handles.

North African hunters flourished on the shores of the Mediterranean. The fluctuations of colder and warmer climates in Libya caused the zone of well-watered, coastal bush country to expand or to contract as climatic conditions changed. At the beginning of the Upper Paleolithic, for example, the wild ox was a favored quarry of Libyan hunters, but the gazelle and the wild horse were taken in much larger numbers after 30,000 B.C., when the Weichsel glaciation began its final onslaught in northern latitudes.

* See pages 389–390 for notes to Chapter 10.

To the west, in what is now Algeria, the coastal plains were isolated from cultural influences to the north by the Mediterranean and to the south by the Sahara. Upper Paleolithic peoples are thought to have arrived in northwest Africa somewhat later than in the Near East, Neanderthal hunters apparently surviving to later than 27,000 B.C. in this region.[3]

The first modern populations, whose culture has been named the "Oranian," hunted bears, deer, and such antelope as the gnu and haartebeest, and enjoyed a dry climate somewhat similar to that of modern Algeria. They may have settled in North Africa as early as 14,000 years ago. The Oranian culture is mostly confined to the coastal zone, few sites having been discovered in the interior. It was replaced in some areas by another culture, named the "Capsian," of peoples who based their economy on shellfish and who made diminutive stone arrowbarbs and other microlithic tools (Figure 10.1).[4] (See also Table 10.1.)

Oranian
10,000–
6000 B.C.

Capsian
8000–
6500 B.C.

the sahara

The Sahara itself was at least in part stunted grassland during the cooler phases of the Weichsel. Innumerable Paleolithic sites are known from the desert, many clustered around the dried-out beds of Pleistocene lakes. Middle Paleolithic hunters were quite numerous in the Sahara, and their characteristic, tanged, "Aterian" points have been found all over the desert (Figure 10.2).[5] Upper Paleolithic peoples did not settle the desert to any degree, and it was not until 15,000 B.C. or even later that the hunting populations of the Sahara abandoned Middle Paleolithic technology and adopted microlithic tools, bows and arrows, and composite tools of stone and bone or wood.

Aterian
Older than
30,000–
15,000 B.C.

sub-saharan africa

With the coming of modern man, the diverse African environment was fully utilized for human occupation for the first time. *Homo erectus* had favored more open country, living in savannah and grassland environments and ignoring for the most part the economic challenges of the rain forest.

His successors occupied both the desert and the semiarid country of northeast and southern Africa and also the dense forests of the Zaire basin as well as savannah country.[6] Climatic and vegetational shifts in the Upper Pleistocene were a major influence in man's choice of new habitats. But between 60,000 and 35,000 years ago, African toolkits un-

60,000–
35,000 B.P.

Figure 10.1
The microlith is a small arrow barb or similar implement made by notching a small blade and snapping off the base of the blade after the implement is formed. Microliths were mounted in wooden or bone shafts to form barbed spears or arrows. They were commonly used by hunters in all latitudes. The barbs were light enough to be used with bows and arrows.

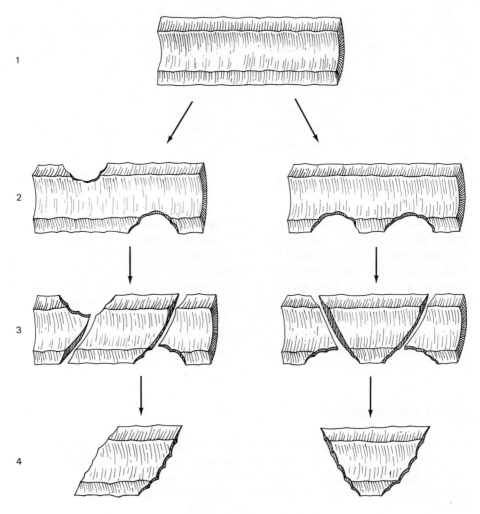

Mode of microlith manufacture

The various stages of microlith manufacture (left). A complete blade is selected (1) and then notched on opposite sides or the same edge depending on the shape of microlith required (2). The blade is then snapped across the notch (3), the middle segment forming the finished implement, in this case a parallelogram-shaped (left) or a trapedzoidal (right) arrow barb (actual size).

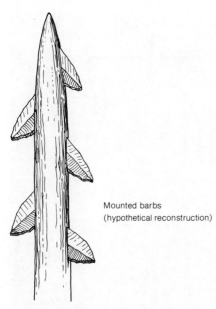

Mounted barbs
(hypothetical reconstruction)

Microliths were commonly mounted in slotted wooden shafts, sometimes forming oblique barbs like the example reconstructed here.

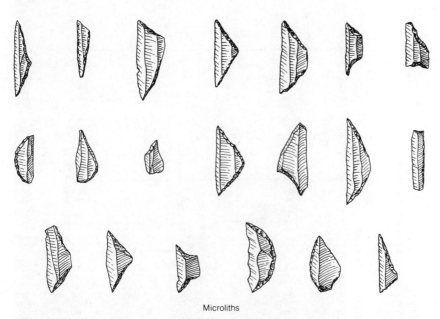

Microliths

Microliths from a Capsian site in Tunisia. These ''geometric'' forms are typical of many late Stone Age hunting cultures in the Old World (actual size).

Table 10.1
Hunter-gatherers in southern latitudes.

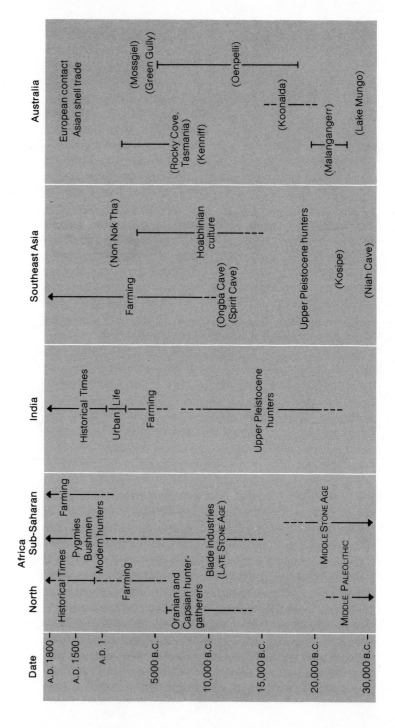

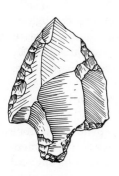

Figure 10.2
  Aterian points (actual size).

derwent a profound change; they began to show regional diversity as if man had begun to perceive the advantages of exploring unfamiliar habitats.

Much evidence for the gradual evolution of human culture in Africa during most of the Middle and Upper Pleistocene is confined to stone tools of interest only to specialists. But by 100,000 years ago a scattered population of hunters, represented by such fossils as Broken Hill man from central Zambia, was widely spread over Africa.[7] The Broken Hill skull is unusually massive in the face and its brow ridges, but in other respects it resembles modern man, as do the limb bones and the pelvis found with the cranium. *Homo sapiens rhodesiensis* was living between 60,000 and 40,000 years ago and was probably capable of occupying the full range of African environments settled by this time (Figure 10.3).

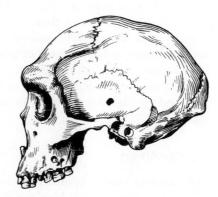

Figure 10.3
  Two views of the skull of Broken Hill man, from Zambia.

During the latter part of the Upper Pleistocene and early Postglacial times, a period of cooler temperatures and lower evaporation throughout Africa was followed by an interval of warmer and more humid climate, itself replaced by more arid conditions about 3000 B.C. Until about 10,000 years ago many hunters in Africa were still making the prepared cores and flake tools characteristic of Middle Paleolithic cultures. These were replaced in part by tools made by blade technology, which became increasingly common after 15,000 B.C.

15,000 B.C.

By the end of the Pleistocene, African hunters were depending on stone arrowbarbs as well as on tiny scraping tools and adzes to supplement a predominantly wooden toolkit.[8] Microlithic tools are found throughout more open country in Africa, most of them being associated with hunting camps occupied by users of bows and arrows, a hunting weapon apparently introduced into sub-Saharan Africa toward the end of the Pleistocene. In more densely forested regions the hunters had no use for lightweight toolkits and relied on heavy picks and a variety of woodworking tools to help them exploit their forest environments.

5000 B.C. to
Modern Times

We find increasing specialization in economic activities. The hunters of the savannah relied on vast herds of antelopes and other mammals for much of their food supply. Other bands settled on the shores of large rivers and lakes, exploiting the rich fish resources in their waters. This valuable and reliable source of protein encouraged more permanent settlement and specialized ways of making one's living. The Stone Age peoples of the forest areas near the Zaire (Congo) River did not have the game resources available to the woodland savannah people of eastern, central, and southern Africa. While they were able to take some game, such as buffalo, elephant, and monkeys, in their forest environment, they relied on vegetable foods and wild roots for much of their livelihood.

The world-famous rock art of eastern, central, and southern Africa has preserved for us, in all its vividness, the incredible richness of the African environment in prehistoric times.[9] Stone Age hunters are depicted pursuing vast herds of antelope, sometimes using the skins of their quarry as decoys (Figure 10.4). A jumble of peaceful mammals, the quarry of prehistoric hunters, march in fascinating herds across the walls of granite rock-shelters in the remote African interior. Domestic scenes, ceremonies, and the material culture of these hunters are depicted in the paintings.

the bushmen

The surviving remnants of African Stone Age populations can be found in the Bushman hunting bands of Botswana in southern Africa and in

Figure 10.4
A running Bushman hunter from Ho Khotso, Lesotho, southern Africa, from a late
Stone Age painting colored in purple-red. The figure is 21 centimeters (about 8 ins.)
high.

the Pygmies of the Zaire forest, two hunting peoples adapted to quite
different ecological situations.[10] Three thousand years ago the hunting
populations of central and southern Africa remained undisturbed in the
incredibly rich environment that was their home. Then immigrants, who   A.D. 100
were farmers and cattle herders, began to settle in many of their favorite
hunting grounds, taking over the water holes and camping places of the
Stone Age populations (Chapter 14). Some hunters adopted the new
economies, marrying into the Negro populations who brought farming
to the savannah and forests. Other hunters were wiped out by the newcomers, because they were unable to compete on equal terms with the
farmers.

Some bands retreated into drier areas or dense forest regions unsuit-
able for agriculture and domestic stock. There they prospered on a small
scale until recent times, but the sportsmen of nineteenth-century Africa   A.D. 1850
decimated the hunting grounds much more effectively than the African
farmers who had ousted the Bushmen centuries earlier. The Bushmen
were forced to rely more heavily on wild vegetable foods as their game
meat supplies diminished.

indian hunters

"In India," wrote the great British archaeologist Sir Mortimer Wheeler, "it is more than ordinarily difficult to set Paleolithic man squarely on his feet. That he abounded for a great many thousands of years is sufficiently evident from the unnumbered lumps of stone which he split and shaped and left for us . . . of his physical aspect we know nothing. His solitary memorial is an infinitude of stones."[11]

?15,000 B.C.   The Upper Pleistocene hunters of the Indian subcontinent are represented by a multitude of stone tool scatters, especially in large river valleys such as those of the Ganges, Narmada, and Krishna in southern India. Microlithic tools are characteristic of these industries, many the remains of composite tools such as stone-tipped arrows and mounted scrapers. The artifacts are rough compared with African and European equivalents; the hunters who made them lived mostly in central and southern India. Their sites are noticeably rare in the Punjab and northern plains, as well as in northeast India and Bangladesh.

The dates of these Indian hunters are highly uncertain, but some idea of their economy was obtained from the Langhnaj site in Gujarat, where a buried land surface was covered with vast numbers of microliths and grinding stones made of sandstone that were perhaps used for pulverizing wild vegetable foods. The bones of rhinoceroses, deer, bovines, pigs, horses, and fish came from the same settlement.[12] Some other related encampments near Madras were those of hunters and fishermen who settled near an old coastline some 5.6–9.1 meters (20–30 ft.) higher than the modern shoreline.

?10,000 B.C.   The tendency toward smaller tools found among Paleolithic hunters is repeated here in India. But the origins of the cultural tradition behind them remains obscure, for the tiny arrowbarbs do not have a likely ancestry in the earlier flake industries of the subcontinent. It may be that the hunters of the Arabian grasslands passed into India, bringing with them new implements of the chase such as the bow and stone-tipped arrow which was adapted to open country and the pursuit of large herds of game.

southeast asia

Mainland and offshore Southeast Asia are among the largest areas of blank territory on the prehistoric map. It is only recently that they have been recognized as being of great significance to human history. When we move eastward into Southeast Asia, we again venture into the vast territory occupied by long-lived chopping tool cultural traditions, already well established in Middle Pleistocene times. Again we lack systematic archaeological research.

The indigenous hunting populations of Southeast Asia during the later Pleistocene were still making chopper tools with jagged edges, achieved by removing several flakes from either side of a pebble. They used few blades, relying on simple flake tools for their toolkit. During the Weichsel glaciation, low sea levels would have exposed the Sunda shelf, a vast land platform now covered by saltwater. People in Malaya and Thailand could move with comparative ease between the mainland and the islands of Borneo, Java, and Sumatra.

Early hunters certainly lived in Borneo during the Weichsel. We know something of their activities from British archaeologist Tom Harrison's excavations in the Great Cave of Niah.[13] The cave is enormous: it is 244 meters (800 ft.) wide at the entrance and 61 meters (200 ft.) high in places, and it extends over 10.5 hectares (26 acres). Over 3.6 meters (12 ft.) of deposits came from its floor, two major occupation zones being separated by a sterile zone 1.8 meters (6 ft.) down.

The earliest Niah people occupied the cavern about 40,000 years ago, hunting both modern mammal species and an extinct anteater. They made simple choppers and flake tools, used no fine blade tools. The skull of one hunter found near the bottom of the Niah deposits was identified beyond doubt as *Homo sapiens;* he is entirely modern in appearance, but clearly distinct racially from early western European or early northern Chinese remains. If the date for the early Niah occupation is confirmed by other samples, this skull is one of the earliest representatives of modern man known to science. The upper levels at Niah were first occupied between about 32,500 and 19,500 years ago. The occupants of Niah continued to make pebble choppers, small flake artifacts, and some bone objects.

Late Pleistocene hunter-gatherers lived on other Southeast Asian islands, too — Palawan, the Philippines, the Celebes, and New Guinea — but Stone Age archaeological research in these areas has hardly begun. Kosipe in the New Guinea highlands was occupied by late Pleistocene hunter-gatherers who used not only struck flakes but also axes or adzes and "waisted" blades, some of them with ground surfaces (Figure 10.5).[14] These are the earliest known ground stone tools in the world, having been radiocarbon dated to between 23,000 and 26,500 B.P. Edge grinding has always been regarded as a characteristic attribute of farming peoples, whose more sedentary lives permitted them the leisure to spend time making ground-edged tools. This theory must clearly be abandoned, for

?40,000 B.P.

32,500 B.P.

26,500 B.P.

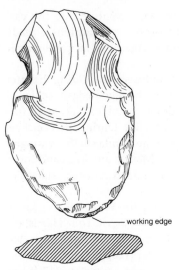

working edge

Figure 10.5
Waisted ax/adze blade from Kosipe, New Guinea (one-half actual size).

ground-edged tools are also known from Japan in late Pleistocene times and probably date to at least 15,000 years ago in mainland Southeast Asia, which can certainly no longer be regarded as a quiet cultural backwater during the Pleistocene.

hoabhinian peoples

Toward the end of the Pleistocene many hunter-gatherers of mainland Southeast Asia were using a distinctive toolkit based on flaked pebbles and enjoying a culture adapted to a humid tropical envrionment. The term "Hoabhinian" has been applied to the sites of these people, but only recently has any attempt been made to define the label more closely.[15]

Hoabhinian
15,000–
3000 B.C.

Hoabhinian tools were first discovered in the 1920s in mountain caves near Hoa Binh in North Vietnam. Subsequently many similar sites have been unearthed in the mountainous parts of northern Southeast Asia, mainly in caves by small streams. American archaeologist Chester Gorman has recently excavated a Hoabhinian site at Spirit Cave in northern Thailand.[16] He was able to establish a firm chronology for his site; it was perhaps first occupied by Hoabhinians about 11,000–12,000 B.C. Ongba

Cave in west-central Thailand has yielded two dates for Hoabhinian layers around 9,000 B.C. Spirit Cave was abandoned in the eighth millennium B.C., but some Hoabhinian peoples were still using a modified version of their original material culture as late as 3500–3000 B.C. Thus this long-lived Southeast Asian cultural adaptation not only had its roots in the Pleistocene but also flourished during the millennia when food production became a significant way of life in Southeast Asia (see Chapter 15).

Hoabhinian sites have been found on the coasts of Malaya, Sumatra, South China, and North Vietnam. The low sea levels of the late Weichsel exposed vast coastal plains and new seacoasts for human exploitation. These areas were flooded again by the higher sea levels of the Postglacial; many excellent hunting grounds were inundated, leaving only a limited picture of early Hoabhinian life. No Hoabhinian sites have yet been found on the lowland alluvial plains of Southeast Asia, which were, however, extensively cultivated in later millennia after the beginnings of cereal agriculture.

The coastal people lived on shellfish, sharks, sting rays, and shallow coastal fish, and hunted large mammals such as rhinoceroses, pigs, and deer, as well as the dugong and turtle. Pigs, deer, wild oxen, rhinoceroses, elephants, and monkeys were hunted inland, together with small rodents, and freshwater fish and shellfish were caught. Some seashells, traded from the coast, were found in inland Malaysian caves. The lower levels of Spirit Cave yielded some vegetal remains, including almonds, betel nuts, peas, and candle nuts.

Hoabhinian toolkits are disconcerting, for they defy classification into discrete tool types. The most common artifacts are crude scrapers made on pebbles, choppers, and rough flakes obviously used for cutting and scraping. Hunting weapons are noticeably absent; they were undoubtedly made of wood or other perishable materials. Bamboo is abundant in the Hoabhinians' homeland and must have been a major resource for tools and utensils.

The Hoabhinian peoples lived through a period of great cultural and economic changes in Southeast Asia, and we shall describe the origins of agriculture and metallurgy among them later. Early inland Hoabhinians exploited mountain ridge and river valley animals as well as forest game, while their coastal relatives lived off the resources of the seashore rather than the deep ocean waters. By the time that Spirit Cave was occupied, however, the Hoabhinians were acquainted with many plant species that are either tended or domesticated in Southeast Asia today. Asians were already set on a course toward food production rather than hunting and gathering.

Figure 10.6
  An Australian aborigine with his lightweight hunting kit.

australia and australians

Since Victorian times, a wealth of speculation has surrounded the origins
of the earliest Australians (Figure 10.6).[17] The past thirty years have seen
the beginnings of scientific investigation into the prehistoric Australians,
for this remote landmass offers a unique opportunity for the study of
prehistoric and living hunter-gatherers (Figure 10.7).[18]

first settlement

During the Middle and Upper Pleistocene the islands of Southeast Asia
formed a basically homogeneous industrial complex that involved the

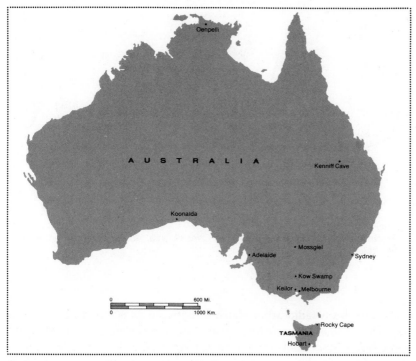

Figure 10.7
Australian sites mentioned in the text.

manufacture of chopping tools as well as trimmed scrapers and other flaked artifacts. Both chopping tools and flakes have been found in the Celebes and possibly in a very early site in the Philippines. During the Weichsel glaciation the Southeast Asian mainland, Java, Borneo, and Palawan were joined together in one landmass, but the Celebes and Australia probably were not, although the body of water between them was much reduced.

Startling evidence for the incredible conservatism of stone tools in Asia during the late Pleistocene came from Tabon Cave on Palawan, where a crude stone technology based on flakes and choppers was in use from at least 40,000 years ago up to approximately 7000 B.C. A somewhat similar sequence extending from 40,000 years ago to 8000 B.C. came from the Niah Cave in Borneo.[19]

It is thought that the earliest settlement of Australia took place over 30,000 years ago, but it is fair to say that the evidence is still extremely inadequate. At Malangangerr and Nawamoyn near Oenpelli in northern Australia, a series of sites with ground-edge adzes, and flake and core

40,000 B.P.

30,000 B.P.

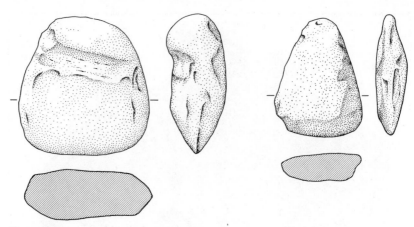

Figure 10.8
Pleistocene ground-edge axes from the Oenpelli area, Australia — three views (one-half actual size).

tools have been radiocarbon dated to between 24,800 and 21,450 years ago (Figure 10.8). A partially cremated human skeleton, 16 hearths, and some heavy stone tools came from a former lake shore at Lake Mungo in New South Wales. These finds are related to a sequence of radiocarbon dates between 30,250 and 32,750 B.P.[20]

One of the most dramatic discoveries has been in Koonalda Cave, close to the south coast of Australia, where engravings have been found in a completely dark chamber dating back at least 18,000 years, as old as much Upper Paleolithic art in western Europe.[21] Koonalda was a quarry site where hunters obtained flint from 61 meters (200 ft.) below ground. Recent research has extended the occupation of the cave back to approximately 22,000 years ago, which would place the first settlement of Australia in the height of the Weichsel glaciation. It is very likely that many of the earliest hunting settlements have been buried by rising sea levels.

Crude flake tools, which are thought by some scholars not to have been mounted on handles (unlike later ones), were used over a wide area of Australia in the late Weichsel, and several regional variations in stone technology emerged. The Kenniff Cave in east-central Australia was occupied 10,000 years ago by makers of a scraper industry which displays considerable variation. Another industry was in Green Gully near Keilor in southern Australia, where the tools were in use later than 17,000 years ago but before 4000 B.C. (Figure 10.9).[22] The crude flake tool tradition lasted long after sea levels had risen above their Weichsel levels. There is an astonishing uniformity about the dependence of these early stone

16,000 B.C.

8000 B.C.

technologies on crude flakes, which seem unlikely to have been mounted as spears and similar tools.

Very few traces of Pleistocene human fossils have come from the continent, and, of those that have, many are of dubious age. The famous Keilor cranium is estimated to date to between 8,000 and 15,000 years ago; unfortunately, it was not found in a stratified layer. A male-female burial at Green Gully dates to 4510 ± 190 B.C., while another site at Mossgiel dates to c. 2850 B.C. or earlier. The Kow swamp site, 120 miles (193 km.) north of Melbourne, has yielded over 30 skeletons with thick skulls, large jaws, and other "archaic" features. This site has been radiocarbon dated to between 8,000 and 10,000 years ago. Several physical anthropologists have demonstrated that the few early Australian skulls show some traits that recall those of the late Pleistocene men found in Java and other areas of Southeast Asia, where, it has been noted, a modern *Homo sapiens* skull dating to 40,000 years ago was found at Niah Cave.[23]

Archaeological research in Southeast Asia has so far been too sparse to demonstrate any close connections between the toolkits of the earliest Australians and those of their Asian contemporaries. No one challenges the accepted theory, however, that Australian origins lie in Asian ancestry.

Some differences can be expected, for the earliest Australians had to

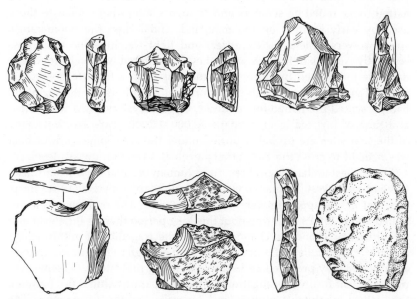

Figure 10.9
Crudely flaked tools from Green Gully, Keilor, Australia (one-half actual size).

adapt to new environmental conditions. Furthermore, the indigenous fauna was drastically different from that of tropical Southeast Asia. Carnivores were less common, and pouched animals like the kangaroo must have provided a large source of game meat. Archaeologists are becoming increasingly interested in the effects of hunters on the extinction of large marsupials known to have lived in Australia during late Pleistocene times. They also surmise that the effects of humanly set bush fires, as well as the overexploitation of game and vegetable foods, may well have upset and drastically modified the often harsh environments of the Australian interior.

While many of the earlier flake tool traditions survived the later millennia of Australian prehistory, the arrival of various technological innovations drastically modified aboriginal toolkits. Ground-edged axes from the third millennium B.C. are found throughout Australia. Boomerangs, spearthrowers, flake points, and a range of microlithic tools spread through different parts of Australia after 3000 B.C.[24]

the tasmanians

When European voyagers first visited Australia they found hunting peoples living on Tasmania, separated from the Australian mainland by the stormy waters of the Bass Straits. The Tasmanians lasted precisely eighty years after their first contact with Western civilization.[25] They had no hafted tools, relied on scrapers and choppers somewhat similar to those used by early hunters on the mainland, and lacked the boomerangs, spearthrowers, shields, axes, adzes, and light-weight stone tools possessed by Australian hunters when they first entered written history. The dog was introduced by Europeans and was soon a favorite possession of the Tasmanians, although their northern neighbors on the mainland had possessed the Dingo for centuries. Obviously, Tasmania was settled at a time of low sea level, perhaps 10,000–11,000 years ago, but many of the first sites are probably buried under the sea. Some form of boat was needed to cross the Bass Straits, even at a time of low sea level.

The earliest archaeological record of human occupation is from Rocky Cove in northwest Tasmania, where a shell heap, 3 meters (10 ft.) deep, was first in use approximately 6170 ± 160 B.C.[26] The midden was abandoned about 1500 B.C. Throughout this long period there is little evidence of cultural or economic change. One of the tragedies of anthropology is that the Tasmanians did not survive long enough to be studied systematically, for they provided an example of living prehistory. It seems very probable that future investigations will demonstrate cultural ties between the earliest inhabitants of mainland Australia and the Tasmanians. The

6000–
1500 B.C.

latter did not receive later cultural innovations that spread into Australia after the sea levels rose.

foreign contacts

The history of foreign contact with the aborigines is an important and pervasive theme of the closing centuries of Australian prehistory. The earliest contacts appear to have been from Southeast Asia, for the shores of northwestern Australia abound in the trepang shell, otherwise known as *bêche de Mer*.[27] This shell was made into soup as well as being used as an aphrodisiac in China. Bands of shell collectors were already frequenting northern Australian coasts when they first came into contact with British explorer Matthew Flinders in 1803. It is likely that this trade has a history extending back over many centuries, but archaeologists have only just begun to study it.

Both Chinese and Arab merchants may have ventured to the inhospitable northern coast, but they left no signs of their visits. As early as 1623, Dutch explorer Jan Carstenz collected specimens of hunting weapons, and by the middle of the eighteenth century his fellow countrymen had traversed all but the eastern coastline of Australia. In 1770 the celebrated Captain Cook and Sir Joseph Banks landed at Botany Bay near the site of modern Sydney, and the gradual decimation of the native hunters of Australia began.

Nineteenth-century views of the aborigines, some of the last surviving hunter-gatherers whose roots lie in the Pleistocene, can aptly be described in the words of William Thomas writing in 1838: "The aboriginal inhabitants of the Colony of Victoria are an Erratic Race, their wandering habits, however ... arise as much from necessity as choice, they have no other alternative for subsistence but by wandering over the country in which Providence has placed them."[28]

Today, by the nature of its unique archaeological record and the wealth of its rich ethnographic sources, Australia promises to be one of the major laboratories of archaeological research in decades to come.

11

early americans

In A.D. 986 one Biarni Heriulfson, the owner of a trading vessel plying between Norway and Iceland, got lost on his way to Greenland and sighted an unknown land "level and covered with woods." Biarni would not let his people land and turned back to Greenland. Nothing else is known of the first Western voyager to set eyes on North America.[1]* His name has been eclipsed by that of Leif Ericson who set sail for the west fifteen years later, landed in Labrador, and wintered at L'Anse-aux-Meadows in northern Newfoundland. Leif's camp was uncovered by Helge Ingstad in 1964. In 1004/5 Leif's brother Thorvald wintered in Labrador, where he was fatally wounded in the first skirmish between Western Europeans and a band of indigenous Americans in canoes. The Norsemen called the natives *Skrellings,* or "barbarians," but the latter succeeded in driving out the foreigners; the first attempts at Western colonization were a failure.

Five centuries later, Christopher Columbus landed in the Caribbean; soon French and English voyagers were exploring the North American coast. These early explorers found flourishing populations of hunters, fishermen, and farmers in what they euphemistically called the New World. American history since the fifteenth century has been the story of continual interaction and conflict between peoples with historic roots in the New World and colonists from other lands.

american origins

Ever since the earliest colonization of the Americas, people have speculated about the origin of the pre-Columbian populations of the Western

166   * See pages 390–392 for notes to Chapter 11.

Hemisphere. There have been many claimants for the peopling of the New World.[2] Canaanites, Celts, Chinese, Egyptians, Phoenicians, and even the Ten Lost Tribes of Israel have been proposed as ancestors of the native Americans. By the early nineteenth century, field research and museum work had begun to replace the wild speculations of earlier scholars. People began to dig in Indian mounds. The long-forgotten temples of Mesoamerica were rescued from the rain forest by Spanish and American explorers.

A wise and sober scholar named Samuel Haven summarized the various myths and legends about the origins of the pre-Columbian Indian in an essay on American archaeology published by the Smithsonian Institution in 1856.[3] He was one of the first to conclude that the New World was initially settled from across the Bering Strait, designating the earliest Americans as northeastern Asiatics who migrated into North America at an unknown date. Most archaeologists now agree with Haven that the first Americans set foot in the New World by way of the Bering Strait or from Kamchatka via the Commander and Aleutian islands. The former route is more widely accepted, for the Bering Strait formed a land bridge between Asia and Alaska at times during the Wisconsin (equivalent to Weichsel) glaciation (Figure 11.1).

Many New World peoples owe much of their culture to hunting traditions that evolved as early as the closing stages of the Weichsel glaciation. In areas where agriculture was impossible or at best a marginal activity, hunting and gathering persisted until recent times. One such region was the Arctic North, where perennial frost and an adverse environment inhibited any form of food production. In the desert West, too, many peoples survived on a diet of seeds, ground acorns, and similar foods.

The archaeological record of the earliest human settlement of the Americas is still thin after more than a century of research. A scarcity of sites, however, is hardly surprising, for the earliest American populations cannot have been large, and, as hunter-gatherers, their campsites are not likely to have been either permanent or substantial enough to survive except under unusually favorable circumstances (Figure 11.2).

Despite widely publicized claims to the contrary, no one has yet found any traces of Lower or Middle Pleistocene hominids in the New World. Nor do living nonhuman primates provide possible New World ancestors for early hominids. A solid body of scientific opinion has examined all the occupation sites claimed to be of this age. None has passed the test of critical appraisal. *Homo sapiens* appears to have been the first human to reach the New World. All skeletal remains found in the Americas belong to modern man (Table 11.1).

A high antiquity for human settlement in the Americas was not widely accepted until the late 1920s. In 1926, J. D. Figgins of the Denver Museum of Natural History found a peculiarly "fluted" stone point at Folsom, New

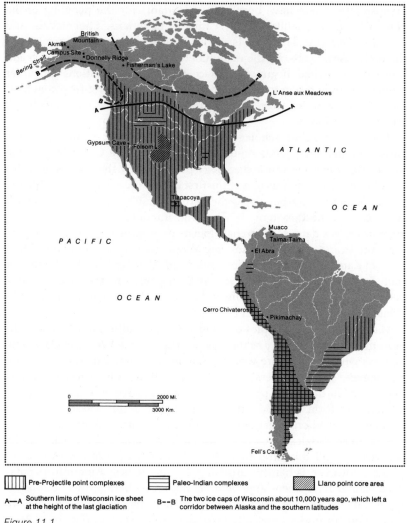

Figure 11.1
Archaeological sites mentioned in Chapter 11.

Mexico, of a type quite unknown in modern contexts.[4] The following year he found another fluted head between the ribs of an extinct type of bison near Folsom. So skeptical had scientists been about his original discovery that Figgins insisted on excavating the second point in the presence of a committee of fellow archaeologists who authenticated and accepted the antiquity of his find. The Folsom kill site yielded the skeletons of 23 extinct bison and 19 projectile heads, indisputable proof of the contemporaneity of early Americans with long-extinct animals.

Figure 11.2
Subsistence patterns among hunters and gatherers in the period after 5000 B.C.

ice sheets and land bridges

In Chapter 9, we showed that human settlement in Siberia and north-eastern Asia intensified during the Weichsel glaciation. Few traces of earlier hunters have come from Siberia, and indeed it has been argued that it was not until the technology of shelter and clothing was sufficiently

Table 11.1
Highly simplified chronological table of hunter-gatherers in the New World.

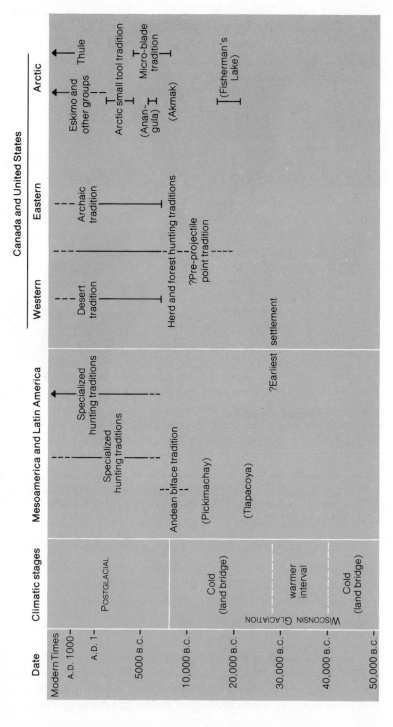

advanced to cope with the climatic extremes of Siberia that man was able to settle the arctic tundra.

Small bands of hunter-gatherers were living in Siberia and northeastern Asia during the last Weichsel cold snap, at a time when sea levels were as much as 52 meters (170 ft.) lower than today. For two prolonged intervals in the past 50,000 years, sea levels were so low that a land bridge existed where the Bering Strait now separates Asia and Alaska. The low-lying plain was a highway for such Asian mammals as the caribou and the mammoth, as well as for man, who presumably ventured eastward toward Alaska in pursuit of game. At its maximum extent, the land bridge extended from the Aleutian Islands in the south to beyond the northern coast of Alaska and Siberia.

The Bering Strait was dry land between about 50,000 and 40,000 years ago and again from 27,000 to 8000 B.C. Great ice sheets covered much of North America during the later phases of the Wisconsin glaciation, extending in a continuous barrier from the Atlantic to the Pacific, effectively blocking any southward movement by man or beast. Southerly corridors through the ice were clear for only a few thousand years before and after the glacial maximum. The Bering Strait Land Bridge was submerged about 8000 B.C. Since then man has had to reach the New World by water, and its aboriginal societies developed in near isolation until the arrival of European colonists and missionaries.[5]

Bering Land Bridge 50,000– 40,000 B.C. 27,000– 8000 B.C.

alaska

We lack many traces of human occupation on the coasts of the Bering Strait or in Alaska dating to the Wisconsin glaciation. Fieldwork conditions are particularly difficult in Alaska, so intensive archaeological reconnaissance is still in its infancy. But Pleistocene deposits in Alaska have yielded abundant traces of edible game, for much of the region was unglaciated, even at the height of the last glaciation. The land bridge area and Alaska were both effectively part of Asia during most of the Wisconsin glaciation. Any hunting bands to the south of the ice sheets were effectively isolated from the outside world for long periods of time.

At least three groups of late Pleistocene sites have been found in Alaska. The oldest occurs at various sites in northern Alaska, in particular at Fisherman's Lake where retouched flakes or blades removed from prepared cores are dated to between 21,000 and 16,000 B.C. The stone tools found in these Alaskan sites have their closest similarities with artifacts from Mal'ta, Irkutsk, and Afontova gora II (Chapter 9), which date to between 20,000 and 12,000 B.C. But these resemblances should not be regarded as close ones, given our incomplete knowledge of both Alaskan and Siberian archaeology.[6]

21,000– 16,500 B.C.

?8000 B.C.   Akmak, one of a complex of settlement sites found at Onion Portage, Alaska, is the earliest site in an 8000-year-long cultural sequence from a river valley that has been a migration route for herds of caribou ever since the time of the earliest human settlement in the region. The site itself consists of a scatter of stone tools on an ancient land surface, perhaps the remains of a permanent settlement area. The tools include heavy chopping and scraping implements, knives, skin-working tools, and many blades and microblades, the latter probably used as insets for weapon points.

Akmak has been radiocarbon dated to about 8000 B.C. The artifacts from the site have some general resemblances to Siberian blade tools and core implements, indicating some general historical relationships between the Akmak tools and the late Paleolithic artifacts in Siberia. But the similarities between the two areas cannot be pressed too hard in our present state of very incomplete knowledge.

Two later complexes of Alaskan and Canadian sites are more recent than Fisherman's Lake. The second group of sites is found in central and northern Alaska. All contain small stone tools made from blades removed from small cores. The stoneworking techniques are closely similar to those practiced in Japan between about 12,000 and 8000 B.C. and in central Siberia at about the same time. Neither the Campus site nor the Donnelly Ridge settlements, to mention two important sites in this group, have been dated, but their chronological bracket is thought to be between 10,000–   10,000 and 8000 B.C.
8000 B.C.   The third group of sites, found east of the Canadian Rockies, includes both bifacially flaked projectile points and conically flaked cores. These artifacts serve to link this group with later tool assemblages in the Arctic, and may be roughly contemporary with the second group.

the earliest hunters

Considerable controversy surrounds the dating of the earliest American hunters. Formerly, many scholars preferred a comparatively recent date for the first settlement, about 13,000 years ago (after the retreat of the ice sheets). By that time, however, the indigenous hunting cultures were so distinctive that they have no links with Asian toolkits, as one would expect if the first settlement across the strait had been that recent. The distinctive features of early American toolkits probably resulted from the isolating factors imposed by the ice sheets, with human settlement occurring at a much earlier date, when access from north to south from the Arctic was possible.

The earliest, widely accepted association of human artifacts with the bones of extinct animals comes from the Tlapacoya site near Mexico City.[7] Some crudely flaked stones and extinct fauna have been radiocarbon dated to 24,000 ± 500 and 22,200 ± 2,600 years ago. A scatter of other early sites has been discovered between Idaho and Latin America; all of them have yielded large, heavy choppers, scrapers, planing tools, and knives but none of the fine, bifacially flaked projectile heads so characteristic of other early hunting societies.[8] Humanly struck tools have been located in caves, in river gravels, and in lake beds. Unfortunately, many finds are badly documented or of doubtful geological date. The artifacts themselves are frequently so generalized that they could well be the work of more recent stoneworkers. Few sites are well dated, and stratigraphical evidence is not easy to come by. If the evidence of surface finds is anything to go on, a crude "nonprojectile point tradition" was widely distributed throughout the Americas by 12,000–13,000 years ago. It is unfortunate that the toolkits of those early hunters are so hard to identify.

26,000–23,000 B.P.

23,000 B.P.

11,000 B.C.

Somewhat more is known of the Latin American hunters.[9] Pikimachay Cave in the Peruvian highlands has yielded two assemblages of stone artifacts found in association with the bones of extinct animals such as the ground sloth. Radiocarbon dates from the earlier levels ranged between 12,750 and 20,000 B.C., with a conservative estimate of their age ranging between 13,000 and 14,500 B.C. The later assemblage dates to c. 12,200 B.C. The El Abra rock-shelter near Bogotá, Colombia, has yielded stone tools which have been radiocarbon dated to slightly earlier than 10,000 B.C. Cut and burned bones of extinct animals have come from Muaco and Taima-Taima in north-central Venezuela. Associated C14 dates range between 11,000 and 14,000 B.C. Cerro Chivateros on the central Peruvian coast was occupied by three successive groups of hunters, the second of which was living at the site about 8500 B.C. Similar stone tool collections have been found in coastal and highland Ecuador, northern Chile, northwestern Argentina, and northern Uruguay. Many stone tools were undoubtedly used for woodworking and the manufacture of other artifacts that have perished owing to their organic nature. No one has yet been able to establish any close relationship between the early South American peoples and the first settlers of North America.

?14,000 B.C.

more hunting bands

Toward the end of the Wisconsin glaciation, the high plains area east of the Rockies lay immediately to the south of the ice sheets. The plains abounded with large herds of mammoths, bison, camels, and horses at this time. By the tenth millennium B.C., we find small kill sites of mammoth hunters scattered over the plains. The Clovis site in New Mexico is one of the most famous, for it has yielded not only the remains of mammoths but also a distinctive form of projectile head known as the Clovis point, which was used by hunters in the chase.[10] Clovis points were carefully flaked on both sides and then were given a "fluted" grooved base that facilitated the hafting of the point on a wooden handle (Figure 11.3).

Within the plains areas where big game hunters flourished, numerous varieties of hunting cultures began to appear. The various styles of projectile head include Eden, Folsom, Midland, Plainsview, and Scottsbluff, as well as other minor types including the celebrated Cody knife that was probably used for skinning (Figure 11.3). Many plains bands relied on big game drives and communal hunting for much of their livelihood.[11] Both the bison and the mammoth were formidable prey for hunters equipped only with spears. We have a remarkably complete knowledge of their hunting methods thanks to discoveries of kill sites where herds of bison were driven down narrow arroyos and then dispatched by waiting hunters. So vivid are the reconstructions of some hunts that we even know the direction of the wind on the day the kill took place. The hunters'

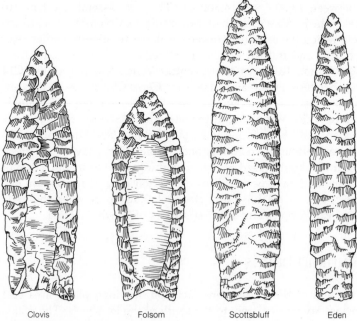

Clovis   Folsom   Scottsbluff   Eden

Figure 11.3
Points from plains cultures (all actual size).

toolkits are scattered around the carcasses of their quarry: scraping tools, stone knives, and numerous flakes used for dismembering game (Figure 11.4). Much of their material culture was perishable, evidently made of wood or bone.

Projectile points are found over an enormous area of North America, from Nova Scotia to northern Mexico. Most sites come from the high plains, but as the Pleistocene ice retreated northward, bands of hunters moved with the Pleistocene game into more northern latitudes, as well as moving toward the Atlantic and Pacific coasts. Not all projectile-head users were big game hunters. Away from the plains, more diversified hunting strategies replaced game drives, with fishing and gathering playing an important role in the economy.

A major variant of the projectile point comes from Mesoamerica and is known as the Lerma point (Figure 11.5). Lerma points are lancehead-shaped and have nonfluted (ungrooved) bases. Pleistocene mammoths have been recovered in Mesoamerica that were associated with these characteristic projectile heads, which are also found in Latin America.

The contemporary hunting populations of South America are little known, except for a widespread stoneworking tradition, the Andean Biface, which may date to between 12,000 and 7000 B.C. Spearheads, large bifaces, and scrapers are typical of hunting sites known over a vast area from Venezuela to Chile. The diversified hunting economies of the Andean Biface Horizon must have varied considerably from region to region, with some bands placing major emphasis on big game while others were predominantly fishermen and shellfish gatherers.

12,000–
7000 B.C.

The many variations in human culture during the millennia after 12,000 B.C. can be attributed to steady population growth and to changes in the Postglacial environment. New hunting territories were exploited where new adaptations were necessary. Fluctuations of climate caused changes in vegetational zones and rainfall patterns, which affected game distributions and the availability of traditional food resources. The net result was greater diversity in hunting and gathering populations.

specialized hunters and gatherers

As the world climate warmed up at the end of the last glaciation, major changes resulted in New World environments. The western and southwestern United States became drier, while the East Coast and much of the Midwest was densely forested. The large Pleistocene mammals of earlier times became extinct, but the bison remained a major food source.[12] In the warmer southeast, the more favorable climate was reflected by drier conditions that resulted in less standing water, markedly

Figure 11.4
A layer of excavated bison bones from the Olsen-Chubbuck site in Colorado, where a band of hunters stampeded a herd of bison into a narrow arroyo.

Figure 11.5
  Points found with mammoths in Mexico. The length of the middle point is 8.1 centimeters (about 3 ins.) long.

seasonal rainfalls, and specialization toward fishing or intensive gathering as opposed to big game hunting.

The big game hunters of the High Plains concentrated on the bison and continued to hunt this beast until the nineteenth century A.D. In the northwest, some big game hunters began to take advantage of seasonal salmon runs in the fast-moving rivers of this area, setting a trend for highly specialized hunter-gatherer economies later in prehistory.

A shift in economic emphasis took place in the arid West and Southwest. The great basin west of the Rockies was the scene of a gradual alteration in an economic strategy in which hunting played a rarer part. The emphasis was on smaller animals such as rabbits, squirrels, and antelopes. At the same time the gathering of vegetable foods assumed the dominant role in economic life, combined with some fishing and, in maritime areas, the exploitation of shellfish. We are fortunate that arid conditions in Utah, Nevada, and elsewhere have preserved many plant and vegetable foods eaten by these early desert hunter-gatherers. By 7000 B.C. a distinctive desert form of culture had been developed over much of the western United States by small bands camping in caves, rock-shelters, and temporary sites.

Desert Tradition 7000 B.C.

The excavations at Danger Cave in Utah and at the Gypsum and Lovelock sites in Nevada reveal that the hunters were making nets, mats, and baskets, as well as cordage (Figure 11.6).[14] They were using digging sticks to uproot edible tubers, and much of their toolkit consisted of grinding stones used in the preparation of vegetable foods. Those who lived in this way were obliged to be constantly on the move, searching for different vegetable foods as they came into season and camping near scanty water supplies.

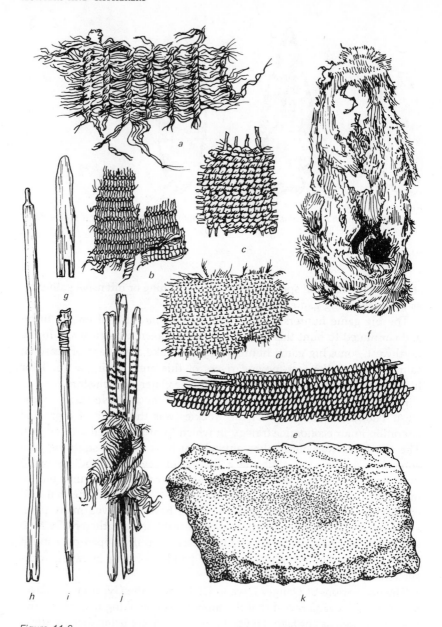

Figure 11.6
Artifacts from Danger Cave, Utah, which were preserved by the dry conditions: (a-b)
twined matting; (c) twined basketry; (d) coarse cloth; (e) coiled basketry; (f) hide
moccasin; (g) wooden knife handle, 7.4 centimeters (4.5 ins.) long; (h) dart shaft,
41 centimeters (16 ins.) long; (i) arrow shaft with broken projectile point in place, 84
centimeters (33 ins.) long; (j) bundle of gaming sticks, 29 centimeters (11.5 ins.) long;
(k) milling stone.

The basic features of desert life in the western United States survived virtually unchanged into the eighteenth and nineteenth centuries A.D. when many hunting groups were practically exterminated by expanding European settlement. A particularly celebrated case of coastal adaptation is in the West that of the Chumash Indians of southern California, who achieved a relatively high population density by virtue of their skillful exploitation of the abundant seafood resources of the Santa Barbara Channel and offshore islands.[15] The ultimate origins of their culture extend back many thousands of years into the early prehistory of North America.

The more densely wooded parts of the eastern United States supported hunters with a much more diversified economy than that of earlier big game hunters. The term "Archaic tradition" has been coined to refer to these woodland hunter-gatherers. It is a purely archaeological label designed to group together regional variations within the eastern woodland hunters of North America.

The Archaic tradition began in the eastern United States between 7000 and 5000 B.C. and lasted until the second millennium B.C.[16] The Archaic people exploited more vegetables and less game for food. In those localities where it was possible, fish and shellfish became dominant features of the diet. Ground axes were in wide use, and the more northern hunters relied on gouges for woodwork. Between the fifth and sixth millennia B.C., the Archaic people began to develop extensive trading networks that handled seashells from the Florida coast and a wide variety of exotic raw materials. One of the most widespread trade items was copper, collected from rich outcrops near Lake Superior; it was traded in the form of crude weapons and tools, such as spearheads, knives, and pins, as far away as New England, New York, and the southeastern United States (Figure 11.7).[17]

Archaic 7000– 5000 B.C.

Within the general Archaic tradition there were many minor variations, reflecting specialized ecological adaptations or particularly successful economic strategies. Much of the Archaic hunting tradition has survived until modern times, especially in the northern parts of the eastern United States and in Canada, where the first explorers found hunters and gatherers living in much the same way as the Archaic people had millennia before.[18]

Specialized hunter-gatherers also began to emerge in Central and South America as climatic conditions changed. Space limits preclude discussing the various specialized hunting groups whose sites have been excavated between Mexico and Tierra del Fuego. One characteristic adaptation was centered around the Andes, while another flourished on the uplands of eastern Brazil.[19] As in North America, the intensified hunting and gathering are reflected by a concentration of the human population

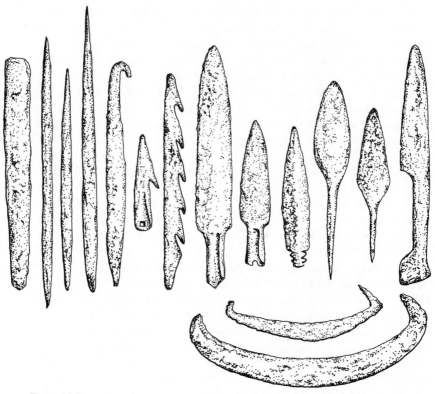

Figure 11.7
Copper artifacts from the Archaic period, made from native copper, which were traded
over enormous distances (about one-half actual size).

in favored localities such as the shores of lakes and seacoasts, where there
was an unusual abundance of resources. Sophisticated gathering and
hunting strategies were used to ensure food at all seasons. An insight
into such strategies was obtained in the Tehuacán Valley, Mexico, and
is described in Chapter 16.

Some of these specialized hunters and gatherers remained at the simple
hunting and collecting level because of the limitations of their environment and a plentiful supply of natural resources that precluded the necessity for economic change. But in some areas in Mesoamerica and on
the coast and highlands of Peru, hunter-gatherer bands became the vehicles of dynamic cultural change and gradual economic experimentation
that inevitably led to food production and, ultimately, to the rise of New
World civilizations.

The southernmost extremities of Latin America were inhabited until

Figure 11.8
 A nineteenth-century drawing of a Fuegan Indian of the Tekeonica tribe.

recent times by scattered bands of hunters and fishermen who were
regarded by eighteenth-century explorers as some of the most primitive
and backward people on earth (Figure 11.8). Charles Darwin reacted
strongly to the Fuegans of that area: "It is a common subject of conjecture
what pleasure in life some of the lower animals can enjoy: how much

more reasonably the same question may be asked with respect to these barbarians."[20]

The Ona, Yaghan, and Alacaluf peoples have been vividly described by early missionaries who settled among them. They lived in small bands, using only the crudest of shelters made of skins or grass and driftwood, with only skin mantles for body covering during the height of the Antarctic winter. Shellfish, some game, fruits, berries, and fish provided them with a simple diet, and their crude tools included none of the more sophisticated weapons made by more northern hunters. Tierra del Fuego, however, was occupied remarkably early, and it is thought that the Fuegian tradition emerged as early as 4000 B.C. if not earlier. Many of the roots of these most southerly prehistoric humans lie back in early hunting cultures that elsewhere were replaced by more advanced farming culture thousands of years before.

arctic cultures

The arctic regions of North America were, in a sense, a province apart from the rest of the New World, partly because of their harsh climate. But within the mainland areas of the North and the Aleutian Islands some of the richest hunting and gathering societies in the world flourished for thousands of years (Figure 11.9).

anangula and the aleuts

Anangula
6500–
5700 B.C.

Anangula Island in the Aleutians has been occupied by maritime hunter peoples for at least 4,000 years, and probably as early as 6500–5700 B.C.[21] All the available archaeological, geological, physical, and linguistic evidence points to a single population system, thought by some scholars to be that of the Aleuts. The economic orientation on Anangula was toward fishing, sea mammals, and birds, an economic strategy developed in an isolated and stable environment. The Anangula site itself lies on a cliff 20 meters (65.5 ft.) above the present sea level, a position that was still on the coast when the sea level was much lower and the Bering Land Bridge was in existence. Anangula was occupied for at least 500 years and was probably a permanent village occupied by at least 100 people. Unfortunately, no organic remains were recovered, but blade and flake tools thought to be used for incising or grooving bone or wood came from the settlement. Chaluka, a later site nearby, carried the story of hunting occupation up to recent times. Anangula itself cannot be compared with either Japanese or mainland Alaskan sites with any reliability, for the distances are enormous. But the site is important, for it shows

Figure 11.9
The earliest known picture of an Eskimo sketched in 1576. This hunter from Frobisher Bay carries his kayak paddle, bow, and arrow.

that the Aleutian islanders enjoyed one of the richest maritime hunting cultures in the world but remained isolated from other societies until recent centuries.

the mainland

8000–
4000 B.C.

A cultural tradition involving microblades and a variety of projectile points was prevalent in Alaska from about 8000 to 4000 B.C. and extended southward into subarctic regions. Another, and better-known, stone tool technology, the Arctic Small-Tool tradition, developed in western Alaska between 3000 and 4000 B.C. and lasted until about 1000 B.C.; it was used across the Arctic as far as Greenland. The type site of the Arctic Small-Tool tradition is at Iyatayet on Cape Denbigh.[22] Small pressure-flaked tools, quite different from those of earlier millennia, are typical of Arctic Small-Tool sites. J. L. Giddings, the discoverer of Iyatayet, described the inhabitants as sea-mammal hunters who used harpoons against walrus and seals, and their pressure-flaked arrowheads against migrating caribou. Bone and ivory evidently were already being extensively used, but no specimens have been found. The Arctic Small-Tool tradition probably originated on the Bering Land Bridge coast, although its technology shows some Asian links.

Arctic
Small–Tool
4000–
1000 B.C.

Aleut cultural traditions appear to have considerable antiquity, and Eskimo culture goes back at least 2,000 years. The latter may even go back to Land Bridge times. A clearly identifiable Eskimo culture was flourishing by 1000 B.C. in Greenland.

Most of the early American Eskimos, such as the Kodiaks, lived in rectangular houses partly buried below the ground and entered by means of a passage — a form of dwelling characteristic of arctic hunting cultures in Siberia. The Eskimos made pottery but still used stone, bone, and antler for their tools. Several regional variations have been distinguished on the basis of art styles and the design of such implements as harpoon heads; variants centered on such localities as St. Lawrence Island and Point Barrow.[23]

Thule
A.D. 1000

In the far northeast, the Thule culture was centered on Hudson Bay and northern Canada and eventually reached as far as Greenland.[24] The Thule culture probably originated in Alaska or farther east and shared many common features of culture and economy with its neighbors to the west. The new culture spread rapidly along the northern coast of the New World about A.D. 1000, blanketing earlier cultural traditions. There was some local development of Thule culture in the central Arctic, and subsequently a flow of cultural influences returned to northern Alaska in recent times. The distinctive Thule art styles in bone and ivory have, in places, survived until modern times, even though the Thule people were some of the first to meet European voyagers.

As early as the tenth century A.D., Viking seamen came in contact with Eskimos living in southern Greenland; their habits are recounted in the Nordic sagas. The Thule people learned about iron from the Norsemen and began to use the metal for tips of weapons. Most modern Eskimo culture in the Arctic North owes its origins to Thule and earlier traditions, which demonstrates again the long antiquity of hunting and gathering in the Americas.

*"Agriculture is not to be looked on as a difficult
or out-of-the-way invention, for the rudest savage,
skilled as he is in the habits of the food-plants he gathers,
must know well enough that if seeds or roots
are put in a proper place in the ground they will grow."*
Sir Edward Tylor

farmers

12

the harvest is plenteous

"The pastures are clothed with flocks; the valleys also are covered over with corn; they shout for joy, they also sing," rejoices the writer of Psalm 65. He was extolling the virtues of agriculture only a few millennia after food production had become a new way of life for Near Eastern hunter-gatherers. Sometime near the end of the Weichsel glaciation, man became a producer of his own food rather than merely a powerful hunter among other hunters. Mankind could now influence his environment and sometimes control its ecological balance with drastic long-term consequences for the history of mankind.

food production and its consequences

It is difficult for us, buying our food from supermarkets, to appreciate the awesome consequences of this shift in human economic practices. The impact of agriculture and domestic animals on human history has been as drastic as that of the Industrial Revolution and the motorcar. For 99.5 percent of our long existence we were hunters and gatherers, living in bands, tied to an existence determined by the seasons of vegetable foods or the annual migrations of game. Our territorial perspectives were those of a few hundred square miles, delineated in part by the distribution of water, fruit trees, and game, as well as our walking abilities. The human population of the world was probably only a few million at the end of the Pleistocene epoch, for the carrying capacity of even the most favorable hunting territory was small by modern standards.[1]*

The new economies proved successful. They spread to all corners of the world, except where environmental factors such as extreme heat or aridity rendered agriculture or herding impracticable, or where people chose to remain as hunters and gatherers. In some places, food production was the economic base for urbanization and literate civilization. But most human societies did not go further than subsistence-level food production until the industrial power of nineteenth- and twentieth-century Europe led them into the machine age.

Food production has resulted in much higher population densities, for the domestication of plants and animals can result in a form of economic strategy that both increases and stabilizes the available food supplies. Farmers use concentrated tracts of territory given over to agriculture and to the grazing of cattle or small stock, if mixed farming is practiced. Their territory is much smaller than that of hunter-gatherers, although pastoralists need enormous areas of grazing land for seasonal pastures. Within a smaller area of farming land, property lines are carefully delineated, as individual ownership of land and problems of inheritance of property arise. Shortages of land can lead to property disputes and perhaps to the founding of new village settlements on previously uncultivated soil.[2]

More permanent settlements brought other changes in their wake. The portable and light-weight material possessions of many hunters were replaced by heavier toolkits and more lasting houses (Figure 12.1). Grindstones, implements of tillage, and axes with ground and polished edges were essential parts of farming culture, each of them used for specific purposes. New social units came into being as more permanent home bases were developed; these social linkages reflected ownership and inheritance of land and also resulted from the constant association of family groups, which previously had been separated during much of the hunting year.

Food production led to changes in human attitudes toward the environment. Cereal crops enabled man to store his food, creating surpluses for use in winter months (Figure 12.1). The hunter exploited game, fish, and vegetable foods, but the farmer altered the environment by the very nature of his exploitation. Shifting agriculture entailed the felling of trees and the burning of vegetation to clear the ground for planting. The same fields were then abandoned after a few years to lie fallow, and more woodland was cleared instead. The original vegetation began to regenerate, but it might be cleared again before reaching its original state. Voracious animals stripped pastures of their grass cover, then heavy rainfalls denuded the hill slopes of valuable soil, and the pastures were never the same again. Whatever the level of his agricultural technology, the farmer had an effect on his environment, if only with the fires he lit to clear scrub from his gardens and to fertilize the soil with wood ashes.

Figure 12.1
A pole-and-mud hut typical of the Middle Zambezi Valley, Africa (left). Such dwellings, often occupied for fifteen years or more, are more permanent settlements than the windbreak or the tent of the hunter-gatherer. Right: a grain bin in an African village, used for cereal crops. The storage of food is a critical part of a food-producing economy.

Although food production resulted in higher population densities, the growth rates of both herds and human populations were controlled by such factors as disease, available food surpluses, water supplies, and particularly famine. Early agricultural methods depended heavily on careful soil selection. The technology of the first farmers was hardly adequate for extensive clearance of the dense woodland under which many good soils lay, so this reduced the amount of potentially cultivable land to a dramatic extent. Gardens were probably scattered over a much wider territory than is necessary today, with modern plowing and other advanced techniques. Indeed, one authority on African agriculture has estimated that, even given advanced shifting agriculture, only 40 percent of typical soil of moderate fertility in Africa is suitable for such cultivation.[3] This figure must have been less in the early days of agriculture, when simpler stone tools and fewer crops were available.

In regions of seasonal rainfall like the Near East, sub-Saharan Africa, and parts of Asia, periods of prolonged drought are commonplace. Famine was probably a real possibility as population densities rose. Many early agriculturalists must have watched the sky with concern and must frequently have experienced crop failures in times of drought. Their small stores of grain from the previous season would have been inadequate to carry them through another year, especially if they had been careless with their surplus grain.

The result must have been a forced shift in economic strategy. Even today some farmers are obliged to rely heavily on wild vegetable foods and hunting to survive in bad years.[4] Many hunting bands collect intensively just a few species of edible plants in their large territories. They are aware of many other edible vegetables, but fall back on them only in times of stress. These foods normally serve to carry a comparatively small population through to the next rains.

Unfortunately, the same is not true of a larger agricultural population, which quickly exhausts wild vegetable resources and depletes game within the much smaller territory used for farming and grazing. The result, especially if the drought lasts over a period of years, can be famine, death, and a reduction in population. We may speculate that famines were not unknown in the early days of agriculture, although archaeological evidence is lacking.

domestication: the causes

"It is vain to hope for the discovery of the first domestic corn cob, the first pottery vessel, the first hieroglyphic, or the first site where some other major breakthrough occurred. Such deviations from the preexisting pattern almost certainly took place in such a minor accidental way that these traces are not recoverable. More worthwhile would be an investigation of the mutual causal processes that amplify these tiny deviations into major changes in prehistoric culture."[5] With these few words University of Michigan archaeologist Kent Flannery summarized the basic problem of causes. Why did man choose to grow his own crops? What processes caused the acceptance of the new inventions and their adoption in thousands of different human societies?

Speculations about the origins of agriculture go back over a century.[6] Early efforts are typified by a somewhat idealistic approach to basic causes. Anthropologist H. L. Roth was explicit in 1887: "When man began to harvest and carry the (wild) crop to the camp, many seeds were scattered on the track and thus there would be some foundation for supposing that the cultivation of edible grasses began near the home for the time being. . . ."[7] To many archaeologists the origins of agriculture became one of those brilliant ideas that come to mankind occasionally, an innovation of genius whose impact was revolutionary.

Another school of thought hypothesized that increased desiccation at the end of the Weichsel glaciation, as climatic zones moved northward out of the Near East, led to enforced concentrations of man and animals in oases where permanent water supplies were to be found. There, intensive interaction took place between man and certain plants and animals, including wheat, barley, goats, and sheep. The so-called oasis theory received wide respectability in the hands of such archaeologists as V. Gordon Childe,[8] who became interested in the origins of agriculture and urban life in the Near East as a direct result of his work on European archaeology. In 1928, he published one of his most famous books, *The Most Ancient East*, in which he committed himself to economic interpretations of archaeological data. He proposed two major economic revolutions in prehistory, a Neolithic Revolution and an Urban Revolution. The Neolithic Revolution was described as an economic revolution that "opened up a richer and more reliable supply of food, brought now within man's own unaided efforts." He described the period during which that revolution took place as one of "climatic crisis affecting precisely that zone of arid sub-tropical countries where the earliest farmers appear." Desiccation at the end of the Pleistocene epoch caused man to congregate in the same oases as his prey, which then fed on the stubble from man's fields, so that a symbiotic relationship developed. The oasis theory is no longer favored, for no evidence for extensive desert conditions in the Near East at the end of the Pleistocene has been turned up by geologists or other fieldworkers.

Harold Peake and Herbert J. Fleure were two scholars who attempted to locate the area in which food production began.[9] They pointed to the Near East, especially to the hilly regions overlooking "the Fertile Crescent," a term coined by Henry Breasted to refer to Egypt and the Mesopotamian delta, which were once thought to be the earliest centers of food production. The hills were the natural habitats of the wild species of plants and animals that were subsequently domesticated.

It was not until the late 1940s that systematic fieldwork into the origins of food production began. Robert J. Braidwood of the University of Chicago mounted an expedition to the Kurdish foothills of Iran to test the theories of Childe, Peake, and Fleure.[10] The geologists and zoologists on the expedition produced field evidence which caused Braidwood to reject the notion of catastrophic climatic change at the end of the Pleistocene, despite some minor shifts in rainfall distribution. Nothing in the environment, he argued, predetermined such a radical shift in human adaptation as that proposed by Childe. Braidwood envisaged the economic change as resulting from the "ever increasing cultural differentiation and specialization of human communities." Man had begun to understand and manipulate the plants and animals around him in a series of "nuclear zones," one of which was the hilly flanks of the Zagros Mountains and the upland areas overlooking the lowlands of the Near East. This hypothesis is based on an assumption that the human capacity for experimentation or receptiveness of new ideas made it possible for man to domesticate animals — but it does not explain why food production was adopted.

In 1952, Carl O. Sauer published a remarkable essay on agricultural origins, a form of ecological analysis of food production.[11] He saw the origins of food production as a change in adaptation, a change in the way in which culture and environment interacted. Sauer was interested in early centers of food production and proposed Southeast Asia as a major center of domestication, where root crops were grown by semisedentary fishing folk. Few scholars now accept Sauer's theory that the idea of domestication was diffused from Southeast Asia to the Near East.

An ecological approach to the origins of food production has become increasingly pervasive in recent years. Robert Adams cautioned his colleagues to remember that the origins of agriculture were a process as well as an event. It was necessary to concentrate on studying local adaptations within small areas, for they provided the best way of understanding the complicated interactions between cultural and environmental variables.[12]

Lewis Binford rejected Braidwood's contention that human nature caused the adoption of agriculture and argued that demographic stress favored food production.[13] At the end of the Pleistocene, he hypothesized, there was a flow of population from some of the world's seacoasts into less populated areas inland as a result of environmental change. The population movements led to demographic stress in certain areas of the world where potentially domesticable plants and animals were to be found. The development of agriculture was adaptively advantageous for the inhabitants of these regions. Like Braidwood's hypothesis, Binford's theory is a theory of cause that suffers from several weaknesses, not the least of them being the repeated fluctuations of sea level that occurred in earlier interglacials. Why did they not lead to similar demographic stress and culture change?

Kent Flannery has developed a systems hypothesis to explain the *mechanisms* of the transition to food production.[14] He argues that the process of transition was a gradual one. In a classic paper on Mesoamerican archaeology, Flannery maintained that the adaptation of the preagricultural peoples of Mesoamerica who later became agriculturalists was not to a given environment but to a few plant and animal genera whose range crosscut several environments. Using pollen and animal bone analyses from preagricultural sites, Flannery listed the different animals and plants upon which these people depended. The list included century plant leaves, various cactus fruits, deer, rabbits, wild waterfowl, and wild grasses, including corn. Foods like the century plant were available the year-round. Others, like mesquite pods and deer, were exploited during the dry season, but cacti were eaten only during the rains.

To obtain these foods the people had to be in the right place at the right season, and the right time depended on the plants rather than on the people. The hunters had to plan their schedule around the seasons. In other words, their food procurement system was scheduled. A minor change in any part of the food procurement system was reflected in the group's scheduling and might preclude exploiting those foods whose seasonality conflicted with the new schedule.

Genetic changes in two food plants, corn and beans, through time made these plants increasingly important to the people who used them. Both plants became slightly more productive, and this slight increase in productivity acted as a positive feedback for their procurement systems. Gradually more and more time was spent on beans and corn, and the groups had to reschedule their activities to accommodate this change. Because a group could not be in two places at once, those foods that were procured at times when corn and beans had to be planted or harvested would necessarily be neglected, and a negative feedback might be said to have operated on their procurement systems.

In another paper Flannery considered the problems of Near Eastern food production.[15] He stressed that what was important was not the planting of seeds or the herding of animals but the fact that man moved out to niches to which he was not adapted and removed certain pressures of natural selection that now allowed more deviants to survive and eventually selected for characteristics which were not beneficial under natural conditions. According to Flannery and his colleague Frank Hole,[16] about 20,000 years ago men began to shift from a predominantly hunting way of life to one in which small game, fish, and vegetable foods, including cereals, were utilized. This shift from specialized hunting to a broader economic base was accompanied by several preadaptations to hunting, including the use both of ground stone tools for crushing pigments and tough grass seeds and of storage pits as well. Seasonal utilization of the environment was typical of many parts of the Near East and Mesoamerica, with different wild foods being scheduled at separate seasons. But what caused this state of equilibrium between culture and environment to be upset?

Flannery took Binford's demographic model, in which population growth in some areas of southwestern Asia placed major stress on the optimum habitats inhabited by the seasonal hunters and gatherers of the hilly flanks and the Palestine woodlands. The population increases resulted in the splitting off of new groups into more marginal areas where the inhabitants tried to produce artificially, around the *margins* of the optimum zone, stands of cereals as dense as those in the heart of the zone.

The implications of this hypothesis are as follows. First, the hunter-gatherer populations in the optimum areas increased before the origins of food production. This can be tested in the archaeological record by searching for evidence of denser settlement and for traces of larger sites yielding traces of intensive hunting and collecting. Second, the earliest evidence of food production will appear on the margins of the hilly flanks and the woodland areas of Palestine in sites where the material culture of the inhabitants is strikingly similar to that of the hunter-gatherers in the best areas. Lastly, it follows that there will be more than one center of domestication of both plants and animals. The advantage of Flannery's hypothesis is that it can be tested in the field, although the testing process is likely to be both arduous and time-consuming. The demonstration of population increases before the advent of food production will be particularly hard to demonstrate, if indeed such increases took place.

British archaeologists Eric Higgs and Michael Jarman have proposed a hypothesis based on the assumption that throughout the Weichsel glaciation and at least in Europe and the Near East, "there is evidence for close man/animal relationships, wherein the animals concerned changed according to the environmental changes, but a symbiotic relationship was maintained."[17] It is absurd, they argue, to look for the beginnings of food production in one area — their hypothesis does not imply the "invention" of food production. The assumption that the Near East was an innovating center arises from the notion that all Paleolithic people were hunter-gatherers, a far from proven proposition. Higgs and Jarman regard the Near East as an area where the "techniques and symbiosis of the inhabitants of colder regions were adjacent to temperate and subtropical areas in each of which different forms of symbiosis had existed. Collected together and integrated they formed complex, powerful, and expanding economies." In other words they emphasize the study of economy, an approach that deemphasizes the cultural models so fashionable in recent decades.

We have dwelt at some length on hypotheses for the origins of food production. Flannery's systems model is probably the most widely accepted theory at the time of writing, but in itself does not answer the basic problem of cause. Of course we shall never identify the exact point at which plant and animal domestication took place. The fact is that hunters do not lead unpleasant lives. They have as much leisure if not more than the peasant farmer. The phenomena of germination and planting were familiar to hunter-gatherers, but they did not start growing crops — they had no incentive to do so.

We can be sure that strong pressures of food shortage or other factors

affecting the viability of an existing way of life must have caused a deliberate change in economic strategy, one that might well have been abandoned when the crisis was over. Innovations are frequent and usually
short-lived in all human societies. The selective pressures favoring the
adoption of a new and radical basis of food procurement must have been
both strong and increasing over a long period of time to favor the development of food production. Archaeologists need to develop hypothetical
models of the possible causes of food production to complement the
promising systems models of the process of origin once a fundamental
and revolutionary step toward food production had been made, that of
social acceptability.

the domestication of animals and crops

animals

The domestication of animals was first achieved in the Old World, where
potentially domesticable species like the wild ox, goat, sheep, and dog
had well-defined geographical limits in the late Pleistocene. New World
farmers tamed only such animals as the llama, the guinea pig, and the
turkey, and then only under special conditions and within narrow geographical limits. The possession of one's own herds of domesticated
mammals ensured a regular meat supply. There are obvious advantages
to having a major source of meat under one's own control. Later on,
domesticated animals provided a number of by-products, among them
milk, cheese, and butter as well as skins, tent coverings, and materials
for making leather shields and armor. In later millennia, man learned
how to breed animals for plowing, transportation, and traction.

The process of domestication implies a genetic selection that emphasizes special features of continuing use to the domesticator.[18] For example,
wild sheep have no wool, and wild cows produce milk only for their
offspring. Undomesticated chickens do not produce surplus eggs.
Changes in wool-bearing, lactation, or egg production could be bred by
isolating wild populations for selective breeding under human care.
Stated in simple terms, the isolation of wild species from a larger gene
pool produced domestic sheep having thick, woolly coats and domestic
goats providing regular supplies of milk, which formed a staple in the
diet of many human populations.

No one knows exactly how domestication of animals began. During
the Upper Pleistocene, man was already beginning to concentrate heavily
on particular species of large mammals for his diet. The Magdalenians
of southwestern France oriented much of their life toward the pursuit

of reindeer. At the end of the Pleistocene, hunters in the Near East were concentrating on gazelles and other steppe animals. Wild sheep and goats were intensively hunted on the southern shores of the Caspian Sea. Gregarious animals are those most easily domesticated — those which follow the lead of a dominant herd member or which all move together simultaneously.

Hunters would often feed off the same herd over long periods of time, sometimes deliberately sparing young females and immature beasts to ensure the continued survival of their food resource. Young animals captured alive in the chase might be taken back to camp, becoming dependent on those who caged them and partially tamed. A hunter could grasp the possibility of gaining control of the movements of a few key members of a herd who would be followed by the others. Once the experience of pets or restricting game movements had suggested a new way of life, people might experiment with different species.[19] As part of domestication, both animals and humans changed their attitudes toward one another in a subtle way that increased their mutual interdependence.

The nature of archaeological evidence for early domestication is such that nothing survives except the bones of the animals hunted or kept by early man. The differences between wild and domestic animal bones are initially often so small that it is difficult to distinguish one from the other unless very large collections of bones are found. This is especially true of the earliest centuries of domestication, when corralled animals were virtually indistinguishable from wild species.

One way of distinguishing between domestic and wild beasts is to age the animals by using their dentitions. Hunters normally kill animals of all ages but have a strong preference for subadults, which offer the best meat. Given a breeding situation, however, herd owners tend to slaughter sheep and goats at a younger age for meat, especially surplus males, while females are kept until no longer productive as breeding animals. In some early farming sites such as Zawi Chemi in the Zagros Mountains of the Near East, the only way that domestic sheep could be identified was by the young age at which they were slaughtered.[20]

The process of animal domestication was undoubtedly a prolonged one that developed in several areas of the Near East at approximately the same time. Although animal bones are scarce and often provide unsatisfactory evidence of early domestication, most authorities now agree that the first species to be domesticated in the Near East was the sheep — about 10,500 years ago. Sheep are small animals living in herds, whose carcasses yield a high meat supply relative to their size. They can readily be penned and isolated in situations where they can develop a symbiotic relationship with man.

Cattle are much more formidable creatures to domesticate, for their

Figure 12.2
  Bos primigenius, *the aurochs or wild ox, as depicted by S. von Heberstain in 1549.*
  The aurochs became extinct in Europe in 1627, although recent breeding experiments
  have reconstructed this formidable beast.

prototype was *Bos primigenius,* the wild ox much hunted by Stone Age
man (Figure 12.2). Perhaps cattle were first domesticated from wild animals who were penned for food, ritual, and sacrifice purposes. They may
have been captured from wild herds grazing in man's gardens.

crops

The qualities of wild wheat, barley, and similar crops are quite dissimilar
to those of their domestic equivalents. In the wild state, they occur in
dense stands.[21] The grasses can easily be harvested by simply tapping
the stem and gathering the seeds in a basket as they fall off. This technique of harvesting wild grass seeds was used by the California Indians.
It is effective because the wild grain is attached to the stem by a brittle
joint, or rachis. When the grass is tapped, the weak rachis breaks and
the grass falls into the basket.

   The conversion of wild grass to domestic strains must have involved
some selection of desirable properties in the wild grasses (Figure 12.3).
For example, for the extensive cultivation of cereal crops, the yield of
an acre of grass has to be increased significantly before all the work
involved is worth it. If the yield remains low, it is easier to gather wild
seeds and save the labor of cultivation. A tougher rachis must be developed to prevent the seed from falling on the ground and regerminating.
By toughening the rachis, man could gain control over the propagation

Figure 12.3
  The wild ancestor of einkorn (Triticum boeoticum) *(a) is contrasted with cultivated einkorn* (T. monococcum) *(b) (both two-thirds actual size).*

of the grass, sowing it when he liked and harvesting it with a knife blade or sickle.[22]

The crops that were bred had to be adaptable enough to grow outside their normal wild habitats.[23] Early farmers seem to have grown cereals with remarkable success, but a success that probably came only after long periods of experimentation in different localities.

technology and agriculture

The technological consequences of food production were, in their way, as important as the new economies.[24] A more settled way of life and the decline of hunting led to more permanent settlement, lasting architectural styles, and more substantial housing. People used the raw materials most abundant in their environment to build with. The early farmers of the

Near East employed dried mud to make small houses with flat roofs, useful as sleeping quarters during the hot season. Some less substantial houses had reed roofs. In the more temperate zones of Europe where wetter climates were the rule, timber was used to build thatched-roof houses of various shapes and sizes. Early African farmers often built huts from grass, sticks, and anthill clay. In contrast, nomadic pastoralists in the northern steppes made skin tents for shelter during icy winters.

Grain storage bins, jars, or pits became an essential part of the agricultural economy for stockpiling surplus food supplies against periods of famine (Figure 12.2). The bins might be made of wattle and daub, clay, or timber. Basket-lined silos protected valuable grain against rodents.

The hunter had used skins, wooden containers, gut pouches, and sometimes baskets for carrying wild vegetable foods. But farmers needed containers to store grain and water. They were soon making clay pots by coiling rolls of clay or building up the walls of vessels from a lump and firing them in simple hearths. Clay vessels were much more durable than skin or leather receptacles. Some pots remained in use for several decades before being broken and abandoned. Pottery did not appear simultaneously with the beginnings of agriculture, however. For example, hunter-gatherers on the Japanese islands were making simple clay pots as early as 8000 B.C.; the Jomon people lived a semisedentary life by their shell middens, using clay vessels long before agriculture became part of their way of life. Although pottery appeared with the first agriculture on the Chinese mainland, it was invented independently in the Near East during the sixth millennium B.C.[25]

Agriculture involved new tools for tilling soil and for clearing brush. Although the earliest farmers tended to select lighter and looser soils for their crops, they used stronger working edges on their axes and adzes than did their hunting forebears. Ground and polished stone axes and adzes mounted in wooden handles became common. Trade networks in ax stones developed rapidly, extending over enormous areas. Prehistoric farmers were soon exercising increasing choice and discrimination over raw materials for ornamentation and toolmaking. One such material was obsidian, a black volcanic rock prized for its toolmaking properties and as an ornament since Pleistocene times.[26]

The beginnings of agriculture not only solved the problem of obtaining food but made man more aware of opportunities for modifying his environment whenever he wished. Food production was certainly a gradual and pervasive revolution in the history of the world.

13

the origins of food production: europe and the near east

Note: This chapter is written using the new tree-ring calibrated radiocarbon dates rather than the conventional radiocarbon chronology used in many chapters of the book. For your convenience we have placed C14 dates in Roman type with the calibrated reading in italic type below. This will enable you to make comparisons with other areas using conventional radiocarbon chronology. For calibration formulae used, see V. R. Switzur, "The Radioactive Calendar Recalibrated," *Antiquity*, 1973, 47, 186, pp. 131–137. See also Table 13.2 on page 212 which lists radiocarbon dates with their equivalent corrected dates.

Asia Minor has long been the subject of vigorous archaeological inquiry as successive generations of scholars have sought to investigate biblical history and the origins of Mediterranean civilization. The use of domesticated plants and animals formed the economic foundation for the Mesopotamian city-state as well as for our own civilization. Yet systematic research into the origins of food production in the Near East is a phenomenon of recent decades.[1]* We have already touched on the theories of Gordon Childe,[2] Braidwood,[3] and others relating to the origins of agriculture in the Near East.[4] It is time to review the archaeological evidence for early agriculture throughout the western parts of the Old World.

* See pages 393–395 for notes to Chapter 13.

lowland farmers

Both the Kurdish foothills and the Jordan Valley have yielded traces of a gradual economic and technological shift from hunting and gathering to cultivation (Figure 13.1). At the end of the Pleistocene, both highlands and coastal plains were occupied by hunters of wild sheep and goats, gazelles, wild oxen, and other mammals. The toolkits included small microliths and some grinding stones for preparing wild vegetable foods. These hunters were cave dwellers who flourished between c. 13,000 and 9000 B.C. (C14).[5]

Hunting
Cultures

13,000–
9000 B.C.

Natufian

The fertile regions on the fringes of the coastal plain and in the Jordan River valley supported bands of gazelle hunters at the end of the Pleistocene. But cultural changes were soon underway, reflected in the "Natufian" culture (named after a cave in Israel) found both in the Mount Carmel caves and in open sites covering a wide area of the coastal strip from southern Turkey to as far south as the fringes of the Nile Valley.

The gazelle was hunted to the exclusion of all other mammals, but fishing was also a major activity at many sites. More significantly, however, a high proportion of the diet came from harvesting cereal grasses. The toolkit includes flint sickle blades whose cutting edges bear a char-

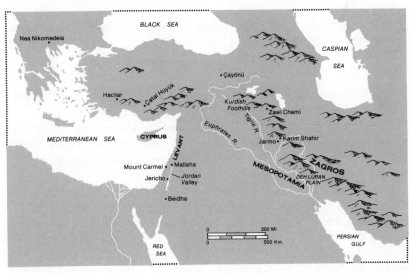

Figure 13.1
Archaeological sites in the Near East.

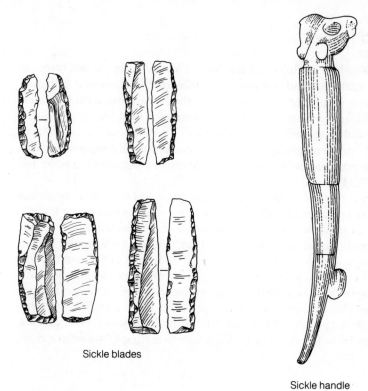

Sickle blades

Sickle handle

Figure 13.2
Natufian sickle blades and a bone handle for such blades, bearing a deer's head (about one-half actual size).

acteristic gloss formed by friction against grass stalks — and the bone handles in which the sickle blades were mounted (Figure 13.2).

Natufians began to live in fairly permanent settlements. Mallaha in northern Israel covers at least half an acre and contains circular houses with stone foundations. Stone bowls, mortars, paved floors, and many burials were found in this substantial settlement.[6]

8000 B.C.   By 8000 B.C. (C14), Natufian culture had developed to the extent that the town at Jericho needed defenses. The very first settlement at Jericho had been a small Natufian camp built around the bubbling spring that formed the locus of settlement there for many thousands of years.[7] Some farmers had occupied the site before the eighth millennium B.C.; they made stone tools in the Natufian tradition.

The early Jerichans built massive defense walls around their town. A rock-cut ditch over 2.7 meters (3 yds.) deep and 3.2 meters (10 ft.) wide was bordered by a finely built stonewall complete with towers (Figure 13.3). Their beehive-shaped huts were clustered within the shelter of the defenses. These early town dwellers had to muster a substantial force to build their defenses. The communal labor of wall-building required both political and economic resources on a scale that would have been unheard of a few thousand years earlier. Why walls were needed remains a mystery, but they may have been for defensive purposes, resulting from group competition for scarce resources.

The economic strategy that supported this activity is still imperfectly known, but probably included extensive trade in obsidian. Another site, Beidha, has produced many specimens of wild barley, which must have been either gathered in enormous quantities from natural stands or sown deliberately. The emmer wheat seeds from Beidha show a wide range in size as if the processes of domestication had only recently begun.

Figure 13.3
The excavated remains of the great tower of early Jericho.

Several other minor crops were either grown or gathered. Large numbers of young goats were also found, their ages implying a selective slaughtering pattern that strongly suggests domestication rather than hunting.[8]

the hilly flanks in the near east

Late Paleolithic hunters were living in highland caves as late as 9000 B.C. (C14), hunting wild goats and collecting a range of vegetable foods. The first traces of the new economies are dated to around 9000 B.C. at open camping sites such as Karim Shahir and Zawi Chemi Shanidar, where people lived in round, semisubterranean houses. At Zawi Chemi, many wild sheep had been killed when immature, as if the inhabitants had either fenced in the grazing grounds of wild sheep, penned herds, or even tamed sheep to the extent that they could control the age at which they were killed.[9]

Karim Shahir
9000 B.C.

7000 B.C.   At least by 7000 B.C. (C14), toolkits and settlement patterns throughout the Near East had undergone substantial modification. Grinding stones and reaping equipment were in regular use, and more permanent villages were occupied by larger communities than before. Unfortunately, we still lack firm evidence of agriculture from this critical period in human history. Wild goat and sheep bones are common finds, as are carbonized wild grasses, including those of potential domesticates. The Zawi Chemi sheep bones show that man was at least on his way to producing his food, and well aware of the implications of intensive exploitation of game and vegetable foods.

village farming

The processes of experimentation were certainly complete by 7000 B.C., when village life became more widespread. A fairly intensive agricultural economy was widely distributed over southwest Asia by 6000 B.C., fostered by extensive trade networks that distributed obsidian, which was much prized for ornaments and sickle blades. Farming villages dating to this time flourished at Jericho and along the Syrian and Palestinian coasts.

Jarmo
?6750–
5000 B.C.   One of the most famous early villages is Jarmo, in the Zagros foothills southeast of Zawi Chemi Shanidar, dated to the seventh millennium B.C.[10] Jarmo consists of little more than a small cluster of some twenty-five houses built of baked mud, which formed an irregular huddle separated by small alleyways and courtyards. Storage bins and clay ovens were an integral part of the structures. The Jarmo deposits yielded abundant

traces of agriculture: seeds of barley, emmer wheat, and various minor crops were found together with the bones of sheep and goats. Hunting had declined in importance with only a few wild animal bones testifying to such activity. But the toolkit still included Stone Age–type tools together with sickle blades, grinding stones, and other paraphernalia of cultivation.

The lowlands to the southwest of the Kurdish foothills form a vast alluvial delta watered by the Tigris and the Euphrates rivers. As we shall see in Chapter 18, it was these delta areas which played a leading part in the development of urbanization in the Near East. As early as 7500 to 6750 B.C. (C14), however, goat herdsmen were wandering over the Deh Luran plain east of the Tigris River.[11] In the late winter and spring they harvested wheat, but nine-tenths of their vegetable diet came from wild plants.

7500–6750 B.C.

After 6750 B.C., the Deh Luran people relied more heavily on cereal crops and less on wild seeds, and goats were still important in their diet. Their multiroomed houses were clustered in small villages. In the sixth millennium, pottery was introduced, and sheep became more important. A thousand years later, irrigation agriculture first came into use, setting the villagers clearly on the road to urban life. By this time, man had drastically modified his environment so that his dependence on wild plants and hunting significantly diminished.

anatolia

Toward the end of the eighth millennium B.C., some scattered farming villages began to appear in the headwaters of the Tigris River and to the west in Anatolia. At Çayönü in southern Turkey, a small community of food producers roughly contemporary with Jarmo used tools resembling those from the Levant and Zagros regions. Obsidian was in plentiful supply and native copper was hammered into simple ornaments. Domestic pigs and sheep were in use.[12]

The first evidence of food production on the Anatolian plateau to the west extends back to about 7000 B.C. But there is no reason why farming should not have flourished even earlier in the rolling highlands of Turkey. British archaeologist James Mellaart excavated a remarkable early farming village at Hacilar, in southwestern Anatolia, which was founded about 7000 B.C.[13] Seven phases of village occupation took place at Hacilar before its inhabitants moved elsewhere. They lived in small rectangular houses with courtyards, hearths, and ovens. The walls of the rooms were plastered and burnished with pebbles, and were sometimes decorated with geometric designs.

Hacilar 6500 B.C.

No pottery was used at Hacilar, but basketry and leather containers probably were. Barley and emmer wheat were cultivated, while some wild grass seeds were also eaten. The bones of sheep or goats, and cattle and deer are present, but no evidence exists for the domestication of any animal except the dog. Hacilar was a simple and unsophisticated settlement, probably typical of many such communities in the Near East in the early millennia of farming.

Çatal Hüyük
6500–
5600 B.C.

The simplicity of Hacilar is in dramatic contrast to the Çatal Hüyük mound, some 200 miles (322 km.) to the east, also excavated by the Mellaart.[14] Çatal Hüyük covers an area of 13 hectares (32 acres); it consists of a town of numerous small houses, built of sun-dried brick, that were designed to back onto one another, occasionally separated by small courtyards. Roofs were flat, and the outside walls of the houses provided a convenient defense wall for Çatal Hüyük (Figure 13.4). The town was rebuilt at least twelve times after about 7000 B.C., presumably when the houses began to crumble or the population swelled.

Çatal Hüyük owed its existence to cultivation and trade of various cereal crops, including barley and einkorn and emmer wheats. The inhabitants relied on hunting, too, but did not have many metal objects except for some hammered copper ornaments. They used flint and obsidian for sickle blades, spearheads, and other simple tools. Clothing

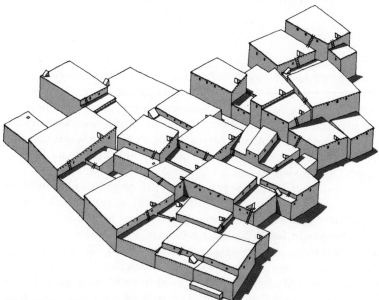

Figure 13.4
Schematic reconstruction of houses and shrines from Level VI at Çatal Hüyük, Anatolia, showing their flat-roof architecture and roof entrances.

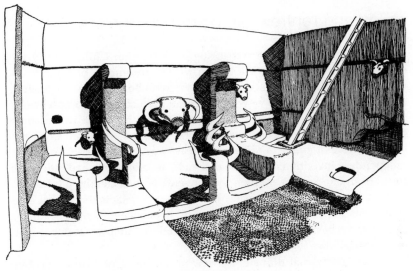

Figure 13.5
 Reconstruction of the east and south walls of Shrine VI.14 at Çatal Hüyük, Anatolia,
 with sculptured ox heads, horn cores, benches, and relief models of bulls and rams.
 The shrine was entered by the ladder at the right.

was made from skins and textiles, and basketry and pottery were used
as containers.

A most remarkable feature of Çatal Hüyük was its artistic tradition,
preserved in the form of paintings on carefully plastered walls, some of
them parts of shrines (Figure 13.5). Most of the figures depicted were
women or bulls. Others paintings show women giving birth to bulls.
Many art themes concerned fertility and the regeneration of life, and
figurines of women in childbirth have been found.

The Çatal Hüyük cultural tradition seems to have lasted virtually unchanged throughout the duration of the occupation of the settlement. The
village itself does not seem to have had any political authority outside
its immediate neighborhood, and it was not until much later that the
highlands of Anatolia came under any form of unified political authority.

Much of Çatal Hüyük's prosperity resulted from its monopoly of the
obsidian trade from quarries in nearby mountains. Syrian flint was imported for making daggers; seashells came to Çatal Hüyük from the
Mediterranean for conversion into ornaments. Trade in raw materials and
ornaments between Anatolia and southwestern Asia continued to flourish
in later millennia, as metallurgy and other attributes of urban life took
a firmer hold in the Near East.

childe and renfrew: european chronology

"Europe," wrote the great archaeologist V. Gordon Childe nearly fifty years ago, "is indebted to the Orient for the rudiments of the arts and crafts that initiated man's emancipation from bondage to his environment."[15] Childe based his view of European prehistory on comprehensive studies of local chronologies and artifact styles. He made two assumptions in interpreting European prehistory: first, the appearance of a new cultural development in different areas was not necessarily due to independent invention; and second, if such developments had indeed diffused from one area to another, then inventions had stemmed from Near Eastern sources and Europeans had been the recipients. Childe's assumptions soon became widely accepted, his concept of the "irradiation of European barbarism by Oriental civilization" almost passing into archaeological law.

Childe's somewhat diffusionist view of European prehistory has been substantially altered by later researches. No longer do people think of vast hordes of farmers and metallurgists flooding from Asia into Europe, bringing the inventions of an innovative East to barbarian peoples to the north and west. The Europeans of prehistoric times possessed their own distinctive cultures and societies.

Gordon Childe made most of his studies before the development of radiocarbon dating. Since his death in 1957, a complex European radiocarbon chronology has been developed (summarized in Table 13.1). Until radiocarbon dating came along, all dates prior to 3000 B.C., the date when Egyptian historical chronologies begin, had been guesswork. The new radiocarbon dates agreed well with the older estimates back to about 2500 B.C. (C14), but pushed the chronology of early farming villages and the origins of agriculture both in Europe and in the Near East back far earlier than had been expected. Nevertheless, the "diffusionist" view of European prehistory did not seem to be affected, for agriculture still began in the Near East earlier than in temperate Europe, although there were some serious dating anomalies within the broad scheme.

The calibration of radiocarbon dates with tree-ring chronologies (Chapter 1) caused British archaeologist Colin Renfrew to develop a much revised time scale for European prehistory between 1500 and 5000 B.C.[16] Renfrew's research has had a disastrous effect on the diffusionist theory. European radiocarbon dates of the third millenium B.C. have been recalibrated to several centuries earlier than before. But Egyptian historical chronology from 3000 B.C. now agrees more closely with radiocarbon dates. Formerly, the latter when cross-checked against objects of known historical age were several centuries too recent. Fortunately, archaeol-

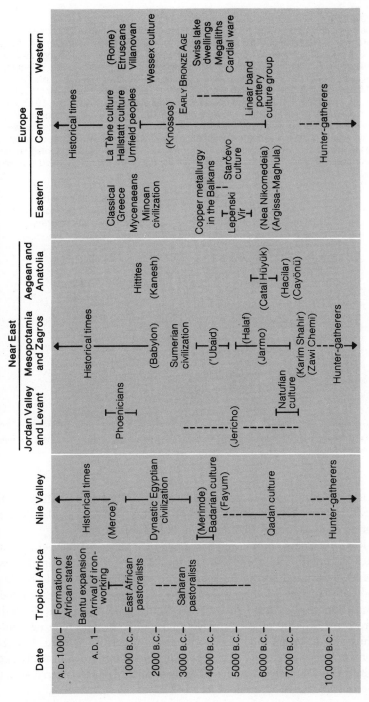

Table 13.1
A summary of the origins of food production in Africa, the Nile Valley, the Near East, and Europe (highly simplified).[a]

[a]Temperate Europe's chronology is calibrated.

Table 13.2
The calibration of radiocarbon dates. With the exception of Chapters 13 and 18–22, radio-carbon dates in this book are uncalibrated to allow for errors due to variations in the amount of C14 in the atmosphere. This correction is made by using tree-ring readings as a basis for calibration of radiocarbon dates to correspond with actual dates in years. The dates were not calibrated because we were unable to locate a sufficiently widely accepted conversion table to use. While this book was in proof, Dr. V. R. Switzur published a most useful article on the subject: "The Radiocarbon Calendar Recalibrated" (*Antiquity*, 1973, 47, 186, pp. 131–137), which includes suitable tables. We have added a simple conversion table to allow the reader to make approximate calibrations. This table should be treated as an approximate guide to the degree of variation in radiocarbon dates from about 7,000 years ago to the present. A mean reading for the various calibration figures quoted by different laboratories is used. *Readers concerned with accuracy are strongly advised to consult the original paper by Dr. Switzur.*

Radiocarbon date (Half-life of 5730 years)	Corrected age in years, using average of corrected ages from two laboratories[a]
A.D. 1837	A.D. 1777
A.D. 1587	A.D. 1538
A.D. 1087	A.D. 1131
A.D. 588	A.D. 649
262 B.C.	257 B.C.
512 B.C.	553 B.C.
1012 B.C.	1152 B.C.
1512 B.C.	1867 B.C.
2012 B.C.	2355 B.C.
2512 B.C.	3058 B.C.
3012 B.C.	3565 B.C.
3512 B.C.	4207 B.C.
4012 B.C.	4686 B.C.
4512 B.C.	5166 B.C.
4762 B.C.	5365 B.C.

[a]These dates give approximate variations at about 500–year intervals. In addition, there are numerous minor variations.

ogists had continued to use the historical dates for the dating of much Near Eastern, Aegean, and Cretan prehistory. The new calibrations supported the wisdom of this decision. (See Table 13.2.)

Renfrew's new chronology has moved the dates for temperate Europe back in time to the extent that the traditional diffusionist links between the Near East and Europe have been ruptured (Figure 13.6). Using historical dates for the Mediterranean, now in agreement with calibrated radiocarbon results, has caused what Renfrew aptly calls a "fault line" across the Mediterranean and southern Europe. The new chronology, which we have adopted here, still needs much refinement, but it has transformed our notions of a European prehistory much less affected by cultural developments in the Near East and Mediterranean basin than had been hitherto assumed.

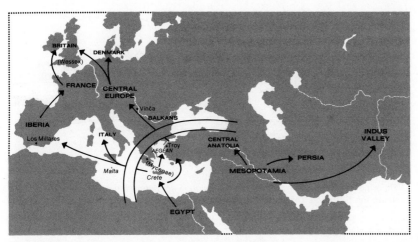

Figure 13.6
The chronology of Europe and the calibration of radiocarbon chronology. Under the uncalibrated chronology, the traditional view of European prehistory saw agriculture and other innovations spreading northwestward from the Near East and eastern Mediterranean into continental Europe. The calibrated chronology has hardly affected the dates after 3000 B.C. for the eastern Mediterranean and sites to the southeast of the fault line marked on the map. The calibrated dates after 3000 B.C. for sites to the west and northwest of the fault line have been pushed back several centuries by calibration, so that the old notion of innovation from the east is replaced by new theories postulating less eastern influence.

european farmers

The temperate zones to the north and west of Greece and the Balkans provided contrasting environments to the seasonal rainfall areas of the Near East. Timber and thatch replaced the mud brick used effectively in Near Eastern villages (Figure 13.7). Agricultural techniques had to reflect the European climate. The initial development of agriculture in Europe coincided with the warm, moist Atlantic phase (Table 4.4). Midsummer temperatures were at least 2° C warmer than now.[17] The forest cover was mainly mixed oak woodland, more shady tree cover that reduced the grazing resources of larger game animals like deer and wild cattle. As a result, hunter-gatherer populations may have shifted to coastal and lakeside settlements where fish, waterfowl, and sea mammals were readily available.[18]

The earliest evidence of food production in Europe comes from the Argissa-Maghula village mound in Greek Thessaly, where domestic cattle, sheep, and pig bones found in the lower levels of the site have been

Figure 13.7
Thatch and timber used in European housing. Reconstruction of a lakeside village at Aichbühl, Germany. (After Schmidt.)

7000 B.C.   radiocarbon dated to c. 7000 B.C. (Figure 13.8).[19] These are presently the earliest tame cattle in the world. These early dates for cattle and pig domestication are strong arguments for an independent development of domestication of animals in southeastern Europe. The Argissa-Maghula farmers were cultivating emmer wheat and barley and keeping sheep for some time before they began to use pottery. Hunting was still an important activity.

Nea Nikomedeia   A village flourished at Nea Nikomedeia in Macedonia as early as 6100
?6000 B.C.   B.C.[20] The inhabitants lived in houses made from timber, wattle, and daub. They used polished stone axes and adzes to clear their gardens in which they planted wheat, barley, and other crops.

The earliest agricultural people of the Balkans settled in compact villages of single-room dwellings built of baked mud plastered on poles and wicker. Many settlements were occupied over long periods of time. Farming villages occur on brown forest soils and alluvial river plains. The economy was based on the cultivation of wheat and barley and the domestication of sheep and goats. Ruth Tringham has argued that cereal agriculture reached southeastern Europe from the Near East, basing her hypothesis on the apparent lack of continuity between earlier hunting artifacts and the new farming cultures.[21] A number of culture traits, including *Spondylus* shells (a characteristic Mediterranean mussel much valued because it could be used for ornamentation), clay seals and figurines, and reaping knives, show continuing connections with the Med-
Starčevo   iterranean world. The Starčevo site near Belgrade has provided a vivid
?5500 B.C.   picture of the economic life and pottery styles of this widespread farming culture.

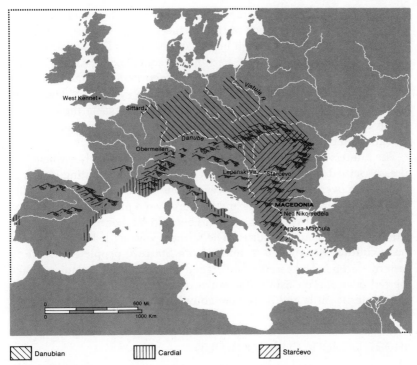

Danubian   Cardial   Starčevo

Figure 13.8
Archaeological sites in temperate Europe and the distribution of Linear (Danubian)
pottery, Cardial ware, and Starčevo and related cultures.

lepenski vir

The settlement of Lepenski Vir lies on the banks of the Danube at the
bottom of the gorges that form the famous Iron Gates of southwest Ru-
mania. Lepenski Vir is situated near a whirlpool by the river bank where
fish abound, feeding on the small organisms churned up by the swirling
water.[22] The slopes of the gorge were covered with pine-juniper-birch
forest, which flourished in a relatively wet and cool climate.

Between about 5800 and 4900 B.C. small groups of hunter-gatherers
lived on the south bank of the Danube at Lepenski Vir. They hunted
forest animals such as the aurochs with the aid of domesticated dogs,
traps, and snares. Fishing was an important source of food, with large
carp providing a major part of the diet, apparently clubbed with stones
or trapped in weirs.

?5800–
4900 B.C.

The hunters built rows of trapeze-shaped houses on small terraces cut in rows facing the river. Each of the six successive levels used the same terraces. The inhabitants rebuilt houses on the ruins of earlier structures, with the doors facing the river. Each house contained a hearth pit lined with stones, and burials were sometimes deposited near the fireplaces. A block of water-rounded limestone carved with eyes and a mouth and even scales was placed at the end of the house opposite the entrance. These carvings are unique finds in European hunting societies and are thought to represent either humans or fish.

The hunters of Lepenski Vir were flourishing when early farmers had already settled in other parts of eastern Europe. The hunting camps at the site are overlain by later (Starčevo) occupation, for the same locality was inhabited by both hunters and farmers over a prolonged period. The rich fish and forest resources around Lepenski Vir contributed to stable settlement over many centuries. The farmers who settled at the site had many cultural attributes in common with Starčevo people elsewhere in eastern Europe. The farmers still relied heavily on forest animals like the red deer and on fishing for much of their diet. Pottery was in use, and domestic cattle and dogs were abundant.

linear pottery culture group

Farther north, in the loess plains and the valley of the Danube we find the most distinctive early European farming tradition, centered on the middle Danube and extending as far west as southern Holland and eastward toward the Vistula River and the upper Dneister. These people were the Danubians (Linear pottery culture group), famous to generations of European archaeologists because of their characteristic pottery.[23] The Danubians made round-based vessels which have lines (Figure 13.9), spirals, and meanders carefully incised on the clay. They cultivated barley, einkorn, emmer wheat, and a number of minor crops including flax. These they planted on the fertile loess soils of central Europe using a simple form of shifting agriculture that was wasteful of land but led to a rapid settlement of the loess zones from the Danube to the Low Countries. Cattle, goats, sheep, and dogs were fully domesticated, and domestic herds formed an important part of Danubian diet.

The Danubians were living in southern Holland by 4800 B.C. (C14), and introduced food production to northwestern Europe at a considerably later date than it appeared in areas to the southeast. By the fifth millennium B.C., Danubian villages contained rectangular houses from 20 to 50 meters (18 to 46 yds.) long, which were made of timber and thatch and presumably sheltered stock as well as several families.

Danubian

4800 B.C.
5370 B.C.

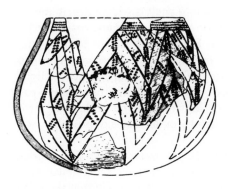
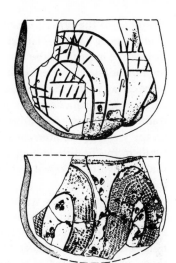

Figure 13.9
Danubian Linearbandkeramik *(Linear pottery) from Sittard, Holland, with characteristic line decoration (one-fourth actual size).*

Originally, the Danubians probably stemmed from the Starčevo culture group, and practiced their wasteful agricultural techniques on the loess lands. Growing populations, however, obliged some of them to move onto heavier and poorer soils. We find regional developments of Danubian culture developing in different parts of central Europe. Some farmers had to rely more heavily on hunting and gathering, for the soils of their gardens did not yield sufficient food to support their families. Defensive earthworks begin to appear, as if vigorous competition for land resulted in intertribal stress.

While the Danubians were settling in central Europe, other peoples were moving onto the Russian plains in the east. People somewhat similar to the Danubians occupied farming settlements in the Ukraine and around the Dneiper River. Like the Danubians, they lived in rectangular houses and reached the height of their prosperity during the period of the "Tripolye" culture when many villages were fortified by placing the houses in a circle.

mediterranean and western europe

As the Danubians were cultivating the plains of western Europe, the new farming economies were becoming established around the shores of the Mediterranean. Extensive bartering networks from one end of the Mediterranean to the other exchanged seashells, obsidian, exotic stones, and, later, copper ore. A characteristic type of pottery decorated with the distinctive imprint of the *Cardium* (scallop) shell is widely distributed on the northeastern shores of the Mediterranean, on Adriatic coasts, and as far west as Malta, Sardinia, southern France, and eastern Spain (Figure 13.10).[24] *Cardium*-decorated wares spread widely as a consequence of trading. The new economies were soon flourishing among people living on the western Mediterranean shores, who were partly converted to pastoralism by the fifth millennium B.C. Cereal crops and cattle were introduced to western France and Switzerland around 4000 B.C., probably from the Mediterranean.

During the very dry winter of 1853/54, the water level in Lake Zurich, Switzerland, fell to a record low. The inhabitants of Obermeilen were astonished to find stone axes, pottery, and wooden piles in the lake-shore mud. Dr. Ferdinand Keller of Zurich examined the finds and diagnosed them as the remains of a lake dwelling.[25] Keller immediately dug the Obermeilen site. Other lake dwellings were found on the shores of Lakes Geneva and Neuchâtel, which proved to be a mine of information on early European farming.

?4000 B.C.
4680 B.C.

3000 B.C.
3560 B.C.

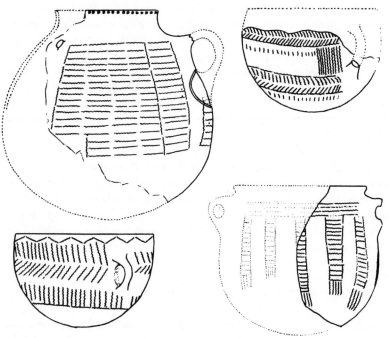

Figure 13.10
Cardium-shell impressed pottery from southern France (one-fourth actual size).

The lake-shore settlements were occupied by cattle-owning farmers, who cultivated barley, wheat, peas, beans, and lentils. They also grew small apples, perhaps used to make cider. Flax was cultivated for its oily seeds and for its fiber employed in making textiles, which, like basketry, was a highly developed art in this culture. The houses were built on damp ground between the lakes' reed beds and the scrub brush of the valley behind. Small rectangular huts were replaced by larger two-roomed houses. Some villages grew to include between twenty-four and seventy-five houses clustered on the lake shore, a density of population considerably above the average for the hamlets of Norman Britain, for example, which usually contained about thirty households. The Swiss farming cultures were mirrored by scattered agricultural communities between the Mediterranean and the English Channel, far beyond the western frontiers of Danubian territory.

As early as 4000 B.C., some French farmers were building large communal tombs of stone, known to archaeologists as "megaliths" ("large stone" in Greek). Megaliths are found as far north as Scandinavia, in Britain, Ireland, France, Spain, the western Mediterranean, Corsica, and Malta. For years, archaeologists thought that megaliths had originated in the eastern Mediterranean about 2500 B.C. and that the distinctive tomb architecture had spread westward into Spain with colonists from the Aegean, who had carried a custom of collective burial and their religion with them. Megalithic tombs were then believed to have been built in western Europe, witnesses to a lost faith perhaps spread by pilgrims, missionaries, or merchants. With their massive stones and large burial chambers, megaliths remained one of the mysteries of European prehistory (Figure 13.11).[26]

3000 B.C.
3560 B.C.

This popular and widely accepted hypothesis was seriously weakened by radiocarbon dates from France that turned out to be earlier than others from western Europe. Furthermore, the new calibrated dates have made Spanish megalithic sites and their associated culture date to as early as c. 4000 B.C., much earlier than their alleged prototypes in the Aegean. Thus, megaliths were being built in western Europe at least a millennium before massive funerary architecture became fashionable in the eastern Mediterranean. This remarkable form of freestanding architecture stands as a unique, local European creation.

Agriculture and domestic stock were in use in southern Scandinavia and on the north European plains by 3500 B.C. A vigorous hunting and gathering cultural tradition had flourished on the shores of the Baltic for thousands of years.[27] Then it seems that some hunters adopted the new economy from the Danubian farmers on their southern boundaries, because pollen diagrams from Scandinavian bogs show a striking disturbance in the natural forest cover at this time. The forest cover, especially

3500 B.C.

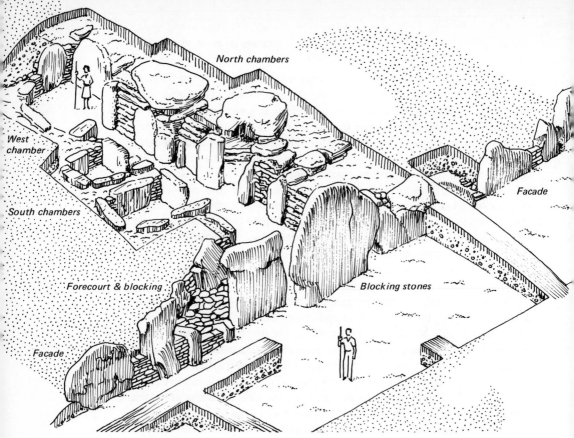

Figure 13.11
The interior of a megalithic chamber tomb at West Kennett, England, dating to the middle of the third millennium B.C. (After Piggott.)

elm trees, in the diagrams diminishes; cereal grasses and the pollen of typical cultivation weeds appear for the first time. Layers of charcoal fragments testify to forest clearance by burning. The drop in elm cover is thought to mean the use of that tree for cattle fodder.

The general features of this early farming activity are familiar to us — the growing of cereal crops and the grazing of stock, sizable settlements of rectangular houses, and forest clearance with polished stone axes. Danish archaeologists have experimented with stone axes and adzes and found them remarkably effective for felling trees (Figure 13.12).[28] The farmers began building sizable family tombs. They developed a characteristic form of clay beaker with a flared neck, later widely distributed over central and northwestern Europe.

The British Isles stand at the extreme northwest corner of Europe, the receiving end, as it were, of culture traits from many diverse peoples. Before 4000 B.C. farming communities were established in southern Brit-

3000 B.C.
3560 B.C.

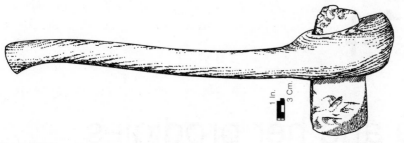

Figure 13.12
  A reconstructed polished stone ax with wooden handle, a copy of an example found
  in a Danish bog — a highly effective instrument for forest clearance. The stone is
  original.

ain. Communal burial chambers and large cattle camps with extensive
earthworks came into use. British sites reflect cultural influences from
both western France and Scandinavia. Flourishing barter networks carried
stone blades, and the material to make them, throughout England. Similar
exploitation of flint and other stone outcrops is a persistent feature of
early European farming.[29]

By 4000 B.C. or thereabouts, stone-using peasant farmers were well
established over most of temperate Europe. Many Stone Age hunters had
adopted the new economies; other still made their living by hunting and
gathering alongside the farmers. Both subsistence patterns survived side
by side for many centuries. In Scandinavia, for example, fishermen and
fowlers of the Ertebolle culture absorbed some new economic practices
without making any major change in their traditional way of life. They
traded fish for grain products grown by their farming neighbors, and lived
on the outskirts of cleared farmlands.

But by the time that farming and cattle herding were familiar economic
strategies in the West, new advances in human technology had sparked
cultural and social innovation in the Near East. Man had begun to live
in cities, to write about himself, to develop new political structures. Another chapter in human history had already begun.

3500 B.C.
4200 B.C.

14

africa and her prodigies

For more than three-quarters of its course, the magnificent Nile River meanders through arid desert country. Virtually all its water comes from highland Ethiopia, mostly down the Blue Nile. Between mid-August and mid-October, the summer floodwaters of the Blue Nile reach Egypt, flooding over the banks of the main river. A layer of silt from far upstream is deposited in the valley, ensuring the continued fertility of the rich soils on the Nile floodplain. Lush vegetation crowds the banks of the Nile, providing a sharp contrast with the surrounding desert.

The wonder of the Nile has attracted man for thousands of years, exciting even the most sober traveler. The famous Karl Baedeker compiled a series of great nineteenth-century travel guides that are still bibles to many tourists. Even that conservative observer wrote: "The verdant crops and palms which everywhere cheer the traveller as soon as he has quitted the desert . . . lend to the site of Ancient Thebes the appearance of a wonderland, richly endowed with the gifts of never-failing fertility."[1]*

hunters on the nile

The Nile Valley was a rich environment for human settlement in late Pleistocene times. The Nile 12,000 years ago already was flowing through desert country, although intervals of higher rainfall did occur there, the last between about 11,000 and 9,000 B.C. At that time the Nile Valley was occupied by hunting and gathering populations, which made much use of wild grains and seeds as well as large game animals, fish, and birds (Figure 14.1).[2]

* See pages 395–396 for notes to Chapter 14.

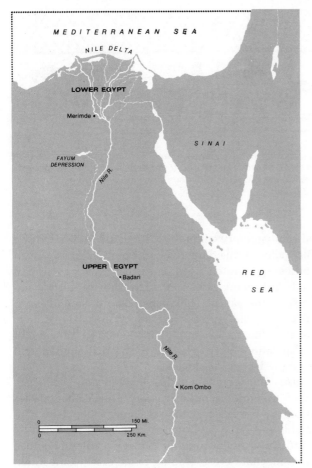

Figure 14.1
Archaeological sites in the Nile Valley mentioned in Chapter 14.

One such culture, named the Qadan, flourished between c. 12,500 and 4550 B.C. The Qadan is best known from small microlithic tools found on riverside campsites near the Nile. In the earlier stages of the Qadan, fishing and big game hunting were dominant activities (Figure 14.2). But large numbers of grindstones and grinding equipment came from a few localities, as if the gathering of wild grains was already important. Some Qadan settlements were probably large and occupied over considerable periods of time. The dead were buried in cemeteries in shallow pits covered with stone slabs. Some pits contained two bodies. In six instances, small stone tools were actually embedded in the bones of the skeletons, for some Qadan people had met a violent end.[3]

Qadan
?12,500–
4550 B.C.

Figure 14.2
Ancient Egyptians hunting the rich Nile fauna, drawn from tomb paintings at Beni Hassan. The hunters have spread large nets to trap the game (in the background) and are pursuing gazelles and wild cattle with dogs and bows and arrows. Some wild sheep are caught in the nets.

Other distinct and contemporary cultural traditions are known to have prospered in the Nile Valley at this time. Around Kom Ombo, upstream of Qadan country, Stone Age hunters lived on the banks of lagoons and flood channels of the Nile, seeking game in the riverside woodlands and on the plains overlooking the valley. They fished for catfish and perch in the swamps. Here again, wild grasses were important in the hunter-gatherer economy of the Nile Valley from about 13,000 B.C.[4] No doubt animal and human populations were attracted to the rich environment of the Nile throughout the Upper Pleistocene.

The valley is an unusual phenomenon, in that its water supply depends on the seasonal floods from Ethiopia, not on rainfall. Thus its boundaries are severely constricted by the desert, confining human populations to the Nile banks. A highly favorable environment was being exploited by hunters with a bow and arrow toolkit superior to that of earlier millennia, so population densities inevitably rose, leading to increased competition for a habitat that was the only means of survival for the people of the valley. They could not move away from the river, for the arid deserts could not support them. The only solution was more specialized exploitation of natural resources, but there is no evidence that the peoples of the Nile had begun to cultivate their own food before southwest Asian food crops were introduced into the Nile Valley.

fayum and merimde

The earliest farming settlements in what is now Egypt date to the early fifth and late fourth millennia B.C. They were discovered by British archaeologist Gertrude Caton-Thompson on the shores of a former lake

4400 B.C.

in the Fayum depression to the west of the Nile Valley.[5] The sites belong to a time when the deserts were better watered and partly covered with stunted grasslands.

The Fayum settlements were transitory and lacked the substantial houses found in contemporary settlements in the Near East. The farmers may have used crude matting or reed shelters. They stored their grain in silos lined with baskets. The arid environment has preserved traces of their coiled baskets as well as the grains of emmer wheat and flax. Sheep and goats roamed the shores of the lake, and cattle and pigs were probably domesticated. The Fayum people engaged in little trade and lived at a simple subsistence level by the shores of their lake. They fished and hunted both crocodiles and hippopotamuses.

The well-established farming culture of the Fayum cannot be regarded as the earliest to flourish in the Nile Valley. So far, however, only farming sites dating to later millennia have been found on the floodplain. But Fayum agriculture was based on Asian crops and domesticated animals, which were apparently introduced to the Nile Valley sometime in the fifth millennium or earlier (Figure 14.3).

One floodplain settlement is the village of Merimde near the Nile Delta, where a cluster of oval houses and shelters were built half underground and roofed with mud and sticks.[6] An occupation mound 2 meters (7 ft.) high was accumulated over a period of some six hundred years from c. 4130 B.C. Simple pottery, stone axes, flint arrowheads, and knives

Fayum (margin)

Merimde ?4130– 3530 B.C. (margin)

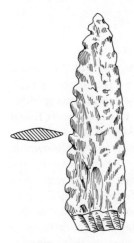

Flint sickle blade

Hollow-based arrowhead

Figure 14.3
Fayum artifacts (both one-half actual size).

were in use. Agriculture and the cultivation of cereal crops is evidenced by grains stored in clay pots, baskets, and pits. Dogs, cattle, sheep or goats, and pigs were kept. This general level of culture at a subsistence level may well have been characteristic of large areas of the Nile flood-plain for some thousands of years.

Other farmers who flourished in the Upper Nile are largely known to us from cemetery burials. Like their northern neighbors they used bows and arrows in the chase, many of them tipped with finely flaked arrowheads. Emmer wheat and barley were cultivated, while cattle and small stock provided much of their meat supply. Settlements again were typified by transient architecture, but the dead were buried with some ceremony. Linen shrouds were used, and the bodies covered with skins. The women wore ivory combs and plaited their hair. This culture, named the Badarian after a village near where the first settlements were found, is thought to be broadly contemporary with Merimde.[7]

Badarian
4000 B.C.

The inhabitants of both the Merimde and Badarian villages tended to camp on high ground overlooking the Nile Valley and do not appear to have exploited the floodplain as intensively as did later Egyptians. The uniformity of the Nile environment is such that we can expect future discoveries to reveal similar farming cultures over many miles of the Nile Valley. Not until the early fourth millennium B.C. did Egyptians first begin to settle on the floodplain itself, perhaps making use of irrigation to increase the yield of their gardens and to support much higher population densities (Figure 14.4).

3800 B.C.

the sahara

During the early millennia of Egyptian agriculture much of the Sahara was stunted grassland, and occasional, vast, shallow lakes contained fish and crocodiles. Saharan grasslands supported sparse populations of Stone Age hunter-gatherers. Traces of their hunting camps have been found by the shores of long-dried-up Pleistocene lakes deep in the desert.[8]

The grasslands were a favorable environment for cattle-owning nomads as well. By 4600 B.C., sheep and goats were being kept on the Libyan coast.[9] Domestic cattle bones have been found in Saharan caves dating to as early as 5500 B.C. It is thought that farmers were living in the Sahara at least a thousand years earlier, but some uncertainties still surround this early chronology. We can be sure that herds of cattle were roaming the Sahara by the fifth millennium B.C. Whether they were introduced into the desert or domesticated there from wild cattle remains to be seen.[10] The Saharan pastoralists have left a remarkable record of their lives on the walls of caves deep in the desert. Wild animals, cattle,

4600 B.C.

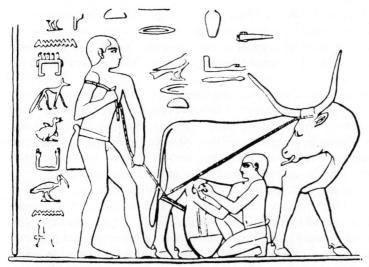

Figure 14.4
  Ancient Egyptians milking a cow, from the tomb of Kagemni, Saqqara, c. 2330 B.C.
  (one-sixth actual size).

goats, humans, and scenes of daily life are preserved in a complicated
jumble of artistic endeavor extending back perhaps to the seventh millennium B.C.[11]

The increasing aridity of the Sahara after 3000 B.C. forced many of the   3000 B.C.
pastoralists to move southward to the northern fringes of sub-Saharan
Africa. The Saharan cattle people are thought to have used domestic
crops, experimenting with such African summer rainfall cereals as
sorghum and millet as they moved southward out of areas where wheat,
barley, and other cereal crops used in the Mediterranean basin could be
grown.[12]

sub-saharan africa

At the end of Pleistocene times the indigenous inhabitants of sub-Saharan
Africa were already adapted to a wide range of specialized environments.
Some lived by intensive fishing, others by gathering or hunting, depending on the nature of their environment. Indeed, in a primitive way the
techniques of food production may have already been in use on the
fringes of the rain forests of western and central Africa, where the common use of such root plants as the African yam led people to recognize
the advantages of growing their own food.[13] Certainly the yam can easily

be germinated simply by replanting the tops. This primitive form of "vegeculture" may have been the economic tradition onto which the cultivation of summer rainfall cereal crops was grafted as it diffused southward from the grassland areas on the southern borders of the Sahara.

950 B.C.   By the first millennium B.C., the time at which Europe and the Near East were beginning to enjoy the benefits of iron tools, Stone Age food producers were already living on the East African highlands of Kenya, northern Tanzania, and parts of West Africa.[14] Unfortunately, we know little about these early African farmers, nor do we know how deeply they penetrated into the vast rain forest areas of the Congo basin.

A.D. 100   But it was not until the beginning of the Christian era and the arrival of ironworking that food production and domestic animals spread throughout the African continent. For thousands of years after the Near East started to enjoy literate civilization, Bushmen hunters and gatherers flourished on savannah woodlands. Much of Africa, though the cradle of mankind and home of cultural innovation, was unexploited by more advanced agricultural societies until very recent times.[15]

15

rice, roots,
and ocean voyagers

"As the cradle of earliest agriculture I have proposed Southeastern Asia. It meets the requirements of high physical and organic diversity, of mild climate with reversed monsoons giving abundant rainy and dry periods, of many waters inviting to fishing, of location at the hub of the Old World for communication by water or by land. No other area is equally well situated or equally well furnished for the rise of a fishing farming culture." This emphatic statement was penned by a geographer, Carl O. Sauer, in 1952 as part of an essay on agricultural origins that has become a minor, if controversial, classic.[1*] When he wrote it, almost nothing was known about early agriculture in Southeast Asia. Not much more is known now, but we can identify this vast region of the world as a major center of early food production (Table 15.1).

Most people who have speculated about early Asian farming agree on the theory that the first garden culture probably developed in a permanently humid tropical region with rich flora and abundant coastal or freshwater fish. Early gardening may have been the work of individual farmers who planted the tops of root plants such as taro and yams in riverside or forest plots. Fishermen who gardened on the side have been given tentative credit for early cultivation in the monsoon area of Asia, extending from southeastern India to Southeast Asia. Archaeological researches have just begun to provide some background support for this hypothesis.

Table 15.1
Early agriculture and human settlement in Asia and the Pacific.

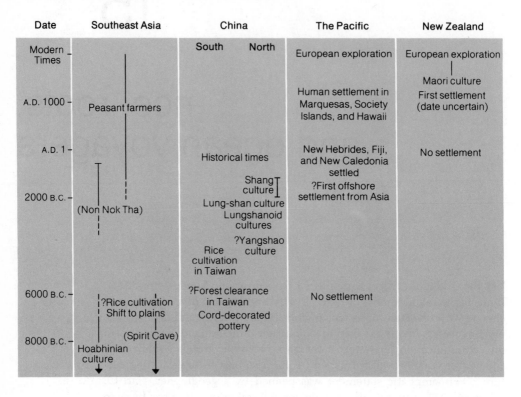

Date	Southeast Asia	China South North	The Pacific	New Zealand
Modern Times			European exploration	European exploration
				Maori culture
A.D. 1000	Peasant farmers		Human settlement in Marquesas, Society Islands, and Hawaii	First settlement (date uncertain)
A.D. 1		Historical times	New Hebrides, Fiji, and New Caledonia settled	No settlement
2000 B.C.	(Non Nok Tha)	Shang culture Lung-shan culture Lungshanoid cultures	?First offshore settlement from Asia	
		?Yangshao Rice culture cultivation in Taiwan		
6000 B.C.	?Rice cultivation Shift to plains	?Forest clearance in Taiwan Cord-decorated pottery	No settlement	
8000 B.C.	(Spirit Cave) Hoabhinian culture			

southeast asia: spirit cave and non nok tha

American archaeologist Chester Gorman has recently excavated Spirit Cave in northern Thailand (Figure 15.1), situated in a limestone cliff overlooking a small stream in highland country.[2] The inhabitants exploited the vegetable foods around the stream, water life itself, as well as deer, pigs, and small mammals. The lowest levels of Spirit Cave were formed earlier than 11,000 years ago. Hoabhinian tools, including characteristic flakes and small choppers (Chapter 10), came from these horizons and remained in use for a long time.

Hoabhinian 9000 B.C.

Chester Gorman was able to recover considerable quantities of seeds from Hoabhinian levels. Among the foods eaten by the inhabitants were almonds, betel nuts, broad beans, peas, gourds, water chestnuts, peppers, and cucumbers. Most of these are potentially domesticable foods. At the

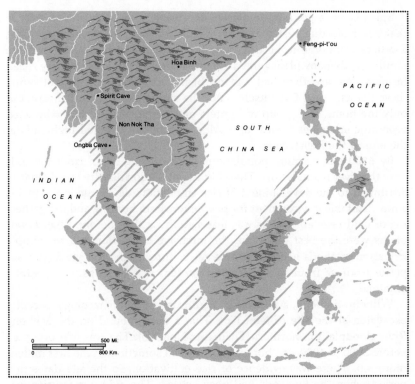

Figure 15.1
Early farming sites in Southeast Asia mentioned in Chapter 15. The low sea level areas at the end of the Weichsel glaciation are shaded.

very least the Hoabhinians of Spirit Cave were making sophisticated use of a broad range of vegetable foods. In fact, the botanists studying the seeds from the cave may show that they are from domesticated plants. If they are, then the Spirit Cave people are the earliest known cultivators of vegetable foods yet known to science, as Spirit Cave agriculture precedes that of Near Eastern farmers by at least 2,000 years.

In about 6800 B.C. there was a major change in the material culture   6800 B.C.
of the Spirit Cave people. Some new tools came into use, including rectangular stone adzes and ground slate knives. Pottery was introduced for the first time; it was made by sophisticated techniques that could not have been invented at Spirit Cave. Much of the pottery is marked with cord impressions. The slate knives found in the upper levels of Spirit Cave show strong resemblances to similar, later artifacts used for harvesting rice in parts of Indonesia and may be suggestive of cereal cultivation near the site.

Spirit Cave is not unique merely because it is the only site of its type that has been dug systematically. It tells us that 11,000 years ago cave dwellers were able to occupy their homes the year around. They were familiar with many plant genera that today are commonly grown by Asian farmers. Perhaps they had already begun to experiment in cultivating these plants. Spirit Cave itself is not the cradle of Asian agriculture, but only the home of a group of hunters and perhaps cultivators who used economic strategies typical of a wide area of the forested highlands at the end of the Pleistocene.

6500 B.C.
By 6500 B.C., farming populations were moving down from the hills onto the river plains below. This shift in population density may be partly attributed to the development of rice cultivation, which made the plains a most suitable environment for people to whom hunting and the gathering of wild vegetable foods was less significant than before. River floodplains were the best places for the intensive cultivation and the simple irrigation methods needed for rice agriculture. High crop yields, far superior to those from small highland gardens of root crops, were readily obtained.

Wilhelm Solheim, a pioneer in Southeast Asian archaeology, recently excavated at the site of Non Nok Tha, a deep mound on the Mekong River floodplain in northern Thailand.[3] Non Nok Tha was first occupied

Non Nok Tha
3500–500 B.C.
before 3000 to 4000 B.C., but was abandoned sometime in the first millennium A.D. There was evidence of rice cultivation, so the site dates to a period when the lowlands had been settled. The evidence for rice was in the form of grain impressions found on the pots from the lowest levels. Bones of domestic cattle, too, were discovered in excavating these same horizons.

Non Nok Tha represents a different stage in economic development than Spirit Cave. The inhabitants were sedentary farmers depending on rice and cattle for most of their diet. Hunting and gathering were less important than in earlier millennia when highland sites were occupied all year round. Copper smelting was apparently practiced, and cattle were domesticated by the fourth millennium B.C., fully as early as in the Near East.

Southeast Asia did not suffer from the drastic climatic changes of northern latitudes. With the exception of major changes in sea level, there were no prolonged droughts or major vegetational changes to alter the pattern of human settlement. By the later Upper Pleistocene, however, some Asians were exploiting their environment more intensively than ever before, an essential prelude to the agriculture of later millennia. The same processes of experimentation with plants and animals took place in Southeast Asia as elsewhere when new agricultural economies took hold for the first time.

southern china: taiwan

Fortunately, the researches of Chinese-American archaeologist Kwang-chih Chang into the archaeology of southeastern China have provided additional information on early agriculture in Southeast Asia, for the monsoon areas of South China belong within the same broad environmental zone as those of the Thai discoveries. Jih-yüeh-T'an Lake in central Taiwan has provided a critical pollen record that covers the period of early agriculture.[4] Tropical vegetation covered the lowlands of Taiwan 8,000 years ago, as sea levels rose and the climate became warmer. The pollen diagram reveals a marked change in the Jih-yüeh-T'an vegetation about 10,000 years ago. It shows a definite increase in the number of secondary trees (the species that grow after the primary forest growth has been cut down). Many charcoal fragments are also found, clear indications of forest fires, perhaps lit to clear brush. The botanists believe that they were the result of human interference with the natural vegetation, changes that might have resulted from agriculture.

6000 B.C.

The period of warmer climate just referred to coincides with the presence of hunting peoples who also relied heavily on fish and shellfish for their livelihood.[5] They made pots decorated with cord-impressed motifs. Significantly, their cord-decorated pottery is mirrored by related forms both in Thailand and in northern China.

About 4,200 years ago groups of rice cultivators appeared in Taiwan, themselves related to northern Chinese farmers of the "Lungshanoid" tradition described later in this chapter. Their appearance is marked in the pollen diagrams by clear signs of more intensive agriculture. Several species of cultivation weeds, of the types that grow with rice crops, appear in the pollen samples. These weeds were absent in earlier levels, when agriculture was not extensive enough for them to flourish.

2250 B.C.

yangshao and early chinese farming culture

As early as the eighteenth century, people respected Chinese civilization as the most ancient in the world. "A young Chinese seems to me an antediluvian man renewed," wrote one scholar.[6] The impression of considerable antiquity fostered by students of earlier times has been confirmed by archaeological researches in the twentieth century.

By the end of the Weichsel glaciation, scattered bands of hunter-gatherers were inhabiting wide areas of the Far East. Some were fishermen and shellfish gatherers; others hunted or lived off wild vegetable

8000 B.C.

foods. We do not know exactly what tools they used or how they lived.

The Huangho Valley and the central regions of the Huangho (Yellow) River valley formed a major center of early agriculture, sometimes referred to as the North China Nuclear Area (Figure 15.2). The nuclear area is a small basin, forming a border between the wooded western highlands and the swampy lowlands to the east.[7] Pollen analysis of Postglacial deposits in China has provided abundant evidence that there was a prolonged period of warmer climate from about 8,000 to 4,000 years ago, when the rainfall and warm climate were sufficient to make the nuclear area a favorable locality for agriculture.

The loess soils of this environment were formed during the glacial periods of the Pleistocene. The fine, soft-textured earth was both homogeneous and porous and could be tilled by simple digging sticks. Because there was a concentrated period of summer rainfall, cereal crops, the key to northern Chinese agriculture, could be grown successfully. A number

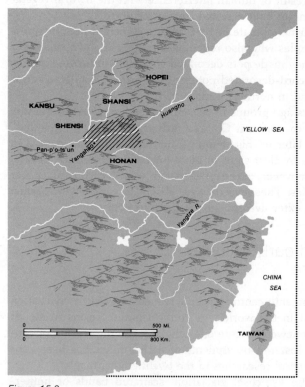

Figure 15.2
   One approximate nuclear area (shaded) of early Chinese agriculture. Yangshao sites occur both within the nuclear area and outside it.

of indigenous plants were also available for potential domestication, including the wild ancestors of foxtail millet, broomcorn millet, sorghum, hemp, and the mulberry. Ancient Chinese farmers developed their own cultivation techniques, which persisted for thousands of years before irrigation was developed. Although irrigation gradually became the basis of the agricultural economies of Egypt, the Indus Valley, and Mesopotamia, it did not achieve importance in northern China until much later.[8]

The earliest millennia of northern Chinese agriculture are still a complete blank on the archaeological map, but we can assume that the inhabitants of the Huangho region passed through a long phase of experimental cultivation and intensive exploitation of the indigenous flora before developing their own distinctive agricultural techniques. Early farming villages are associated with coarse cord-marked pottery, found on the banks of the Huangho River in western Honan Province and on the lower Weishui River. Perhaps these cord-marked vessels are related to the cord-decorated pottery traditions of Southeast Asia and Taiwan.

Some of the earliest traces of agricultural settlement were first found in the 1920s on the low-lying loess soils in the middle reaches of the Huangho River, especially at a site named Yangshao.[9] Similar villages have been found over a wide area of the Huangho River basin, which in geographical terms is fully as large as that of early centers of agriculture in Egypt and Mesopotamia. Radiocarbon dates for Yangshao sites released to date belong in the period 3950–3300 B.C.[10]

Yangshao

3950– 3300 B.C.

Many Yangshao villages were undefended settlements built on ridges overlooking the floodplains, sited to avoid flooding or to allow maximal use of floodplain soils. The villagers lived in fairly substantial round or oblong houses that were partly sunk into the ground. Yangshao houses had mud-plastered walls, timber frames, and steep roofs (Figure 15.3). Usually there were cemeteries outside the villages; sometimes the villages boasted a special area for pottery kilns where the characteristic Yangshao painted funerary vessels favored by the householders were manufactured.

The Yangshao people moved their settlements at regular intervals, but returned to the same village sites again and again. Using hoes and digging sticks, they cultivated foxtail millet as a staple crop. Simple dry-land slash-and-burn farming techniques probably supplemented riverside gardens. Irrigation may have been practiced as early as the fifth millennium B.C., however. Dogs and pigs were fully domesticated. Cattle, sheep, and goats were less common. Hunting and gathering were still significant activities as was fishing, for which hooks and spears were employed.

Each Yangshao village was a self-contained community, thousands of which flourished in the river valleys of northern China. The Yangshao farmers were distributed over a comparatively limited area of northern China from eastern Kansu in the west to Huangho and northwestern

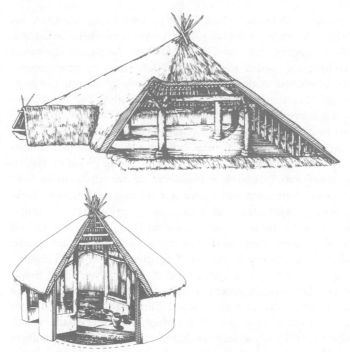

Figure 15.3
Reconstructions of Yangshao huts from Pan-p'o-ts'un, China.

Honan in the east. Many regional variations of Yangshao culture remain to be distinguished, but the salient features of a characteristic, and thoroughly Chinese, culture are already clear. The earliest Chinese farmers had already developed a distinctive naturalistic art style (Figures 15.4 and 15.5). The unique Chinese cooking style, with its reliance on steaming, is attested by the discovery of cooking pots identical to specialized cooking vessels of later millennia. Jade was being worked; hemp was used for making fabrics; skilled basketry was practiced; even the Chinese language may have roots in Yangshao. Of the indigenous origins of Chinese cereal agriculture there can be little doubt, although long-established trade routes to the West may have brought new ideas to the Far East, including some crops, especially in later millennia.

lungshanoid cultures

Lungshanoid
2500 B.C.

Sometime before 2500 B.C. Lungshanoid cultures began to develop with a far wider distribution than the Yangshao.[11] The Lung-shan culture was

Figure 15.4
Yangshao pottery from Kansu Province, China (about one-fourth actual size).

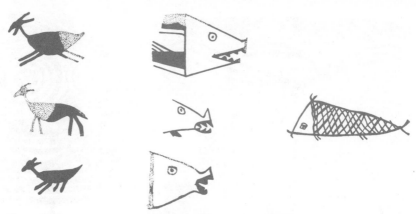

Figure 15.5
Animal and fish motifs on Yangshao pottery from Pan-p'o-ts'un, China.

perhaps based on rice cultivation as well as on domestic animals, fishing, hunting, and gathering. We can speculate that rice was probably first domesticated in the south, on fertile floodplains where lush water meadows could provide high crop yields without too much effort and where wild rice already flourished. The new crop may have been introduced from the south, soon transforming Yangshao economies, decreasing reliance on dry-land agriculture.

The Lungshanoid peoples had their roots in the Yangshao cultural tradition but represented a more advanced version of it, adapted to a wider range of environmental situations. Rice growing gave the northern farmers greater adaptability. Lung-shan peoples soon developed in the nuclear area and on the coast and southward to the latitude of Taiwan (Figure 15.6). At least six regional variants of Lungshanoid culture have been distinguished. Their village settlements follow a pattern of river valleys and seacoasts, each regional variant being connected to others by a network of waterways. Their inhabitants probably spread southward into eastern and southeastern China from the nuclear area, perhaps as a result of population pressure in the north. Stone knives and sickles used for rice agriculture appear in large numbers. Carpenters' tools, bone, horn, and shell artifacts are common (see also Figure 15.7).

Rice cultivation spread rapidly throughout Southeast Asia, not only on the mainland but also through the offshore islands and far into the Pacific. Perhaps Lungshanoid people were among those who spread the new economies eastward and southward from Mainland China. The success of the new cereal crops also played a part in the early development of Chinese states.

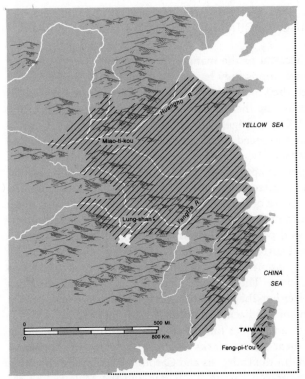

Figure 15.6
The approximate distribution of the Lungshanoid cultures in China (shaded area).

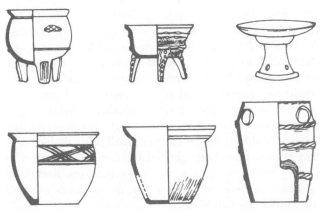

Figure 15.7
Some typical Lungshanoid vessels used for cooking and other purposes, from Miao-ti-kou, China (scale not recorded).

early man in the pacific

"Who can give an account of the manner in which they were conveyed hither, what communications they have with other beings, and what becomes of them when they multiply on an isle. . . ." French explorer Louis de Bougainville was among the first to speculate about the origins of the Polynesian islands.[12] His voyages and those of the celebrated Captain Cook revealed to an entranced world a myriad of tropical isles peopled by romantic, tall savages who lived a life of ease and tropical plenty. Historian J. C. Beaglehole aptly described the sequel: "And now rose up, indeed, within Natural History, something new, something incomparably exciting, Man in the state of nature; the Noble Savage entered the study and the drawing room of Europe in naked majesty, to shake the preconceptions of morals and politics."[13] An atmosphere of the "never-never" and tropical bliss still surrounds the South Seas today, when we can fly from Los Angeles to remote Tahiti in eight hours or from Auckland to Hawaii in the same time. The industrial progress of two centuries has done little to dispel either the myths of Polynesia or the controversies regarding the origins of the Pacific islanders.

Captain Cook was one of the first to speculate on the origins of the Polynesians: "They bear strong marks of affinity to some of the Indian tribes, those that inhabit the Ladrones and Carolina Islands; and the same affinity may again be traced among the Battas and the Malays," he remarked soberly.[14] Not all Cook's successors have been so restrained in their speculations. Pacific studies have been the scene of wild hypotheses and fierce debates. The classic academic controversies of diffusion versus evolution (Chapter 2) have been fought on Pacific battlefields.[15] The arguments surround an American or an Asian origin for the Polynesians and the means by which Melanesia and Polynesia were settled (Figure 15.8).

Most authorities now look to Asia for the origins of Melanesian and Polynesian populations. They point to the island fruit and root crops, based on the cultivation of breadfruit, coconut, sugarcane, taro, and yams, with the sweet potato an additional food whose origin is still uncertain. All these crops except the sweet potato are of Southeast Asian origin. Chickens, dogs, and pigs were also valued as food and were domesticated in Asia before being introduced to the Pacific. Small animals like pigs and chickens could readily have been carried from island to island in canoes, as could easily germinating root plants like the yam. Both food sources allowed a sizable population to inhabit many hundreds of small islands separated by miles of open water.[16]

The Pacific islanders show no features attributable to American Indian stock. Their physical attributes had probably stabilized before any cultivators left the Asian mainland. Their languages have much in common

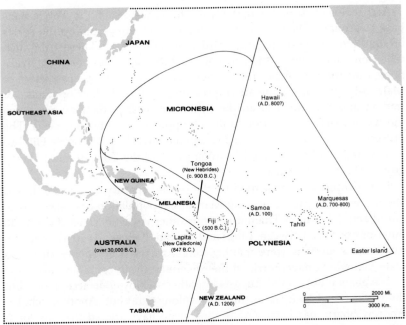

Figure 15.8

The settlement of the Pacific Islands. The chronologies, based on the few available radiocarbon dates, are provisional. Melanesia, Micronesia, and Polynesia are demarcated by the boundary lines on the map. (After Chard.)

with Thai and other Southeast Asian dialects and bear no resemblance to native American speech. Artifacts such as ground and polished axes and adzes, shell fishhooks, and canoes can be paralleled in general terms on the western shores of the Pacific.

A diametrically opposed viewpoint is that Polynesia was populated by waterborne colonization from the Americas, with migrating waves of Indians floating westward to new lands from Peru. This long-lived hypothesis was resurrected dramatically in 1947 by Thor Heyerdahl, who sailed his *Kon-Tiki* raft from Peru to Polynesia.[17] His argument was that Polynesia had been settled by South American Indians who sailed westward on the trade winds in search of a new home. Unfortunately, no one has been able to support Heyerdahl's hypothesis with firm data in the form of artifacts of American origin. Peruvian pottery has been found on the Galapagos Islands, but no South American Indian cultures have yet been unearthed in Polynesia itself.[18] The overwhelming evidence of archaeology and anthropology points to a Southeast Asian origin for Polynesian culture, although the possibility of fleeting contacts with the Americas cannot be ruled out.

3000 B.C.

1000 B.C.

Archaeologist Robert Suggs traces the ancestors of the Polynesians back to groups of fishermen living in the river valleys and on the coasts of southern China during the third millennium B.C.[19] These tribesmen relied on simple agriculture, fishing, shellfish, and pigs for their livelihood, and they were skillful seamen. Their language was a dialect of Malayo-Polynesian. Population pressures, political developments, or trading opportunities caused the fishermen to shift their homes down the Asian coast and offshore to the Philippines and into Melanesia. The process of colonization proceeded astonishingly rapidly, with Fiji and New Caledonia being settled by 1000 B.C., and the Tongan and Samoan groups shortly afterward.

The Marquesas were settled by the second century B.C., and Tahiti at about the same time. A growing Marquesan population colonized Easter Island and the eastern Tuamotus, while other voyagers crossed the 2,200 miles of open sea between Tahiti and Hawaii. Between 1800 B.C. and 200 B.C., the Polynesians were making long voyages over open water on a scale that would have horrified their Mediterranean contemporaries.

The general outlines of Suggs's hypothesis enjoy wide acceptance, but the navigational abilities of the early colonists do not. Another scholar, Andrew Sharp, has been among those who have argued that the long-distance voyages of early Polynesians were one-way, accidental trips, when canoes were blown out to sea.[20] Early navigators, he argued, were helpless to counteract the effects of ocean currents. His views have been sharply challenged by those who have studied the well-developed maritime technology of the Polynesians.[21] They point out that nearly all the long-distance trips attributed to the Polynesians were in a north-south direction, which, navigationally speaking, involved simple dead-reckoning calculations and a simple way of measuring latitude from the stars. Recently, anthropologist Ben Finney made detailed studies of Polynesian canoes and navagational techniques; his findings support a notion of deliberate one-way voyages, sparked as much by necessity — drought or warfare — as by restless adventure.[22] Evidence for the carrying of women, animals of both sexes, and plants for propagation, however, shows that deliberate colonization was the aim.

pacific archaeology: western polynesia

Radiocarbon dating and excavation are fleshing out and modifying the simple hypotheses of Pacific settlement outlined here. Little archaeological evidence has yet come from the islands east of New Guinea, settled by the time of the Upper Pleistocene.[23] The Lapita site on New Caledonia contained a distinctive style of pottery bearing intricate incised designs radiocarbon dated to c. 847 B.C. Similar vessels have been found in the New Hebrides and in Fiji, and there seems little doubt that people with Lapita pottery had penetrated into Polynesia by the end of the twelfth century B.C. A settlement at Enta on Tongoa in the Central New Hebrides was occupied by c. 900 B.C., but potsherds from this region are distinct from the Lapita vessels and bear no resemblance to those found on other islands. Polished stone axes and adzes (Figure 15.9) were in common use, and shell adzes, choppers, and scrapers also formed an essential part of the material culture. Pigs, dogs, and chickens, along with agricultural products, formed the basis of the diet. In addition, shellfish was an important element. Thus, western Polynesia was first settled at least 3,000 years ago by peoples with no metals who enjoyed a simple level of village farming culture.

900 B.C.

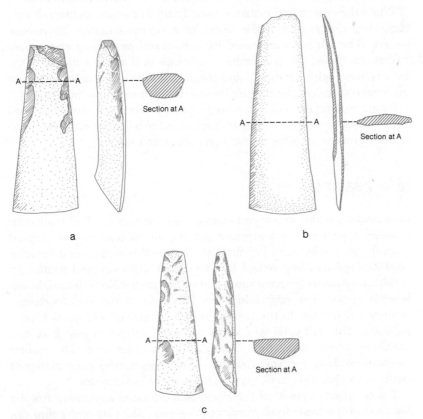

Figure 15.9
  Adzes from various South Sea areas: (a) North Island of New Zealand; (b) South Island of New Zealand; (c) Marquesas. All were mounted on wooden handles (about one-fourth actual size).

eastern polynesia

A.D. 800

The time depth for human settlement in eastern Polynesia is probably not much more than 2,000 years, although a few early sites have been found. Securely dated sequences of human occupation extend back to A.D. 700–800 in the Marquesas and Society Islands, and Hawaii has sites dating back to about the same time period.[24] The eastern Polynesian environment was ideal for growing breadfruit and other tropical crops with minimal effort by the inhabitants. Fishing was a constant activity, testified to by bone and shellfish hooks that are common artifacts throughout eastern Polynesia. The result was that the people enjoyed major agricultural surpluses and abundant leisure time, which was absorbed by religious concerns, as evidenced by extensive temple ruins.

When the French and British visited Tahiti in the late eighteenth century, they chanced upon the center of a vigorous eastern Polynesian society. The islands were ruled by a powerful hereditary clan whose power was based on its members' religious skill and warlike abilities. Society was highly stratified, and religion, which included an emphasis on human sacrifice, played a major role in the lives of the inhabitants.[25]

Future excavation will undoubtedly paint a picture of remarkably diverse Polynesian cultures, spread from island to island by navigators and seamen familiar with the subtle signs of sea and sky.[26]

new zealand

A.D. 1200

New Zealand is the largest and among the most remote of all the Pacific islands; it possesses a temperate climate, in contrast to the tropical warmth enjoyed by most Polynesians. Despite this ecological difference, New Zealand was first settled by Polynesians who voyaged southward within comparatively recent times and settled on the North Island. Maori legends speak of a migration from Polynesia in the mid-fourteenth century A.D. (Figure 15.10). Settlers may have arrived 400 years before, including Toi Ete'huatai who came to New Zealand in search of two grandsons blown away from Tahiti during a canoe race. The earliest radiocarbon dates for New Zealand archaeological sites are a matter of controversy, but date back only to the present millennium.[27]

The temperate climate of the North Island formed a southern frontier for most of the basic food plants of Polynesia. The yam and gourd can only be grown there, but the sweet potato could be cultivated in the northern part of the South Island, provided that adequate winter storage pits were used. The Polynesian coconut never grew in New Zealand. The

Figure 15.10
A portrait of a Maori warrior drawn during Captain Cook's voyages in the eighteenth century. The elaborate tattoos on the face were heraldic symbols of great significance to the Maori.

earliest settlers relied heavily on hunting, fishing, and gathering during the early centuries of human occupation. Even in later times, while some peoples specialized in food production, others did not, especially in the

South Island, where much settlement was based on the coasts close to abundant ocean resources.

Early New Zealand hunters were lucky. They found great flocks of flightless Moa birds, cumbersome and helpless in the face of systematic hunting. Moas were soon exterminated by the Maori, as the birds formed a staple part of their diet. Fish, fern roots, and shellfish, too, were important throughout New Zealand's short prehistory. Systematic cultivation resulted in higher population densities and more permanent settlements in the North Island from the mid-fifteenth century A.D. onward. Two hundred years later, the classical phase of Maori culture began, reaching its height in the decades before 1800.

The earliest New Zealanders used adze blades and fishhooks of unmistakable Polynesian form. By the fifteenth century, Pacific designs had been replaced by native New Zealand adzes (Figure 15.9), barbed fishhooks, and other innovations. Maori culture itself can be identified as early as the fifteenth century; during the classical period, agricultural surpluses resulted in the accumulation of wealth. Unlike Polynesia, where religion was a strong unifying force, the Maori diverted their attentions to warfare (Figure 15.10). Under the leadership of powerful chiefs who measured their prestige in terms of war, the Maori built large fortified encampments of *pa's*, protected with earthworks. Their obsession with warfare is thought to have resulted from pressure on cleared agricultural land, caused by rapidly increasing population densities and a shortage of adult male labor for forest clearance.[28]

A.D. 1400

Maori material culture included a wide variety of weapons as well as a vigorous artistic tradition, which was reflected especially in canoe ornamentation. The earliest explorers and white settlers found the Maori to be formidable opponents who resisted the annexation of their lands and the process of colonization with ferocity. The native population was decimated as white settlement took place, but, after the last Maori war ended in 1872, the native population gradually began to assume a happier role in New Zealand society.

A.D. 1872

16

new world agriculture

"The soile is the most plentifull, sweete, fruitfull and wholesome of all the world," enthused Elizabethan sea captain Arthur Barlow of Virginia in 1584. He tells us that the Indians raised three crops of maize a year from North American soil, remarkable testimony to the skill of indigenous farmers. An impressive array of New World plants had been cultivated by the early Americans before the arrival of the European voyagers. Some American staples such as maize, manioc (often called cassava, a root crop), potatoes, and tobacco rapidly passed into Old World economies, just as European crops took hold in the New World.

american agriculture

Much archaeological inquiry has been devoted to the origins of American agriculture (Table 16.1). Diffusionist hypotheses have been particularly fashionable. The Egyptians and the Israelites, among others, have been held responsible for the introduction of agriculture to the Americas. In fact, however, the Indians domesticated such a range of native New World plants that an Old World origin for American agriculture seems impossible. A long period of systematic experimentation with domesticable plants leading to the deliberate cultivation of cereal and root crops occurred separately in the New World.

The differences between New World and Old World food production are striking. Old World farmers were able to tame herds of wild goats, sheep, and cattle, which were indigenous to much of Asia and Europe. Although mountain goats and sheep are found in the Rockies, they were never tamed. In the Eastern Hemisphere, cattle were used for plowing,

Table 16.1
Early agriculture in the New World.[a]

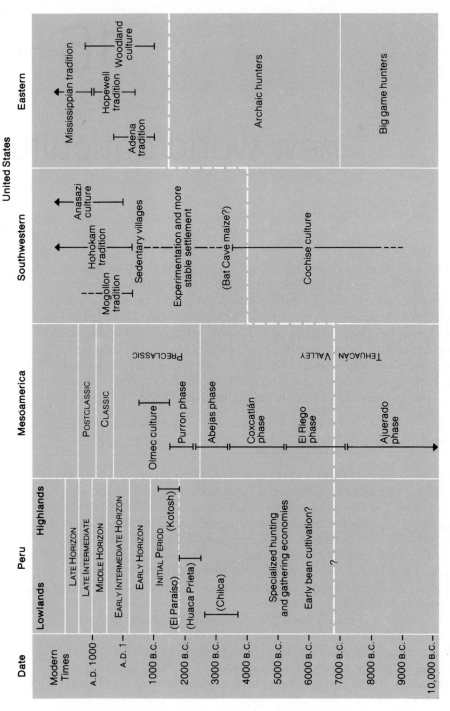

[a]The broken line across the table marks the change from hunting and gathering to agriculture.

riding, and load-carrying. Leather, meat, milk, and wool could be obtained from Old World herds.

In contrast, the pre-Columbian Indians had few domesticated animals to provide a domestic meat supply or to assist with agriculture or load-carrying. The early Peruvians domesticated the llama of the Andes Mountains, prized for its meat and load-carrying abilities. Tame alpacas provided wool. Dogs appear in the Americas, but the domestic fowl, so frequent in Old World villages, was absent, its place taken in North America by the raucous and unruly turkey.[1]* The guinea pig which was also tamed in the Andes served as an excellent substitute for the rabbit.

But American Indians domesticated a remarkable range of plants, nearly all of which are distinctive New World forms indigenous to the Americas. Cotton, gourds, and two or three other crops are common to both the Old World and the New World but were probably domesticated independently. Root crops such as manioc and sweet and white potatoes were particularly important to many Americans, and formed the staple diet for many early South American farming cultures. Chili peppers were grown as hot seasonings, taking the place of mustard and pepper used in the Old World. Among the other edible seeds were amaranth, sunflowers, cacao, peanuts, and several types of beans. Gourds, squashes, pumpkins, and tobacco were in common use. Beans provided an important complement to corn in the farmers' diet.

The most important staple crop of all was Indian corn, properly called maize, the only important wild grass in the New World to be fully domesticated and formed into a staple food crop by the early Americans. It remains the most important single food crop in the Americas today, being used in its over 150 varieties as both food and cattle fodder. One major concern of American archaeology has been to discover the place where maize was first cultivated. Some people believe that maize and other crops were first domesticated in a nuclear area where experimentation was favored, and then were spread to neighboring regions. Others feel that separate experiments were conducted in several localities, with substantial contact between them resulting in the diffusion of agriculture all over the Americas. The latter theory enjoys greater popularity.

Geographer Carl Sauer, who was mentioned in Chapter 15, has also speculated about the origins of New World food production.[2] He makes a fundamental distinction between seed and root agriculture, the latter being predominantly a South American phenomenon and the staple crops being manioc and potatoes. Sauer argues that seed crops were first grown on a larger scale in Mesoamerica, while root crops may have been farmed at an early date in the Caribbean lowlands of South America. Archaeol-

* See pages 397–399 for notes to Chapter 16.

ogists, however, have tended to think that the two major nuclear areas were Mesoamerica and the highlands of the central Andes, because these regions have yielded long and elaborate sequences of human cultures that culminated in sophisticated political and economic confederacies. Field evidence in favor of Sauer's Caribbean hearth is virtually nonexistent, but his hypothesis has hardly been tested.[3]

mesoamerica: tehuacán

During the millennia immediately following the Pleistocene, many different specialized hunting and gathering cultures emerged in the New World. Some were societies for whom gathering was a vital and major element in their diet. Traces of early experimentation with the deliberate growing of such crops as maize and squash have come from a number of regions in Mexico, noticeably from Sierra Madre, Sierra de Tamaulipas, and Tehuacán in Puebla (Figure 16.1).

American archaeologist Richard MacNeish uncovered a remarkable sequence of gathering and farming cultures in the Tehuacán Valley.[4] This dry, highland region contains many caves and open sites and is sufficiently arid to allow the preservation of seeds and organic finds in archaeological deposits. For a number of years MacNeish and his colleagues had been searching for the origins of cultivated maize. Botanist Paul Mangelsdorf had earlier hypothesized that the wild ancestor of maize was a corn covered with a light husk that would have allowed the seeds to disperse at maturity, something man seeks to prevent by breeding the domestic strain with a tougher husk (Figure 16.2).[5]

MacNeish soon found domestic maize cobs dating back to about 3000 B.C. But it was not until he began digging in the small Coxcatlán rockshelter in the Tehuacán Valley that he found maize that met Mangelsdorf's specification. Coxcatlán contained twenty-eight occupation levels, the earliest of which dated to about 10,000 B.C. MacNeish eventually excavated twelve sites in Tehuacán, which gave a wealth of information on the inhabitants of the valley over nearly 12,000 years of prehistory. The cultural terms that follow were devised by him.

The Tehuacán people lived on wild vegetable foods and by hunting for thousands of years, developing economic strategies that involved seasonal emphasis on different wild food sources. Jack rabbits, birds, turtles, and other small animals were hunted or trapped. The hunters collected a variety of wild plants as they came into season at different times of the year. MacNeish named this phase of Tehuacán's history, which dates from approximately 10,000 to 7200 B.C., the "Ajuereado." Only occasionally did the Ajuereado people kill any of the extinct horses or deer whose

Ajuereado
10,000–
7200 B.C.

Figure 16.1
Archaeological sites and culture areas mentioned in Chapter 16.

bones occur in some caves. The inhabitants of Tehuacán were already forced to rely on more intensive exploitation of vegetable foods.

About 7200 B.C. plant foods began to become increasingly significant. Hunting was de-emphasized in favor of the intensive collecting of plant foods. During the dry season, small camps of these "El Riego" people camped throughout the valley, exploiting such vegetable foods as were edible. During the rains, families came together in larger bands when more food was available. Milling and grinding stones assumed a greater

El Riego
7200–
5200 B.C.

importance in the toolkit. The people collected squashes, chili peppers, and avocados; some of these may have been cultivated sporadically.

Coxcatlán
5200–
3400 B.C.

Several important changes took place in the "Coxcatlán" phase, which lasted from 5200 to 3400 B.C. The Coxcatlán people cultivated a long list of plants, including maize, amaranth, beans, squashes, and chilis. Gathering and hunting were still practiced, since only 10 percent of their diet came from cultivated gardens. Settlements were more permanent and larger. Maize cobs found at Coxcatlán are still strongly reminiscent of the hypothesized wild ancestor of wild corn and may have been partially domesticated (Figure 16.2).

Abejas
3400–
2300 B.C.

The following "Abejas" phase lasted from 3400 to 2300 B.C. and was the one during which agriculture finally became firmly established. Up to 30 percent of Tehuacán's food supply came from domestic sources,

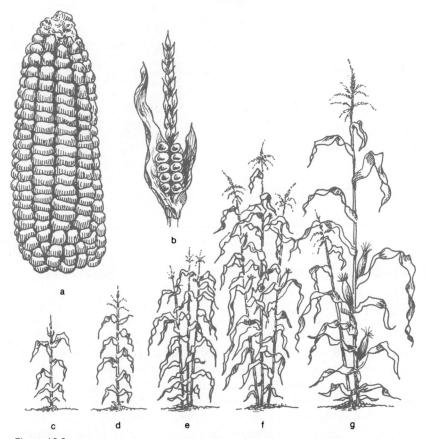

Figure 16.2
The development of maize: (a) a typical ear of modern maize; (b) probable appearance of extinct wild maize; (c–g) evolution of the domesticated maize plant.

including maize cobs which were larger than those of Coxcatlán and were clearly the descendants of the earlier wild strains. The people lived in far more permanent settlements, many of which were sited on river terraces where more suitable conditions for agriculture occurred. Most folk were firmly anchored by their agriculture and were dependent on their crops to a far greater extent than their predecessors.

About 2300 B.C., the "Purron" phase began, which was remarkable for the first making of clay pots in Tehuacán. During the next eight hundred years the inhabitants of the valley became completely dependent on agriculture, while their hunting and gathering declined to insignificant proportions. Soon afterward, more complex village settlements are found, as well as the first religious structures. Tehuacán was gradually drawn into the fabric of Mesoamerican civilization (see Chapter 22).

Purron
2300 B.C.

The sequence of events at Tehuacán is by no means unique, for other peoples were also experimenting with new crops. Other hybrid forms of maize are found in Tehuacán sites, forms which were not grown locally and can only have been introduced from outside. Dry caves elsewhere in northern Mesoamerica have paralleled the cultural events in Tehuacán. Before 5000 B.C., gourds, peppers, and squashes were domesticated, while beans were tamed soon afterward and maize was fully domesticated around 3000 B.C.[6]

Plant domestication in Mesoamerica was not so much an invention in one small locality as a shift in ecological adaptation deliberately chosen by peoples living in regions where economic strategies necessitated intensive exploitation of vegetable foods as large game became extinct and more arid conditions occurred at the end of the Pleistocene.

Cultural progress was rapid once maize cultivation became a foundation of economic life. By 1000 B.C., agriculture was well established in the valley of Mexico, which was at that time partly filled by a great lake surrounded by prosperous villages. The villagers were cultivating maize, beans, and squashes by using stone axes and digging sticks. They hunted deer, peccary, small birds, and rodents. Pottery was in use. Plant gathering still remained a major feature of village life. By 400 B.C., shrines and ceremonial centers were being built in the villages, the shrines often being placed on earthen mounds. We find emerging some motivating force or political power, which encouraged both communal works and powerful religious cooperation.

early agriculture in coastal peru

A parallel move toward food production took place in Peru and probably elsewhere in South America as well.[7] The archaeology of Peru is better

Table 16.2
Approximate times of the domestication of some plants in the New World.[a]

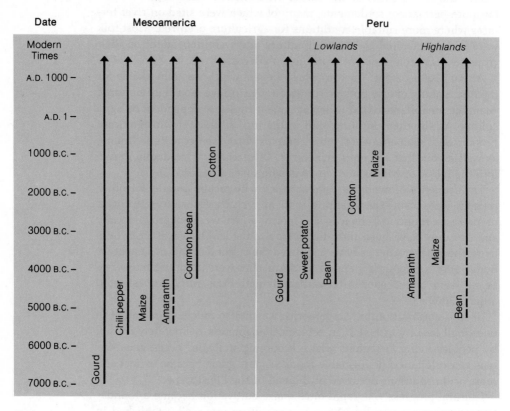

[a]Broken lines indicate possibly earlier chronological ranges.

known than that of other South American countries, which accounts for the greater abundance of dates for early agriculture there (Table 16.2).

The Peruvian coast forms a narrow shelf at the foot of the Andes, crossed by small river valleys that descend from the mountains to the sea. These valleys are a series of oases in the desert plain, with deep, rich soils and blooming vegetation where water is plentiful. For thousands of years Peruvians have cultivated these valley floors, building their settlements, pyramids, and palaces at the edges of their agricultural land. Since preservation conditions in this arid country are quite exceptional, the archaeological record is correspondingly complete.

A great array of crops was grown in these valleys, including maize, manioc, beans, squashes, and cotton, sometimes using very limited irrigation. An agricultural diet was supplemented by the immensely rich sea

life of the Peruvian coast, which fed on the plankton of the cold Humboldt
current. In both highlands and lowlands, effective exploitation of small
basin and valley environments led to the growth of population, intensive
gathering, and greater social and cultural complexity in fertile areas.[8]

Between about 4200 and 2500 B.C., Peruvian coastal peoples depended
on marine resources — fish, sea birds, and mollusks — for much of their
diet. During the warmest and driest climatic period after the Pleistocene,
the coastal people tended to move closer to the shore, dwelling in larger
and more stable settlements. Concomitant with the shift to more permanent coastal dwelling was the development of sophisticated equipment
for deep-sea fishing. 4200–
2500 B.C.

A typical coastal camp of this period flourished at Chilca, 45 miles
(72 km.) south of present-day Lima. Frederic Engel excavated a series of
refuse heaps there and radiocarbon dated the earlier Chilca occupation
between 3800 and 2650 B.C.[9] When the site was in use, it probably lay
near a reedy marsh, which provided both matting and building materials
as well as suitable sites for small gardens. The Chilca people lived off
sea mollusks, fish, and sea lions; they apparently hunted few land mammals. They cultivated jack and lima beans, gourds, and squashes, probably depending on river floods as well as rainfall for their simple agriculture. Chilca
3800–
2650 B.C.

One remarkable Chilca house was uncovered: a circular structure, it
had a dome-like frame of canes bound with rope and then covered with
bundles of grass (Figure 16.3), and the interior was braced with bones
from stranded whales. Seven burials had been deposited in the house
before it was intentionally collapsed on top of them. The skeletons were
wrapped in mats and all buried at the same time, perhaps in consequence
of an epidemic.

Chilca toolkits are poorly preserved. They include fishhooks of bone
and cactus spines, and some simple shell beads. Other coastal sites of
this period have yielded further burials, traces of squashes, gourds, and
chili peppers. The diet was strongly maritime in emphasis; the transition
to fully sedentary agriculture was still in the future.

The succeeding millennia of coastal history saw the establishment of
many permanent settlements near the ocean; the people combined agriculture with fishing and mollusk-gathering. Domesticated cotton first
appears somewhere around 2500 B.C. Squashes, peppers, lima beans, and
other crops remained as staple foods until recent times. Maize and other
basic foods were still unknown. Agriculture remained a secondary activity much later than it did in Mesoamerica. 2500 B.C.

One later site is Huaca Prieta, a sedentary village that housed several
hundred people on the north coast of Peru between 2500 and 1800 B.C.[10]
The vast Huaca Prieta refuse mound contains small one- or two-room 2500–
1800 B.C.

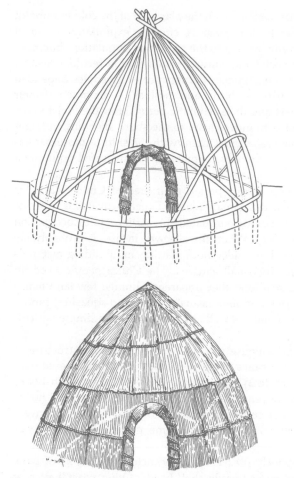

Figure 16.3
A reconstruction of a Chilca house. (After Donan.)

houses built partially into the ground and roofed with timber or whale-bone beams. In addition to domesticated plants, some wild seeds were also gathered. Nets weighted with stone sinkers were used for fishing. The inhabitants of Huaca Prieta were remarkably skillful cotton weavers who devised a sophisticated art style with animal, human, and geometric designs.

Maize makes its first appearance on the coast at Playa Culebras, another important and contemporary settlement south of Huaca Prieta.[11] Playa Culebras and other settlements show a greater emphasis on permanent architecture, not only in the form of domestic buildings but also as large ceremonial structures. A whole complex of stone and mud mortar platforms lies at El Paraíso on the floodplain of the Chillón Valley, some distance from the sea. At least one mound was a series of complexes of interconnected rooms built in successive stages. Settlements such as El Paraíso were obviously dependent on agriculture to a greater extent than earlier sites. By the time the temple complexes were built there, after 1800 B.C., loom-woven textiles and pottery had come into widespread use. All the major food plants that formed the basis of later Peruvian civilization were now in use.

1800 B.C.

the andean highlands

We know little about the early history of agriculture in the Andes, for we lack the excavations on dry sites that have yielded such riches in Mesoamerica and on the Peruvian coast. The highlands were certainly the center of domestication of beans as early as 6000 B.C. as well as the native white potato. Maize was early an important crop in the Andes. Llamas were probably domesticated at an early date.

Of importance for the study of early agriculture is the Kotosh site near Huanuco, in a temperate climate about 6000 feet above sea level.[12] Two large mounds dominate Kotosh. They consist of a mass of superimposed buildings reaching a total height of 13 meters (43 ft.). The earliest level in one mound contained a temple built on a small platform. Its stone and mud mortar walls were plastered with clay. This initial stage of Kotosh occupation has been named the "Mito" phase and was overlain by a later occupation which included pottery dating to between 1800 and 1140 B.C. The earliest occupants of Kotosh used flaked projectile heads, polished stone axes, and various tools of bone. Some charred seeds came from the temple buildings, but have not yet been identified. The presence of temples and other substantial structures at Kotosh is a sure sign that the inhabitants were dependent on agriculture, as substantial food surpluses would have been needed to support the labor of building them.

Mito
1800–
1140 B.C.

The story of early agriculture in the highlands will eventually come from the deposits of caves and other settlements where the necessary botanical information awaits discovery. A critical issue for South American agriculture is the interchange of newly domesticated plants between the highland and lowland areas of the continent. For example, maize is much older in Mesoamerica than in Peru. Its domesticated form appears in Mexican caves by 3400 B.C., but does not occur on the Peruvian coast until about 2000 B.C. While the highlands, lying within the original natural habitat of wild corn, may have been an early center of maize domestication, it is equally likely that the crop was brought to the Andes in about

2000 B.C. and crossed with local wild forms. Whatever happened, however, the new crop was certainly diffused rapidly to the coast and other parts of the continent. Domestic corn evolved rapidly in South America, for the distinctive Peruvian varieties were soon diffused northward to Mesoamerica, and have been found in archaeological deposits there.

early farmers in north america: the southwest

By 4000 B.C., the southwestern portions of the United States were populated by hunters and gatherers whose culture was oriented toward desert living. A distinctive Archaic hunting and gathering culture known as the Cochise flourished in southeastern Arizona and southwestern New Mexico from about 9000 B.C. onward.[13] The Cochise people gathered a wide range of plant foods, including yucca seeds, cacti, and sunflower seeds. They used small milling stones, basketry, cordage, nets, and spearthrowers. Many features of their material culture survived into later times, when cultivated plants were introduced into the Southwest.

Cochise
9000 B.C.

The Bat Cave in New Mexico contained primitive pod corn in levels estimated to date to as early as 3500 B.C.[14] Later horizons have yielded more advanced maize cobs, as if the same evolutionary development of corn was taking place in Cochise country as in Tehuacán and other Mexican localities. Gathering, however, remained a major economic activity. Cochise sites are centered in upland valleys, whose ecology is somewhat similar to that of Tehuacán.

?3500 B.C.

By 300 B.C., local experimentation and the introduction of new hybrid varieties of maize from the south had led to sedentary villages and much greater dependence on farming. The Mogollon cultural tradition was based on agriculture, had its roots in the Cochise, and acquired pottery from other cultures. At least five stages of the Mogollon have been identified in New Mexico, the earliest beginning about 300 B.C., the fifth ending about A.D. 1350.[15] The Mogollon tradition arose from a grafting of simple agricultural methods onto an earlier gathering economy, and is well known from dry caves in New Mexico. Mogollons were skillful basket and blanket makers. Their toolkit included milling stones, carrying nets, digging sticks, bows and arrows, and characteristic brown pottery. Timber-framed houses covered with mats were normally built in shallow pits, with a narrow pathway serving as an entrance (Figure 16.4). Many Mogollon villages were occupied for long periods of time.

Mogollon
300 B.C.–
A.D. 1350

The Hohokam tradition was contemporary with the Mogollon in Arizona, was also derived from the Cochise, and shared many features with the Mogollon. Hohokam is divided into at least four major stages, begin-

Hohokam
300 B.C.

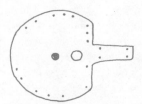

Figure 16.4
  Mogollon house built in a sunken pit, with a sloping path entrance, from the Harris
  Village site, New Mexico.

ning about 300 B.C. Its architecture is distinct from that of Mogollon, with rectangular houses built in pits; the pole framework of the houses were covered with small branches and grass. Many Hohokam sites are concentrated in the Salt and Gila river valleys, arid desert territory where irrigation works were essential for even simple farming. Before A.D. 800, Hohokam peoples built elaborate irrigation ditches, the most sophisticated in North America, which may have originated, like so many other aspects of Hohokam architecture and material culture, in Mesoamerica, with which they traded constantly.[16]

 The most extensive southwestern farming culture is the Anasazi, which was centered in the "Four Corners" area where Utah, Arizona, Colorado, and New Mexico meet. Many people are familiar with the Anasazi from such spectacular settlements as Mesa Verde and Pueblo Bonito. The roots of Anasazi came from the spread of new economies and cultural traits from the south. As early as 1924, Alfred Kidder proposed subdividing the Anasazi culture into eight stages, a classification based on both pottery and other artifacts.[17] Its earliest stages consist of little more than the addition of maize and squashes, brown pottery, and distinctive log-and-mud-mortar dwellings built against cliffs in the earlier, Archaic hunting tradition. Anasazi began about 2,000 years ago, flourishing until modern times. By about A.D. 700 the basic Anasazi settlement pattern had evolved to the point where above-the-ground houses were being substituted for the pit dwellings of earlier centuries. The latter developed into kivas, subterranean ceremonial structures that were a feature of every large village. Large settlements of contiguous dwellings became the rule after A.D. 900, with clusters of "rooms" serving as the homes of separate families or lineages. Large settlements like Pueblo Bonito developed around A.D. 1100, the latter a huge D-shaped complex of 800 rooms rising several stories high around the rim of the arc (Figure 16.5). Kivas and two large plazas were distinctive features of this remarkable settlement.[18]

 The Anasazi enjoyed a relatively elaborate material culture at the height of their prosperity, and made a distinctive white and black pottery,

A.D. 800
or earlier

Anasazi
A.D. 1

A.D. 700

A.D. 1100

Figure 16.5
Pueblo Bonito, New Mexico, was the first site to be dated by tree-ring chronology, to A.D. *919–1130.*

well-formed baskets, and fine sandals. Their distinctive architecture was neither very sophisticated nor particularly innovative. Baked mud and rocks were formed into box-like rooms; a roof of mud rested on horizontal timbers. Room after room was added, as the need arose, using local raw materials and a simple architectural style that was entirely appropriate for its environment.

In the Southwest we find a continuity of farming culture from its very beginnings up to modern times, the only changes being a rapid growth in population, some enrichment of material culture and ceremonial life, and modifications to farming patterns as the population increased. When overpopulation forced families to move to new areas, water was diverted onto fertile soils. The success of the southwestern farmer was due to his skillful use of limited water resources. Soil and water were brought to-

Modern Times

gether by careful damming of drainage streams, floodwater irrigation, and a variety of other water distribution systems. Planting techniques were carefully adapted to desert conditions and short water supplies, resulting in a myriad of tiny gardens supplying the food supply of each family or lineage.

Despite some large settlements and some evidence of organized social life in the form of kivas and irrigation works, the southwesterners never developed the powerful state governments that typified their southern contemporaries in Mesoamerica or their eastern neighbors.

eastern cultivators

As in the West, innovations such as horticulture and pottery were grafted onto the Archaic hunting traditions that had proved so efficient in the eastern United States for many thousands of years (Figure 16.6). These new culture traits made little immediate difference in Archaic ways, for the transition to new economies occurs almost imperceptibly. The appearance of "grit-tempered" pottery has been taken to be an arbitrary archaeological yardstick to signal the end of the Archaic and the beginnings of the "Woodland," a generalized term used to refer to farming sites with pottery and burial mounds in the East.[19] Traces of vegetable foods in early Woodland sites are few and far between, but during the first millennium B.C. maize cultivation began to take hold, probably an introduction from the Southwest and Mexico. Tobacco smoking and weaving were other culture traits of foreign origin. Perhaps some crops such as the sunflower had been independently domesticated in the East before maize arrived. We also find the Woodland people beginning to make pottery and building large burial mounds by 1000 B.C. or slightly later.

2500 B.C.

Woodland
1000–
600 B.C.

At least three broad subdivisions of Woodland have been distinguished in the Midwest and East. One well-known tradition is the Adena centered in southern Ohio, southeastern Indiana, northern Kentucky, West Virginia, and southeastern Pennsylvania. This tradition thrived for a thousand years from about 1000 B.C. (Figure 16.7). A somewhat later development was the Hopewell, which had a distribution in southern Ohio, Illinois, and the Mississippi Valley sometime after 400 B.C. Hopewell artifacts also extend eastward into New York State.[20]

Adena
?1000 B.C.–
A.D. 200

Hopewell
400 B.C.–
A.D. 1000

Both the Adena and Hopewell groups based much of their religious life around elaborate burials and the after life. The most elaborate Adena burials were deposited in open graves for a while. Later the bones were painted brightly before being buried in a tomb under a large earthen mound. The Hopewell people were both gardeners and hunters who ex-

Their rype corne.

Their greene corne

Corne newly sprong.

Their sitting at meate.

The place of solemne prayer

The house wherin the Tombe of their Herounds standeth.

SEGOTON

A Ceremony in their prayers with strange testures and songes dansing abowt posts carued on the topps lyke mens faces.

0 ——— 8 Ft.

0 ——— 2.5 M.

Figure 16.7
A reconstruction of an Adena house, based on the post-hole pattern shown at left.

ploited large and small game as well as fish and mollusks and cultivated maize, especially on river floodplains. Extensive trading networks carried raw materials and Hopewell artifacts all over the eastern United States. In this way, hammered copper ornaments from the Lake Superior region were distributed all over the southeast.

Around A.D. 1000 a new eastern farming tradition, the Mississippian, emerged, at least in part, from Woodland roots.[21] The Mississippian reached its greatest development in the Mississippi Valley, and extended into southeastern Missouri, southern Illinois, Georgia, Alabama, and Kentucky. The influence of this more advanced culture, however, was felt over a much wider area. Some Mississippians lived in larger towns that were centered around conspicuous rectangular temple mounds and large open spaces; this reflecting a major concern with religious and ceremonial matters (Figure 16.8). The summits of large earthen mounds

Mississippian A.D. 1000– Modern Times

Figure 16.6
Eastern American agriculture (opposite). The celebrated sixteenth-century artist John White's drawing of the Indian village of Secoton on the Atlantic seaboard in North Carolina. Note the hunters at top left and the cornfields in three stages of growth on the right. This picture first appeared in Thomas Hariot's A briefe and True Report of the New Found Land of Virginia, published in London in 1590.

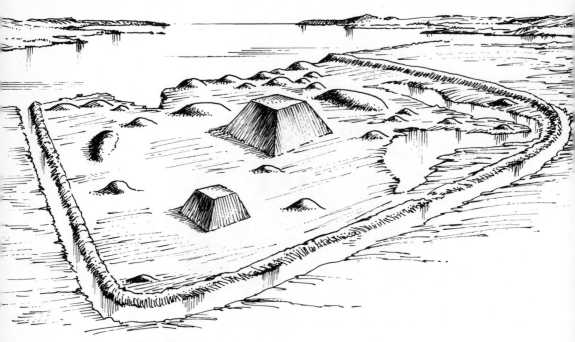

Figure 16.8
Mississippian mound group at Holy Bluff, Mississippi — an artist's impression of the complex.

were capped with temples built of timber and thatch, surprisingly modest buildings given the size of some of the mounds. The most impressive manifestation of Mississippian culture is centered around vast mound complexes like Cahokia in East St. Louis, Illinois.[22]

The Mississippians had few technological advantages over their predecessors. Their leaders seem to have had the political capacity to organize huge earthwork projects involving hundreds, if not thousands, of people. They developed a distinctive art style that features lively representations of dancing figures, snakes, and humans.

The Mesoamerican connections with Mississippian ceremonial centers are undeniable. The great mounds, the elaborate temples built on them, and some features of their art recall Mexican notions and traditions. But the causes of such influences must remain a matter of speculation. They may have resulted from the initial influence of a few foreigners with strong religious charisma who drastically modified the social structure of many peasant societies in the Midwest. While such theories are attractive, it is only fair to say that no Mesoamerican artifacts have come from Mississippian settlements.

A Mississippian ceremonial center would have been an imposing sight, the great mounds capped by thatch-roofed temples dominating the river floodplain for miles around. Carved figures stood on the temple roofs, looking down on the plaza where dances, ball games, and other ceremonies were held. The countryside around the plaza was dotted with villages set in the midst of cultivated plots. A large farming population supplemented extensive slash-and-burn agriculture with hunting, fishing, and gathering — a mode of subsistence that survived with little modification until the arrival of the Pilgrim Fathers.

In the early eighteenth century, French explorers witnessed the funeral rites of Tattooed-serpent, a Natchez chief whose culture had its origins in the Mississippian.[23] At least six people, including his two wives, his doctor, and a servant were ritually strangled during the burial and mourning ceremonies. Tattooed-serpent was buried inside the temple with his wives, the remainder of the victims outside it or in local shrines. The chief's house was burned as soon as he was buried.

Modern Times

By this time, Natchez culture was changing, and the burial ceremonies of Tattooed-serpent were probably a pale imitation of those of earlier chiefs. But the religious institutions of the Mississippian survived into modern times among such tribes as the Creek and the Choctaw, supported by the constant and arduous labor of thousands of farmers.

*"The great tide of civilization has long since ebbed,
leaving these scattered wrecks on the solitary shore.
Are those waters to flow again, bringing back the seeds
of knowledge and of wealth that they have wafted
to the West? We wanderers were seeking what they had left
behind, as children gather up the coloured shells
on the deserted sands."   Austen Henry Layard*

IV
cities
and civilizations

17

civilization:
the problem of causes

There is no particular, exact moment at which civilization first appears in world history. Indeed, every society has its own concept of civilization. The ultimate origins of Western civilization, if defined by literacy and a preference for urban life, go back to the very beginnings of towns and city-states in Egypt and Mesopotamia. In terms of human history, the most important consequences of urban life were in the political and social spheres. With the emergence of urban societies the ground rules of human life were so rapidly changed that for the first time one of the major problems of the twentieth-century world appeared — a deep gulf of misunderstanding between the man who lives comfortably in a city and the peasant society upon which he relies for his food and ultimately his survival.

Why did man begin to congregate in larger communities and city-states, institutions that are basically parasitic, dependent on farming societies for grain supplies, meat, and raw materials? Before looking at different early civilizations we should pause to examine the problem of causes.

Everyone who has studied the prehistory of human society agrees that the emergence of civilization in different parts of the world was a major event in human progress. The world "civilization" has a ready, everyday meaning. It implies "civility," a measure of decent behavior that is widely accepted as the mask of a "civilized" person. Such definitions of civility are inevitably ethnocentric or in the form of value judgments. They are hardly useful to students of prehistoric civilizations concerned with basic definitions and causes.

Although there are almost as many definitions of civilization as there are archaeologists, most scholars consider civilization a stage of human cultural development, one that has dimensions of time and space and is defined by its artifacts and other cultural attributes. But civilization differs from other archaeological culture groupings in that it has certain special attributes. Such attributes have been the subject of intense debate and speculation for at least a century.

a search for cause and process: the urban revolution

Notions of human progress have lurked behind explanations for the emergence of civilization and urban life ever since the days of Herbert Spencer in the nineteenth century. Victorian anthropologists thought of their own civilization as the ultimate pinnacle of human progress, with the hunter-gatherers at the base of the pyramid of progress. Evolution has continued to dominate much thinking about the origins of civilization, for many anthropologists have sought to discover a single process that would explain the development of complex societies. One approach has been to look for regularities between early civilizations that developed in broadly similar environments like those of the Near East and the Nile, for example. (See Figure 17.1.)

Diffusionists, on the other hand, have sought to derive all civilization from a common source, normally centered in Ancient Egypt (Chapter 2). Such explanations, dramatized perhaps by the *Kon-Tiki* and the *Ra* expeditions, are much less fashionable than they were thirty years ago. Diffusionist theories are just too simplistic to describe the complex evidence for early civilization in such widely separated areas as China, the Near East, and Mesoamerica.

One of the pioneer attempts to define the criteria of civilization was that of V. Gordon Childe. He postulated an Urban Revolution centered around the development of the city, a densely populated settlement whose farmers supported a small army of craftsmen, priests, and traders with massive food surpluses. "The first step towards escape from the rigid limits of . . . barbarism was the establishment of a metallurgical industry . . . that not only provided farmers with superior tools and weapons, but . . . overturned the barbarian social order, based on kinship, and evoked a new population of full-time specialists. The latter is my excuse for calling it the Urban Revolution."[1]* Childe argued that the techniques of mining, smelting, and casting were far more exacting than the normal

* See page 399 for notes to Chapter 17.

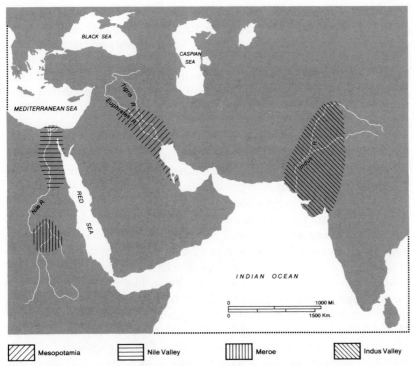

Figure 17.1
  The location of the four major areas of urban civilization discussed in Chapters 18–19.

tasks of the peasant farmer. Thus, full-time craftsmen were essential, and they were supported by the food surpluses of the peasants. The products of the craftsmen had to be distributed, and raw materials obtained from outside sources, reducing the self-reliance of peasant societies. Agricultural techniques became more sophisticated as an increased yield of food per capita was needed to support the nonagricultural population. Irrigation increased productivity, leading to centralized control of food supplies and the mechanisms of production and distribution. Taxation and tribute led to the accumulation of capital. A new class-stratified society emerged. Writing was essential for record-keeping and the development of exact and predictive sciences. Transportation by water and land was part of the new order. A unifying religious force dominated urban life as priest-kings and despots rose to power. Monumental architecture testified to their activities.

Gordon Childe thought of the Urban Revolution as a critical point in a gradual process of cultural, economic, and social change. The notion of an Urban Revolution dominated archaeological and historical literature for years. But the revolution hypothesis has serious flaws as an all-embracing definition of civilization and an explanation of its causes. Childe's criteria are far from universal. Some highly effective and long-lasting civilizations like those of the Maya and the Mycenaeans never had cities.[2] The Maya, for example, built elaborate ceremonial and religious centers that were surrounded by a scattered rural population clustered for the most part in small villages. Writing is absent from the Inca civilization of Peru. The Mayan and Aztec scripts seem to have been little more than devices for administering an elaborate calendar. While a degree of craft specialization and religious structure is typical of most civilizations, it cannot be said that these can form the basis for an overall definition of civilization.

American archaeologist Robert Adams has stressed the importance of the development of social organization and craft specialization during the Urban Revolution. He has raised a number of objections to the Childe hypothesis, arguing that the term implies an undue emphasis on the city at the expense of social change — the development of social classes and political institutions. Many of Child's criteria, like the evolution of the exact sciences, have the disadvantage of being not readily preserved in the archaeological record. Furthermore, Childe's Urban Revolution was identified by lists of traits, although the term implies an emphasis on the *processes* of cultural change through time. Childe considered technological innovations and subsistence patterns to be at the core of the Urban Revolution. Adams oriented his work toward changes in social organization; he described early Mesopotamia and central Mexico as following "a fundamental course of development in which corporate kin groups, originally preponderating in the control of land, were gradually supplemented by the growth of private estates in the hand of urban elites."[3] The eventual result was a stratified form of social organization rigidly divided along class lines.

irrigation — a potential cause?

Most scholars now agree that three common elements on Childe's list seem to have been of great importance in the growth of all the world's civilizations. The first was the creation of food surpluses, used to support new economic classes whose members were not directly engaged in food production. Agriculture as a way of life immediately necessitates the storage of crops to support the community during the lean times of the year. The creation of a surplus over and above this level of production resulted both from increased agricultural efficiency and from changes in the social and cultural spheres as well. Specialist craftsmen, priests, and traders were among the new classes of society to come into being as a result.

Second, agricultural economies probably became more diversified as the subsistence base was widened. The first inhabitants of Mesopotamia did not rely on cereal crops alone for their livelihood. Fishing and hunting were vital parts of the economy, domestic animals assisting with plowing and transport and providing clothing and fertilizer as well as meat. The ancient Egyptians relied on husbandry, especially in the Nile Delta. The diversity of food resources not only protected the people against the dangers of famine but also stimulated the development of trade and exchange mechanisms for food and other products and the growth of distributive organizations that encouraged centralized authority.

The third significant development was intensive land use, which probably increased the total agricultural output. Intensive agriculture is normally taken to imply irrigation, often hailed as one fundamental reason for the emergence of civilization. Archaeologists have long debated the significance of irrigation to the origin of urban life. Julian Steward and Karl Wittfogel, for example, have argued that the emergence of irrigation was connected with the development of stratified societies.[4] The state bureaucracy had a monopoly over hydraulic facilities; in other words, the social requirements of irrigation led to the development of states and urban societies. Robert Adams takes a contrary view.[5] He feels that the introduction of great irrigation works was more a consequence than a cause of the appearance of dynastic state organizations, however much the requirements of large-scale irrigation subsequently may have influenced the development of bureaucratic organizations.

Adams's view is based on studies of prehistoric irrigation in Mesopotamia, as well as observations of irrigation in smaller-scale societies. Large-scale irrigation had its roots in simpler beginnings, perhaps based on simple cooperation between neighboring communities to dam streams and divert water into fields where precious seeds were sown. The Northern Paiute of eastern California diverted mountain streams into ditches several miles long. The Hohokam of the Southwest built hundreds of miles of large canals that served different communities. Such comparatively simple irrigation schemes, while often on a large scale, are a different proposition from the elaborate networks of canals needed by the city-states in Mesopotamia.

The floodplain of the Tigris and the Euphrates rivers, with its long, harsh summers could only be cultivated by irrigation canals, canals that had to be dug deep enough to carry water even when the rivers were at their lowest levels. No means of lifting water was developed until Assyrian times, so the earliest inhabitants of the delta were obliged to dig their canals very deep and to keep them that way. Silting, blockage, and flooding were constant dangers, requiring enormous expenditures of man-hours to keep the canals in working order. In terms of man-hours, it paid the earliest delta farmers to live within a limited geographical area where canal digging was kept to an essential minimum. But even then the organization of the digging work would have required some centralized authority and certainly more restructuring of social life than the simple intercommunity cooperation typical of many smaller agricultural societies who used irrigation.

The construction and maintenance of small-scale canals requires no elaborate social organization nor population resources larger than those of a single community, or several communities acting in cooperation. Large-scale irrigation requires technical and social resources of a quite different order. Huge labor forces had to be mobilized, organized, and fed. Maintenance and supervision require constant attention, as do water distribution and the resolution of disputes over water rights. Those living downstream are at the mercy of those upstream, so large-scale irrigation works are only viable as long as those who enjoy them remain within the same political unit. A formal state structure with an administrative elite is essential to irrigation on this scale.

Robert Adams has found that there was little change in settlement patterns in Mesopotamia between prehistoric times and the end of the third millennium B.C. or even later.[6] Irrigation was conducted on a small-scale basis. Natural channels were periodically cleaned and straightened; only small-scale artificial feeder canals were built. Maximum use was made of the natural hydrology of the rivers. Most settlement was confined to the immediate vicinity of major watercourses. Irrigation was organized through individual peoples. Large-scale artificial canalization did not take place in Akkad until after the rule of Hammurabi (c. 1790 B.C.), or even in Sumer until Early Dynastic times, long after the emergence of urban life. The same is true of ancient Egypt, where large-scale artificial canal construction seems to have been the culmination of a long process of evolution of intensive agriculture. Adams also claims that the local and small-scale terracing and irrigation led to the gradual evolution of large-scale irrigation in north coast Peru, but he admits that his data are inadequate.

In summary, irrigation seems to have played a lesser role in the development of urban life and city-states than has sometimes been alleged. Its beginnings, like so many human endeavors, were on a small scale. But, as Malthus pointed out in his famous *Essay on Population*, there is obviously a relationship between density of population and food supplies. This relationship is not necessarily as simple as the Malthusian explanation, but an increased food supply undeniably permits population growth. The gradual evolution of irrigation techniques to a large-scale, state-controlled operation was, to some degree, a logical outcome of small-scale hydrological operations.

a systems approach to civilization

Everyone seems to agree that the emergence of civilization was a gradual process during a period of major economic and social change. Childe's Urban Revolution is now seen as an operating definition that does not apply to all civilizations. Many have fallen back on quite arbitrary working definitions of urban life and civilization like that proposed by American anthropologist Clyde Kluckhohn: towns of 5,000 people or more, a written language, and monumental ceremonial centers. This is the working definition we use in *Men of the Earth,* similar in intent to the arbitrary terms of reference for different settlement types which appear in the Glossary.[7]

British archaeologist Colin Renfrew has chosen to take the matter further, to search for what he calls "something more central to the idea of civilization than a mere choice of its symptoms."[8] In other words, he is looking for the essential "flavor" of a civilization, that distinctive zest that we encounter when visiting a strange country or eating in a foreign restaurant. He drew attention to a paragraph written by that great scholar of Near Eastern archaeology Henri Frankfort: "The individuality of a civilization, its recognizable character, its identity which is maintained through the successive stages of its existence . . . we recognize in it a certain . . . consistency in its orientation, a certain cultural 'style' which shapes its political and judicial institutions as well as its morals. I propose to call this elusive identity of civilization its form. It is the form which is never destroyed, although it changes in course of time."[9] We are all familiar with the "form" of our own civilization, an intangible feeling we have about our own institutions, however much we admire or detest them.

Renfrew, in a long analysis of Minoan and Mycenaean civilization, has developed a potentially unifying concept to explain what we mean by civilization and what different civilizations have in common. He sees "the process of the growth of a civilization as the gradual creation by man of a larger and more complex environment . . . whereas the savage hunter lives in an environment not so different in many ways from that of other animals . . . civilized man lives in an environment very much of his own creation. Civilization, in this sense, is the self-made environment of man, which he has fashioned to insulate himself from the primeval environment of nature alone."[10]

Mankind's artifacts are intermediaries between man and his natural environment. Renfrew speaks of a "web of culture so complex and dense" that most of man's activities now relate to an artificial environment rather than the natural one. He then goes on to develop a systems approach to the emergence of civilization. American archaeologist Kent V. Flannery was among the first to apply systems theory concepts to archaeological data in an important paper on Mesoamerican agriculture, in which he described five food procurement systems in terms of the mechanisms that regulated them.[11] Renfrew, like Lewis Binford, Flannery, and others, regards human culture as a system or part of a system.

The components of the system are the members of the society involved, their artifacts, and natural objects in the environment. Each interacts with the others, the limits of the system being defined arbitrarily. The systems approach emphasizes the interrelationship between man and his environment, allowing for man-made changes in the environment as well as for natural change. Renfrew describes five interconnected subsystems of interacting elements that make up his overall cultural system: subsistence, technology, social behavior, symbolic expression (religion, art, language, science), and trade and communication.

When a culture is not changing, its subsystems are in a state of equilibrium. Each subsystem is self-regulating. It will stabilize and react to a sudden development like a dry year or famine or crop failure, but in the main a continuity and a coherence are maintained, which result in the inheritance of behavior by succeeding generations. This is a fundamental cause of innate conservatism in human society.

Renfrew argues that civilization is the result of innovation that became part of normal human behavior: "In seeking to explain civilization we are seeking to analyze how and why man's total environment changed and how he came to produce the artificial environment which encompasses man in every dimension of his existence." The natures of innovations are such that they grow all the time, like mutations in living organisms. Their appearance is not critical, but the response of human society is, for if the innovation is rejected there is no change. If it is accepted, then future change along related lines is more likely. "Conventional" behavior that controls the mechanisms of all societies successfully inhibits much innovation, a large part of it, of course, disadvantageous to society.

Renfrew points out that changes in one field of human activity can sometimes favor changes in other subsystems by positive feedback. The changes in one or more systems can enhance the change in the original subsystem. This "multiplier effect," as Renfrew calls it, was a vital mechanism in the emergence of civilization. The multiplier effect of positive feedback between and within linked subsystems produced a rapid rate of innovation and structural change in society that was much faster over a long period of time, the period of the so-called Urban Revolution.

It follows that previous developments in the emergence of civilization did not in themselves cause urban life. All the developments were interconnected. No one major innovation caused civilization; each development was linked to another. The growth of population depended on increased food supplies, higher productivity on the part of farmers, a development linked in its turn with the radical alteration of social organization. When major change can occur in several subsystems, a cultural takeoff may occur, during which most subsystems of the society involved will change considerably. Such changes took place during the emergence of civilization in several different parts of the world, principal among them Mesopotamia, Egypt, the Aegean, the Indus Valley, China, Mesoamerica, and Peru. All men have the inherent capability and potential to develop the institutions of civilization, but it was in these areas that vigorous human civilizations first arose. In the chapters that follow we shall summarize the evidence for each.

18

mesopotamia
and the first cities

Note: In Chapters 18 through 22, calibrated radiocarbon dates and historical dates (datings obtained from documentary sources) appear in italic type in the page margins, and uncalibrated radiocarbon dates are in Roman type, as in other chapters.

"And it came to pass, as they journeyed from the East that they found a plain in the land of Shinar, and they dwelt there. And they said to one another, 'Go to, let us make brick and burn them thoroughly.' And they had brick for stone and slime had they for mortar. And they said, 'Go to, let us build a city and a tower whose top may reach into heaven and let us make a name lest we be scattered abroad on the face of the whole earth.'" These words were set down in Genesis, Chapter 11, sometime around 800 B.C., and give an account of the earliest founding of urban society in the world. This biblical account of the first settlement of Mesopotamia is little more than a folk legend written down at a time when people had vivid memories of floods inundating valuable farmland and oral traditions of the struggles of the earliest settlers on the sandy plains.

The delta regions and floodplain of the Tigris and Euphrates rivers form a hot, low-lying environment, much of it inhospitable sand, swamp, and dry mud flats bordered by dense stands of reeds. Yet this region was the cradle of man's earliest urban civilization (Table 18.1). The floodplain is bounded by the two rivers, and "Mesopotamia" in Greek means "the land between two rivers" (Figure 18.1). From north to south, Mesopotamia is approximately 600 miles (965 km.) long and some 250 miles (402 km.) wide. The crucial developments that led to urban civili-

Table 18.1
Old World civilizations and earlier cultures.[a]

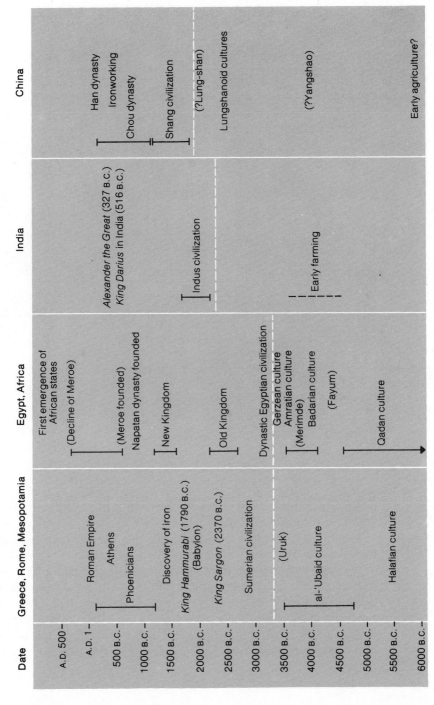

Date	Greece, Rome, Mesopotamia	Egypt, Africa	India	China
A.D. 500 —				
A.D. 1 —	Roman Empire	First emergence of African states		Han dynasty
500 B.C. —	Athens	(Decline of Meroe)	Alexander the Great (327 B.C.)	Ironworking
	Phoenicians		King Darius in India (516 B.C.)	Chou dynasty
1000 B.C. —		(Meroe founded) Napatan dynasty founded		
1500 B.C. —	Discovery of iron	New Kingdom		Shang civilization
2000 B.C. —	King Hammurabi (1790 B.C.) (Babylon)		Indus civilization	(?Lung-shan)
2500 B.C. —	King Sargon (2370 B.C.)	Old Kingdom		Lungshanoid cultures
3000 B.C. —	Sumerian civilization	Dynastic Egyptian civilization		
3500 B.C. —	(Uruk)	Gerzean culture Amratian culture (Merimde)		(?Yangshao)
4000 B.C. —	al-'Ubaid culture	Badarian culture	Early farming	
4500 B.C. —		(Fayum)		
5000 B.C. —		Qadan culture		
5500 B.C. —	Halafian culture			Early agriculture?
6000 B.C. —				

[a]The table gives the approximate dates for the emergence of civilization in various parts of the Old World (the broken line delineating this emergence), relates prehistoric cultures to historical events, and shows the antecedents of the civilizations.

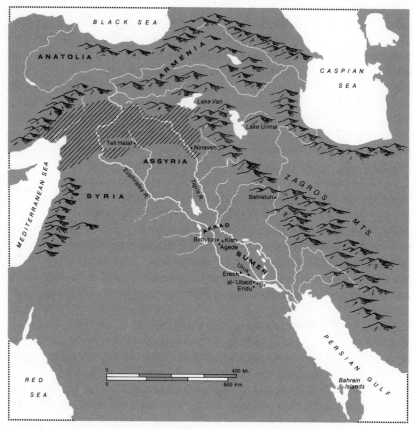

Approximate distribution of Halafian painted pottery and related wares

Figure 18.1
Mesopotamian sites and the distribution of Halafian pottery.

zation largely took place in the southern parts of the delta, in the area
known to the ancient world as Sumer.

Even in Classical times Herodotus and other Greek writers were aware
that Mesopotamia was the cradle of their civilization. The fertile soils
of the delta were famous for their yields of wheat produced by skillful
irrigation. Early travelers recognized former sites of great cities that were
easily picked out on the flat plains, for they formed small hills, or tells,
as a result of successive reoccupation of the same town sites century after
century.[1]* The available raw materials in the delta were mud brick and
reed. Successive rebuilding of houses on the same site led to a rapid

* See pages 399–400 for notes to Chapter 18.

Figure 18.2
The mound or tell of Nimrud in Mesopotamia excavated by Sir Austen Henry Layard in the nineteenth century. This drawing appeared in his Discoveries in the Ruins of Nineveh and Babylon.

accumulation of large occupation mounds. Today archaeologists can dissect these mounds to obtain long sequences of cultural history extending back to the time when the first human populations settled between the rivers (Figure 18.2).

As early as the seventeenth century A.D., European travelers were bringing back exciting accounts of strangely inscribed clay tablets that were recognized as a hitherto unknown type of writing, cuneiform (Figure 18.6). Although German scholar Georg Friedrich Grotefend succeeded in deciphering the script in 1802, his findings were never published. It was left to a later generation of scholars, most famous among them being Sir Henry Rawlinson, to reconquer the complex script in the 1840s. Rawlinson was a remarkable character who began his assault on cuneiform by copying the famous trilingual inscription of the Persian King Darius, which had been hewn on a rock face at Behistun in 516 B.C.

In the 1840s, Paul Botta and Henry Layard dug furiously in the delta, trying to uncover as many monumental sculptures and spectacular antiquities as they could.[2] Their finds were exhibited in European museums and published in best-selling travel books. Thus a picture of early Sumerian civilization emerged from the total obscurity in which it had rested for centuries.

the first cities

"The country life is to be preferred, for there we see the works of God, but in cities little else than the works of men." Thus wrote William Penn, one of the early American colonists. The question arises: how did these "works of men" come into being?

5500 B.C.

About 5500 B.C. many of the village farmers of the Near East began to make a characteristic style of painted pottery, abandoning the monochrome wares they had made before. The new fashion spread from southwestern Turkey around the shores of Lake Van and as far east as the Zagros Mountains. The most brilliantly painted pottery was made

Halafian

in northern Iraq by the inhabitants of Tell Halaf (Figure 18.1), whose enormous kilns produced bowls, dishes, and flasks adorned with elaborate, stylized patterns (Figure 18.3) and representations of men and animals. Many variations in painting style flourished as trade increased in obsidian, semiprecious stones, and other luxury materials between widely separated communities. Villages were still politically autonomous and self-supporting, depending on cereal crops and herds of sheep and goats. As populations grew, so did the number of villages scattered over the plains; life was possible without advanced agricultural methods.[3]

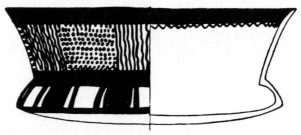

Figure 18.3
Painted Halafian vessel from Iraq (about one-fourth actual size).

During the period that painted pottery was at the height of fashion, farmers began to settle on the Mesopotamian floodplains. The delta, lacking metals and virtually stoneless, was an area with no animals suitable for domestication and no indigenous cereal crops. But the deep silt of the plains was extremely fertile if irrigated with water from the Tigris and Euphrates. As farmers began to move onto the plains they were faced with the task of constructing canals to ensure the survival of their crops.

Suitable building materials for houses had to be improvised from the sand, clay, palm trees, and reeds that abounded between the rivers. For farmers to settle on any scale in this region required not only the technology for irrigation but also the social and political discipline to organize canal digging and waterworks. Canals had to be dug to divert rivers and streams. The clogging silt of the delta had to be cleared from canals each year, a task requiring constant, backbreaking effort.

The first inhabitants of the delta settled on river banks with every incentive to concentrate their gardens within limited areas to minimize their irrigation efforts. Early irrigation does not seem to have involved huge community projects but, rather, the clearing of clogged natural channels and the construction of small-scale feeder canals for gardens already situated to take advantage of natural drainage. These simple irrigation works made it possible to grow vegetables in addition to cereal crops. Cattle were probably penned in lush pastures, conceivably on a communal basis. The fish and waterfowl that abounded were important dietary supplements. Fruit of the date palm may have formed a vital staple.

The first inhabitants of Mesopotamia are known to us from the small village of al-'Ubaid.[4] This small settlement was built on a low mound which was covered with huts made of mud brick and reeds, sometimes with roofs formed from bent sticks. The al-'Ubaid people relied on hunting and fishing as well as cereal crops for their livelihood. They reaped their grain with sickles made of clay or fitted with flint blades. Cattle and other domestic stock were herded on the floodplain. But this somewhat unprepossessing village community does not give us a true picture of 'Ubaid culture, for many people with a similar way of life lived in substantial settlements that could be called small towns. One of them, the mound at Eridu, has been excavated on a large scale.

al-'Ubaid

Eridu was first occupied in about 4750 B.C. at a time when the Tell Halaf people were still making their painted pottery in the north.[5] The first inhabitants lived in small houses with rectangular ground plans. While economic practices probably differed little from those at al-'Ubaid, from the very earliest Eridu levels we find evidence of shrines and temples. By the time the 'Ubaid people were replaced by more advanced farmers around 3500 B.C., Eridu temples had grown to considerable size, contained altars and offering places, and had a standardized plan with a central room bounded by rows of smaller compartments.

4750 B.C.

3500 B.C.

The 'Ubaid culture was fully developed by 4350 B.C. and spread over all Mesopotamia. Its cities and temples were supported by an economy organized around the power of the priests and their temples. At every 'Ubaid settlement of any size, temple buildings dominate the town. One senses that religion had a pervasive influence on 'Ubaid life, that society was controlled, as were economic matters, by priestly rulers who came to power as a result of religious preeminence or economic ability.

technological advances

Technological advances were equally dramatic as the new structures of society imposed demands on the farmer and on the specialist craftsman. 'Ubaid occupation levels are found in the lowest horizons of such famous mounds as Ur of the Chaldees, but the later development of 'Ubaid culture is best glimpsed at the mound of Warka (Uruk), where new styles of pottery are found, perhaps introduced from the northern highlands.[6] Much larger temples, several of them set on platforms that raised them above the town, were in use.

Uruk
3500 B.C.

3500 B.C.   Copper tools and ornaments began to appear in Mesopotamia. On the plateau to the north, coppersmiths had been working for centuries, making small pins and awls. Other peasant societies were also aware of the properties of native copper. Egyptian farmers made small pins from soft native copper picked up as surface rocks. The American Indians of the Lake Superior region, who traded hammered copper ornaments over enormous distances, possessed no knowledge of the melting properties of the metal. But the low melting point of copper was soon recognized by peoples who were familiar with the firing of pottery and the use of pot kilns (Figure 18.4).

Copper is a fine, lustrous metal much prized for its ornamental properties. Its economic advantages in terms of sharp cutting edges are less obvious. But, when blacksmiths learned how to alloy copper with tin to make bronze, metal technology began to assume importance in warfare and domestic life.

Around 3500 B.C., cast copper ornaments, axes, and other tools appeared in small numbers in Mesopotamian archaeological sites. The 'Ubaid towns of the southern delta lacked the new metal, for farmers were still using fired clay to make sickles and socketted axes. By 3000 B.C., copper specialists had begun to work in most Mesopotamian cities, smelting and casting weapons and ornaments of high standard. Mesopotamian blacksmiths had to obtain all their metals by trade. Some cities attempted to maintain a monopoly on bronze weapons and tools by training specialist craftsmen and controlling trade in tin ingots and bronze artifacts. The development of bronze weapons can be linked to the rise of warfare as a method of obtaining political ends.

3000 B.C.

3200 B.C.   By 3200 B.C., Mesopotamian temples were even more elaborate. They rose on stepped platforms or "ziggurats" high above the floodplain, an architectural style famous from Eridu and other celebrated excavations (Figure 18.5). Cities had walls, indicating that a need for protection had arisen as territorial boundaries expanded and small city-states began to compete against each other. Archaeologists have found the first traces of pictographic writing in the form of temple accounts (Figure 18.6). The Mesopotamian state had reached a point where its rulers had to keep an accurate account of the input and output of their people.

sumerian civilization

By 2900 B.C., Sumerian civilization was in full swing in the southern delta. In archaeological terms this is reflected in an increase in wealth.[8] Metal tools became much more common and domestic tools as well as weapons proliferated. Technologically speaking, they were far in advance of earlier tools. Smiths began to alloy copper with tin to produce bronze. Wheeled chariots and wagons formed part of the equipment of armies and farmers. With a shift in political power from the priests to the kings, Mesopotamian rulers became more despotic, concentrating the wealth of the state and controlling subjects by military strength, religious acumen, and taxation, as well as economic incentive.

Early Dynastic 2900 B.C.

The power base of the cities depended in part on intensive agriculture, something that irrigation and the fertile Mesopotamian soils had encouraged to the extent that rural populations increased sharply as the agricultural capacity of the floodplain increased. The plow was developed, an invention that depended on the availability of draft oxen trained to pull it through the soil to give a deeper furrow and thereby increase agricultural yields. Plows were never in use in the New World, where draft animals were not domesticated, nor did the rice farmers of Asia have much use for such a tool. But its use permitted higher yields of cereal crops and the support of larger urban and rural populations in the Western world.

Trade, too, was an essential lifeline for early Mesopotamian cities. Specialized craftsmen serving priests and kings created demands for all sorts of raw materials: metals, timber, skins, ivory, and precious stones like malachite. Many of these raw materials could be found only in the remote highlands to the north of Mesopotamia. Wheeled vehicles and boats became vital elements in trade and warfare. Crude wheels were being used to make pots very early in the development of urban life, and soon wagons and chariots were furnished with heavy or lightweight wheels. Horses, asses, and oxen were employed to draw heavy loads.

Flourishing trade routes developed along the delta waterways, especially up the placid Euphrates, which was easily navigable for long distances. This great river, whose ancient name Uruttu meant copper, transmitted raw materials from the north and trade goods from the Persian Gulf to the Mediterranean. Well before 3000 B.C., the Euphrates joined

Figure 18.4
  Copper and bronze metallurgy. Bronze is an alloy of copper and tin that provides a much tougher working edge on a finished artifact. Bronze rather than copper caused the revolution in agricultural and military technologies, resulting from the use of metallurgy.

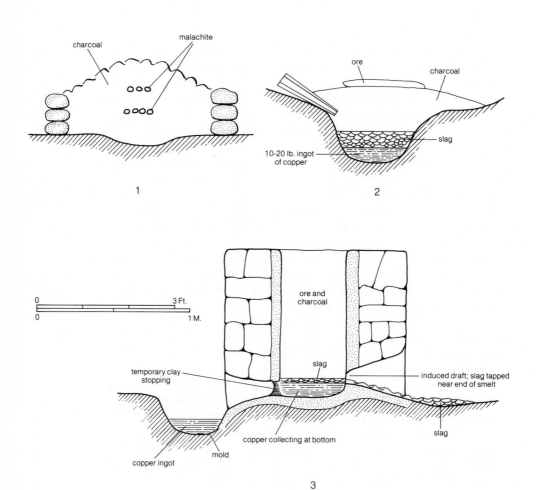

Copper-smelting hearths: (1) open fire; (2) a hearth from Israel; (3) Roman copper-smelting furnace for production of stamped "bun" ingots. Before smelting was invented, two high-temperature techniques were available to early man: pottery kilns and melting native metals over open fires. Smelting requires much higher temperatures, obtained either by a natural draft chimney or through the use of bellows. Animal skins make excellent bellows bags, and an artificial draft is likely to have been used at an early date. Conceivably, the technique of smelting was discovered through the accidental melting of copper in a pottery kiln.

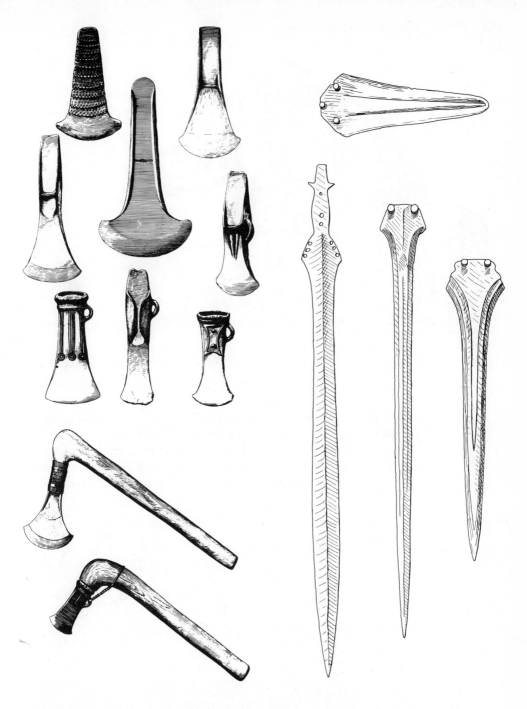

Copper and bronze implements from prehistoric Europe: simple flat axes and flanged and socketed axes (left), with two of them (bottom left) showing method of mounting onto a handle; a dagger and sword blades (right) (various scales).

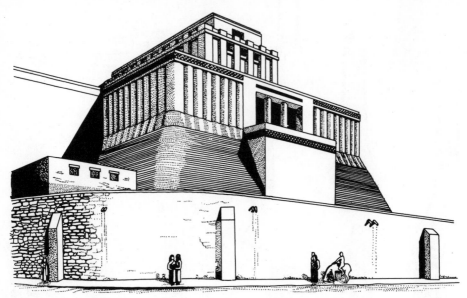

Figure 18.5
Reconstruction of an Uruk temple at Eridu. Note the platform architecture and the drainage holes in the walls.

many scattered towns together, transmitting to all of them the products of Sumerian craftsmen and a modicum of cultural unity.

Political authority was still effective only at the city level, with the temple's priests the only logical authority for controlling trade, economic life, and political matters; thus, many of the priests' concerns were

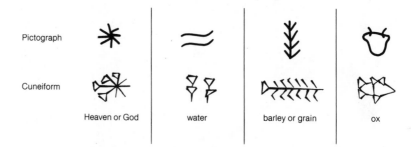

Figure 18.6
Cuneiform writing evolved from pictographs or symbols representing common objects. This drawing compares the original pictograph with the earliest cuneiform equivalent. The word ''cuneiform'' is derived from cuneus in Latin, meaning a wedge, after the characteristic wedge impression of the script.

worldly. But by this time population densities had risen to the limit that the available land in the delta could support. Irrigation systems were enlarged as people began to concentrate in larger cities, abandoning many smaller towns. The motive for this shift was as much defense as population increase, for both inscriptions and the archaeological record speak of warfare. Armies were raised to protect trade routes, enforce monopolies, and secure additional food supplies. The onerous tasks of defense and military organization passed into the royal hands of despotic kings supposedly appointed by the gods who led urban populations in raids against neighboring city-states.

2800 B.C.

By this time the delta was populated by a multitude of small city-states, each state and ruler vying with the others for status and prestige. Such states as Erech, Kish, and Ur of the Chaldees had periods of political strength, prosperity, and sometimes obscurity. Some nurtured powerful rulers. British archaeologist Sir Leonard Woolley caused a sensation in the 1930s when he found the Royal Graves at Ur, the burials of Sumerian kings who were accompanied to the other world by warriors, charioteers, guards, servants, and women. One tomb contained the remains of fifty-nine people who had been slaughtered to accompany their king.[9]

Sumerian civilization prospered within Mesopotamia until about 2500 B.C. Then urban centers sprang up in the north in Assyria, which began to compete with delta cities for trade and political power. Rulers with greater territorial ambitions sought to rule over wider areas. In about 2370 B.C., a Semitic-speaking leader, Sargon, founded a ruling dynasty at the town of Agade, south of Babylon. This northern house soon established its rule over Sumer and Assyria by a series of military campaigns and skillful commercial ventures. After a short period of economic prosperity, the new kings were toppled by highland tribesmen from the north. Mesopotamia entered into a period of political instability. But by 1990 B.C., the ancient city of Babylon was achieving prominence under Semitic rulers, which culminated in the reign of the great king Hammurabi in 1790 B.C.

2500 B.C.

2370 B.C.

1990 B.C.

1790 B.C.

Hammurabi set up a powerful commercial empire centered on Mesopotamia and extending as far afield as Assyria and Zagros. The unity of his empire depended on a common official language and a cuneiform writing system for its administration. Small city-states for the first time had an influence on world culture far greater than their geographical territory would appear to justify, an influence based on economic and political power maintained by despotic rule and harsh power politics. By this time, the influence of Mesopotamia was such that the weapon types used by Babylonian armies had spread as far afield as Russia, Europe, and the western Mediterranean.

the consequences of urbanization

The consequences of city life in the Near East were more lasting in terms of man's relationships with man than they were in terms of relations with the environment.[10] Although urbanization was based on some changes in exploitation patterns of the environment, man's dependence on his environment was freed even further by new political and cultural institutions and by new social structures. More balanced economics were based on diversified resources as well as on trade in foodstuffs, which allowed organizational action to counter famines or the effects of extreme weather. The planning of food supplies reduced the city dweller's dependence on the day-to-day whims of his environment.

Trade became increasingly important as raw materials were carried hundreds of miles from village to city, from mine to craftsman. The cities depended on one another for economic prosperity, competed for natural

Figure 18.7
Warriors ascending a mountain to a besieged city near a river, from Austen Henry Layard's Monuments of Nineveh.

resources, and inevitably drifted into territorial quarrels which in their turn raised problems of political unity. Manufactured goods became more plentiful, and agricultural production benefited from better tools. Community irrigation projects and architectural schemes became more common, sometimes coming under the aegis of centralized political authority as, for example, in the Nile Valley (Chapter 19).

The long-term effects of urban life on the natural environment of Mesopotamia were severe. Overirrigation caused a gradual salting effect in the soils of the delta, which resulted in greater dependence on salt-resistant crops like barley. Agricultural economies became more dependent on a single crop, thus reducing the self-sufficiency of peasant villages and increasing their vulnerability to famine. Heavy taxation and increasing state control of farmlands were symptoms of increasing bureaucratic interference in agriculture. In times of political instability or warfare, the administrative structure fell apart, causing chaos and starvation among both rural and urban populations. The cities themselves fed on the rural populations, drawing their growing populations from the countryside; their own people were constantly decimated by a high infant mortality rate because of bad sanitation and overcrowding.

The consequence of urbanization was a greatly increased human capacity to alter the environment. The Mesopotamian delta was virtually a man-made environment by 2000 B.C., an environment that was devastated again and again as the pursuit of political power and wars of conquest became recurring themes of human history (Figure 18.7). Man's interactions with the natural environment had been obscured by his own handiwork.

19

pharaohs, chiefs,
and indus merchants

To many people, Egypt *is* early civilization, the fountainhead for all later civilized life. This essentially diffusionist view of the origins of civilization was argued persuasively by Grafton Elliot Smith and his disciples many years ago.[1]* There is something basically attractive about the notion of Egypt as the cradle of mankind: a world of exotic pharaohs and hiero-glyphics, spectacular pyramids, and royal tombs. In fact, however, civili-zation, in the sense of literacy, urban life, metallurgy, and specialist craftsmen, reached Egypt comparatively late, at about the time the Cre-tans built Knossos.

Unlike Mesopotamia, where the vast delta was first settled by farmers obliged to use irrigation techniques, the Nile farmers prospered on inten-sively cultivated gardens naturally irrigated by the river itself. About 3700–3600 B.C., larger settlements were built on the floodplain, the fields fertilized by the late summer floods when the river waters spilled out over the farmlands. The large-scale production of cereal crops could vir-tually be guaranteed in an environment where the Nile did most of the work. Furthermore, the arid climate of the desert fringes allowed indefi-nite storage of harvested grain.

3700 B.C.

pre-dynastic societies

Amratian
3600 B.C.

By 3600 B.C., the way of life for the average Egyptian probably differed little from that in some Upper Nile villages today (Figure 19.1). Wheat

* See pages 400–401 for notes to Chapter 19.

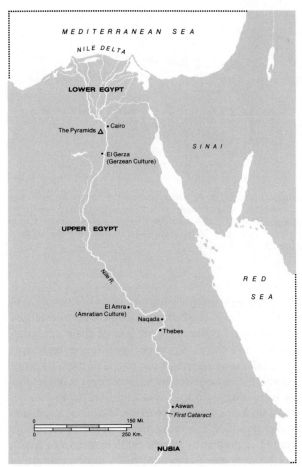

Figure 19.1
  The Nile Valley.

and barley were cultivated in riverside fields. Dogs, small stock, cattle, and pigs were sources of meat, supplemented by the rich Nile fauna. These Amratian (or pre-Dynastic) people were the successors of the Badarians (Chapter 14).[2] Amratian settlements with a material culture somewhat similar to that of earlier centuries have been found scattered on the Nile floodplain. Although pottery was still being made, elegant stone vessels in alabaster and basalt were also in use; craftsmen were also producing beautiful ground and pressure-flaked spearheads, dagger blades, and arrowheads.

The Amratian culture had a number of variations, one of which is named the Gerzean, a more developed pre-Dynastic culture confined to

Gerzean
3400 B.C.

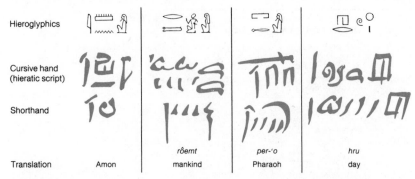

	Amon	rôemt mankind	per-'o Pharaoh	hru day
Hieroglyphics				
Cursive hand (hieratic script)				
Shorthand				
Translation				

Figure 19.2
Egyptian writing is commonly referred to as hieroglyphics, the familar symbols that appear on formal inscriptions and on tomb walls. In fact, Egyptian scribes developed cursive hands that were used in everyday life. The examples above show formal hieroglyphic script (top line) and below it both the cursive style and the scribe's shorthand, which was used for rapid writing.

the northern parts of Upper Egypt and the southern parts of Lower Egypt to the very fringes of the Nile Delta. The Gerzean people were specialized farmers who enjoyed a wealthier economy than that of their predecessors.[3] For the first time we find traces of copper working, a technique introduced from Asia. Metalsmiths were making pins, flat axes, daggers, and simple knives. The volume of trade seems to have risen considerably as a result of the new technology. Copper was imported from sources as far away as Sinai, while lead and silver came from Asia. The proportion of luxury goods rose and included the local manufacture of faience, a form of glass widely traded in prehistoric times. Settlements were larger, and the social structure became more elaborate, with some evidence of social classes.

Most significant of all, however, is the appearance of a number of objects of unmistakable Mesopotamian or Asian origin. The site of Naqada II yielded a single cylinder seal of unmistakable Mesopotamian form, and some arrowheads and artifact forms recall Asian specimens.[4] As Egyptian art began to develop we find that many Mesopotamian motifs appear on tablets, knives, and walls. Hunting scenes, mythical beasts, and even Mesopotamian-style pots are depicted in earlier Egyptian art.

At approximately this time, too, architectural styles changed. Mud bricks, first used in Mesopotamia, came into use along the Nile. Some of the monumental architectural styles recall early buildings from Mesopotamia. But, even as early as 3000 B.C., Egyptian farming cultures and the large settlements on the Nile had a characteristic African flavor that served to distinguish them sharply from west Asian society. For example, the cylinder seal became part of Egyptian culture, but was soon adorned with Egyptian symbols rather than Mesopotamian motifs.

About this time the late pre-Dynastic people began to use hiero-glyphic writing. Hieroglyphics were written on papyrus documents, painted on clay or wood, and carved on public buildings.[5] Many of the symbols were pictorial, others phonetic. Only the consonants were writ-ten down in Egyptian writing. The vowel sounds were omitted, although they were pronounced. With practice, reading this form of script is easy enough, and a smpl tst 'f ths srt shld shw ths qt wll. Many authorities feel that Egyptian writing was ultimately derived from Mesopotamian sources. Presumably the motives for its use were convenience and an increased need for accurate accounts (Figure 19.2).

the origins of egyptian civilization

Scholars have argued for many years about the origins of Egyptian civili-zation.[6] Formerly they thought that the cities of the Nile were founded by foreigners who invaded the valley and set up their own city-states, which soon assumed an Egyptian atmosphere. Current opinion favors a period of intensified cultural contacts throughout the eastern Mediter-ranean in the fourth millennium B.C., following the development of sea-going ships. As a result, new ideas and techniques permeated Egyptian culture at a time when the native population of the Nile Valley was beginning to realize a staggering economic potential.

Sometime around 3000 B.C., the Egyptians organized themselves suffi-ciently to make use of the Nile floods for intensive agriculture. The floodplain population had risen perhaps as high as 200,000 people. A combination of new ideas from Mesopotamia and intensified agricultural production undoubtedly accelerated the move toward more unified polit-ical and economic units in the Nile Valley. From its earliest inception the Egyptian nation extended from the Mediterranean far southward into northeast Africa. But, unlike the city-states of Mesopotamia, Egypt was from the beginning a unified political reality, once the process of urbani-zation had begun.

According to legend, this unification was carried out by a ruler named Menes who founded the first Dynasty of Pharaohs and joined Upper and Lower Egypt. In fact, this process is more likely to have taken a consid-erable amount of time and, if Egyptian art is any guide, transpired partly as a result of considerable fighting, some by foreigners. In any case, by about 3200 B.C., Egypt had become a unified political state under the rule of a divine king.[7] A state over 600 miles (965 km.) long, Egypt developed

Dynastic period
3200 B.C.

its own bureaucracy, extensive trading contacts, and an architectural style of glory and magnificence that has survived to astonish the tourist and scholar of the twentieth century.

the egyptian state

Egypt was the first state of its size in history, predating nation formation among the Sumerians by many centuries.[8] Pharaohs ruled by their own word, following no written laws, unlike the legislators of Mesopotamian city-states. The origins of the kingship go back into prehistoric times; they perhaps were connected with rainmaking and land fertility. The pharaoh had power over the Nile flood, rainfall, and all people, including foreigners. He was a god in his own right, respected by all people as a divine and tangible god whose being was the personification of *Ma'at*, or "rightness." Thus his pronouncements were law, in practice regulated by a massive background of precedent set by earlier pharaohs. Egyptian rulers lived a strictly ordered life. As one Greek writer tells us: "For there was a set time not only for his holding audience or rendering judgement, but even for his taking a walk, bathing, and sleeping with his wife; in short, every act of his life." The great pyramids of the Nile stand as dramatic reminders of how the entire Egyptian nation supported the vast labor of building these edifices commemorating their divine rulers (Figure 19.3).

The mother of the pharaoh enjoyed a powerful position in the kingdom, for matrilineal inheritance was the rule in the court. The eldest son of the pharaoh was his heir, his eldest daughter the royal heiress, her dowry the kingdom itself. Royal heir and heiress were thus supposed to marry each other to perpetuate divine rule, an incestuous institution often defeated by infant mortality.

A massive, hereditary bureaucracy effectively ruled the kingdom, with rows of officials forming veritable dynasties. Their records tell us that much official energy was devoted to tax collection, harvest yields, and hydraulic engineering. An army of some 20,000 men, many of them mercenaries, was maintained at the height of Egypt's prosperity. The Egyptian empire was a literate one; that is to say, trained scribes who could read and write were an integral part of the state government. Special schools trained writers for careers in the army, the palace, the treasury, or a host of other callings. Learning hieroglyphics was a tedious task, even harder in later times when classic Egyptian was no longer spoken, only written for official purposes (Figure 19.4).

Despite the number of scribes and minor clerics, a vast gulf separated those who could read and write from the uneducated peasant worker.

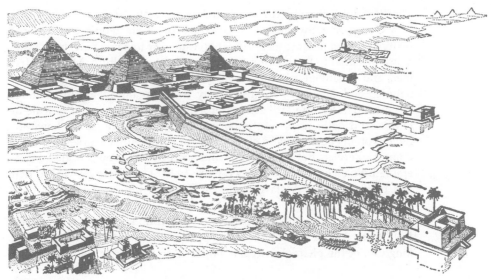

Figure 19.3
  A reconstruction of the pyramid complexes of several pharaohs of the later Old King-dom.

Figure 19.4
  A steward reading an inventory from a papyrus roll prepared by his scribes, to the left, from a tomb at Saqqara, c. 2330 B.C.

The life of a peasant, with never-failing harvests, was easier than that of a Greek or a Syrian farmer, although the state required occasional bouts of forced labor to clear irrigation canals or to haul stone, both tasks being essential to the maintenance of Egyptian agriculture. Minor craftsmen and unskilled laborers lived more regimented lives, working on temples and pharaohs' tombs.[9] Many were organized in shifts under foremen. There were strikes, and absenteeism was common. A scale of rations and daily work was imposed. Like many early states, however, the Egyptians depended on slave labor for some public works and much domestic service. But foreign serfs and war prisoners could wield considerable influence in public affairs (Figure 19.5). They were allowed to rent and cultivate land. A slave could be freed by his owner merely by a witnessed declaration.

The Egyptian empire was endowed with abundant natural resources. Gold from Arabia and Nubia and copper from Sinai were plentiful. The kingdom of the pharaohs became powerful in the ancient world through

Figure 19.5
A Syrian mercenary and his wife are shown being waited on by their Egyptian servant, from Amarna, c. 1355 B.C.

its minerals and the skill of its craftsmen. The power of its pharaohs and
the effectiveness of its government were proverbial. Economic prosperity
was assured by the remarkable Nile and its lifegiving floods. Long-term
stability was supported by an efficient system of governance in which
hereditary officials controlled the affairs of state by a massive weight of
precedents from earlier centuries.

The period of the New Kingdom (1570–c. 1180 B.C.) was the golden *1570* B.C.
age of Egyptian history.[10] We know the names of the pharaohs. Their
personal possessions have survived. We can gaze on their mummified
features. Their deeds are praised in inscription and papyrus. A vigorous
artistic tradition of sculpture, furniture, glass, and fine ornaments is
known from royal tombs. All manner of exotic imports flooded into the
Nile Valley when Egyptian armies conquered Asian lands. Mercenaries
manned the royal regiments as success went to Egyptian heads. By 1380 *1380* B.C.
B.C., the power of the pharaohs began to decline, for the stultifying bureaucracy had sapped initiative and led to the copying of older ways.
Soon the Nile Valley became an uneasy colony of Asian empires, eventually becoming a Roman province and an important center of the Christian
church.[11] But the legacy of a remarkable and stable civilization survives
in the richness of archaeological treasures that have fired public imagina-
tion for centuries.

egypt and the emergence of african states

meroe

What were Egypt's relationships with the vast African continent that
bordered the Nile? Her influence on her southern and Saharan neighbors
was surprisingly small, for her ties were closer to the Mediterranean
world than to Black Africa. The pharaohs exercised political control only
as far south as the First Cataract, near what is now the Aswan Dam. But
the areas to the south were an important source of ivory for ornaments
and of slaves for the divine rulers.

Around 900 B.C., however, an unknown governor of the southernmost *900* B.C.
part of Egypt founded his own dynasty and ruled a string of small settlements extending far southward into what is now the Sudan. The capital
at Napata began to decline because of overgrazing of the fragile grasslands by the Nile. The inhabitants moved southward and founded a town *590* B.C.
called Meroe on a fertile floodplain between the Nile and Atbara rivers
(Figure 19.6). There they developed their own thriving urban civilization
which was in contact with peoples living far to the east on the southern

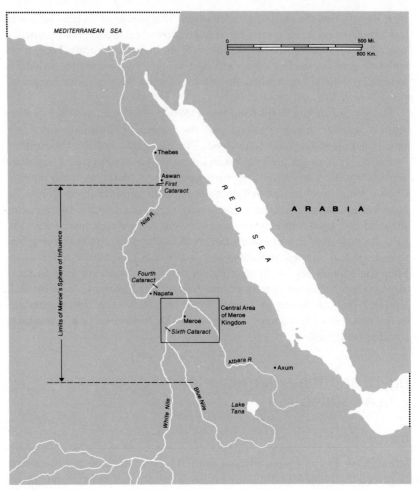

Figure 19.6
Meroe and the Nile Valley.

fringes of the Sahara.[12] They gained prosperity from extensive commerce in such trade items as copper, gold, iron, ivory, and slaves. At least sporadic contacts were maintained with the Classical world. The empire declined in the early centuries after Christ, following raids from the kingdom of Axum, centered on the Ethiopian highlands.[13] The fertile grasslands around Meroe were overgrazed, too, and the increasing aridity A.D. 300 of the countryside made urban life a difficult undertaking. Some of Meroe's prosperity may have been based on ironworking, for deposits of this vital material were abundant near the capital. Iron artifacts are, however, fairly rare in the city itself.

north africa

The North African coast had long been a staging post for maritime traders from the eastern Mediterranean. During the first millennium B.C., the Phoenicians set up ports on the coast.[14] The colonists came into contact with well-established barter networks that criss-crossed the Sahara.[15] The desert is rich in salt deposits that were controlled by the nomadic peoples who lived there. They came in touch with Negro tribesmen living to the south of the desert who bartered salt for copper, ivory, gold, and the other raw materials that Africa has traditionally given to the world. Soon, long-distance trading routes connected North Africa with tropical regions, well-trodden highways which provided much of the wealth of Greek and Roman civilizations during the height of their powers.

Most of the Saharan trade was in the hands of nomadic tribesmen, middlemen between Black Africa and the bustling markets of the Mediterranean. Then, in Roman times the camel was introduced to the Sahara. Veritable "ships of the desert," they enabled merchants to organize sizable camel caravans that crossed the Sahara like clockwork. The result was more direct contact with the Mediterranean world and a much greater volume of trade.[16]

A.D. 350

ironworking and african states

Ironworking had reached West Africa by the fourth century B.C., perhaps via the Saharan trade routes.[17] The new metallurgy, unlike that of copper, spread rapidly over sub-Saharan Africa within a few centuries. The spread of iron was connected in part with the dispersal of Bantu-speaking peoples over much of eastern, central, and southern Africa. Bantu languages are now spoken by most of the inhabitants of tropical Africa.[18] The original dispersal area of Bantu tongues may have been north of the Zaire forest (Figure 19.7).

300 B.C.

This spread of the new language coincides with the arrival of negroid peoples both in the Zaire forest and on the savannah woodlands to the east and south of it. Ironworking farmers were living near the great East African lakes by the third century A.D., by the banks of the Zambezi River at approximately the same time, and crossing the Limpopo into South Africa during the first millennium A.D. They introduced farming and domestic animals into wide areas of Africa, absorbing, eliminating, or pushing out the indigenous Bushman hunter-gatherers (Chapter 10).[19]

A.D. 250

A.D. 400

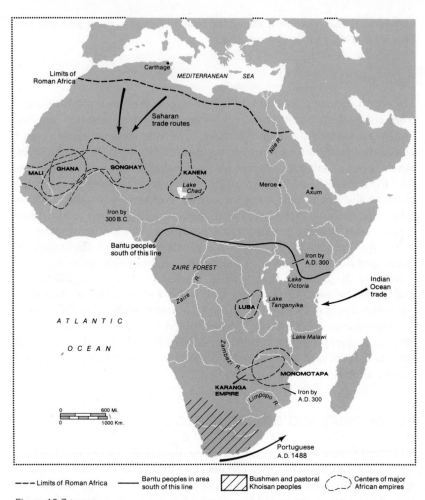

Figure 19.7
Iron and trade in Africa, from 600 B.C. to A.D. 1488. Distribution limits on this map are approximate.

The Bantu farmers used shifting agriculture and careful soil selection to produce a diet based on sorghum, millet, and other cereal crops. They kept cattle, and sheep or goats and relied on hunting and gathering for much of their diet. Their architectural styles and pottery have a clear but indirect relationship with those of many present-day rural black Africans. Many of modern Africa's cultural traditions undoubtedly owe their origins to the Bantu-speaking farmers who brought agriculture, iron, and, perhaps, a flourishing art tradition to much of the continent.

ghana, mali, and songhay

The past thousand years have seen the proliferation of prosperous African states ruled by leaders whose power was based on religious ability, entrepreneurial skill, and control of vital raw materials.[20] The West African states at the southern edges of the Sahara, such as Ghana, Mali, and Songhay, based their prosperity on the gold trade with North Africa. The Saharan trade passed into Islamic hands at the end of the first millennium A.D., and Arab authors began describing the remarkable African kingdoms that were flourishing south of the desert. The geographer al-Bakri drew a vivid picture of the kingdom of Ghana, whose gold was well known in northern latitudes by the eleventh century. "It is said," he wrote, "that the king owns a nugget as large as a big stone."

ghana

The kingdom of Ghana straddled the northern borders of the gold-bearing river valleys of the Upper Niger and Senegal.[21] No one knows exactly when it first came into being, but the kingdom was described by Arab writers in the eighth century A.D. The prosperity of the Ghanians depended on the gold trade and on the constant demand for ivory in the north. Salt, kola nuts (used as a stimulant), slaves, and swords also crossed the desert, but gold, ivory, and salt were the foundations of Ghanian power. Islam was brought to Ghana sometime in the late first millennium, the religion serving to link the kingdom more closely to the desert trade. The king of Ghana was a powerful ruler, who, wrote al-Bakri, "can put 200,000 men into the field, more than 40,000 of whom are bowmen."

Ghana was a prime target for Islamic reform movements, whose desert leaders cast longing eyes on the power and wealth of their southern neighbor. One such group, the Almoravids, attacked Ghana in about A.D. 1062, but it was fourteen years before the invaders captured the Ghanian capital. The power of Ghana was fatally weakened, and the kingdom fell apart into its component tribal parts soon afterward.

A.D. 1062

mali

The kingdom of Mali emerged some two centuries later, after many tribal squabbles.[22] A group of Kangaba people under the leadership of Sundiata came into prominence about A.D. 1230 and annexed their neighbors' lands. Sundiata built his new capital at Mali on the Niger River. He founded a vast empire that a century later extended over most of sub-

A.D. 1230

Saharan West Africa. The fame of the Malian kings spread all over the Muslim world. Timbuktu became an important center of learning. Malian gold was valued everywhere. When the king of Mali went on a pilgrimage A.D. *1324* to Mecca in A.D. 1324, the price of gold in Egypt was reduced sharply on account of the king's liberal spending. Mali appeared on the earliest maps of West Africa as an outside frontier of the literate world, providing gold and other luxuries for Europe and North Africa.

The key to the prosperity of Mali was the unifying effects of Islam. Islamic rulers governed with supreme powers granted by Allah, and ruled their conquered provinces through religious appointees or wealthy slaves. Islam provided a reservoir of thoroughly trained, literate administrators, too, who owed an allegiance to peace, stability, and good trading practices.

songhay

A.D. *1325*   About A.D. 1325 the greatest of the kings of Mali, Munsa Musa, brought the important trading center of Gao on the Niger under his sway.[23] Gao was the capital of the Dia kings, who shook off Mali's yoke around A.D. 1340 and founded the Kingdom of Songhay. Their state prospered increasingly as Mali's power weakened. The great chieftain Sonni Ali led A.D. *1464–* the Songhay to new conquests between A.D. 1464 and 1492, expanding *1492* the frontiers of his empire deep into Mali country and far northward into the Sahara. He monopolized much of the Saharan trade, seeking to impose law and order with his vast armies to increase the volume of trade that passed through Songhay hands. Sonni Ali was followed by other competent rulers who further expanded Songhay. Its collapse came in A.D. *1550*   the sixteenth century.

karanga and zimbabwe

Powerful African kingdoms also developed in central and southern Africa. The Luba kingdom of the Congo and the Karanga empire between the Zambezi and Limpopo rivers were led by skilled priests and ivory traders who also handled such diverse raw materials as copper, gold, seashells, cloth, and porcelain. Their power was based on highly centralized political organizations and effective religious powers, which channeled some of their subjects' energies into the exploitation of raw materials and long-distance trade.

The Karanga peoples lived between the Zambezi and Limpopo in what is now Rhodesia, and developed a remarkable kingdom whose viability was based on trade in gold, copper, and ivory and on their leaders' religious acumen.[24] The Karanga leaders founded their power on their role as intermediaries between the people and their ancestral spirits, upon whom the people believed the welfare of the nation depended. Around A.D. 1000, the Karanga began to build stone structures, the most famous of which is Zimbabwe, built at the foot of a sacred hill in southeastern Rhodesia. Zimbabwe became an important commercial and religious center. Its chiefs lived in seclusion on the sacred hill, known to archaeologists as "the Acropolis." In the valley below sprawled a complex of homesteads and stone enclosures, which were dominated in later centuries by the high, free-standing stonewalls of the Great Enclosure, or Temple (Figure 19.8).

A.D. 1000

At least five stages of occupation have been recognized at Zimbabwe, the first of them dating to the fourth century A.D., when a group of farmers camped at the site, but built no stonewalls. They were followed by later occupants who constructed the Great Enclosure in gradual stages and

Figure 19.8
The Zimbabwe ruins, Rhodesia, an important trading and religious center of the Karanga peoples of south-central Africa in the second millennium A.D. Most of the Great Enclosure, or Temple, was built by A.D. 1500.

built retaining walls on the Acropolis. The heyday of Zimbabwe was between A.D. 1350 and 1450, when imported cloth, china, glass, and porcelain were traded to the site. Gold ornaments, copper, ivory, and elaborate iron tools were in common use. A distinctive artistic tradition in soapstone also flourished at Zimbabwe.

Zimbabwe fell into decline after A.D. 1450, probably as a result of environmental deterioration due to overpopulation in an area where agricultural resources were relatively poor.[25] In addition, political confederacies, whose leaders had come into contact with Portuguese explorers in the sixteenth century, rose to prominence in the north.

foreign traders

Much of the history of Africa concerns the exploitation of its peoples and raw materials by foreign traders and explorers. The East African coast was visited by Arabs and Indian merchants who used the Monsoon winds of the Indian Ocean to sail to Africa and back within twelve months on their prosperous trading ventures. The Portuguese skirted Africa's western and southeastern coasts in the fifteenth century, establishing precarious colonies ruled from Portugal and based on the exploitation of raw materials.[26] Some parts of Africa, however, had no contact with the outside world until the coming of Victorian explorers and missionaries, who met remote and exotic peoples as they strove toward elusive goals, including such geographical prizes as the source of the Nile.[27] But the origins of recent colonial exploitation of Africa and the keys to its present patchwork of peoples and cultures lie firmly in prehistoric times.

the indus civilization

Sometime after the appearance of urban life in Mesopotamia and the beginnings of Dynastic rule in Egypt, another distinctive urban civilization developed to the east of the Mesopotamian delta in the fertile Indus Valley. The Indus civilization, which developed in part as a result of contacts with centers of higher civilization in the West, probably affected more of the world's population than did either the Mesopotamian or the Nile civilizations.

In Chapter 10 we summarized the Stone Age cultures of India and showed that this subcontinent was inhabited by small bands of hunters and gatherers with a microlithic toolkit at the end of the Pleistocene epoch. It is suspected that the arts of agriculture and pastoralism reached northwest India from the Near East sometime before 3500 B.C.,[28] although nothing is known of the origins of agriculture in India. The first farmers probably used simple copper implements and made painted pottery on slow, hand-turned wheels. By 2500 B.C. this type of farming culture was widely distributed over much of what is now Pakistan. The general pottery tradition and other cultural traits have many links with regions to the west, and some distinctive pottery motifs are reminiscent of those found on Sumerian sites in Mesopotamia. The earliest farmers of northwestern India probably played a key role in the diffusion of new inventions and the forging of fresh trade links between India and western centers of urban civilization.

Until fifty years ago, the traditional view of early Indian history made no mention of prehistoric urban communities. Most scholars considered that the first cities were built by the descendants of pastoral nomads from the north, who came to India about 1500 B.C., overran a large native population, and introduced the Sanskrit language. These people brought with them a large reservoir of oral traditions, often incorporated in the form of sacred hymns that were not written down until the eighteenth century A.D. The nomads' oral records contained vague references to the *Dasus*, or aboriginal population, that was said to live in great cities, to possess temples, and to be skilled in the arts. These references were discounted until the 1920's when British archaeologist Sir John Marshall began excavating two city mounds at Harappa and Mohenjo-daro in West Pakistan. He found traces of an entirely unknown urban culture, whose distribution extended over an enormous area of northeastern Pakistan. The Indus civilization was subsequently identified as a whole new chapter in Indian history, confirming at least in part the traditions of the hymns.

The earliest dated levels of the Indus civilization, belonging to a time when cities were already thriving, have been radiocarbon dated to approximately 2000 B.C. or even later. But the origins of the Indus civilization extend back somewhat earlier. Harappa and Mohenjo-daro continued to flourish until the eighteenth century B.C., when a gradual decline in their prosperity ensued.

Thanks to forty years of intermittent excavations, much of it in the hands of Indian scholars and other well-known archaeologists like Sir Mortimer Wheeler, considerable data are available about the Indus civilization.[29] Most of our knowledge comes from the excavations at Harappa and Mohenjo-daro; the latter lies 140 miles (225 km.) northeast of Karachi, while the former is 400 miles (644 km.) farther to the northeast, near the Ravi River (Figure 19.9). Both are situated by major rivers, which provided water for irrigation and seasonally flooded the large riverside gardens.

These cities have a circumference of up to three miles (4.8 km.) and, like Mesopotamian towns, are clustered around conspicuous ceremonial

2500 B.C.

2000 B.C.

1700 B.C.

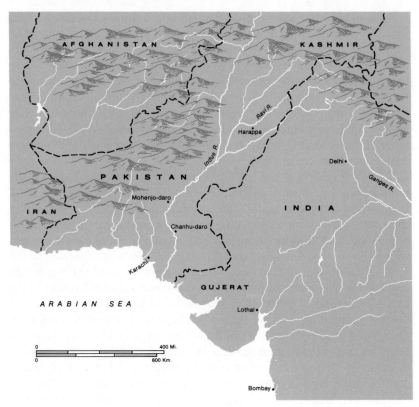

Figure 19.9
The Indus civilization sites. Shaded landmasses are over 1,000 meters (3,300 ft.) above sea level.

centers. The citadel at Harappa, for example, was enclosed by brick walls adorned with defensive towers and encompassed an area 550 meters (600 yds.) across. Both towns are laid out on a rectangular grid pattern, with streets crisscrossing each other with regularity. Drains and wells were part of the cities' design (Figure 19.10).

The more prosperous inhabitants lived in houses with courtyards built of fired brick and with complete sanitation facilities and storage rooms. The workmen's quarters consisted of humble, mud-brick cottages situated near brick kilns, smelting furnaces, and other work areas. Vast public granaries testify to a strongly centralized government, one that maintained rigid control over the cities and the surrounding countryside.

However, we know nothing of the political mechanisms that enabled these vast cities and centers like them to flourish for so long. Whatever the character of those who inhabited the fortified citadels at Harappa and

Figure 19.10
A typical street in Mohenjo-daro.

Mohenjo-daro, it is certain that the rulers' political control was such that they had a finger on every aspect of the people's lives. Whether priests, despotic kings, or monks, their power was based on economic control, religious leadership, and despotism, too.

The economy of the Indus cities throughout their history was based on wheat, barley, cotton, and a range of secondary crops. Cattle, water buffalo, asses, horses, and camels were already domesticated, known through pictures on clay seals (Figure 19.11). Though the subsistence base of the Indus civilization was firmly based on mixed farming, much of their prosperity was due to far-ranging commercial activities. Cotton cloth must have been a staple element in Indus Valley trade. Merchants employed it as a medium for obtaining exotic raw materials such as gold, tin, copper, silver, and alabaster, but metal was rarely used by Indian craftsmen. Many of these substances came from the north, from Afghan-

Figure 19.11
  An Indus Valley seal, bearing a humped bull.

istan, Kashmir, and Iran. Contacts with Mesopotamia are known to have formed part of the Indus trade because Indus Valley pots, seals, beads, and small trinkets have been found in Mesopotamian cities as early as the time of King Sargon, about 2370 B.C. Much of the trade in luxuries and raw materials between the two river valley civilizations took place by sea through middlemen living in what is now Bahrein.

At the height of its power, the Indus civilization was the largest in the Old World in geographical terms. Its territory extended over 1,000 miles (1,610 km.) from north to south, with an indented coastline over 700 miles (1,126 km.) long. In recent years other cities have been excavated, including a port at Lothal in Gujerat and the important settlement of Chanhudaro. Both show the same standardization and unity of the Indus civilization. This is a remarkable phenomenon, for the Indus territory was far larger than that of patchwork city-states.

The rulers and bureaucracy of the civilization developed a pictographic writing on clay seals, again presumably in response to a need for accounting devices. Unfortunately, however, it has yet to be deciphered, and we still know nothing of the powerful rulers of northwestern India who were able to command the loyalty of a larger population than any others had done before.

We still do not know how the Indus civilization arose. Some regard it as a colonial offshoot of Sumerian civilization, citing parallels in ceremonial centers, trading and farming practices, and general features of city life, even though the latter flourished much earlier than the Indus cities. Others believe that village farmers in the early third millennium B.C. received a number of vital technological, cultural, and societal ideas from the west that encouraged them to coalesce into larger economic and social units, a unifying religious or political force providing them with the incentive to exploit potentially fertile river valleys. But this remarkable civilization, like other early urban societies, had as its economic base a floodplain watered by large rivers whose overflows periodically renewed the fertility of their agricultural soils.

The closing centuries of life at Harappa and Mohenjo-daro show a gradual decline in the prosperity of the cities, culminating in the abandonment of Mohenjo-daro in the eighteenth century B.C. No one is sure why this decline took place, but signs of flooding in its last years become more prevalent. Hydrologist Robert Raikes has hypothesized that the Indus River was blocked by earthquake action downstream of Mohenjo-daro. The blockage formed a huge lake that periodically flooded the city, until it was abandoned.[30]

Although some centers of the Indus civilization lingered on in later centuries, the population of India became a predominantly peasant one, a plethora of peasant societies inhabiting much of the subcontinent with little semblance of political unity. Ironworking was introduced by the Persian King Darius when he campaigned in India in 516 B.C.

516 B.C.

Alexander the Great ventured to the Indus in 327 B.C. His death five years later led to a nationalistic revolt under the leadership of Chandragupta. This leader founded the first ruling dynasty which was able to unite the Indus Valley with that of the Ganges to the east, another great river valley, but one which had not experienced the same flowering of urban society as the Indus and had supported cities from only about 1000 B.C. By 500 B.C., Buddha had begun to preach, and the Indian subcontinent was on the threshold of historical times.

20

european society in transition

The temperate latitudes of Europe lie just to the north of the eastern Mediterranean, whose coasts and seaways were the haunts of traders and the sites of small and prospering towns and villages shortly after 3000 B.C. What did Europe have to offer to Mediterranean cultures? How did metallurgy begin and urban life reach temperate regions? The answers to these questions are intimately connected to the vicissitudes of Bronze Age communities on the Aegean and elsewhere. (See Figure 20.1.)

As we discussed in Chapter 13, Gordon Childe's notion of *ex oriente lux*, or "light from the East," is no longer an apt description of European prehistory, partly because of new chronological evidence. The Europeans of prehistoric times possessed their own distinctive cultures and societies. But at times they came in contact with new ideas from the Near East or the Mediterranean basin, which led to technological change or fresh trading opportunities. Such fleeting contacts are a far cry from the ardent diffusionism of earlier archaeologists.[1*] In this chapter we shall survey the progress of European society from about 3000 B.C. until the beginnings of urban life (Table 20.1).

anatolia and the hittites

A long agricultural tradition had been established in Anatolia by the time that metallurgy and urban life began to take hold there. Culture change

* See pages 401–403 for notes to Chapter 20.

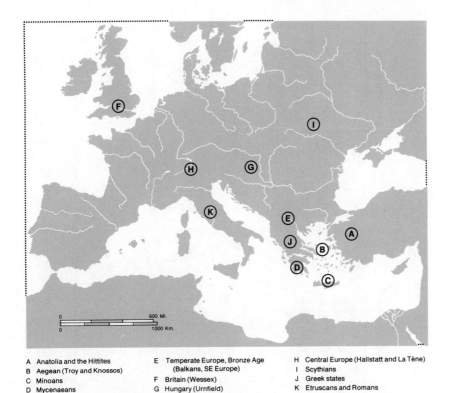

A Anatolia and the Hittites
B Aegean (Troy and Knossos)
C Minoans
D Mycenaeans

E Temperate Europe, Bronze Age
   (Balkans, SE Europe)
F Britain (Wessex)
G Hungary (Urnfield)

H Central Europe (Hallstatt and La Tène)
I Scythians
J Greek states
K Etruscans and Romans

The Phoenicians in the eastern Mediterranean (Lebanon) are not shown on this map.

Figure 20.1
   The culture areas described in this chapter are shown in geographical terms and are
   labelled alphabetically in the sequence in which they are covered in the text. Detailed
   maps appear throughout the chapter.

was slow until the Assyrians set up trading stations in the highlands, designed to regulate and control copper and other valuable raw materials needed by urban societies to the south.[2] Bronze metallurgy began around 3000 B.C., at which time the exploitation of Anatolia's mineral wealth was well underway, benefitting not only Near Eastern cities but also their maritime trade.   *3000* B.C.

The highlands were probably ruled by various dynasties of chieftains, trading and quarreling among themselves and living in fortified towns. Caravan routes and cargo ships were forging regular trading contacts throughout Anatolia. By 1900 B.C., a sizable Assyrian merchant colony   *1900* B.C. was flourishing on the outskirts of the city of Kanesh (Figure 20.2), where regular donkey caravans moved southward from the highlands toward Mesopotamia.[3]

Table 20.1
The prehistory of European society.

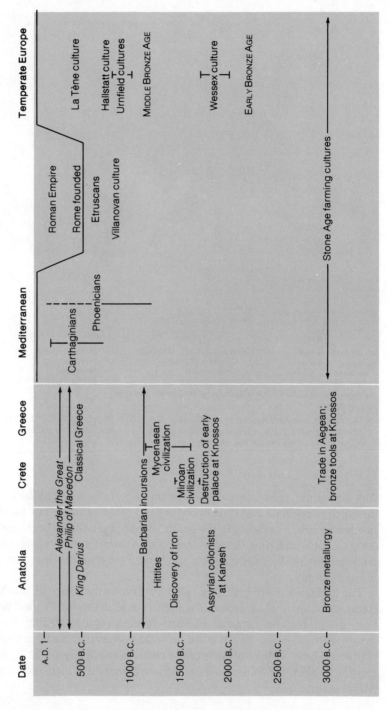

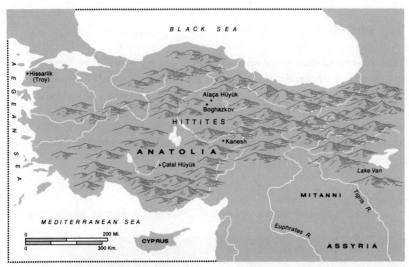

Figure 20.2
Anatolian sites mentioned in the text.

About this time, distinctive Hittite names first appear in mercantile records, as a small number of these able newcomers apparently entered Anatolian government and soon rose to political dominance.[4] The origins of the Hittites are shrouded in mystery, but small numbers of them are thought to have entered Anatolia from northern latitudes. They were an ambitious people, remarkable for their genius at military and political organization. With foreign policies aimed at conquering new territory and controlling trade routes, the Hittite empire, with its great capital of Boghazköy was a powerful element in Near Eastern politics by 1300 B.C. Its able kings used their wealth and commercial power to play off Egypt and Assyria against each other. But Hittite rule did not survive long, for their empire was overthrown by barbarian Phrygians from the north and west about the twelfth century B.C.

One major achievement of Hittite rule was the discovery of iron, thought to have been smelted first in the highlands immediately to the south of the Black Sea by the mid-second millennium B.C. The military advantages of this tough new metal were obvious, and the Hittite kings jealously guarded their secret. But eventually foreign mercenaries in their armies carried iron-smelting techniques to their homelands; knowledge of how to produce this most important of metals spread rapidly throughout the Near East and into Europe, bringing political consequences in its wake.

Hittite empire
1300 B.C.

Phrygian
1200 B.C.

?1450 B.C.

the aegean

?3000 B.C. The Aegean islands were sparsely inhabited by Stone Age farmers, for the rainfall is uncertain and the soils are poor. Soon after copperworking was introduced to mainland Greece around 3000 B.C., the Aegean assumed a more important role. Copper, obsidian, marble, and other valuable commodities were found on the Cyclades. Hardy settlers, who were also skillful mariners, traded their island products over the length and

Figure 20.3
Gold mask of a bearded man from Shaft Grave V at Mycenae, Greece, sixteenth century B.C.

breadth of the Aegean and far westward in the Mediterranean to Malta, Sicily, and Spain. Their ships, although of considerable size, had no windward ability; they could only sail downwind. Oars were used in periods of calm or of headwinds. During the Bronze Age, mariners were already accustomed to long, open-water voyages in search of metals and other forms of material prosperity. The Cretans and the Greeks were among those who sought to control the Aegean trade, with brilliant results.

troy and knossos

"A kind of radiance, like that of the sun or moon, lit up the high roofed halls of the great king. . . . The interior of the well-built mansion was guarded by golden doors hung on posts of silver which sprang from the bronze threshold. . . . On either side stood gold and silver dogs . . . to keep watch over the palace of the golden hearted Alcinous and serve him as immortal sentries never doomed to age."[5] Thus did the Greek writer Homer describe the palace of a legendary Greek king. Homer's *Iliad* and *Odyssey* have sparked the imaginations of generations of classical scholars and laymen alike. The legendary tales originated in prehistoric times before Greece became the epitome of Western democracy. Homer himself lived early in the first millenium B.C., his works being among the first expressions of the Western mind to appear in literary form.

Nineteenth-century archaeologists were fascinated by the Homeric epics and sought to identify the site of Troy and the palaces of its legendary heroes. But the discovery of the great Bronze Age civilization of Greece and Troy was the work of Heinrich Schliemann, a German businessman who retired at the age of forty-six to pursue his passion for archaeology.[6] Convinced that the site of Homer's Troy was the mound of Hissarlik near the Bosporus, he dug there at intervals from 1871 to 1890. The results were spectacular. He found the remains of great palaces, a citadel, and accomplished gold work; he was convinced that Hissarlik was indeed the site of Homer's Troy.

Then Schliemann turned his attention to the famous walled settlement of Mycenae on the Greek mainland. His excavations were rewarded with five spectacular shaft graves containing the remains of great chieftains adorned with weapons inlaid with copper and gold and gold face masks (Figure 20.3). He claimed they were the burials of legendary Homeric heroes.

As scholars continued Schliemann's work after his death in 1890, people began to speculate about the origins of Mycenaean civilization. Schliemann himself had favored Crete as a possible site for Mycenaean ancestry. At the time of his death, he was negotiating to dig at Knossos, fabled site of the legendary King Minos. After a German scholar had noticed the prevalence of carved seal stones inscribed with a form of writing in Crete, interest quickened. In 1896 a celebrated British archaeologist, Sir Arthur Evans, completed an exhaustive study of the seals and agreed with Schliemann that the Mycenaeans had originated in Crete.

Four years later Evans began to dig at Knossos and immediately uncovered the palace of Minos, a vast structure that covered two acres (0.8 hectares).[7] The excavations lasted for over thirty years and resulted in the discovery of a hitherto unknown prehistoric Minoan civilization with remarkable art, powerful rulers, and extensive trading connections.

the minoans

Prehistoric settlement in Crete was centered on the low-lying land adjoining the northern coast of the island. The first prehistoric inhabitants of Crete are known to us from a few stratigraphical pits at Knossos, where 7 meters (23 ft.) of Stone Age farming villages, consisting of ten building levels, underlie the Minoan civilization.[8]

6100 B.C.   The first farmers settled at Knossos around 6100 B.C., at about the same time that Çatal Hüyük was founded in Anatolia (Chapter 13). Pottery was first used soon afterward. The farmers lived in villages of sun-dried mud and brick huts which had rectangular ground plans containing 3730 B.C.   storage bins and sleeping platforms. By 3730 B.C., there are increased signs of prosperity and traces of rare, far-flung trading contacts, reflected in Egyptian stone bowls found in Stone Age levels. The origins of these farming cultures may well lie in Anatolia.

3000 B.C.   About 3000 B.C., a unique flowering of Aegean Bronze Age culture began with the introduction of small copper objects and the appearance of the first palace at Knossos.[9] About this time the olive tree and the grapevine had been domesticated, in addition to the emmer wheat and small stock of earlier times. Both olive trees and grapevines can be cultivated in places where cereals will not grow and thus do not compete for prime farming soil. This increased agricultural productivity, and provided the possibility of settlement on Aegean islands, where olives and grapes but not cereal crops could be grown. Agricultural economies became more diversified, and local food surpluses could be exchanged locally. Some measure of economic interdependency resulted, which eventually led to the development of redistribution systems organized by the palaces in Crete and elsewhere in the Aegean near the major centers of olive production.

Stone Age farmers had been largely self-sufficient except for limited obsidian trading. But the advent of metallurgy led to increased contacts within the Aegean area as demands for manufactured goods and metal tools increased. Interest in metal had a major impact on the Aegean, resulting in some cultural homogeneity brought about through trade, gift exchange, and perhaps piracy. The development of metalworking seems to have been a local process, although some specialized techniques may have been acquired from elsewhere. A wide range of day-to-day tools, weapons of a high standard, and beautiful luxury objects came into being as Aegean smiths refined their skills. Specialist craftsmen worked in the palaces, producing all manner of artifacts for the people. They lived in stone buildings with well-designed drainage systems and possessed wooden furniture.

Colin Renfrew has made out a convincing case for describing both Minoan and Mycenaean societies of Bronze Age times as civilizations.[10] He points to their sophisticated art and metalwork, to the complex palaces organized around specialist craftsmen, and to their developed redistribution networks for foods. The Minoans and Mycenaeans did not build vast temples like those at Tikal in Guatemala or those in Egypt. Nor did they live in cities. Palaces and elaborate tombs were the major monuments. Renfrew looks for the origins of Minoan and Mycenaean civilization within Greece and the Aegean, the result of local social change and material progress rather than external population movements. His theory is in sharp contradistinction to earlier hypotheses that called for the migration of new peoples into Greece from the north or for the diffusion of new culture traits from Anatolia or the eastern Mediterranean.

Sir Arthur Evans distinguished no less than nine periods of Minoan civilization; these periods have subsequently been refined by other scholars.[11] We know that the early palaces were finally destroyed in 1700 B.C., probably by an earthquake. Even before this, Cretan objects were being traded to Egypt and have been found in archaeological sites there. The high point of Minoan civilization occurred between 1700 and 1450 B.C., when the palace of Knossos reached its greatest extent. This remarkable structure was made largely of mud brick and timber beams with occasional limestone blocks and wood columns.[12] Some buildings had two stories, the plaster walls and floors of the palace were usually painted dark red. The walls and even the floors of the palace frequently were decorated, initially with geometric designs, and after 1700 B.C. with vivid scenes or individual pictures of varying size. Sometimes the decorations were executed in relief; in other cases, colors were applied to the damp plaster (Figure 20.4).

Figure 20.4
Reconstruction of the Throne Room at Knossos, Crete. The wall paintings are modern reconstructions from fragments found at the site and may be inaccurate in detail.

Artistic themes included formalized landscapes, dolphins and other sea creatures, and scenes of Minoan life. The most remarkable art depicted dances and religious ceremonies, including acrobats leaping vigorously along the backs of bulls (Figure 20.5). The famous writer Mary Renault has vividly reconstructed Cretan life at Knossos in a series of novels that bring Minoan culture to life.[13]

At the height of its prosperity, Crete was self-supporting in food and basic raw materials, exporting foodstuffs, cloth, and painted pottery all over the eastern Mediterranean. The Cretans were renowned mariners. Their large ships transported gold, silver, obsidian, ivory, and ornaments from central Europe, the Aegean, and the Near East, and ostrich eggs were probably traded from North Africa. The key to their political power seems to have been in their trading ability, which gave them widespread contacts and a virtual monopoly over maritime traffic.

1500 B.C. In 1500 B.C. a volcano on the island of Thera, 70 miles (113 km.) from Crete, exploded violently and seems to have had some destructive effect on Minoan civilization, which, however, was already showing signs of

1450 B.C. decline.[14] Fifty years later many Minoan sites were destroyed and abandoned. There are also signs of destruction and fire at Knossos. Warrior

?1400 B.C. farmers, perhaps from mainland Greece, established sway over the em-

Figure 20.5
A Minoan bull and dancers, as painted on the walls of the Palace of Knossos. The ox has a piebald coat and was a domesticated form. (After Arthur Evans.)

pire and decorated the walls of Knossos with military scenes. Seventy-five years later the palace was finally destroyed by fire, and the center of the Aegean world moved to the Greek mainland, where Mycenae reached the height of its power.

1375–1350 B.C.

the mycenaeans

When Heinrich Schliemann found the pre-Classical cultures of Greece and the Aegean, he claimed he had made a reality of the Homerian epic. He believed that the events in the *Iliad* and the *Odyssey* actually occurred, that archaeologists would be able to identify the actual burials of Agamemnon and other heroes. Schliemann in fact discovered prehistoric peoples whose deeds were vaguely remembered in Homer's days and were woven into long epic poems. The limitations of archaeological research and a lack of contemporary historical documents make it certain that the identity of the Mycenaean chiefs will always be shrouded in mystery. Schliemann's finds belong to the Greek Bronze Age, whose origins go back into what archaeologists call Middle Helladic times.

Mycenaean civilization began to flourish about the sixteenth century B.C., during Late Helladic times. Mycenae rose to political prominence because of its economic strength and extensive trading contacts. Minerals were in constant demand in the central and eastern Mediterranean, especially the tin used for the alloying of copper to make bronze. Both copper and tin were abundant in central Europe, and the Mycenaeans developed the necessary contacts to obtain regular metal supplies.

Mycenaean 1600 B.C.

Baltic amber, a yellow-brown fossil resin that when rubbed seems to become "electric," was being passed southward to the Mediterranean by the time the Mycenaeans became interested in central Europe (Figure 20.6). The magic properties that they believed amber to possess made it highly prized, so this substance was in constant demand.[15]

Amber was found in the royal graves at Mycenae. Its leaders' demands for the resin dominated much trade in Europe for many centuries, certainly until Mycenae declined in the twelfth century B.C. Well-established trade routes based on copper, tin, and amber ran across the Brenner Pass toward the Elbe River, then from the Adriatic to Greece by sea.

Mycenae itself was a strongly fortified citadel, an important center of warrior kings who rode in light chariots pulled by horses (Figure 20.7). Schliemann's Shaft Graves, with their gold and copper ornaments and weapons, found inside the famous Lion Gate at Mycenae testify to the wealth of the Mycenaean chieftains. So powerful were those rulers that *1400 B.C.* they probably destroyed Knossos in 1400 B.C., thereafter developing extensive trading contacts over the eastern Mediterranean as the prosperity of Mycenaean life reached its peak.

Mycenaean writing showed strong Minoan influences. The rulers of

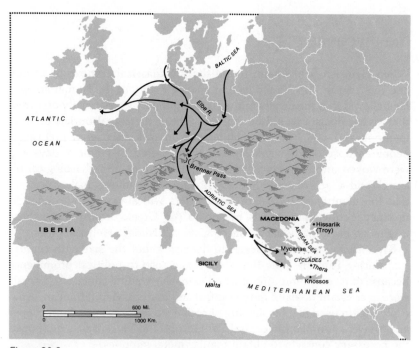

Figure 20.6
Amber trade routes in Europe and to Mycenae. Northern coastlines were the primary sources of amber.

Figure 20.7
Impression of a warrior fighting an enemy with a dagger, from an engraved gold ring, Shaft Graves, Mycenae, Greece.

Mycenae used a form of script written in the Greek language, known as Linear B.[16] Eighty-nine characters make up Linear B, forty-eight of which can be traced back to Minoan writing, Linear A. While Linear B is almost certainly derived from Linear A, the latter probably originated in the simple pictographic script of the earliest Minoans (Figure 20.8). The terms "Linear A" and "Linear B" were coined by Sir Arthur Evans when he first studied Minoan writing. Linear B was in more widespread use than A, partly because the Mycenaeans exerted greater political and economic power than their Cretan neighbors.

Mycenae continued to dominate eastern Mediterranean trade until the twelfth century B.C., when its power was destroyed by warrior peoples from the north. In the same century, other northern barbarians destroyed the Hittite kingdom in Anatolia. These incursions into the Mediterranean world were caused by unsettled political conditions in Europe, at least in part the result of population pressures and tribal warfare.

1150 B.C.

temperate europe in the bronze age

Older views of European prehistory held that the techniques of metallurgy diffused into more northerly latitudes from the Mediterranean

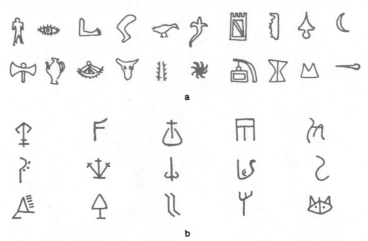

Figure 20.8
Early forms of writing: (a) Cretan pictographic script; (b) Linear A signs.

basin. Childe and others argued that the constant demands for copper and tin from central Europe led to a much wider diffusion of metallurgy and of bronze tools themselves. Soon metal became cheaper and more abundant, but its use was mostly limited to axes, spears, and ornaments.

The calibration of radiocarbon dates has resulted in a radically new chronology for the European Bronze Age. It places the appearance of metallurgy in the Balkans earlier than the first metal tools in Greece and the Aegean. Colin Renfrew has argued that the farmers of southeastern Europe invented the techniques of copper smelting independently, perhaps, as both he and Ruth Tringham have pointed out, as a result of improvements in pottery firing techniques that led to experimentation with copper ore.[17] Copper metallurgy, but not bronze, first appears around *4000 B.C.* 4000 B.C. and developed over a long period.

The development of bronze metallurgy in Europe was a somewhat later event, occurring during the third millennium B.C. Implements made of the new alloy were initially very rare, but their tough working edges were vastly superior to earlier tools. Most peasant societies, however, continued to use the stone tools that had effectively cultivated European soils for millennia.

the wessex culture

?2000–1700 B.C. One highly distinctive Early Bronze Age culture developed in southern Britain. The Wessex culture is perhaps most famous for its associations

Figure 20.9
Stonehenge photographed from the air before the restoration work of 1958, when the appearance of the site was radically altered to cater to large numbers of tourists.

with Stonehenge, the remarkable structure of freestanding stones in Wiltshire (Figure 20.9).[18] Richly adorned burials of warrior chieftains were laid under small burial mounds that stand out on the undulating landscape. Elegant stone battle-axes, metal daggers with wooden handles decorated in gold, and amber and gold ornaments accompanied the dead. The Wessex culture had its roots in earlier farming cultures, but the metal tools are somewhat reminiscent of Central European bronzework. Wessex bronze daggers date to a full millennium before Mycenae.

bronze age chieftains

Eventually, bronze weapons became more plentiful, as trading connections with the Mediterranean opened up new opportunities for European peasants. The intensification of trade inevitably led to trading monopolies and the concentration of wealth in the hands of a comparatively few individuals. Warlike tribes ruled by minor chiefs began to assert their authority, as population pressures on agricultural land intensified.

The rivalries of petty chiefs and warrior bands resulted in considerable political instability in central Europe. New alliances of small tribes were created under the leadership of powerful and ambitious chiefs, themselves once minor chieftains. Some warrior groups began to impinge on *1150* B.C. the fringes of the Mediterranean, destroying Mycenae and the Hittite empire.

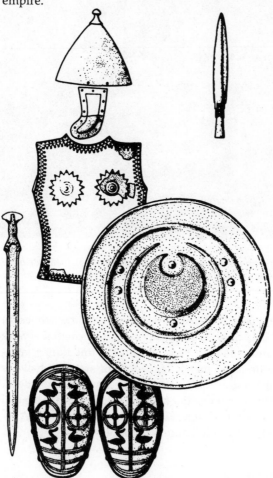

Figure 20.10

Late Bronze Age armor and weapons from central Europe, assembled to make a warrior's outfit. Each artifact was found in a different grave or hoard (one-twelfth actual size).

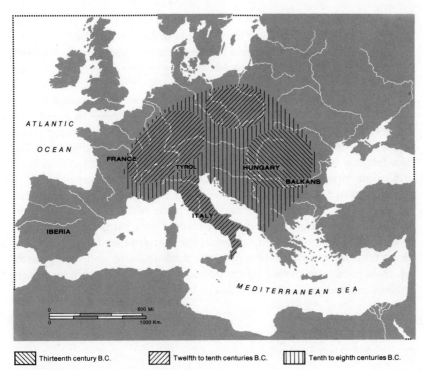

ATLANTIC

OCEAN

FRANCE

TYROL

HUNGARY

BALKANS

ITALY

IBERIA

MEDITERRANEAN SEA

0   600 Mi.

0   1000 Km.

Thirteenth century B.C.	Twelfth to tenth centuries B.C.	Tenth to eighth centuries B.C.

Figure 20.11
Approximate distribution of Urnfield cultures in Europe.

One powerful group of warrior tribes was centered in western Hungary; they are known to archaeologists as the "Urnfield" people, largely because of their burial customs. Their dead were cremated and their ashes deposited in urns. Huge cemeteries of urn burials are associated with fortified villages often built near lakes. Urnfield people began to make full use of horse-drawn vehicles and new weaponry. Skilled bronze smiths turned out carefully hammered sheet metal helmets and shields. The Urnfield people also used the slashing sword, a devastating weapon which was far more effective than the cutting swords of earlier times (Figure 20.10).

Around 800 B.C., the Urnfield people began to expand from their Hungarian homelands. Within a couple of centuries, characteristic slashing swords and other central European tools have been dated in sites in Italy, the Balkans, and the Aegean. By 750 B.C., Urnfield peoples had settled in southern France and moved from there into Spain (Figure 20.11). Soon Urnfield miners were exploiting the rich copper mines of the Tyrol in Austria. Bands of miners used bronze-tipped picks to dig deep under

Urnfield culture
?1000 B.C.

800 B.C.

750 B.C.

the ground in search of copper ore. Their efforts increased the supplies of copper and tin available to the peasants of central Europe.[19]

After 1200 B.C., the copper and amber trade with the Aegean declined, as a result of the fall of Mycenae. Many more copper and bronze artifacts became available for domestic consumption. Some new tool forms were introduced by central European smiths, including socketed axes, a variety of woodworking tools, and the ard (a scraping plow drawn by oxen). The ard was a particularly important innovation, for it allowed deeper plowing, more advanced agricultural methods, and higher productivity. The new farming techniques were vital, for there were more mouths to feed, and prime farming land was at a greater premium than ever before.

The pattern of European trade changed in response to greater demands for metal tools. Itinerant smiths and merchants peddled bronze weapons and axes all over Europe. Sometimes traders were caught in tribal raids or local wars, so they buried their valuable merchandise for safety. Some never returned to collect their precious stock-in-trade, and their hoards, which have been recovered by archaeologists, give an eloquent testimony to the unsettled political conditions of the later Bronze Age.[20]

european ironworkers: hallstatt and la tène

The Urnfield people lived in the center of a complicated network of trade routes that carried not only metals but also salt, grain, gold, pottery, and many other commodities. Sometime after 1000 B.C., the new techniques of ironworking spread into central Europe. The existing Bronze Age trade routes accelerated the diffusion of iron technology. As iron tools spread into the country north of the Alps, new societies arose whose leaders exploited the potential of the new metal.

hallstatt

Hallstatt culture
730 B.C.

One such culture was the Hallstatt, so named after a site near Salzburg, Austria.[21] Halstatt culture emerged in the seventh and sixth centuries B.C., and owed much to Urnfield practices, for the skillful bronze working of earlier times was still practiced. But some immigrants from the east, carrying long iron swords, may have achieved political dominance over earlier inhabitants. However, bronze was still the dominant metal used for horse trappings, weapons, and ornaments. Chiefs were buried in large burial mounds within wooden chambers, some in wagons.

The Hallstatt people and their culture spread widely through former Urnfield territories as far north as Belgium and the Netherlands and into

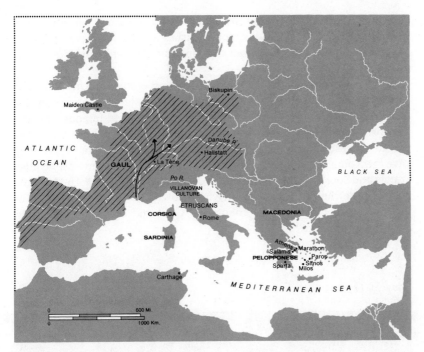

Figure 20.12
  Distribution of Hallstatt Iron Age cultures (shaded area) in Europe during the seventh to fifth centuries B.C. The map also shows the trade routes in southern France and the Mediterranean sites mentioned later in this chapter, Pazyryk is omitted.

France and parts of Spain (Figure 20.12). Many Hallstatt sites are particularly noticeable for their defensive nature. One famous settlement is the palisaded town of Biskupin, Poland, a fortress built in the middle of a swamp.

The Hallstatt peoples in the west began to develop contacts with Greek merchants centered on the French Riviera, who had established well-travelled trade routes up the Rhone River into central Europe. A significant import was the serving vessel for wine; skins of Mediterranean wine were carried far into central Europe, as Hallstatt chieftains discovered the joys of wine drinking.

la tène

By the last quarter of the fifth century B.C., a new and highly distinctive Iron Age culture, La Tène, had developed in the Rhine and Danube valleys.[22] An aristocratic clique of chieftains centered on the Danube valley enjoyed implements and weapons elaborately worked in bronze

La Tène culture
450 B.C.

and gold. Much of their sophisticated art had roots in Classical Greek and Mediterranean traditions, for Hallstatt craftsmen were quick to adopt new motifs and ideas from the centers of higher civilization to the south.

350 B.C.   La Tène technology was a specific adaptation of ironworking to woodland Europe. The culture extended northward into the Low Countries and Britain in the fourth century. La Tène art is justly famous, and the hill forts and defensive settlements of this Iron Age culture are widespread in western Europe (Figure 20.13). Their superior iron technology gave the Romans the short sword, for La Tène peoples survived long after France and southern Britain had been conquered by Rome.[23] The La Tène people were the fierce tribesmen whose towns Julius Caesar sacked in *55 B.C.*   his northward travels, as he conquered Gaul and brought Britain into the Roman Empire.

Figure 20.13
Aerial photograph of the earthworks at Maiden Castle, Dorset, England.

the scythians

The vast area of rolling grassland and steppe extending from China to the Ukraine was not settled by farming peoples until they were able to develop a culture enabling them to survive in an environment with extreme contrasts of climate and relatively infertile soils. The carrying capacity of the land is such that a vast territory is needed to support herds of domestic stock. The Scythians and other steppe people were nomads who settled on the steppe during the first millennium B.C., relying on the horse and wagon for mobility, living in stout felt tents, and subsisting largely on horse's milk and cheese, as well as on food from hunting and fishing. *?750 B.C.*

We are fortunate in having a great deal of data about the vigorous society of the Scythians, proto-Turks, and Mongols, largely gained from the spectacular frozen tombs of Siberia. The Scythians were feared by many. They were vividly described by Greek writer Herodotus: "Their customs . . . are not such as I admire. . . . The skulls of their enemies whom they most detest they treat as follows. Having sawn off the portion below the eyebrows, and cleaned out the inside, they cover the outside with leather. When a man is poor, this is all that he does; but if he is rich, he also lines the inside with gold: in either case the skull is used as a drinking cup."[24] With such a practice, it was certainly wise not to tangle with the Scythians.

Russian archaeologist Sergei Rudenko has excavated several Scythian burial mounds at Pazyryk in northeastern Siberia.[25] The chiefs of Pazyryk were elaborately tattooed, wore woollen and leather clothes, and employed skillful artists to adorn their horse trappings and harnesses with exuberant, elaborate stylized animal art. A powerful chief was accompanied to the next world by his wife and servants, horses and chariots, and many of his smaller possessions. *400 B.C.*

The Scythians lived to the north of the well-traveled trade routes of Greek merchants, but their territory was constantly being explored and sometimes colonized by settled farmers, whose own lands were becoming overpopulated or overgrazed. Enormous areas of steppe were needed to support even a small band of horsemen, for just a slight increase in population could drastically affect the food supplies of the original inhabitants. The result was constant displacement of populations as the Scythians sought to expand their shrinking territory to accommodate their own population pressures. The Scythians were a potent political force on the northern frontiers of the Mediterranean world throughout Classical and more recent times.

the mediterranean after mycenae

1200 B.C. After the fall of Mycenae in 1200 B.C., small townsmen on the Greek mainland continued to trade as their Mycenaean predecessors had, enjoying a monopoly of commerce within the Aegean and the Black seas.

600– 700 B.C. By the seventh and eighth centuries B.C., small colonies of Greek settlers lived on the northern and western shores of the Black Sea and along the north coast of Anatolia, and developed trade in gold, copper, iron, salt, and other commodities. Other Greeks voyaged westward and settled in southern France; they soon developed a brisk trade in wine and other commodities with central Europe.

The geography of Greece is such that fertile agricultural areas are often separated by ranges of mountains. As a result, the traders and seamen of the Aegean islands and the Greek mainland formed a network of small city-states that competed with each other for trade and political power. Athens was one of the larger and more prosperous states. The island of Sifnos in the Aegean was famous for its gold and silver. Paros marble was known all over the eastern Mediterranean. Milos provided obsidian for many centuries.

Greek states unified only in times of grave political stress, as when the Persian king Darius sought to add Greece to his possessions. His

490 B.C. defeats at Marathon (490 B.C.) and ten years later in a naval battle at Salamis ensured the security of Greece and permitted the development of Classical Greek civilization. Athens was foremost among the Greek states.[26] She became mistress of a league of maritime cities, which she soon turned into an empire. This was the Athens that attracted wealthy immigrants, built the Parthenon, and boasted of Aeschylus, Sophocles,

450 B.C. and other mighty playwrights. Classical Greek civilization flourished for fifty glorious years.

But throughout the brilliant decades of Athenian supremacy, bickering rivalry with the city of Sparta in the Peloponnese had flickered unabated. A deeply felt animosity between the two cities had its roots in radically different social systems. Sparta's government was based on military discipline and a rigid class structure. Athenians enjoyed a more mobile society and a democratic government.

The long-drawn-out rivalry culminated in the disastrous Peloponne-

430 B.C. sian war from 431 to 404 B.C. that led to the emergence of Sparta as a dominant political force on the mainland. The contemporary historian Thucydides has ably documented the history of the war which left disar-

359 B.C. ray in its wake.[27] Greece soon fell under the sway of Philip of Macedonia, whose rule between 359 and 336 B.C. began to develop political unity. This enabled his son Alexander the Great to bring much of the Mediterranean and Asian world under Greek influence, paving the way for the uniform government of imperial Rome.

the phoenicians

While the Greeks were developing their trading endeavors in the Aegean and Black seas, other maritime peoples were also emerging as vigorous traders. The Phoenicians of Lebanon first rose to prosperity by acting as middlemen in the growing trade in raw materials and manufactured products.[28] Phoenician ships carried Lebanese cedarwood and dye to Cyprus and the Aegean area as well as to Egypt. After the decline of Mycenae they took over much of the copper and iron ore trade of the Mediterranean. Their trading networks later extended far to the west, as they ventured to Spain in search of copper, tin, and the purple dye which was extracted from seashells and much used for expensive fabrics. By 800 B.C. Phoenician merchants were everywhere. They were using a fully alphabetical script by the tenth century B.C.[29]

1200 B.C.

800 B.C.

Phoenicians not only traded widely but set up small colonies that served as their vassals and acted as marketplaces for the hinterland of Spain and North Africa. Some settlements achieved independence from home rule. The greatest was the North African city of Carthage, which challenged the power of the Roman Empire.

the etruscans

The maritime activities of the Greeks and Phoenicians were expanding at the same time that skilled bronze workers and copper miners in northern Italy were developing a distinctive but short-lived urban civilization.

In about 1000 B.C., some Urnfield peoples from central Europe had settled south of the Alps in the Po Valley. They developed a skilled bronze-working tradition, whose products were traded far into central Europe and throughout Italy. This "Villanovan" culture emerged in the ninth century B.C. and was soon in touch with Greek colonies in southern Italy and perhaps with the Phoenicians.[30] Ironworking was introduced to the Villanovans about the ninth century. Iron tools and extensive trading contacts enabled the Villanovans to attain political control over much of northern and western Italy. They established colonies on Elba and Corsica. Some centuries of trade and other contacts culminated in a literate Etruscan civilization.

1000 B.C.

850 B.C.

Etruscan
650 B.C.

Like Classical Greece, Etruscan civilization was more a unity of cultural tradition and trade than a political reality.[31] The Etruscans traded widely in the central Mediterranean and with warrior peoples in central Europe. Etruscan culture was derived from the Villanovan, but it owed a considerable amount to eastern immigrants and trading contacts that brought a degree of oriental influence to Italian towns.

Etruscan territory was settled by city-states with a large measure of independence, each with substantial public buildings and fortifications. The decentralized political organization of the Etruscans made them vulnerable to foreign raiders. Warrior bands from central Europe were able *450 B.C.* to overrun some Etruscan cities in the centuries after 450 B.C. Etruscan prosperity began to crumble.

By the time of Etruscan decline, however, the Mediterranean was a civilized lake. Phoenician colonists had founded Carthage and other cities in North Africa and Spain and controlled the western Mediterranean. The rulers of Greece and Egypt and later Philip of Macedon controlled the east, while the Etruscans were in control of most of Italy and many central European trade routes.

the romans

The Etruscans had been the first to fortify the seven famous hills of Rome. *509 B.C.* In 509 B.C., a foreign dynasty of rulers was evicted by the Romans, who *295 B.C.* began to develop their own distinctive city-state.[32] By 295 B.C., the power of Rome had expanded to the extent that it dominated the whole of Italy. After two vicious wars with the Carthaginians of North Africa, where the expansionary desires of two great commercial states collided head on, Carthage was laid waste and the Romans quietly annexed its prosperous North African territories.[33] This territorial expansion provided much of the grain that the Roman emperors used to feed their teeming urban populations.

During the first two centuries B.C., Roman rule extended into the Near East and Egypt; the Mediterranean was completely under Roman control. Julius Caesar was the general responsible for the annexation of western *59 B.C.* Europe, conquering Gaul in a series of brilliant campaigns from 59 to *A.D. 43* 51 B.C., while Claudius subjected southern and central Britain from A.D. 43 to 47.

The Romans dominated Europe as far eastward as the Danube until *A.D. 117* A.D. 117, when their power began to decline as the ambitions and sophistication of the Iron Age tribes living on the fringes of Roman territory began to increase. The "barbarians" on the fringes of the empire were mainly peasant farmers who had obtained iron by trading and intermarriage with La Tène peoples. Many served as mercenaries in the Roman armies, acquiring wealth and sophistication.

A shortage of farming land and an increasing disrespect for Rome caused many Germanic tribes to raid Rome's European provinces. The raids were so successful that the imperial armies were constantly campaigning in the north. In A.D. 395, after the death of the emperor Theodosius, the Roman Empire was split into eastern and western divisions. Large-scale barbarian invasions from northern Europe ensued. Fifteen years later a horde of Germanic tribesmen from central Europe sacked Rome itself; then the European provinces were completely overrun by warrior peoples. Other Germanic hordes disturbed North Africa and crossed much of Asia Minor, but left little lasting mark on the history of those areas.

A.D. 395

A.D. 410

christianity and european civilization

The final spread of literate civilization to Europe owes much to the spread of Christianity. In the early fourth century A.D., it was recognized as the official religion of the Roman Empire. It survived in scattered outposts in England after the barbarian invasions of western Europe. Charlemagne and other west European rulers had reestablished Christianity as a vital force in western Europe by A.D. 800.[34]

A.D. 325

A.D. 800

A century later, the Vikings of Scandinavia and the Magyars of Hungary ravished much of the Atlantic coast and the frontiers of the Frankish empire, but by A.D. 1300, a more stable political situation had enabled Christianity to spread deep into Russia. The newly found unity of Christendom enabled European armies to resist the inexorable spread of Islam.

A.D. 1300

After the death of the Prophet Mohammed in A.D. 632, his followers had engulfed much of the Near East, as well as northwestern India, North Africa, and much of Spain.[35] Islam reached the peak of its territorial power in the tenth century. Two centuries afterward, merchants of the Middle Ages were trading with China again, as the Romans had done a thousand years before. In the fourteenth century, however, the Chinese began to embark on a policy of isolation. The policy partly resulted from continuing blockades and harassment by Muslim powers. Ambitious European merchants hoped to circumvent the Muslim blockade by finding alternative routes to China. Fifteenth-century Spanish and Portuguese adventurers began a search for sea routes to China. By the late fifteenth century the Portuguese had rounded the Cape of Good Hope and reached India, and Christopher Columbus had seen the New World. These voyages opened a new chapter in human history, the ultimate result of which was the end of prehistoric times for the world's population.[36]

A.D. 1488

21

the cities of asia

"During the age of Shen Nung, men cultivated food and women wove clothing. People were governed without a criminal law and prestige was built without the use of force. After Shen Nung, however, the strong began to rule over the weak and the many over the few. Therefore, Huang Ti administered internally with penalties and externally with armed forces."[1]* The passage we have just quoted is one of many legends surrounding a major folk hero, the famous Huang Ti (or the "Yellow Emperor"), who is credited with the founding of Chinese civilization. He is alleged to have reigned in 2697 B.C. But his deeds and those of the Hsia dynasty of kings said to have succeeded him are far from adequately documented and remain within the realm of legend. The emergence of the distinctive Shang civilization in the second millennium B.C. is, however, the point at which Chinese history and prehistory meet.

Archaeological researches into early Chinese civilization began centuries ago when nobles and kings dug royal graves for vases and fine bronzes. The collection of antiquities became a fashionable pursuit. People realized that Chinese civilization had a long history, but had no idea where the earliest cities would be found. Some clues were provided by nineteenth-century peasants who found innumerable fragments of decorated bone in their fields near Hsiao-t'un in the Anyang region of northern Honan Province. These curious bones were ground up by local druggists for use as medicines. Chinese archaeologists recognized the finds as Shang dynasty oracle bones. They began to look for archaeological traces of the legendary Shang kings.

In 1928, Tung Tso-pin and, later, Li Chi began digging at Hsiao-t'un and uncovered many details of a rich and diverse Shang city. The Hsiao-

* See page 403 for notes to Chapter 21.

t'un excavations were the training ground of a whole generation of Chinese archaeologists, many of whom subsequently worked on other Shang sites. Over fifty years of research have resulted in the investigation of over 130 Shang settlements centered in the former territory of the Yangshao people but extending southward to the Yangtze basin and to the west into eastern Kansu and Hupei.

lung-shan and the emergence of shang civilization

Many scholars have argued for a foreign origin of Shang civilization, with writing and other attributes of urban life being diffused eastward to the Huangho (Yellow) River. This ambitious theory ignored the distinctively Chinese character of Shang art; it has also been invalidated by recent discoveries of earlier Shang settlements (c. 1850 B.C.) and a long sequence of village and urban life in the Honan region.[2]

Chinese civilization had its roots in village farming cultures, and was based on economic and cultural traditions extending back several thousand years into prehistory. About 2500 B.C., the Lungshanoid Tradition spread widely over northern, central, and southern China (Chapter 15).[3] Each local variant of the Lungshanoid shared features of economy and material culture with other areas. The cultural inventories of the Lungshanoid cultures over a large area of China hint at a rapid spread of rice-growing societies. Inevitably, however, the Lungshanoid tradition began to develop in different ways as a result of contrasting environments and diverse economic strategies.

Lungshanoid Tradition 2500 B.C.

The interior saw the development of local "Lung-shan" ceramic styles, with their roots in the Lungshanoid traditions often found underlying Shang levels and covering occupation levels of the Yangshao farmers (Figure 21.1). (See also Chapter 15.) Radiocarbon dates for Lung-shan sites are virtually nonexistent, but a sample from Honan places Lung-shan-type pottery around 2200 B.C.[4]

Lung-shan cultures ?2000 B.C.

A number of elements in Lung-shan culture foreshadowed the emergence of Shang civilization. Lung-shan peasants were already living in sizable permanent settlements, far larger than the villages of earlier millennia. This clustering of population was partly in self-defense, for fortifications were common, a clear sign of warfare and raiding parties. Lung-shan villages sheltered some specialized craftsmen, for gray pots and jade ornaments are found in occupation levels of the period. There is also evidence of social ranking and trade.

In archaeological terms, the transition to full Shang civilization is marked both by a continuity in economic strategies and by a similarity

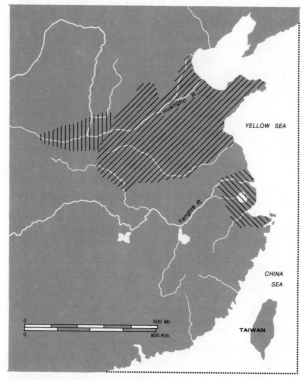

Figure 21.1

Distribution of Lung-shan cultures in China. Each shaded area represents a different regional variant of Lung-shan (not discussed in detail in the text). Compare with Figure 15.2.

of ritual practices such as ancestor worship and scapulimancy.[5] Staple crops and domestic animals remained the same, but the Shang people added water buffalo to their herds. Much of the population continued to live in semisubterranean houses clustered in large villages, which were sometimes built near large ceremonial complexes.

shang civilization

Shang
1850 B.C.

The cradle of Shang civilization has not yet been precisely identified, although Shang-type remains are found stratified directly on top of Lung-shan remains at numerous localities in North China (Figure 21.2).

Many changes introduced by the Shang people were political and social in nature: urban settlement patterns were common, bringing in their train

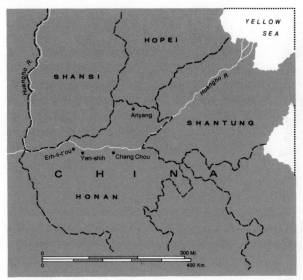

Figure 21.2
Shang archaeological sites mentioned in the text. Erh-li-kang and Hsiao-t'un are near Anyang.

some form of centralized government, much wider trading contacts, and greater necessity for keeping records; new techniques of warfare were developed, in which chariots played a leading role; class distinctions became more prominent as an elite aristocracy played a leading role in economic and political life. Writing was another Shang innovation, as was bronze working.

The history of writing in China is remarkable, for the analytic system of Chinese scribes has been in use for at least 4,000 years.[6] Chinese writing uses characters rather than the abstract alphabet used in the Western world (Figure 21.3). According to writing experts, the Shang inscriptions are in a script that had undergone a long period of development. They argue either that earlier writing has not survived because it was written on perishable materials or that it still awaits discovery. Other scholars think it was an artificially created script, possibly influenced by cuneiform, thus accounting for the transitional nature of Shang writing. We have no means of checking on any of these theories. Most Shang writings consist of archaic Chinese characters found on oracle bones and bronzes at Anyang. Some inscriptions are little more than proper names or labels of religious significance. The oracle texts, which are a little longer, are thought to contain both the questions posed by clients and the priests' responses.

Bronze working is a remarkable attribute of Shang civilization. Sophis-

Figure 21.3
 An inscription cast into a Shang bronze vessel, showing the Shang script.

ticated techniques such as casting were in use from the earliest centuries of the Shang. For this reason, some scholars have argued that the techniques of metallurgy were introduced to China from the West, where they had flourished for some time. But whatever the influences from outside, native Chinese style, design, and technique are strongly developed from the first appearance of bronze technology. Some knife and dagger forms as well as socketed axes do recall similar types widely distributed over the central Russian plains, and detailed analogies between pieces of Shang art and Russian finds may indicate considerable cultural contact and trade between the eleventh and fifteenth centuries B.C.

The well-known Sinologist Noel Barnard is convinced, however, that Shang bronze metallurgy shows little similarity to Western practices and was invented in China.[7] Abundant deposits of copper and tin occur in North China and were readily available to innovative craftsmen

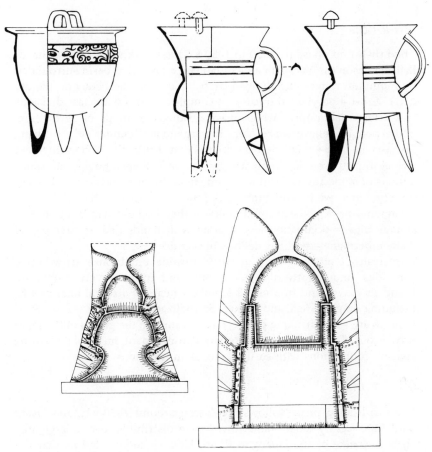

Figure 21.4
Shang bronze vessels (top) from Cheng Chou, China (no scale available), and diagrams (bottom) of clay molds for casting such vessels (about one-fifteenth actual size).

anxious to copy traditional art forms and artifacts in a new medium. Shang bronze workers are justly famous for their intricate vessels and fine casting technique (Figure 21.4).

stages of shang culture

At least three broad stages of Shang civilization have been identified, with a certainty that this tripartite scheme will be complicated in the future.[8]

erh-li-t'ou

Erh-li-t'ou
?1850–
1650 B.C.

The Erh-li-t'ou phase (c. 1850 to 1650 B.C.) is best known from archaeological sites in the Yen-shih area of Honan, a low-lying basin surrounded by mountain ranges and drained by tributaries of the Huangho (Figure 21.2).⁹ Erh-li-t'ou yielded traces of a complex society with class divisions and a large labor force which used advanced methods of agriculture. Some people believe that T'ang, the legendary founder of the Shang Dynasty in 1766 B.C., made his capital, Po, at Erh-li-t'ou. The settlement was of impressive size, dominated by a large T-shaped house with foundations of stone and walls of mud and sticks. Smaller rectangular houses, pottery kilns, wells, and numerous burials adorned with pottery and ornaments have come from the site. Other bodies were deposited in storage pits or occupation levels, often with hands tied or after partial dismemberment — perhaps deliberate sacrifices.

Specialist craftsmen were at work, turning out bronze arrowheads, fishhooks, and spearheads. Jade, stone, and turquoise ornaments are found in graves and houses. The pottery bears stylized animal motifs, including dragons, fish, and snakes. Specialized cooking vessels are common; so are wine-drinking pots, typically found in the graves of the more prosperous. Cord-impressed pottery is also abundant, much of it showing stylistic connections with earlier Lung-shan traditions.

erh-li-kang

Erh-li-kang
1650–
1400 B.C.

The Erh-li-kang phase follows Erh-li-t'ou around 1650 B.C., and lasted until 1400 B.C. By then, Shang towns were distributed over a large area on both banks of the Huangho River. Literary sources tell us that the Shang kings changed their capital several times before finally settling at Anyang after 1400 B.C. One such early capital was at the modern city of Cheng Chou, a major center of Shang civilization during the Erh-li-kang phase.

Cheng Chou was a very large city indeed, with a centrally situated ceremonial and administrative area that now lies under the modern town. A walled rectangular enclosure, some 1.3 miles (2.1 km.) from north to south and a mile (1.6 km.) across, surrounded the ceremonial area. An Chin-huai, a Chinese scholar, has estimated that the earth wall around Cheng Chou was over 9 meters (30 ft.) high, with an average width of 18 meters (60 ft.). His experiments in earthmoving with Shang tools produced a rough calculation that a labor force of 10,000 men would have taken at least 18 years to build the walls of Cheng Chou. Presumably, the royal families, priests, and some selected craftsmen lived in the enclosure, protected by guards and retinue.

Most workmen and peasant farmers who supported this vast ceremonial complex lived around Cheng Chou in small villages scattered through the countryside. Bronze foundries and pottery kilns have been located outside the walls. While some craftsmen lived in substantial houses, with floors of pounded-down earth, most people lived in humble, semisubterranean huts and used far less intricate vessels than the skillfully cast ceremonial bronzes of the Shang kings.

yin

By 1400 B.C., the center of Shang civilization had shifted north of the Huangho River, but the extent of the kingdom remains confined to northern Honan and parts of Hopei and Shantung. The Yin phase of Shang civilization, lasting until 1100 B.C., is best known from the great capital city of Anyang, the seat of twelve Shang kings over nearly 300 years. The Anyang area had been occupied for centuries before it became the center of Shang settlements. Despite nearly two decades of excavations, tantalizingly little has been written about the royal capital.

A huge ceremonial district at Hsiao-t'un near Anyang was built on the banks of the Huan River.[10] The north end of Hsiao-t'un was occupied by fifteen large rectangular houses (Figure 21.5). Other rectangular or square structures were built in the middle of this settlement. Many burials were found in their vicinity; included also were the foundations of five gates. A further complex of buildings at the southern end of the precinct may have been a ceremonial area. Hsiao-t'un houses were built with pounded-down earth foundations and a timber framework set on stone pillars. The walls of wattle and daub were topped with thatched roofs (Figure 21.5). Semisubterranean huts nestled near the larger structures, some of them bronze workshops or potters' areas. Others were presumably servants' quarters. Several of the temple structures had been consecrated with human sacrifices found huddled in pits near the foun-

Yin
1400–
1100 B.C.

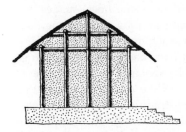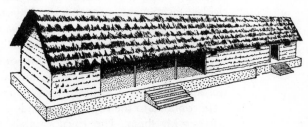

Figure 21.5
A reconstruction of a long house from the ceremonial area at Hsiao-t'un, Anyang, Honan Province, China.

dations. Hsiao-t'un probably served much the same function as the great enclosure at Cheng Chou.

royal graves

The Shang royal graves and cemeteries were discovered at Hsi-pei-kang, north of Hsiao-t'un.[11] Eleven highly elaborate tombs are thought to coincide with the eleven Shang rulers who resided at Anyang at the height of its prosperity.[12] The bodies were laid in huge tomb-like structures up to 9 meters (30 ft.) deep, entered by long ramps on two or more sides. A wooden chamber inside each pit contained the royal coffin, surrounded by human sacrifices, and elaborate ornaments — bronze castings, remarkable stone sculptures of stylized beasts in a distinctive Chinese style, fine clay vessels, jade, and bone objects. Chariots were also buried with the dead. Sacrificial victims were placed both in the pit and on the ramps leading to the grave. Some were decapitated before burial, their heads buried separately from their trunks.

shang life

Shang civilization is epitomized by the organization of Cheng Chou and Anyang. The aristocracy lived in their own compounds, which had ceremonial altars, temples, imposing palaces, and elaborate royal tombs. Administrative powers were exercised from the security of the aristocracy's precincts, where they were surrounded by the paraphernalia of economic, political, and religious prestige.

The royal seats were surrounded by extensive networks of scattered villages whose economic and administrative structures were linked together in such a way that they depended on one another for specialist services. The peasant farmers supported the state by intensive agriculture, for which they used large digging sticks, stone hoes, spades and sickles. Fishing was economically important; hunting occurred perhaps as a royal sport rather than as a subsistence activity.

Chinese-American scholar Kwang-chih Chang has stressed the contrast between the large urban populations of Mesopotamia and the scattered village networks around a Shang capital.[13] While the Shang civilization was a definite break with earlier settlement traditions, its urban centers were confined to the royal compounds and the specialist craftsmen associated with them. The royal capitals supported the aristocracy and priesthood, employed craftsmen, and were the nucleus of political and religious life (Figure 21.6). Scribes recorded official business, and stores of food were maintained. In these senses the capitals performed all the essential functions of the Mesopotamian city-states.

In contrast to the West, the common people were dispersed throughout the countryside, providing the essential subsistence base for a remarkable and highly sophisticated civilization. There were no teeming urban populations of peasants and artisans clustered in metropolitan communities under the shadow of temple or city walls. Communications and basic administrative functions were facilitated by a sophisticated system of writing. The powers of the central government depended on economic and kinship ties, which could deliver huge labor forces to build royal tombs and to staff armies when wars occurred.

Figure 21.6
Oracle bone of the Shang dynasty, from Hsiao-t'un, Honan Province, China.

Shang religious life was controlled by a regular calendar of events. The clannish aristocracy was much concerned with elaborate ancestor worship. A supreme being, Shang Ti, presided over a series of gods, controlling all human affairs. The royal ancestors acted as intermediaries between the Shang rulers and Shang Ti, with scapulimancy and other rites providing communication with the dead. Shang art is remarkable for its animal motifs and human images, sculpted in stone and bronze, as well as in clay, jade, bone, and ivory. This artistic tradition was at least partly dictated by ceremonial specifications connected with burial and other ritual events.

shang and chou

Throughout the life of the Shang civilization, village farming cultures of earlier millennia continued to flourish in other parts of China. Shang culture exercised a vigorous influence on the native populations of central and southern China. The growth of early Chinese civilization was slow, albeit constant.[13]

Chou
1122 B.C.

About 1122 B.C., the capital of the Shang empire was plundered by the Chou people, who lived on the frontiers of the Shensi. So pervasive, however, was the pattern of Shang civilization that the new arrivals soon took over the long-established Shang social and cultural practices. Soon the Chinese acquired many of the basic customs and philosophical tenets that have survived until modern times. Ironworking was invented, apparently independently from the West, in the mid-first millennium. Cast-iron tools were used for cultivation, which further increased the productivity of Chinese farmers.

500 B.C.

Han
221 B.C.

The Chou dynasty divided its territory into a series of feudal states. Not until the last few centuries before Christ was China unified under the Ch'in and Han emperors, who shifted the political power base from Huangho in northern China to the Yangtze River area. During this time, the Chinese came into contact with the Roman Empire and began extensive trading with India. By Roman times, Chinese civilization had been flourishing for over 2,000 years, a distinctive and highly nationalistic culture that survives today.

22

maya, aztec, and inca: early civilizations in the new world

"The great city of Tenochtitlán is built in the midst of this salt lake, and it is two leagues from the heart of the city to any point on the mainland. Four causeways lead to it, all made by hand and some twelve feet wide. The city itself is as large as Seville or Córdova." Thus did the Spanish conquistador Hernando Cortes begin his description of the Aztec capital in the valley of Mexico in A.D. 1519. Cortes provided a vivid description of a prehistoric civilization at the height of its power, a society he destroyed completely within a few years.

A little more than a decade later, Francisco Pizarro destroyed the Inca state, another New World civilization whose riches rivaled that of the Aztec. Both Aztec and Inca were debased by superior technology, and left folk traditions, impressive monumental sites, and large peasant populations behind them. Although Spanish scholars like Garcilaso de la Vega had an inclination for ethnographic observations, we are obliged to rely on nearly a century of intense archaeological research into pre-Columbian sites to write the account of Mesoamerican and Peruvian civilizations that follows.

Who was responsible for the development of American civilizations? Were they of indigenous origin or the work of immigrants from across the Atlantic or Pacific? A large literature surrounds this fascinating question, some of it near nonsense, and other contributions highly provocative. Some diffusionist theories which say inhabitants of such hypo-

Table 22.1
Early civilizations in Mesoamerica and Peru.

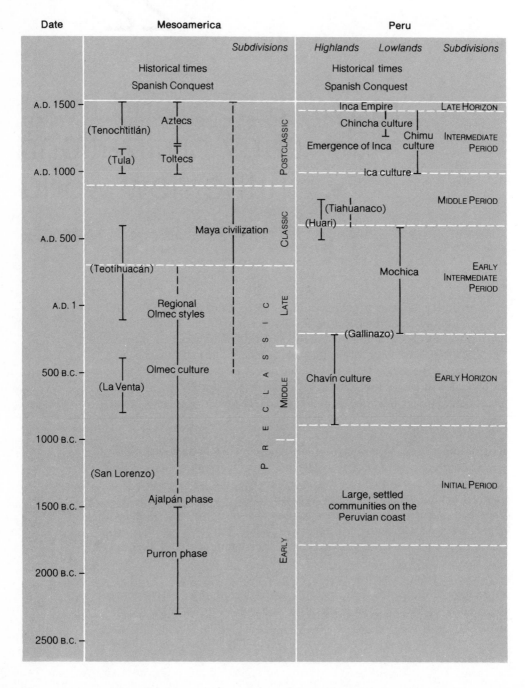

thetical lands as Mu and Atlantis came to America are so extraordinary that they do not merit serious consideration. Many legends speak of early visits by Mediterranean sea captains, ancient Egyptians, and St. Brendan (an Irish abbot whose peripatetic voyages in the sixth century A.D. have been a fruitful source of historical speculation). Betty Meggers and other scholars have sought to derive pre-Columbian pottery from Ecuador from Jomon wares in Japan, talking in terms of trans-Pacific colonization of South America. Most authorities think that the two pottery styles are unrelated but have some chance resemblances.

The practicability of transoceanic voyaging to the New World over the Atlantic has clearly been demonstrated by Thor Heyerdahl with his *Ra* expedition. But he has not proved that such voyages took place. The archaeological evidence for pre-Columbian visitors is practically nonexistent, with the exception of l'Anse-aux-Meadows, a possible Viking settlement in Newfoundland. In summary, there seems little doubt that some Old World visitors did reach America before Christopher Columbus, but the question of whether these visitors were culturally significant is another matter and one that is the subject of intensive debate.[1]*

mesoamerica

Before examining the rise of Mesoamerican civilization, we should look at the nuclear area's rich and diverse environment (Table 22.1).[2] Two mountain chains run down each coast of Mexico, enclosing the Mesa Central, which is bounded in the south by great volcanoes (Figure 22.1). For thousands of years this area has provided good building stone and also volcanic glass for artifacts. The highlands (which include the valley of Mexico) have few outlets to the coasts. A series of shallow, high-altitude lakes nurture waterfowl and fish and provide swampy but fertile soil on their shores. It was in these highland areas that the cultivation of maize first began, an event described in Chapter 16.

The eastern coasts of Mesoamerica are tropical lowlands, rich in both fish and vegetable foods. Humid, dense rain forest covers much of the lowlands, which are interspersed with hilly limestone country and many lakes. Coastal estuaries penetrate deep into the lowlands, merging into swamps and small streams. Long before maize cultivation began, man had settled on river terraces and natural ridges in the forest.

By 1500 B.C., sedentary farming villages were common throughout most of Mesoamerica. Their agriculture relied on a wide variety of plant species, and slash-and-burn farming methods were in wide use in the low-

---

* See pages 404–405 for notes to Chapter 22.

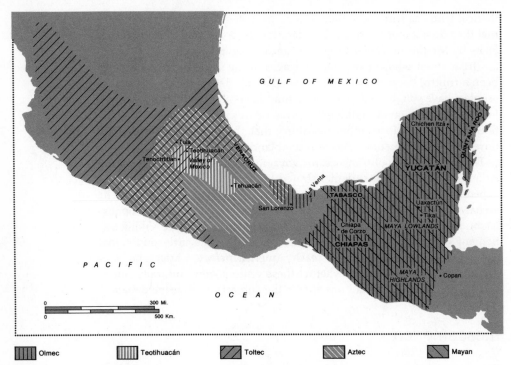

Figure 22.1
Mesoamerican archaeological sites mentioned in Chapter 22. The approximate distributions of various cultures are shown.

lands. Such methods enabled small gardens to be cleared in the forest by cutting the trunks of trees and the brush, and carefully burning branches to fertilize with a layer of wood ash; then maize and other crops were planted with pointed wooden sticks; a few seasons later, the land was abandoned as the soil became exhausted. Thus, every year the farmer had to clear new land, planting less important crops on his older plots or abandoning them to the forest. There was a constant search for new lands, even when slash-and-burn techniques were combined with the use of irrigation or the cultivation of regularly flooded lakeside or riverside gardens.

preclassic peoples

Early
Preclassic
2500–
1000 B.C.

Many centuries elapsed between the origins of village life and the emergence of Mesoamerican civilization. The critical period during which

Mesoamericans began to congregate in larger settlements and build elaborate ceremonial centers has been termed the "Preclassic," or "Formative" period, lasting from approximately 2500 B.C. to A.D. 300.[3] Several Preclassic phases have been identified, the earliest of which marked the appearance of pottery and the first religious centers. The Middle Preclassic is famous for the Olmec culture, appearing from 1200 to 300 B.C. The Late Preclassic is typified by various regional cultures, some displaying Olmec-like features in their art and culture.

The Preclassic period begins with the Purron phase in Tehuacán,[4] between 2300 and 1500 B.C., when pottery first appears in the highland valleys, perhaps modeled on stone originals. The Purron phase was increasingly based on settled villages. By 1500 B.C., the succeeding Ajalpán phase included painted and black fired pots of a type found elsewhere in Mesoamerica, especially in the lower levels of the Chiapa de Corzo site in Chiapas. That settlement shows traces of many successive stages of Preclassic occupation in which stone architecture played an important part in ceremonial life.

Purron
2300–
1500 B.C.

Ajalpán
1500 B.C.

Ceremonial centers emerged in the Middle Preclassic period, marking the transformation of village society into a wider social order as the lives of many communities became concentrated around a common religion. The distinguished American scholar Gordon Willey has argued that the first ceremonial centers developed in response to a population increase and a desire to maintain and symbolize kinship and religious unity. "Some villages," he wrote, "probably the original ones, were revered as homes of leaders and became seats of religious and political authority. They were visited by pilgrims from the surrounding villages, shrines and temples were erected, and the priest-leaders were buried there."[5] As the power of the leaders increased, so did their ability to employ specialist craftsmen, manipulate large labor forces, and engage in trading activities.

Middle
Preclassic
1000–300 B.C.

olmec

The most famous Preclassic culture is that of the Olmec, centered in the lowland regions of southern Veracruz and western Tabasco.[6] There, ceremonial centers achieved a remarkable complexity at an early date. Olmec means "rubber people," and the region was long famous as an important center for rubber production. Although the Olmec homeland is low-lying, tropical, and humid, its soil is fertile, and the swamps, lakes, and rivers are rich in fish, birds, and other animals. Olmec societies prospered in this region for a thousand years from about 1500 B.C., and created a highly distinctive art style. Many of their activities revolved around elaborate ceremonial centers.

Olmec
1500–500 B.C.

san lorenzo

The earliest traces of Olmec occupation are best documented at San Lorenzo, where the Olmec people lived on a platform in the midst of frequently inundated woodland plains. They erected artificial ridges and mounds around their platform, upon which they built pyramids and possibly ball courts and placed elaborate monumental carvings on the ridges overlooking the site. The earliest occupation of San Lorenzo shows few Olmec features, but by 1250 B.C., the inhabitants were already begin-

1250 B.C.   ning to build some raised fields, a task that required enormous labor forces. By that time, too, distinctive Olmec sculpture begins to appear. A century later, magnificent monumental carvings adorned San Lorenzo, distinctive, savage, and often mutilated by the Olmec themselves.

One archaeologist has estimated the population of San Lorenzo at 2,500. The inhabitants enjoyed extensive trading contacts, especially in obsidian and other semiprecious materials obtained from wide areas of Mesoamerica. San Lorenzo fell into decline after 900 B.C. and was surpassed in importance by La Venta, the most famous Olmec site, nearer the Gulf of Mexico.

Figure 22.2
An Olmec altar sculpture from La Venta. The altar is 3.4 meters (about 11 ft.) high.

la venta

The La Venta ceremonial center was built on a small island in the middle of a swamp.[7] A rectangular earth mound, 120 meters long by 70 meters wide and 32 meters high (393 ft. by 229 ft. and 105 ft. high), dominates the island. Long, low mounds surround a rectangular plaza in front of the large mound, faced by a complex of walls and terraced mounds at the other end of the plaza. Vast monumental stone sculptures litter the site, including some of the famous Olmec heads bearing expressions of contempt and savagery; caches of jade objects, figurines, and a dull green rock (serpentine) are common, too (Figure 22.2). Every piece of stone for sculptures and temples had to be brought from at least 60 miles (96 km.) away, a vast undertaking, for some sculptured blocks weigh over forty tons. La Venta flourished for about four hundred years from 800 B.C. After **800–400 B.C.** about 400 B.C., the site was probably destroyed, a deduction made from the fact that many of its finest monuments show signs of having been intentionally defaced.

La Venta is perhaps most famous for its distinctive "Olmec" art style, executed both as sculptured objects and in relief. Olmec sculpture concentrated on natural and supernatural beings, the dominant motif being the "were-jaguar," (Figure 22.3) or human-like jaguar. Many jaguars were given infantile faces, drooping lips, and large, swollen eyes, a style also applied to human figures; some were given almost negroid faces, others resembled snarling demons in their ferocity. The Olmec contribution to Mesoamerican art and religion was enormously significant. Elements of their art style and imagery were diffused widely during the first millennium B.C., southward to Guatemala and San Salvador and northward into the valley of Mexico.

The spread of the Olmec art style and the beginning of the Late Pre- **Late Preclassic** classic in about 500 to 300 B.C. signals the period during which a common **300 B.C.–** religious system and ideology began to unify large areas of Mesoamerica. **A.D. 300** A powerful priesthood congregated in spectacular ceremonial centers, commemorating powerful and widely recognized deities. Distinctive art and architecture were associated with the new religion, whose practice required precise measurements of calendar years and longer cycles of time. Writing and mathematical calculations were developed to affirm religious practices, which served as a unifying political force in the sense that they welded scattered village communities into larger political units. By the time that the Classic Mesoamerican civilizations arose, dynasties of priests and aristocrats had been ruling parts of Mesoamerica along well-established lines for nearly 1,000 years.

Figure 22.3
Ceremonial Olmec ax head depicting a god who combines the features of a man and a jaguar. His face is stylized, with flame-like eyes and a drooping mouth.

the classic period

The cultural achievements of the Mesoamericans between A.D. 300 and 900 were so remarkable that they must rank among the most startling of prehistoric times. The Classic period of Mesoamerican civilization begins with the first "Long Count" dates carved on altars, stairways, or pillars. The Long Count was a method of telling how many days had elapsed since the beginning of time, calculated to have been 3113 B.C., probably a legendary beginning point. The earliest recorded Long Count date is A.D. 292 on a pillar at Tikal, Guatemala; the latest, A.D. 909 from

Quintana Roo.[8] They represent the limits of the Classic period of the Maya, a people connected with the Olmec culture and with a long history of subsistence farming in the lowlands.

During the Classic period, populations increased dramatically, ceremonial centers became even more elaborate, the rich became richer, and the peasants still lived much as they had. More and more human settlement gravitated toward ceremonial centers as craftsmen and specialist traders settled near their masters, and skilled architects directed temple construction. No work was too great. Enormous public works were undertaken for the glorification of the gods. Patient craftsmanship was lavished on sculpture and ritual objects.

Extraordinary heights of cultural sophistication were reached during the Classic period, especially among the Maya peoples of the lowlands but also in the highlands, where the remarkable Teotihuacán people lived in a vast urban complex. Although Teotihuacán and the Maya are the most famous of Mesoamerican civilizations, other regions enjoyed their own distinctive Classic cultures derived from Preclassic cultural traditions.

teotihuacán

Teotihuacán, northeast of Mexico City, was an urban center and the dominant political and cultural center of all Mesoamerica around A.D. 500.[9] The peoples of the valley of Mexico may have lagged behind southern Mesoamerica in cultural terms until the end of the Preclassic, when they built the first mounds on the northern edge of Teotihuacán about 100 B.C. Remarkably, the earliest ceremonial complex covered an area of three square miles (7.8 sq. km.). In succeeding centuries, the site mushroomed to incorporate a huge city.

100 B.C.

Teotihuacán is dominated by the "Pyramid of the Sun" (a modern name), a vast structure made of earth, adobe, and piled rubble. The pyramid, faced with stone, is 64 meters (210 ft.) high and 198 meters (650 ft.) square (Figure 22.4). A wooden temple was probably built on the summit of the terraced pyramid. The long "Avenue of the Dead" passes the west face of the Pyramid, leading to the "Pyramid of the Moon," the second largest structure at the site. The avenue is lined with civic and religious buildings, and side streets lead to residential areas. A large palace and temple complex dedicated to the Plumed Serpent (Quetzalcóatl), with platform and stairways built around a central court, lies to the south of the center of Teotihuacán, across from a central marketplace.

The Avenue of the Dead and the pyramids lie at the center of a sprawling mass of small houses. Priests and craftsmen lived in dwellings

Figure 22.4
The ceremonial center at Teotihuacán, Mexico. The Pyramid of the Sun and the Avenue of the Dead dominate the picture.

around small courtyards; the less privileged lived in large compounds of rooms connected by narrow alleyways and patios. By any standard, Teotihuacán was a city, and at one point housed up to 120,000 people. Although some farmers probably lived within the confines of the city, we also know that rural villages flourished near Teotihuacán. These villages were compact, expertly planned, and administered by city rulers.

Maize, squashes, and beans provided the staple diet of Teotihuacán's teeming population, supplemented by other minor crops and a limited amount of hunting. Substantial agricultural surpluses were essential for the survival of the city. Most archaeologists believe that irrigation techniques were in use, harnessing swamp and river to fertilize the enormous acreages of agricultural land that were needed. Unfortunately, however, irrigation works are difficult to date accurately, and we can only assume that they were in use. The city itself has been described by American archaeologist René Millon as a "pilgrim-shrine-temple-market complex."[10] Obsidian and other raw materials were imported for craftsmen's workshops, the fine products of which were traded widely as barter networks carried Teotihuacán's ceramics to the Gulf Coast and Guatemala.

However, by A.D. 600, just when Teotihuacán's cultural influence was spreading rapidly outside the highlands, the city population declined sharply. Then Teotihuacán was burned, probably by northern barbarians, who destroyed the fabric of one of the most powerful and influential Mesoamerican civilizations. The conquerors of Teotihuacán were one of many northern peoples to press southward into the prosperous farmlands of the highlands. Environmental conditions on the dry northern frontiers of Mesoamerica were such that even simple agriculture was a chancy business, plagued by constant droughts and crop failures. As populations grew, so did competition for agricultural land, hunting grounds, and water supplies. Bands of farmers occasionally moved south toward better-watered country, looking for new territory. The newcomers fell on the prosperous farmers of the highlands, fighting their way southward to Teotihuacán. Some barbarians were rapidly absorbed into Mesoamerican society, but that did not save Teotihuacán from destruction. A.D. 600

the maya

Traces of primordial Mayan culture are discernible in the Yucatan many centuries before this brilliant civilization flourished throughout the southern lowlands and in the Yucatan.[11] Classic Mayan civilization was in full swing by A.D. 300 and was centered around ceremonial centers such as Tikal and Copan, whose earth-filled pyramids were topped with temples carefully ornamented with sculptured stucco. The pyramids were faced with cemented stone blocks. The large temples on top had small, dark rooms because the builders did not know how to construct arches and were forced to corbel their roofs. Tikal was an important trade center and, like other centers, attracted specialized craftsmen who served the priests and the gods (Figure 22.5). Most Mayans lived in scattered villages of humble, thatched houses, supporting the elaborate ceremonies of state by their labors. A.D. 300

The unifying force for the Mayan state was religion. Mayan rulers constantly sought to appease their numerous gods (some benevolent, some evil) at the correct moments in the elaborate sacred calendar cycle. Each sacred year, as well as each cycle of years, was under the destiny of a different deity. The continued survival of the state was ensured by pleasing the gods with sacrificial offerings, some of which were human.

Astronomy was at the center of government and religion. The Mayan priests were remarkable astronomers, who predicted the course of most astronomical events, including eclipses of the sun and moon. Religious

Figure 22.5
  Temple I at Tikal, Guatemala, which dates about A.D. 700.

events were regulated according to a sacred year *(tzolkin)* of 13 months
of 20 days each. The 260 days of the sacred year were unrelated to any
astronomical phenomenon, being closely tied to ritual and divination. The
length of the sacred year was arbitrary and probably established by long
tradition. Tzolkins were, however, closely intermeshed with a secular year
(haab) of 365 days, an astronomical calendar based on the solar cycle. The
haab was used to regulate the affairs of state, but the connections between
sacred and secular years were of great importance in Mayan life. Every
52 years a complete cycle of all the variations of the day and month names
of the two calendars occurred, an occasion for intense religious activity.

The Maya developed a hieroglyphic script that was used for calculating
calendars and regulating religious observations. Thanks to Spanish
bishop Diego de Landa, who recorded surviving Mayan dialects in the
mid-sixteenth century, scholars have been able to decipher part of the
script that was written on temple walls and modeled in stucco. The symbols are fantastically grotesque, mostly humans, monsters, or gods' heads
(Figure 22.6).[12]

The famous site of Copan, founded in the fifth century A.D., was one

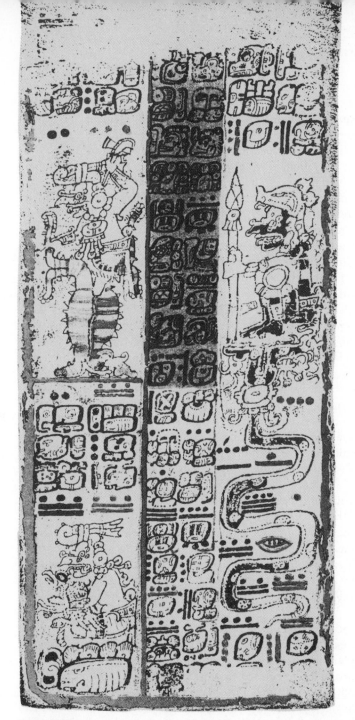

Figure 22.6
Only three Maya codices (books of picture writing) are known to have survived destruction by the Spanish. Here is a page from the so-called Dresden Codex, which records astronomical calculations, ritual detail, and tables of eclipses.

of the major astronomical centers of Mesoamerica. Its pyramids, temples, and pillars are a remarkable monument to the skill of the early American priests. Copan, like Tikal, preserves the essential elements of Mayan ceremonial centers. These include platforms, pyramids, and causeways, architectural features grouped around open concourses and plazas, presumably both for religious effect and also to handle the large numbers of spectators who flocked to the religious ceremonies.

Huge ball courts were built at some centers. They were used for an elaborate ceremonial contest, perhaps connected with the fertility of crops, between teams who competed with a solid rubber ball. The exact details of the game remain obscure, but stone loops protruding from the side walls of the court were presumably designed for the players to knock the ball through, thereby winning the game.

Mayan civilization was far from uniform; each major center maintained its own political identity and ruled a network of lesser religious complexes and small villages. The calendar and hieroglyphic script were common to all, essential to the regulation of religious life and the worship of Mayan gods. Architectural and artistic styles, used in ceramics and small artifacts, varied from center to center as each developed its own special characteristics and cultural traditions. Gordon Willey believes that these local variations "savor of ethnocentrism, a belief on the part of the inhabitants that their particular city-state was superior to all others."[13] Thus the Mayans were unified more by religious doctrine than by political or economic concerns, in much the same way, perhaps, as the spread of Islam unified diverse cultures with a common religious belief (Figure 22.7).

A.D. 900?

Mayan civilization reached its maximum extent after A.D. 600. Then, at the end of the ninth century, the great ceremonial centers of the Petén and the southern lowlands were abandoned. In these areas the calendar was discontinued and the structure of religious life decayed. No one has been able to explain this sudden decline in Petén, which was perhaps brought on by a combination of growing populations, increased pressure on agricultural land, and generally unsettled political and military conditions.

Tribal dislocations may have begun with the fall of Teotihuacán about A.D. 600 and extended farther southward as further incursions from the north disrupted the orderly progress of economic and religious life. J. E. S. Thompson has suggested that the introduction of human sacrifice and more militaristic attitudes into Mayan life may have caused serious dissension between priests and peasants. A combination of all these elements may have caused the collapse of Mayan civilization in Petén. The dissolution of Mayan society there took less than a century, although peasant farmers continued to live near the abandoned religious centers.[14]

Figure 22.7
  A richly clad Mayan priest wears the mask of the long-nosed god. His name is Bird-
  Jaguar. Three persons, probably prisoners about to be sacrificed, kneel before him —
  from Yaxchilán, c. A.D. 75. From The Rise and Fall of Maya Civilization, *by J. Eric*
  S. Thompson. Copyright 1954, 1966, by the University of Oklahoma Press.

toltecs and aztecs

Although by A.D. 900 the Classic period had ended, Mayan religious and
social orders continued in northern Yucatán. The continuity of the ancient
Mesoamerican tradition survived unscathed. Basic economic patterns and
technological traditions were retained, although religious and ideological
patterns and priorities were disarranged. New ceremonial centers were
built, but greater emphasis was placed on war and violence as militaristic
rulers achieved dominance in Mesoamerica.

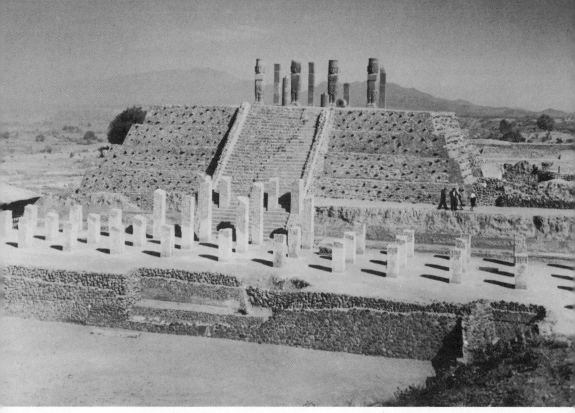

Figure 22.8
The Toltec site at Tula is dominated by a stepped platform with giant columns modeled like warriors.

We have mentioned the unsettled political conditions of the Postclassic period that were caused by population movements and tribal warfare. Many groups of invaders vied with each other for political power until the Toltecs achieved a dominant position in the tenth century. The oral legends of the Aztec rulers, who followed the Toltecs, describe how the Toltecs came into Mesoamerica from the northwest frontiers beyond the civilized world. They settled at Tula, 37 miles (57 km.) north of the valley of Mexico, where they built a ceremonial center dedicated to their serpent god, Quetzalcóatl (Figure 22.8).[15] Tula is notable for its animal sculpture and characteristic pottery styles but it did not have a long life, for around A.D. 1160 some newcomers with a less developed religious organization arrived from the north and destroyed the temples.

Chichen Itzá in northern Yucatán was an important Mayan ceremonial center in Postclassic times. In the tenth century A.D., Chichen Itzá was sacked by Toltec warriors. New architectural elements were introduced to the Maya by the Toltecs, but Mayan hieroglyphs were still used.

Chichen Itzá boasted a sacred pool into which numerous sacrificial offerings were thrown. The site was abandoned in the thirteenth century. But the city of Mayapán rose to prominence in northern Yucatán, a walled settlement clustered around a ceremonial center. At least 12,000 people lived in this Mayan city, which was ruled by the Cocom family. Mayan civilization enjoyed a resurgence in this area, although Mayapán declined during the civil wars of the fifteenth century. The Spanish found Yucatán ruled by numerous petty chiefs a century later.

The militaristic Toltecs were the leading military and political force in Mesoamerica for such a short time that their influence evaporated rapidly when Tula was destroyed. Another period of political chaos in the valley of Mexico ensued, as more barbarians from the north ("Chichimecs") maneuvered for political power. Petty states fought with each other until the Aztecs, one of the last barbarian groups to enter the valley of Mexico, founded their empire at the expense of their rivals.[16] The Aztecs were subject to other highland states for a while after their arrival. They named their capital Tenochtitlán and started building it in A.D. 1325 or 1345; it is now buried under Mexico City.

A.D. 1200

A.D. 1325

In the early fifteenth century the Aztecs began to achieve dominance over the Tepanecs of the valley of Mexico. King Ahuitzotl (1486–1502) embarked on an ambitious campaign of conquest that expanded Aztec power to the Pacific coast as well as to the Gulf of Mexico. Guatemala represented their southern frontier; the valley of Mexico, their northern boundary.

Aztec leaders were revered as semigods. A highly stratified class system supported the power of the king; the ruler was elected from within a limited class group. Much effort was devoted to pleasing the formidable War and Rain gods, Huitzilopochtli and Tlaloc, deities whose benevolence was assured by constant human sacrifices, carried out on the summits of the high temples that dominated Aztec burial centers. These sacrifices reached their peak at the end of 52-year cycles, when the continuity of the world was believed to be assured by bloodthirsty rites.

Tenochtitlán was a spectacular sight in the sixteenth century: "The city has many squares in which markets are continuously held," wrote Cortes. "One square in particular is twice as big as that of Salamanca and completely surrounded by arcades where there are daily more than sixty thousand folk buying and selling."[17] He mentioned special markets for birds and herbs. Barbershops and drugstores, textile and pottery markets, and many other emporia lined the streets. The principal streets were broad and made of stamped earth, and canoe canals penetrated deep into the city. Cortes marveled at the immense temples maintained by an exclusive priesthood. He described forty pyramids, and he admired the stonework "cut into ornamental borders of flowers, birds, fishes and the

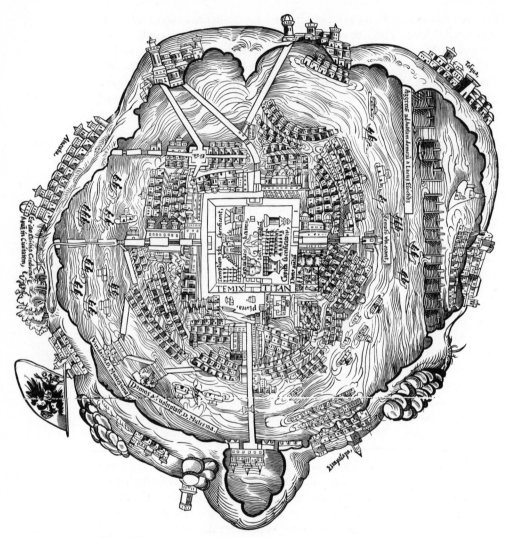

Figure 22.9
The city of Tenochtitlán, as depicted in a German edition of Cortes's account of the conquest of the Aztecs in 1524. The drawing shows the main square, causeways, temples, and parks of the busy capital.

like." Tenochtitlán was a great city even by present standards (Figure 22.9). It was certainly larger, and probably cleaner, than many European cities of the time. The city was maintained by an efficient state government with autocratic powers.

The Aztecs were the dominant people of Mesoamerica at the time of the first Spanish explorations of the New World. From coastal villagers the newcomers heard stories of the fabled rich empire in the high interior. It was not long before the conquistadores pressed inland to check on these stories of gold and other marvelous riches. Hernando Cortes was the first Spaniard to come in contact with the Aztec empire in A.D. 1519. In two short years he succeeded in destroying Tenochtitlán and the Aztec state. The cruel Aztecs had little support from the local people whom they had mercilessly raided for prisoners or subjected in warfare. The Aztecs were astonished when Cortes succeeded in seizing their king, Montezuma. A small handful of explorers armed with a few muskets and horses was able to overthrow one of the most powerful empires in the history of America.

Spanish Conquest A.D. 1519– 1521

From this moment, Mesoamerica enters the purview of written history. Spanish culture spread rapidly throughout Mesoamerica, north into the North American Southwest, and South America. Soon only fragments of the fabulous Mesoamerican cultural tradition remained, as the native population faced a new and uncertain chapter in their history.

peru

the initial period

Between 1800 and 900 B.C., important changes developed in Peruvian life, both on the Pacific Coast and in the highlands.[18] Manioc (a root crop) and peanuts were introduced to coastal villages, while the potato was now being cultivated in the highlands. All the major food plants that formed the basis of Peruvian agriculture in later centuries were in use by 900 B.C. The llama was being herded by the same date. This period of Peruvian prehistory has been named the "Initial Period," initial in the sense that permanent towns began.

Initial Period 1800–900 B.C.

Large, settled communities prospered on the coast during the Initial Period, for natural resources of oceans, rivers, and forests were an important adjunct to agricultural produce (Figure 22.10). A long tradition of permanent settlement was enriched by skillful weaving in the style of earlier centuries. Ceremonial centers of adobe or stone were constructed at such sites as Las Haldas on the northern coast, where a complex of mounds and plazas served as religious and urban headquarters for a dense farming population. Pottery was in common use; monumental art had begun to develop. The major settlements enjoyed political autonomy; no larger states or common religious philosophies yet unified large areas of Peru, although a common cultural tradition had emerged, which formed a foundation for later political and religious developments.

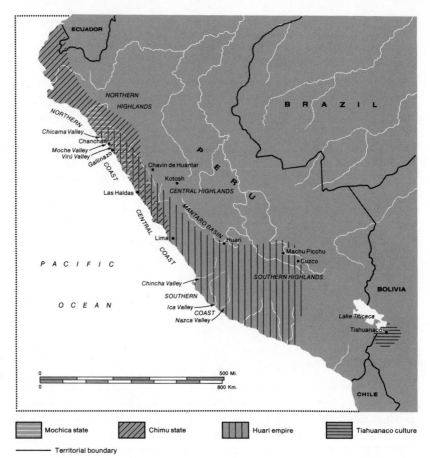

Figure 22.10
*Peruvian archaeological sites mentioned in this chapter. The approximate distributions
of various cultures are shown.*

chavín and the early horizon

Chavín
900 B.C.

Early
Horizon
900–200 B.C.

About 900 B.C., a highly distinctive art style in stone and precious metals
appeared in northern Peru. Within a century this Chavín style had spread
over wide areas of the coast and highlands, forming an "Early Horizon"
in Peruvian prehistory. The Chavín style takes its name from some remarkable sculptures at Chavín de Huántar in the northern highlands.[19]
The site lies in a fertile valley over 5,344 meters (10,000 ft.) above sea
level, centered around elaborate stone platforms decorated with sculptures and clay reliefs. Galleries and small rooms were built inside the

Figure 22.11
Chavín carving on a pillar in the temple interior at Chavín de Huántar.

platforms. The original temple housed a remarkable carving of a jaguar-like human with hair in the form of serpents (Figure 22.11).

Chavín art is dominated by animal and human forms, with jaguar motifs predominating. Humans, gods, and animals are given jaguar-like fangs or limbs. Snakes flow from the bodies of many figures. The art has a savage grace about it that is both grotesque and slightly sinister. Many figures were carved in stone, others in clay or bone.

The Chavín art style is so widely distributed in Peru that it must represent more than merely art for art's sake. Settlements like Chavín de Huántar were important ceremonial centers unifying surrounding farming villages with a common religious concern. Thus, a tradition of settled life was reinforced by a religious philosophy shared by most Peruvians. Chavín flourished for 700 years. It disappeared around 200 B.C., although some stylistic themes (and, presumably, religious philosophies) survived into later times. The influence of Chavín extended into southern Peru. It provided a vital basis for the spectacular cultural developments of the first Peruvian kingdoms which flourished after A.D. 200.

200 B.C.

early kingdoms (early intermediate)

Early
Intermediate
Period
200 B.C.–
A.D. 600

Following the disappearance of the Chavín style, a period of cultural and economic transition ensued in northern Peru. One settlement, Gallinazo, was built on the plains of the Virú Valley as a complex of ceremonial adobe buildings and pyramids, covering at least 1.3 square miles (2 sq. km.).[20] Approximately 5,000 people lived at Gallinazo, with many more farmers dwelling elsewhere in Virú. Large-scale irrigation works were begun in this and other coastal valleys at this time. The population expanded rapidly and more villages and towns were constructed near the field systems and canals. The upper reaches of Virú were guarded by four great forts, a sign of warfare and competition for resources.

Mochica
200 B.C.–
A.D. 600

By 200 B.C., the Mochica state had emerged in northern coastal Peru. It continued to flourish for 800 years. Its origins lay in the Chicama and Moche valleys, where great ceremonial centers were built.[21] At Moche itself, two massive terraced pyramids dominate the landscape, one a temple and burial place, the other probably the headquarters of the Mochica rulers. The Mochica people are best known for their beautiful pottery, especially their "stirrup-mouthed jars." These drinking vessels were created by craftsmen who modeled human portraits, plants, and animals (Figure 22.12). Other Mochica workmen were skillful smiths, casting gold into fine ornaments and making simple copper tools and weapons. Metallurgy, already practiced on a simple level in Chavín times, had achieved a measure of technical sophistication.

The central and southern coasts of Peru were experiencing somewhat similar cultural development while the Mochica state flourished.[22] The valleys of the central coast supported fewer large settlements or towns. Some pyramids were erected at fairly substantial ceremonial centers; burials attest to important leaders who journeyed to the next world accompanied by fine ornaments and human sacrifices. A common pottery style (the Lima), adorned with painted geometric designs, is found in several valleys, possibly indicating common political and economic leadership.

Figure 22.12
 Mochica portrait vessel about 29 centimeters (11.4 ins.) high.

The southern coast was dominated by another pottery style (the Nazca). Nazca vessels, bearing elaborate multicolored patterns, had their origins in earlier local pottery traditions. As on the northern coast, the valley populations were drawn toward large ceremonial centers, whose adobe temples and platforms served as burial places and were surrounded by dwellings.

the middle period: huari and tiahuanaco

By the Middle Period, Peruvian societies were enjoying the benefits of extensive irrigation and terrace agriculture, the latter based on systematic exploitation of hillside gardens. Agricultural populations tended to concentrate around urban centers, the larger of which ruled regional kingdoms. Each small state had its own style of government and local artistic

Middle
Period
A.D. 600–1000

tradition. The states competed with each other for land and food resources; their leaders vied for power and prestige. Times were ripe for
wider economic, political, and social initiatives. The rulers of Tiahuanaco
and Huari in highland Peru were ambitious enough to try.

huari

Huari
A.D. 500–800

An important ceremonial center had been built at Huari in the Manteco
basin before Tiahuanaco achieved importance.[23] Huari lies on a hill, with
huge stonewalls and many dwellings that cover several square miles. Its
inhabitants enjoyed wide trade connections, particularly with the southern coast of Peru. Eventually, Huari political power embraced not only
much of the Peruvian Andes but an enormous span of the coast as far
north as former Mochica country. The Huari empire extended over a far
larger tract of territory than any earlier Peruvian state. Its frontiers were
probably expanded by religious conversion, trade, and especially warfare.
Storehouses and roads were probably maintained by the state, as the
organized control of foodstuffs and labor forces became essential to the
power structure of Huari's rulers. The Huari empire was a political, social,
and religious turning point for the Peruvians. Small, regional states were
replaced by much larger political units. Common religious cults unified
hundreds of ceremonial centers. As urban living and planning became
more important, the government played a leading role in agricultural life,
especially in northern Peru.

Huari itself was abandoned around A.D. 800, perhaps after being destroyed by enemies, but there is no clear evidence of this. The empire
also collapsed, although the widespread Huari art styles continued in use
for another 200 years. But the leaders of Huari had created administrative
and social precedents that were to reemerge in later centuries.

tiahuanaco

Tiahuanaco
A.D. 600

During the first millennium A.D., the highlands supported many small
states whose details are still imperfectly known. Tiahuanaco, at the south
end of Lake Titicaca, was one of the greatest population centers during
the Middle Period.[24] The arid lands in which it lies were irrigated with
water from the lake, supporting a population of perhaps 20,000 living
near the monumental structures at the center of Tiahuanaco. A large earth
platform faced with stones dominates the site. Nearby, a rectangular
enclosure is bounded with a row of upright stones entered by a doorway
carved with an anthropomorphic god. Smaller buildings, enclosures, and
huge statues are also to be found near the ceremonial structures.

Tiahuanaco was flourishing around A.D. 600, with much of its prosperity based on trade around the southern shores of the lake. Copperworking was especially important; it probably developed independently of the equivalent copper technology on the northern coast. The art styles of Tiahuanaco are distinctive and widespread. Such motifs as jaguars and eagles occur over much of southern Peru; so do the anthropomorphic gods depicted at Tiahuanaco, attended by lesser deities or messengers. The influence of Tiahuanaco art and culture is also found in Bolivia, the southern Andes, and perhaps as far afield as northwestern Argentina.

the late intermediate period: late coastal states

Around A.D. 1000, new kingdoms arose to replace the political vacuum left by Huari. At least four states thrived in the coastal valleys, which are dimly recalled in oral legends of the Inca.

Late Intermediate A.D. 1000–1476

The northern coast was dominated by Chimú, with a great capital at Chan Chan in the Moche Valley.[25] The ruins of Chan Chan cover at least 10 square miles (26 sq. km.). Nine great quadrangles of ground were enclosed by thick adobe walls over 12 meters (40 ft.) high. Courtyards, dwellings, and richly furnished graves occur inside the quadrangles. Some dwelling were lavishly decorated, obviously the homes of Chimú nobles. The great enclosure walls were not defensive in nature; they perhaps demarcated living areas for distinct kinship, craft, or religious groups.

Chimu A.D. 1000?– 1476

Chan Chan, from which the empire was administered, represents an important center of Chimú religious and political life. Large rural populations lived nearby in the Moche Valley, occupying enclosures and houses that lack the fine architecture of Chan Chan. The different centers were probably linked to each other by state-maintained highways, themselves used in later times by the Incas. Major irrigation systems ensured agricultural surpluses to support Chimú craftsmen and the aristocratic superstructure of the state. Skillful Chimú copperworkers alloyed tin with copper to make bronze.[26]

The southern coastal peoples of the early second millennium A.D. did not live in large cities like their northern neighbors. They are named after two dominant pottery styles: the Ica and Chincha.[27] The two pottery styles intermingled, as local leaders jockeyed for military and political supremacy on the southern coast. Chincha was dominant after A.D. 1425, perhaps as a result of increased military power that enabled its users to raid far outside the confines of their home valley.

Ica A.D. 1000

Chincha A.D. 1250

A.D. 1425

The decline of Huari and Tiahuanaco in the highlands left no unifying religious or political authorities that dominated more than a few foothill valleys. But the closing centuries of Peruvian prehistory saw the emergence of the Inca empire and a new level of economic, political, and religious sophistication in South America.

the late horizon: the inca state

Late Horizon
A.D. *1476–1534*

The Late Horizon of Peruvian archaeology is also the shortest, dating from A.D. 1476 to 1534. It is the period of the Inca empire, when those mighty Andean rulers held sway over an enormous area of highland and lowland country.[28] The Inca empire began in the Cuzco Valley of the Andes foothills, where humble peasants lived in stone huts. These people are known to have buried their dead in small beehive-shaped tombs.

Inca
A.D. 1200

Oral traditions speak of at least eight Inca rulers who reigned between A.D. 1200 and 1438, but these genealogies are hardly reliable. The ninth Inca king, Pachacuti Inca Yupanqui (1438–1471), was the first well-known leader. He gained control of the southern Peruvian highlands and laid the foundations of Inca power in a series of military campaigns. His successor, Topa Inca Yupanqui (1471–1493), expanded the Inca empire into Ecuador, northern Argentina, parts of Bolivia, and Chile. His armies also conquered the Chimú state whose water supplies Topa already controlled. The best Chimú craftsmen were carried off to work for the court of the Incas. Another king, Huayna Capac, ruled for thirty-four years after Topa Inca and expanded the empire deeper into Ecuador.

At the height of its prosperity, the Inca state represented the culmination of earlier cultural traditions and empire-building efforts. Inca rulers were masters of bureaucracy and military organization, and governed a highly structured state by divine rule. The king, or Inca, was considered divine and ruled with great ceremony; he was surrounded by elite aristocracy of blood relatives and able administrators, who achieved status by ability. An elaborate civil service controlled every aspect of Inca life by means of a large and apparently effective bureaucracy of civil servants.

Military service, farming, road building, and other activities were supported by a ruthless system of taxation, largely in the form of forced labor. All corners of the empire were connected by well-maintained roads constantly traversed by messengers who moved on foot or with llamas. A highly efficient army was armed with spears, slings, and clubs. The Inca used his soldiers to maintain his power. The official road system enabled him to move army units from one end of his kingdom to the other very rapidly. Conquered territories were incorporated into the communications network. Often the defeated ruler would be offered the governorship of his former domains within the framework of the empire. Revolts were prevented by the drastic expedient of moving entire conquered populations from their homelands into new areas.

Inca religion centered around a supreme creator figure, Viracocha. In practice, the Sun God was more actively worshiped. Ritual and divination had much importance. A lunar calendar was maintained by the priests, but no writing was used for the business of state. The Inca relied on the famous quipu, knotted strings, for computing state accounts and inventories.

At the time of the Spanish Conquest, 6,000,000 people are estimated to have been living under Inca rule, most of them in small villages dispersed around religious and political centers. Urban life was not a feature of Inca life, except for some old coastal cities. The ceremonial centers were built of carefully laid stones. Military, religious, and government buildings were constructed on a large scale in the Cuzco area; such centers as Machu Picchu, high in the Andes (Figure 22.13), are famous for their fine masonry structures. But a dispersed settlement pattern is characteristic of the Inca empire.

Figure 22.13
Machu Picchu, seen from above. Machu Picchu was forgotten for 400 years after the Spanish Conquest. It was rediscovered by the American explorer Hiram Bingham in 1912.

The prevalence of village life did not prevent craftsmen from producing major works of art in silver and gold. Bronze was widely used for agricultural implements and weapons. Inca pottery is distinctive, brightly painted in black, white, and red geometrical designs. But, despite the widespread distribution of Inca pots and artifacts, regional pottery styles flourished because subject village potters continued the cultural traditions of earlier centuries.

Spanish
Conquest
A.D. *1525* When Inca Huayna Capac died in an epidemic in A.D. 1525, the empire was plunged into civil war between Huayna's son Huascar and Atahuallpa, a half-brother. Atahuallpa eventually prevailed, but, as he moved south from Ecuador to consolidate his territory, he learned that the conquistador Francisco Pizarro had landed in Peru.

A.D. *1532*

The Spaniards had vowed to make Peru part of Spain and were bent on plunder and conquest. Pizarro arrived in the guise of a diplomat, captured Atahuallpa by treachery, ransomed him for a huge quantity of gold, and then brutally murdered him. A year later the Spaniards were able to capture the Inca capital with a tiny army. They took over the state bureaucracy and appointed Manco Capac as a puppet ruler. Three years later, Manco Capac turned on his masters in a bloody revolt. Its suppression finally destroyed the greatest of the Peruvian empires.

A.D. *1533*

A.D. *1536*

The Spanish conquest ended much of Latin American prehistory. The peasant farmer of earlier times lived on, largely ignored by the conquistadores, too busy building their own Colonial civilization to care about small villages. One wonders what would have happened had the development of New World civilizations continued unchecked by ruthless colonialist ambition.

23

epilogue

"For as long as we can discern, the past has loomed ominously about the lives of men, threatening, demanding and hinting at cataclysm," wrote historian J. H. Plumb.[1]* He asks a pertinent question: are we still justified in trying to explain man's future destiny in terms of the past to strengthen the objectives of society? He concludes that this use of the past is dead. All historians can do is to teach people about the nature of social change, to make them think historically about it.

A similar objective might be appropriate for archaeologists as well. But the nature of the archaeological record is such that explanations in prehistory are harder to formulate. Basic research on the "whys" of world prehistory has hardly begun. We still know little about the processes of cultural change, although ecological and systems approaches to the major questions of human prehistory are already yielding promising results.

Several archaeologists have urged us to use hypothetical models of possible human life styles as a way of understanding, explaining, and predicting human behavior and culture.[2] Such models are worked out from logical analysis of factual data and from processes of mental abstraction. Those who construct such models are in search of lawlike generalizations to explain human history — fundamental props, as it were, of a grand theory of prehistory. Unfortunately, most such generalizations are so vague as to be virtually useless. But one widely accepted generalization sees the theory of evolution as providing a scientific framework for understanding man, his culture, and his relationships with nature.

Evolutionary theory offers a reasonable interpretation of the major developments of world prehistory, provided that one sees the physical environment as a major influence on human behavior. Man has always had to feed and house himself with the resources of his environment. His primary need has been to live with his environment. It follows that overpopulation beyond the limits of the earth's resources will place man in danger of extinction. Man is part of the world's ecological community. Today it is almost platitudinous to argue that ecological balance is essential to mankind's continued survival.

The prehistory of man began with bands of hunters and gatherers in the African savannah over two and a half million years ago. Cultural evolution was slow at first. It took well over a million years for the chopping tool to be replaced by the hand ax. But a gradual increase in technological complexity was accompanied by greater diversity and elaboration of human culture. Human populations rose slowly as basic human behavioral patterns were developed over thousands of years. Acquired cultural skills and knowledge were passed on from generation to generation — in technology, organization, language, and economic strategies. Mankind settled in all manner of environments as the diversity of human life proliferated.

Another half million years elapsed before the world's populations were biologically indistinguishable from ourselves. By 25,000 years ago, *Homo sapiens* had already mastered arctic regions and very extreme conditions of heat and cold. Distinct human physical and racial types had emerged among early men and also among *Homo sapiens.* The differences survive today in a world wracked by racial tensions and competition for political power and resources. Five thousand years ago, perhaps earlier, present-day hunter-gatherers had already been forced into marginal territory by the demands of peasant farmers for land and grazing grass.

The shift from hunting and gathering to food production was another gradual process. Experimentation with domestic crops took place in many areas of the world and led to a shift in human attitudes toward both food and the environment. Growing farming populations placed greater demands on the world's natural resources than did their hunting predecessors. Irrigation methods and terrace agriculture increased crop yields. Herds denuded valuable pastureland and caused the permanent modification of vegetation patterns that had existed for thousands of years. Copper, tin, gold, and iron were soon being exploited; trade in valuable minerals developed rapidly as man increased his dependence on a territory larger than his own village (Figure 23.1).

Hunters and gatherers were normally self-sufficient, obtaining salt from game meat and relying on bone, stone, and wood for toolkits and housing. The farmer with his predominantly carbohydrate diet had to extract salt from boiled grasses or from saline springs. Often he had to trade for salt from deposits far from his village. Metals are not found everywhere, so minerals, too, often had to be bartered from neighbors and more distant sources. Trade fostered links with other communities and the wider world, increasing each man's dependence on other people.

An increased intensity of environmental exploitation developed throughout prehistory. Man began as an insignificant member of the ecosystem and progressed to become the prominent and ultimately dominant one. A pattern of slow cultural change and comfortable subsistence within the confines of the environment changed rapidly within a few thousand years as man developed increasingly powerful skills for controlling and overexploiting his environment.

Initially, a move toward urban dwelling took hold only in a few areas where large political and economic units were unified by a powerful religious force or the need for communal effort to increase agricultural yields. Eventually, towns and cities, each with their jealously guarded territory, formed new and volatile political units. Warfare between them

Figure 23.1
An Algonquin village in North Carolina, surrounded by a defensive palisade. This scene was painted by famous Elizabethan artist John White in 1585. The earlier history of the Algonquin can only be learned through archaeological investigation.

led to new and more sophisticated technologies. Territorial competition went hand in hand with a scramble for increased output to satisfy insatiable demand. Instead of being part of the environment, man had begun to dominate it. By 2000 B.C. he was already set in the pattern of environmental destruction that we are now trying to halt.

The city-states of the Near East were eventually unified into larger empires by such powerful and ambitious leaders as Sargon, Alexander the Great, Cyrus, and Julius Caesar; their efforts led ultimately to the emergence of Western civilization. By then, centuries of peaceful trade and violent warfare had precipitated technological change and had brought an awareness of a wider world unknown in prehistoric times.

Inexorably, Western man extended the frontiers of the "known" world, annexing, destroying, and exploiting prehistoric societies (Figure 23.1). New technologies dominated the simpler tools of earlier times. Missionaries followed in the explorers' wake, seeking new converts and imposing alien gods on peoples who had no need of such spiritual attention. For much of the world, written history began only five hundred years ago with the arrival of Western explorers, and for many people, it began just in the last century. Even today, the *National Geographic* may feature a prehistoric hunting band from the Amazon, the Philippines, or New Guinea taking its first cautious glance at our turbulent civilization. Their "history" is just beginning; one wonders if they would not be more content with their own prehistory.

Twentieth-century Western civilization is rapidly completing the process of destruction by colonial exploitation, wars, jet aircraft, tourism, and foreign aid. Within another fifty years we shall have destroyed most traces of the many human societies whose closest ties lie with prehistory rather than with the Western experience. This will be one of the major tragedies of human history, an event that has happened before in earlier times as hunters vanished in the face of farmers and city-states established trade monopolies over mineral outcrops owned by peasant agriculturalists. Perhaps it is too late to halt the inexorable destruction of the world's weaker societies, for the blandishments of advanced technologies are always attractive to those who have not suffered under them.

One comes away from a study of world prehistory with an overwhelming sense of man's progress, a progress that may seem desirable until one realizes that mankind has a lethal ability to destroy his environment and human life. The tragedy of our atomic world is that man has achieved wonderful solutions to the basic problems of nutrition and defense, but has not achieved control of his own numbers.[3] Our material progress has been so rapid that many of our social institutions still reflect an earlier world where man was a less significant member of the ecological community, a world to which we shall never return.

notes

1
introduction

1. Glyn Daniel's *A Hundred Years of Archaeology*, Duckworth, London, 1950, chap. 1, contains a useful summary of the early development of archaeology.
2. Margaret T. Hodgen, *Early Anthropology in the Sixteenth and Seventeenth Centuries*, University of Pennsylvania Press, Philadelphia, 1964, summarizes the events described in this paragraph.
3. For the antiquity of man, see Glyn Daniel, *The Idea of Prehistory*, Watts, London, 1962. John Green's *The Death of Adam*, Iowa State University Press, Ames, Iowa, 1959, is an informative account of evolution and its impact on Western thought.
4. One of the most famous mound diggers was Sir Austen Henry Layard, archaeologist, diplomat, and politician. See Gordon Waterfield, *Layard of Nineveh*, Murray, London, 1963.
5. T. K. Penniman, *A Hundred Years of Anthropology*, 2nd ed., Duckworth, London, 1952.
6. For a general discussion of culture see: A. L. Kroeber and Clyde Kluckhohn, *Culture: A Critical Review of Concepts and Definitions*, Papers of the Peabody Museum of American Archaeology and Ethnology, vol. 147, no. 1, Cambridge, Mass., 1952. The quotation is from Clyde Kluckhohn and William Kelly, "The Concept of Culture," *in* Ralph Linton (ed.), *The Science of Man in the World Crisis*, Macmillan, New York, 1945, p. 97.
7. A brief summary of the history of archaeology and archaeological theory appears in Brian M. Fagan, *In the Beginning*, Little, Brown, Boston, 1972, chaps. 1, 10, 11.
8. Stuart Piggott, "The Science of Rubbish," *Spectator*, April 9, 1965, p. 482.
9. J. G. D. Clark, *Archaeology and Society*, Methuen, London, and Barnes & Noble, New York, 1965, pp. 94–95.
10. Howard Carter, *The Tomb of Tut-ankh-amun*, Macmillan, London, 1923–1933.
11. James Deetz, *Invitation to Archeology*, Natural History Press, New York, 1967, p. 77.
12. Fagan, *In the Beginning*, pp. 33–36. See also Sir Mortimer Wheeler, *Archaeology from the Earth*, Clarendon Press, Oxford, 1954, chap. 4.
13. Jeremy Sabloff and Gordon R. Willey, *A History of American Archaeology*, Thames and Hudson, London, 1973.
14. Fagan, *In the Beginning*, chap. 2, and Frank Hole and Robert F. Heizer, *An Introduction to Prehistoric Archaeology*, 2nd ed., Holt, Rinehart and Winston, New York, 1969, chaps. 10–13.
15. Colin Renfrew, "The Tree-Ring Calibration of Radiocarbon: An Archaeological Evaluation," *Proceedings of the Prehistoric Society*, 36 (1970): 280–311.
16. D. R. Brothwell and E. S. Higgs, *Science in Archaeology*, 2nd ed., Thames and Hudson, London, 1969.

17. Ivor Noël Hume, *Historical Archaeology*, Alfred A. Knopf, New York, 1968.

18. Industrial archaeology is a new and popular field of research in Europe. For a summary, see R. A. Buchanon, *Industrial Archaeology in Britain*, Pelican Books, Harmondsworth, 1972.

19. Unfortunately, we do not have the space to discuss this vital topic in detail. Key references that are required reading for any archaeologist or potential prehistorian are Hester A. Davis, "The Crisis in American Archaeology," *Science*, 1972, 175, 4019, pp. 267–272, and the same author's "Is There a Future for the Past?" *Archaeology*, 1971, 24, pp. 300–307. On British sites, see Carolyn Heighway (ed.), *The Erosion of History: Archaeology and Planning in Towns*, Council for British Archaeology, London, 1972. Charles R. McGimsey's *Public Archaeology*, Seminar Press, New York, 1972, is essential reading for those interested in legislation and antiquities. See also Clemency Coggins, "Archaeology and the Art Market," *Science*, 1972, 175, 4019, pp. 263–266.

20. Fagan, *In the Beginning*, pp. 68–70.

21. Ibid., chaps. 4, 5. See also Wheeler, *Archaeology from the Earth*.

22. Mary D. Leakey, *Olduvai Gorge*, vol. 3, Cambridge University Press, Cambridge, 1971, gives a comprehensive account of the earlier Olduvai campsites.

23. River gravels were much studied by archaeologists of the 1930s and 1940s. The subject is highly complex; a glimpse of its difficulties can be obtained from K. P. Oakley, *Frameworks for Dating Fossil Man*, Aldine, Chicago, 1964, chap. 7.

24. Two typical cave excavations are described in Jesse D. Jennings, *Danger Cave*, University of Utah Anthropological Papers no. 27, 1957, and C. B. M. McBurney, *The Haua Fteah* (Cyrenaica), Cambridge University Press, Cambridge, 1967.

25. Sir Leonard Woolley, *Ur Excavations*, vol. 2: *The Royal Cemetery*, Publications of the Joint Expedition of the British Museum and of the Museum of the University of Pennsylvania to Mesopotamia, British Museum, London, 1934, pp. 38–39, 41–42.

26. Kwang-chih Chang, *The Archaeology of Ancient China*, 2nd ed., Yale University Press, New Haven, 1968.

27. Sergei I. Rudenko, *The Frozen Tombs of Siberia: The Pazyryk Burials of Iron Age Horsemen*, trans. M. W. Thompson, University of California Press, Berkeley, 1970.

28. For a summary of classification, see Fagan, *In the Beginning*, chap. 7. See also Deetz, *Invitation to Archeology*, chap. 3.

29. Fagan, *In the Beginning*, pp. 306–309.

30. Contemporary archaeology has a major concern with both explanation and quantitative methods. A brief summary is to be found in ibid., pp. 309–315. This should be followed by a study of Lewis R. Binford, *An Archaeological Perspective*, Seminar Press, New York, 1972, and Patty Jo Watson, Steven A. LeBlanc, and Charles L. Redman, *Explanation in Archaeology*, Columbia University Press, New York, 1971. This field of archaeology is still the subject of intense controversy and debate.

2

theories of prehistory: looking at the past

1. Glyn Daniel, *A Hundred Years of Archaeology*, Duckworth, London, 1950, pp. 38–54.

2. Ibid., p. 42.

3. Worsaae was an immensely significant figure in nineteenth-century archaeology. His most famous work is J. J. A. Worsaae, *The Primeval Antiquities of Denmark*, Murray, London, 1849.

4. French archaeologist Gabriel de Mortillet proclaimed that human prehistory was divided into three ages: Stone, Bronze, and Iron, themselves split up into various periods and epochs. Prehistory was a clear demonstration of the progress of man. See Gabriel de Mortillet, *Formation de la nation française*, Paris, 1897.

5. Edward Tylor, *Researches into the Early History of Mankind and the Development of Civilization*, London, 1865; University of Chicago Press, Chicago and London, 1964. Quotation from page 3.

6. Oscar Montelius's *Die Chronologie der ältesten Bronzezeit in Nord Deutschland und Scandinavien* (Brunswick, 1900) is one of his most famous works.

7. See Grafton Elliot Smith, *The Migrations of Early Culture*, Murray, London, 1915, and W. J. Perry, *The Children of the Sun*, Murray, London, 1923, two basic references of the diffusionist school.
8. Brian M. Fagan, *In the Beginning*, Little, Brown, Boston, 1972, pp. 294–298.
9. Ibid., pp. 298–301. Gordon Childe wrote an intensely interesting memoir on his own contribution to archaeology; see his "Retrospect," *Antiquity*, 1958, 32, pp. 69–74.
10. An important paper is Glyn Daniel, "From Worsaae to Childe: The Models of Prehistory," *Proceedings of the Prehistoric Society*, 1971, 37, 2, pp. 140–153. Quotation from V. Gordon Childe, *What Happened in History*, Penguin Books, Harmondsworth, 1942, p. 22.
11. J. G. D. Clark, *Prehistoric Europe: The Economic Basis*, Methuen, London, 1952; and his *Star Carr*, Cambridge University Press, Cambridge, 1954. See also Bruce Trigger, "Archaeology and Ecology," *World Archaeology*, 1971, 2, 3, pp. 321–336.
12. Sir Cyril Fox, *The Personality of Britain*, The National Museum of Wales, Cardiff, 1932. Fox's work has been criticized for being too deterministic.
13. Admirably discussed by Trigger, "Archaeology and Ecology."
14. The results of some recent work are described by various authors in Lewis R. Binford and Sally R. Binford (eds.), *New Perspectives in Archaeology*, Aldine, Chicago, 1968.
15. Richard A. Watson and Patty Jo Watson, *Man and Nature: An Anthropological Essay in Human Ecology*, Harcourt, Brace and World, New York, 1969. This book is essential reading to anyone interested in the broad sweep of world prehistory.

3
understanding evolution

1. The best popular account of Charles Darwin is Alan Moorehead's *Darwin and the Beagle*, Hamish Hamilton, London, 1969.
2. For the controversies and for a general account of evolution, see Ruth Moore, *Evolution*, Time-Life Books, New York, 1964.
3. Darwin himself enlarged on man in his *Descent of Man and Selection in Relation to Sex*, Murray, London, 1871.
4. The best summary of evolution in my mind is E. Peter Volpe's *Understanding Evolution*, William Brown, Dubuque, Iowa, 1970.
5. For more detailed coverage, see I. M. Lerner, *Heredity, Evolution, and Society*, W. H. Freeman, San Francisco, 1968.
6. The literature on race is enormous and at times vitriolic. For a basic summary, start with chap. 4 in Herman K. Bleibtreu's excellent reader, *Evolutionary Anthropology*, Allyn and Bacon, Boston, 1969.
7. One cannot speak of "pure" races, for they are a myth and blatantly absurd, as are the occasional attempts to claim superior intelligence for one group or another that surface occasionally in popular and scientific literature. Regrettably, some governments and, indeed, scientists feel obliged to use arbitrary and frequently unreliable racial classifications as a basis for reconstructing national histories or biased accounts of archaeological sites. Such attempts are both pathetic and usually rightly derided by the gullible public for whom they are intended.

4
the pleistocene

1. In writing this chapter I have drawn extensively on Richard F. Flint, *Glacial and Quaternary Geology*, John Wiley, New York, 1971, and Karl W. Butzer, *Environment and Archaeology: An Introduction to Pleistocene Geography*, 2nd ed., Aldine-Atherton, Chicago, 1971. An elaborate but somewhat outdated work on the Pleistocene is J. K. Charlesworth, *The Quaternary Era*, Edward Arnold, London, 1957. F. E. Zeuner, *The Pleistocene Period*, Hutchinson, London, 1959, is another classic. The beginner is better advised to read I. W. Cornwall, *Ice Ages: Their Nature and Effect*, John Baker, London, and Humanities Press, New York, 1970.

2. Extended discussion in R. F. Flint, "The Pliocene-Pleistocene Boundary," *in* H. E. Wright and D. G. Frey (eds.), *International Studies on the Quaternary*, Geological Society of America, Special Paper no. 84, 1965, pp. 497–533.
3. Louis Agassiz, *Etudes sur les glaciers*, Neuchâtel, 1840. Privately published.
4. James Geikie, *The Great Ice Age and Its Relation to the Antiquity of Man*, W. Isbister, London, 1874.
5. Albrecht Penck and Edward Brückner, *Die Alpen im Eiszeitalter*, Tauchnitz, Leipzig, 1909. Penck and Brückner's glacial terms have now been replaced by Scandinavian labels in general use: Würm = Weichsel, Riss = Saale, Mindel = Elster. Gunz has no equivalent. The interglacial sites described here are typified by the Swanscombe quarry near London, famous for its human remains and thousands of stone tools. See C. D. Ovey (ed.), *The Swanscombe Skull: A Survey of Research on a Pleistocene Site*, Occasional Paper of the Royal Anthropological Institute No. 20, 1964.
6. See Flint, *Glacial and Quaternary Geology*, chap. 16.
7. Ibid., chap. 24.
8. Björn Kurtén, *Pleistocene Mammals of Europe*, Aldine, Chicago, 1968. chap. 2.
9. In writing this description of Pleistocene glaciation, I have drawn heavily on Flint's *Glacial and Quaternary Geology*. Many of the details of the various glacial stages and interglacials still remain more uncertain than is implied here.
10. F. Clark Howell, *Early Man*, Time-Life Books, New York, 1965, pp. 85–100. Also see Chapter 5 of this book.
11. For discussion, see Flint, *Glacial and Quaternary Geology*, pp. 382–384.
12. Dramatic evidence for the flooding of the North Sea came with the discovery of a Stone Age harpoon dredged up in a lump of peat from the bed of the Dogger Bank in 1932; see M. C. Burkitt, "A Maglemose Harpoon Dredged Up Recently from the North Sea," *Man*, 1932, no. 138, p. 132.
13. For a comprehensive summary see Butzer, *Environment and Archaeology*.
14. The analysis of animal bones is described by Raymond E. Chaplin, *The Study of Animal Bones from Archaeological Sites*, Seminar Press, New York, 1971; also Kurtén, *Pleistocene Mammals*. On extinctions, see Paul Martin and H. E. Wright (eds.), *Pleistocene Extinctions: The Search for a Cause*, Yale University Press, New Haven, 1967.
15. Elephants are well described by Kurtén, *Pleistocene Mammals*, chap. 11.

5

the origins of man

1. Thomas Huxley, *Man's Place in Nature and other Anthropological Essays*, Macmillan, London, 1863, p. 77 (1911 ed.). Huxley's prose is elegant and well worth reading for sheer pleasure.
2. The most broadly stimulating book on human evolution is probably Bernard Campbell's *Human Evolution*, Heinemann, London, and Aldine, Chicago, 1967. Many of the controversies surrounding man's relationships to the apes are summarized there. The publication *Perspectives on Human Evolution* provides valuable summaries of recent research at intervals.
3. For the history of human-fossil hunting, see F. Clark Howell, *Early Man*, Time-Life Books, New York, 1965; Maitland A. Edey, *The Missing Link*, Time-Life Books, New York, and Little, Brown, Boston, 1972, is also useful.
4. Another useful volume that summarizes the story of *Homo erectus* and other fossils is John Pfeiffer, *The Emergence of Man*, Harper & Row, New York, 1969.
5. A popular and highly colored account of Dart's work is Raymond Dart, with Dennis Craig, *Adventures with the Missing Link*, Hamish Hamilton, London, 1959.
6. The best popular accounts of the Leakeys' discoveries are to be found in the *National Geographic*, especially "Finding the World's Earliest Men," September 1960, "Exploring 1,750,000 Years into Man's Past," October 1961.
7. Pfeiffer's *Emergence of Man* gives a summary account.
8. We described geochronology in Chapter 2. Accounts of dating methods can be found in Brian M. Fagan, *In the Beginning*, Little, Brown, Boston, 1972, chap. 2.

9. The controversies are summarized by Campbell, *Human Evolution*, and in David Pilbeam, *The Ascent of Man*, Macmillan, New York, 1972.

10. The tarsier is located in north-central Indonesia, a tree-loving animal thought to be a surviving genus of the oldest primates. His limbs are adapted to tree life, yet he displays features such as a fully swiveling neck that point in the direction of the higher primates. See W. E. Le Gros Clark, *History of the Primates*, 4th ed., British Museum, London, 1954.

11. Elwyn L. Simons, *Primate Evolution*, Macmillan, New York, 1972, summarizes the evidence for this theory.

12. George E. Lewis, "Preliminary Notice of New Man-like Apes from India," *American Journal of Science*, 1934, 27, pp. 161–179.

13. *Ramapithecus* is discussed by Pilbeam, *Ascent of Man*, pp. 91–98.

14. The literature is complex, controversial, and highly technical. An easily accessible summary is in Vincent Sarich, "A Molecular Approach to the Question of Human Origins," in Phyllis Dolhinow and Vincent M. Sarich (eds.), *Background for Man*, Little, Brown, Boston, 1971, pp. 60–81.

15. Pilbeam, *Ascent of Man*, pp. 96–97.

16. The theories of evolution and natural selection are clearly described in Ruth Moore, *Evolution*, Time-Life Books, New York, 1964. Readers unfamiliar with these principles are referred to Chapter 3 of this book. A provocative account of human origins is C. F. Hockett and R. Ascher, "The Human Revolution," *Current Anthropology*, 1964, 5, pp. 135–168.

17. Simons, *Primate Evolution*, chaps. 7–9.

18. Jane Van Lawick-Goodall's researches have been widely publicized by the *National Geographic*: "My Life among the Chimpanzees," August 1963, and "New Discoveries among Africa's Chimpanzees," December 1965.

19. In writing this part of the chapter, I have drawn heavily on the writings of Sherwood L. Washburn, including "The Study of Human Evolution," in Dolhinow and Sarich, *Background for Man*, pp. 82–117. See also S. L. Washburn, "Behavior and the Origin of Man," *Proceedings of the Royal Anthropological Institute*, 1967, pp. 21–27.

20. This is a controversial issue. Russell Tuttle has stated that there are no features in human hands that "give evidence for a history of knuckle-walking." See his "Knuckle-Walking and the Problem of Human Origins," *Science*, 1969, 166, p. 953. See also Tuttle's edited volume, *The Functional and Evolutionary Biology of Primates*, Aldine-Atherton, Chicago, 1972.

21. J. R. Napier, "Fossil Hand Bones from Olduvai Gorge," *Nature*, 1962, 196, p. 409. For a general discussion, see Pilbeam, *Ascent of Man*, pp. 62–71.

22. George B. Schaller, *Serengeti: A Kingdom of Predators*, Alfred A. Knopf, 1972, and *The Serengeti Lion*, University of Chicago Press, Chicago, 1972. An important paper is George B. Schaller and Gordon R. Lowther, "The Relevance of Carnivore Behavior to the study of Early Hominids," *Southwestern Journal of Anthropology*, 1969.

23. See, for example, M. W. Fox, "A Comparative Study of the Development of Facial Expressions in Canids: Wolf, Coyote, and Foxes," *Behavior*, 1970, 36, pp. 49–73.

24. Philip Lieberman, "Primate Vocalizations and Human Linguistic Ability," *Perspectives in Human Evolution*, 1972, 2, pp. 444–468. See also Philip Lieberman, Edmund S. Gelir, and Dennis H. Klatt, "Phonetic Ability and Related Anatomy of the Newborn and Adult Human, Neanderthal Man, and the Chimpanzee," *American Anthropologist*, 1972, 74, 3, pp. 287–307.

25. Gordon R. Hewes, *Language Origins: A Bibliography*, University of Colorado, Department of Anthropology, Boulder, 1971.

26. The literature on the Australopithecines is enormous. Raymond Dart's original Taung paper was "*Australopithecus africanus:* The Man-Ape of South Africa," *Nature*, 1925, vol. 115, p. 195. An up-to-date summary of the latest discoveries is given in J. Desmond Clark, *The Prehistory of Africa*, Thames and Hudson, London, and Praeger, New York, 1970, chap. 2. See also W. E. Le Gros Clark, *Man-Apes or Ape-men?* Holt, Rinehart & Winston, New York, 1967, and Karl W. Butzer, *Environment and Archaeology: An Introduction to Pleistocene Geography*, 2nd ed., Aldine, Chicago, 1971.

27. The processes by which physical anthropologists reconstruct the appearance of fossil

hominids are covered in most basic texts on physical anthropology. Try Joseph B. Birdsell, *Human Evolution: An Introduction to the New Physical Anthropology*, Rand McNally, Chicago, 1972.

28. The most thorough study of an Australopithecine ever published is that of the original Bed I skull from Olduvai Gorge, Tanzania. See P. V. Tobias, *Olduvai Gorge*, vol. 2, Cambridge University Press, Cambridge and New York, 1967. Some of these issues are debated in the conclusion of that study as well as in the references given earlier.

29. A steady stream of papers describes the latest East Rudolf finds. Try R. E. F. Leakey, A. K. Behrensmeyer, F. J. Fitch, J. A. Miller, and M. D. Leakey, "New Hominid Remains and Early Artifacts from Northern Kenya," *Nature*, 1970, 226, pp. 223–230. A more popular account, Richard E. Leakey and Gordon W. Graham, "In Search of Man's Past at Lake Rudolf," *National Geographic*, May 1970. See also Richard E. Leakey and Glynn Ll. Isaac, "Hominid Fossils from the Area East of Lake Rudolf, Kenya: Photographs and a Commentary on Context," *Perspectives on Human Evolution*, 1972, 2, pp. 129–140. Richard Leakey's latest and most dramatic discovery is reported by him in: "Skull 1470," *National Geographic*, June 1973, pp. 819–829. See also his paper "East Rudolf Evidence for an Advanced Plio-Pleistocene Hominid," *Nature*, 1973, 242, pp. 447–450. For a summary see Butzer, *Environment and Archaeology*, pp. 417–418.

30. The earlier work at Olduvai was described by L. S. B. Leakey, *Olduvai Gorge*, Cambridge University Press, Cambridge, 1951. Three monographs on Olduvai have subsequently appeared, of which the third is the most significant from our point of view: Mary D. Leakey, *Olduvai Gorge*, vol. 3, Cambridge University Press, Cambridge and New York, 1971. This volume describes the finds in Beds I and II and includes complete accounts of the living floors there.

31. J. Desmond Clark, *Prehistory of Africa*, chap. 2. See also Tobias, *Olduvai Gorge*, vol. 2.

32. Mary D. Leakey, *Olduvai Gorge*, vol. 3, pp. 40–60.

33. Oldowan tools from Olduvai are beautifully illustrated and described by Mary Leakey in ibid. For a wider account of Oldowan finds, see J. Desmond Clark, *Prehistory of Africa*, pp. 70–72, 77–78.

34. For a typical paper, see J. Desmond Clark, "The Natural Fracture of Pebbles from the Batoka Gorge, Northern Rhodesia," *Proceedings of the Prehistoric Society*, 1958, 24, pp. 64–77.

35. Glynn Ll. Isaac, "The Diet of Early Man: Aspects of Archaeological Evidence from Lower and Middle Pleistocene Sites in Africa," *World Archaeology*, 1971, 2, 3, pp. 278–299.

36. Richard B. Lee and Irven DeVore (eds.), *Man the Hunter*, Aldine, Chicago, 1968. This book is a mine of information on hunters.

37. For a more extended abstract see Richard A. Watson and Patty Jo Watson, *Man and Nature: An Anthropological Essay in Human Ecology*, Harcourt, Brace and World, New York, 1969.

6

hand axes and choppers

1. Dubois and his discoveries have been summarized many times. An easily accessible first reference is Edmund White and Dale Brown, *The First Men*, Time-Life Books, New York, and Little, Brown, Boston, 1973. Another secondary reference is John Pfeiffer, *The Emergence of Man*, 2nd ed., Harper & Row, 1972.

2. See M. Boule and H. V. Vallois, *Fossil Men*, Thames and Hudson, London, 1957, pp. 130–146; also Franz Weidenreich, *Apes, Giants, and Men*, University of Chicago Press, Chicago, 1946.

3. About 45 individuals have been identified from cultural levels at Choukoutien, including a skullcap found in 1966.

4. Bernard Campbell, *Human Evolution*, Heinemann, London, and Aldine, Chicago, 1967, pp. 343–348.

5. Mary D. Leakey, *Olduvai Gorge*, vol. 3, Cambridge University Press, Cambridge and New York, 1971.

6. The general characteristics of the Acheulian are described by François Bordes, *The Old Stone Age*, McGraw-Hill, New York, 1968, pp. 51–82.

7. The classical description of the evolution of hand axes at Olduvai Gorge is in L. S. B. Leakey, *Olduvai Gorge*, Cambridge University Press, Cambridge, 1951. This sequence has been modified by later research, partly described by Mary D. Leakey in *Olduvai Gorge*, vol. 3. More information will appear in a future volume of the same series.

8. An able account of African hand ax sites appears in J. Desmond Clark, *The Prehistory of Africa*, Thames and Hudson, London, and Praeger, New York, 1970, chap. 3. See also F. C. Howell and J. D. Clark, Acheulian Hunter-Gatherers of Sub-Saharan Africa, *Viking Fund Publications in Anthropology*, 36, 1963, pp. 458–533.

9. A full account of "eoliths" appears in M. C. Burkitt, *The Old Stone Age*, 3rd ed., Cambridge University Press, Cambridge, 1955, chap. 6.

10. H. de Lumley, S. Gagnière, L. Barral, and R. Pascal, "La Grotte du Vallonet, Roquebrune-Cap Martin," *Bulletin de Musée d'Anthropologie Préhistorique de Monaco*, 1963, 10, pp. 5–20.

11. Described briefly by F. Clark Howell, "Observations on the Earlier Phases of the European Lower Paleolithic," *American Anthropologist*, 1966, 68, 2, pp. 111–140.

12. S. Hazzledine Warren, "The *Elephas antiquus* Bed of Clacton on Sea," *Quarterly Journal of the Geological Society*, 1923, 79, pp. 606–634, and his "The Clacton Flint Industry: A New Interpretation," *Proceedings of the Geologists' Association*, 1951, 62, pp. 107–135. A recent discussion of the Clactonian is in Bordes, *Old Stone Age*, pp. 83–97.

13. R. G. West, "The Quaternary Deposits at Hoxne, Suffolk," *Philosophical Transactions of the Royal Society, London*, ser. 8, 1956, 239, pp. 265–356.

14. C. D. Ovey (ed.), *The Swanscombe Skull: A Survey of Research on a Pleistocene Site*, Occasional Papers of the Royal Anthropological Institute no. 20, 1964.

15. Quoted from Campbell, *Human Evolution*, p. 348.

16. Karl W. Butzer, *Environment and Archeology: An Ecological Approach to Prehistory*, 2nd ed., Aldine-Atherton, Chicago, 1971, pp. 584–585.

17. R. J. Mason, *The Prehistory of the Transvaal*, University of the Witwatersrand Press, Johannesburg, 1962, describes the Cave of Hearths; see also Charles M. Keller, *Archaeology of Montagu Cave: A Descriptive Analysis*, University of California Press, Berkeley, 1973.

18. For dating, see Butzer, *Environment and Archeology*, p. 446. For a site report, see Henry de Lumley, "Decouverte d'habitats de l'Acheuléen ancien, dans des depots Mindéliens, sur le site de Terra Amata (Nice)," *Comptes Rendu de l'Académie des Sciences*, 1967, 264, pp. 801–804, and "A Paleolithic Camp at Nice," *Scientific American*, 1969, 220, pp. 42–50.

19. Two notable examples of African butchery sites are Isimila (Tanzania) and Olorgesaillie (Kenya). For Isimila, see F. Clark Howell, Glen H. Cole, and Maxine R. Kleindienst, "Isimila: An Acheulian Occupation Site in the Iringa Highlands," *Actes du IVe. Congrès Panafricain de Prehistoire et de l'Etude du Quaternaire*, Tervuren, Belgium, 1962; for Olorgesaillie, see G. Ll. Isaac, "New Evidence from Olorgesaillie Relating to the Character of Acheulian Occupation Sites," *Actas del V Congreso Panafricano de Prehistorica y de Estudio del Cuaternario*, Tenerife, 1966.

20. Howell, "Observations on the Earlier Phases," pp. 111–140.

21. J. Desmond Clark, *The Kalambo Falls Prehistoric Site*, Cambridge University Press, Cambridge, vol. 1, 1969, vol. 2, 1973.

22. A good example of an Acheulian site is described in J. Desmond Clark, "The Middle Acheulian Occupation Site at Latamne, Syria," *Quarternaria*, 1967, 9, pp. 1–68.

23. The classic paper on the chopper tools of India and Asia was written soon after the Second World War; see H. L. Movius, "The Lower Paleolithic Cultures of Southern and Eastern Asia," *Transactions of the American Philosophical Society*, 1948, 38, pp. 329–420. A more recent but brief summary is J. M. Coles and E. S. Higgs, *The Archaeology of Early Man*, Faber and Faber, London, 1969, chaps. 18 and 19.

24. Kwang-chih Chang, *The Archaeology of Ancient China*, rev. ed., Yale University Press, New Haven and London, 1968, has a brief account of the Chinese Paleolithic.

25. For a summary, see Higgs and Coles, *Archaeology of Early Man*, pp. 396–401; see also Movius, "Lower Paleolithic Cultures." For chronology, see H. D. Kahlke, "Zur relativen

chronologie ostasiatischer mittelpleistozänen Faunen and Hominoidea-Funde," *in* G. Kurth (ed.), *Evolution and Hominisation*, Fischer, Stuttgart, 1968, pp. 91–118.

26. Glynn Isaac, "Traces of Pleistocene Hunters: An East African Example," *in* Richard B. Lee and Irven De Vore (eds.), *Man the Hunter*, Aldine, Chicago, 1968, pp. 253–261.

27. These arguments have been summarized by Isaac and from the anthropological perspective by Roger C. Owen, "The Patrilocal Band: A Linguistically and Culturally Hybrid Social Unit," *American Anthropologist*, 1965, 67, pp. 675–690.

28. See, for example, Edwin W. Smith and Andrew Dale, *The Ila-Speaking Peoples of Northern Rhodesia*, Macmillan, London, 1920. For a discussion of diet, see Glynn Ll. Isaac, "The Diet of Early Man: Aspects of Archaeological Evidence from Lower and Middle Pleistocene Sites in Africa," *World Archaeology*, 1971, 3, 3, pp. 278–299.

29. Kenneth P. Oakley, "Fire as a Palaeolithic Tool and Weapon," *Proceedings of the Prehistoric Society*, 1955, 21, pp. 36–48.

30. Richard A. Watson and Patty Jo Watson, *Man and Nature: An Anthropological Essay in Human Ecology*, Harcourt, Brace and World, New York, 1969, p. 83.

31. See ibid., pp. 72, 73. Quoted with the permission of the authors and the publishers.

7

homo sapiens

1. Karl W. Butzer, *Environment and Archeology: An Ecological Approach to Prehistory*, 2nd ed., Aldine-Atherton, Chicago, 1971.

2. See C. D. Ovey (ed.), *The Swanscombe Skull: A Survey of Research on a Pleistocene Site*, Occasional Papers of the Royal Anthropological Institute no. 20, 1964.

3. The Steinheim skull is described by Bernard Campbell, *Human Evolution*, Heinemann, London, and Aldine, Chicago, 1967, pp. 348–351.

4. Thomas Huxley, *Man's Place in Nature and Other Anthropological Essays*, Macmillan, London, 1863, chap. 3. His chapter on "Some Fossil Remains of Man" is a classic. Schaaffhausen's comment is from Huxley's chapter 3.

5. Wilfred Le Gros Clark, *The Fossil Evidence for Human Evolution*, 2nd ed., University of Chicago Press, Chicago, 1964, chap. 2, is relevant here.

6. The Mousterian culture is described by François Bordes, *The Old Stone Age*, McGraw-Hill, New York, 1968, chaps. 8–10. A basic report on Le Moustier itself is Denis Peyrony, "Le Moustier, ses gisements, ses industries, ses coches géologiques," *Revue Anthropologique*, 1930, vol. 14. Nearly all the basic references to west European Stone Age sites are in French.

7. Salzgitter Lebenstedt is described by A. Tode, F. Preul, K. Richter, A. Kleinschmidt, and others, "Die Untersuchung der pälaolithischen Freilandstation von Salzgitter-Lebenstedt," *Eiszeitaler und Gegenwart*, 1953, 3, pp. 144–220.

8. Stoneworking techniques such as "Levallois," "disc," and others are described briefly in F. Clark Howell, *Early Man*, Time-Life Books, New York, 1965, pp. 109–122. A broader summary is given in Brian M. Fagan, *In the Beginning*, Little, Brown, Boston, 1972, pp. 188–203. See also Jacques Bordaz, *Tools of the Old and New Stone Age*, Natural History Press, New York, 1970.

9. Lewis R. Binford and Sally R. Binford, "A preliminary analysis of Functional Variability in the Mousterian of Levallois Facies," *American Anthropologist*, 1966, 68, 2, pp. 238–295.

10. Richard G. Klein, "The Mousterian of European Russia," *Proceedings of the Prehistoric Society*, 1969, 35, pp. 77–111.

11. Butzer, *Environment and Archeology*, pp. 463–471.

12. Franz Weidenreich, "The Morphology of Solo Man," *Anthropological Papers of the American Museum of Natural History*, 1951, 40, 1. See also Carleton S. Coon, *The Origin of Races*, Alfred A. Knopf, New York, 1962.

13. J. K. Woo and others, "Fossil Human Skull of Early Palaeanthropic Type Found at Ma'pa, Shaoquian, Kwantung Province," *Vertebrata Paleasiatica*, 1959, 3, pp. 176–182.

14. J. Desmond Clark, *The Prehistory of Africa*, Thames and Hudson, London, and Praeger,

New York, 1970. Chap. 4 has specialist references on Africa as a whole. See also Karl W. Butzer, Michael H. Day, and Richard E. Leakey, "Early *Homo sapiens* Remains from the Omo River Region of Southwest Ethiopia," *Nature*, 1969, 222, pp. 1132–1138.

15. The site reports on Mount Carmel are now somewhat outdated, but they are classics; see Dorothy A. E. Garrod and Dorothea M. A. Bate, *The Stone Age of Mt. Carmel*, vol. 2, Oxford University Press, Oxford, 1939. A more recent summary of Near Eastern prehistory is F. Clark Howell, "Upper Pleistocene Stratigraphy and Early Man in the Levant," *Proceedings of the American Philosophical Society*, 1959, 103, pp. 1–65.

16. On Shanidar, see Ralph S. Solecki, "Prehistory in Shanidar Valley, Northern Iraq," *Science*, 1963, 139, p. 179, and, by the same author, *Shanidar: The Humanity of Neanderthal Man*, Penguin Press, London, 1972.

17. Denis Peyrony, "La Ferrassie," *Préhistoire*, 1934, 3.

18. H. L. Movius, "The Mousterian Cave of Teshik-Tash, South Eastern Uzbekistan, Central Asia," *Bulletin of the American School of Prehistoric Research*, 1953, no. 17; also Richard G. Klein, "Open Air Mousterian Sites of South Russia," *Quaternaria*, 1967, 9, pp. 199–223.

8

the upper paleolithic: hunters in western europe

1. This problem has been ably discussed by David Pilbeam, *The Ascent of Man*, Macmillan, New York, 1972, chap. 8. Although a secondary reference, I would recommend this volume strongly as a source of reliable information and basic publications.

2. Donald R. Brothwell, "Where and When Did Man Become Wise," *Discovery*, 1963, p. 10.

3. M. C. Burkitt, *The Old Stone Age*, 3rd ed., Cambridge University Press, Cambridge, 1955.

4. The new toolkits are described by François Bordes, *The Old Stone Age*, chaps. 2, 12. The reader is also referred to the site reports mentioned by Bordes. Many are well illustrated and give a vivid impression of Upper Paleolithic technology.

5. The early history of Upper Paleolithic research has been described by Glyn Daniel, *A Hundred Years of Archaeology*, Duckworth, London, 1950, pp. 93–96.

6. Edward Lartet and Henry Christy, *Reliquiae Aquitanicae*, Henri Ballière, London, 1875.

7. Gabriel de Mortillet's work is described by Daniel in *A Hundred Years of Archaeology*, Duckworth, London, 1950, pp. 98–104.

8. An interesting basic account of Upper Paleolithic economies is J. G. D. Clark, *Prehistoric Europe: The Economic Basis*, Methuen, London, 1952, chaps. 2, 3. See also Karl W. Butzer, *Environment and Archaeology*, Aldine-Atherton, Chicago, 2nd ed., 1972, pp. 475–482. For the Chatelperronian, see Hallam L. Movius, Jr., "The Chatelperronian in French Archaeology," *Antiquity*, 1969, 43, pp. 111–123.

9. Some scholars have alleged that Upper Paleolithic hunters domesticated the reindeer. A recent fascinating paper on the reindeer problem is Ernest S. Burch, Jr., "The Caribou/Wild Reindeer as a Human Resource," *American Antiquity*, 1972, 37, 3, pp. 339–368.

10. François Bordes, *The Old Stone Age*, McGraw-Hill, New York, 1968, chaps. 11, 12. Abri Pataud is described in Clark Howell's *Early Man*, Time-Life Books, New York, 1965, pp. 164–165; other sites and the basic cultural sequence are discussed by J. M. Coles and E. S. Higgs in *The Archaeology of Early Man*, Faber and Faber, London, 1968, chap. 14. Radiocarbon chronologies for Europe have been summarized by H. L. Movius, "Radiocarbon Dates and Upper Paleolithic Archaeology in Central and Western Europe," *Current Anthropology*, 1960, 1, pp. 335–391. That account is, however, somewhat dated.

   Specialist readers will notice that I am using the terms "Chatelperronian" and "Gravettian" as opposed to the French "Early and Late Perigordian" terminology. The Chatelperronian-Gravettian terminology appears to be more widely used in the United States, and I have therefore adopted it here.

11. Venus figurines are described by A. Leroi-Gourhan, *The Art of Prehistoric Man in Western Europe*, Thames and Hudson, London, 1968.

12. Ferdinand Windels, *The Lascaux Cave Paintings*, Faber and Faber, London, 1965.
13. P. E. L. Smith, *Le Solutréen en France*, Publications de L'Institut de Préhistoire de L'Université de Bordeaux, Memoire No. 5, Imprimeries Delmas, Bordeaux.
14. The original monograph on La Madeleine itself is very rare today: L. Capitan and D. Peyrony, *La Madeleine, Son Gisement, Son Industrie, Ses Oeuvres d'Art*, Librairie Émile Nourry, Paris, 1928.
15. Henri Breuil, "Les Subdivisions du Paléolithique Supérieur et leur signification," *Comptes Rendu de la XIVme Session du Congrès International d'Anthropologie et d'Archéologie préhistoriques*, Geneva, 1912, pp. 165–238.
16. A useful compendium on cave art: Johannes Maringer and Hans-Georg Bandi,*Art in the Ice Age*, Praeger, New York, 1953. See also Peter J. Ucko and A. Rosenfeld, *Palaeolithic Cave Art*, World University Library, New York, 1968. Alexander Marshack believes that man was capable of artistic expression far earlier than the Upper Paleolithic. His *Roots of Civilization*, McGraw-Hill, New York, 1972, is fascinating and thought-provoking.
17. One example of such efforts is W. J. Sollas, *Ancient Hunters*, Macmillan, London, 1911.

9
hunters in northern latitudes

1. Margaret T. Hodgen, *Early Anthropology in the Sixteenth and Seventeenth Centuries*, University of Pennsylvania Press, Philadelphia, 1964, gives a general account of early anthropology. Our quotation comes from Tuan Ch'éng-shih's *Yu-yang-tsa-tsu*, a general book of knowledge, which he compiled in the ninth century A.D. (he died in A.D. 863).
2. George P. Murdock, "The Current Status of the World's Hunting and Gathering Peoples," *in* Richard B. Lee and Irven DeVore (eds.), *Man the Hunter*, Aldine, Chicago, 1968, pp. 13–20.
3. I have relied heavily on Richard G. Klein's *Man and Culture in the Late Pleistocene*, Chandler, San Francisco, 1969. This book contains a clear summary of the Kostenki sites; it also has a list of Russian references.
4. For plans of houses see ibid., figs. 113–119, 142, 170–177, and others.
5. Dolní Věstonice is described by B. Klima, "Paleolithic Huts of Dolní Věstonice," *Antiquity*, 1954, 23, pp. 4–14; also "The First Ground Plan of an Upper Palaeolithic Loess Settlement in Middle Europe and Its Meaning," *in* Robert J. Braidwood and Gordon R. Willey, *Courses toward Urban Life*, Viking Fund Publications in Anthropology, 32, 1962, pp. 193–210.
6. Grahame Clark, *Archaeology and Society*, rev. ed., Methuen, London, and Barnes & Noble, New York, 1965, pp. 94–95.
7. The archaeological literature on Siberia is both scattered and complicated. A basic survey can be found in Chester S. Chard, *Man in Prehistory*, McGraw-Hill, New York, 1969, pp. 132, 176–177. I am very grateful to Professor Chard for his advice on recent Siberian references and dates. A more comprehensive survey is Richard G. Klein, "The Pleistocene Prehistory of Siberia," *Quaternary Research*, 1971, 1, 2, pp. 131–161.
8. M. M. Gerasimov, "The Paleolithic site of Mal'ta (1956–57 excavations)," paper in Russian, *Sovetskayen etnografiya*, 1958, 3, pp. 28–52.
9. Radiocarbon dates for Siberia have been summarized by Richard G. Klein in "Radiocarbon Dates on Occupation Sites of Pleistocene Age in the U.S.S.R.," *Arctic Anthropology*, 1967, 4, 2, pp. 224–226.
10. Kwang-chih Chang, *The Archaeology of Ancient China*, rev. ed., Yale University Press, New Haven, 1968. Choukoutien has been opened up for new excavations since 1949.
11. Pei Wên-chung and others, *Report on the Excavations of Palaeolithic Sites at Ting-ts'un, Hsiang-fen-Hsien, Shansi Province, China*, Peking, 1958.
12. J. M. Coles and E. S. Higgs, *The Archaeology of Early Man*, Faber and Faber, London, 1969, pp. 404–406.
13. A third synthesis of Chinese archaeology, with, however, greater emphasis on the later periods, is Wilfred Watson, *China before the Han Dynasty*, Thames and Hudson, London, and Praeger, New York, 1959.

14. The literature on early Japan is highly technical and scattered in many periodicals. For a start, try H. Befu and C. S. Chard, "Pre-Ceramic Cultures in Japan," *American Anthropologist*, 1960, 62, pp. 815–849. See also notes 15 and 16 and recent numbers of *Arctic Anthropology*.

15. F. Ikawa, "The Continuity of Non-Ceramic to Ceramic Cultures in Japan," *Arctic Anthropology*, 1964, 2, 2, pp. 95–119. See also Richard E. Morlan, "The Preceramic Period of Hokkaido: An Outline," ibid., 1967, 4, pp. 164–220, and Kensaku Hayashi, "The Fukui Microblade Technology and Its Relationships in Northeast Asia and North America," ibid., 1968, 5, pp. 128–190.

16. The Jomon culture is described by Kwang-chih Chang, Chester S. Chard, and Wilhelm G. Solheim, *East Asia in Prehistory*, Aldine, Chicago, 1973. See also Ikawa, "Continuity," and Y. Kotani, "Upper Pleistocene and Holocene Conditions in Japan," *Arctic Anthropology*, 1969, 5, 2, pp. 133–158.

17. Two basic references on Siberia are A. P. Okladnikov, "Ancient Populations of Siberia and Its Culture," *in* M. G. Levin and L. P. Potapov (eds.), *The Peoples of Siberia*, University of Chicago Press, Chicago, 1964, pp. 13–98, and N. N. Dikar, "The Discovery of the Paleolithic in Kamchatka and the Problem of the Initial Occupation of America," *Arctic Anthropology*, 1968, 5, 1, pp. 191–203.

18. Chang, Chard, and Solheim, *East Asia in Prehistory*. Several issues of *Arctic Anthropology*, notably vol. 5, 1 (1968) and vol. 6, 1 (1969), deal primarily with Siberian archaeology.

10

hunters in southern latitudes

1. Richard B. Lee and Irven DeVore, (eds.), *Man the Hunter*, Aldine, Chicago, 1968, and Bridget Allchin, *The Stone-Tipped Arrow*, Barnes & Noble, New York, 1966.

2. This event has been discussed by many authors. A detailed account is given in F. Clark Howell, "Upper Pleistocene Stratigraphy and Early Man in the Levant," *Proceedings of the American Philosophical Society*, 1959, 103. See also J. M. Coles and E. S. Higgs, *The Archaeology of Early Man*, Faber and Faber, London, 1969, chap. 18. The animals hunted by early Near Eastern hunters are discussed by Eric S. Higgs, "Faunal Fluctuations and Climate in Libya," *in* W. W. Bishop and J. D. Clark (eds.), *Background to Evolution in Africa*, University of Chicago Press, Chicago, 1967.

3. C. B. M. McBurney, *The Stone Age in North Africa*, Pelican Books, Harmondsworth, 1960; also Coles and Higgs, *Archaeology of Early Man*, chaps. 11 and 12.

4. The Capsian and Oranian are described in detail by Jacques Tixier, "Typologie de l'Epipaleolithique de Maghreb," *Memoires du Centre de Recherches Archaeologiques, Prehistoriques et Anthropologiques* (Algiers), 1963.

5. A summary of the Aterian will be found in J. Desmond Clark, *The Prehistory of Africa*, Thames and Hudson, London, and Praeger, New York, 1970, pp. 127–129. See also L. Balout, *Prehistoire de l'Afrique du Nord*, Arts and Metiers Graphiques, Paris, 1955, pp. 269–334.

6. Clark, *Prehistory of Africa*, chap. 4.

7. J. Desmond Clark and others, "New Studies on Rhodesian Man," *Journal of the Royal Anthropological Institute*, 1947, 77, pp. 7–32.

8. Clark, *Prehistory of Africa*, chap. 5. Numerous references are given to the technical literature.

9. A good survey is A. R. Willcox, *The Rock Art of South Africa*, Thomas Nelson, Johannesburg, 1963. For detailed analogies with archaeology and modern hunters; see J. Desmond Clark, *The Prehistory of Southern Africa*, Pelican Books, Harmondsworth, 1959, chaps. 9 and 10.

10. On Bushmen, see Elizabeth Marshall Thomas, *The Harmless People*, Alfred A. Knopf, New York, 1959; on Pygmies, see Colin M. Turnbull, *The Forest People*, Doubleday, New York, 1962 (paperback ed.).

11. Sir Mortimer Wheeler, *Early India and Pakistan*, Thames and Hudson, London, and Praeger, New York, 1959, p. 34. I have drawn on his chapters 3 and 4 for this account.

12. H. D. Sankalia and I. Karve, "Early Primitive Microlithic Culture and People of Gujara," *American Anthropologist,* 1949, 51, pp. 28–34.

13. Tom Harrisson, "The Great Cave of Niah," *Man,* 1957, article 211. Anyone seriously interested in Borneo or Thailand should read *Asian Perspectives,* 1972, 13.

14. J. Peter White, K. A. W. Crook, and B. P. Ruxton, "Kosipe: A Late Pleistocene Site in the Papuan Highlands," *Proceedings of the Prehistoric Society,* 1970, 36, pp. 152–171. For the use of stone tools in modern New Guinea, see B. A. L. Cranstone, "The Tifalmin: A 'Neolithic' People in New Guinea," *World Archaeology,* 1971, 3, 2, pp. 132–143. For New Guinea archaeology, see Jim Allen, "The First Decade in New Guinea Archaeology," *Antiquity,* 1972, 46, 183, pp. 180–190.

15. Chester F. Gorman, "Hoabhinian: A Pebble-Tool Complex with Early Plant Associations in Southeast Asia," *Science,* 1969, 163, pp. 671–673. See also *Asian Perspectives,* 1972, 13.

16. Chester F. Gorman, "The Hoabhinian and After: Subsistence Patterns in Southeast Asia during the Late Pleistocene and Early Recent Periods," *World Archaeology,* 1971, 2, 3, pp. 300–320. See also *Asian Perspectives,* 1972, 13.

17. Edward Tylor *Researches into the Early History of Mankind,* Macmillan, London, 1865; University of Chicago Press, Chicago, 1964 ed.

18. The basic source of information on Australian archaeology is Derek J. Mulvaney, *The Prehistory of Australia,* Thames and Hudson, London, and Praeger, New York, 1969. See also Richard A. Gould, "Australian Archaeology in Ecological and Ethnographic Perspective," *Warner Modular Publications, Module # 7,* 1973.

19. Harrisson, "Niah." See discussion in Mulvaney, *Prehistory of Australia,* chap. 5.

20. Ibid., pp. 153–154. See also J. M. Bowler, R. Jones, H. Allen, and A. G. Thorne, "Pleistocene Human Remains from Australia: A Living Site and Cremation from Lake Mungo, Western N.S.W.," *World Archaeology,* 1970, 2, pp. 39–60.

21. F. M. Setzler and F. D. McCarthy, "A Unique Archaeological Specimen from Australia," *Journal of the Washington Academy of Sciences,* 1950, 40, pp. 1-5. See also Mulvaney, *Prehistory of Australia,* pp. 82–83, 130–132, 143. Richard V. S. Wright (ed.), "Archaeology of the Gallus Site, Koonalda Cave," *Australian Aboriginal Studies # 26,* Australian Institute of Aboriginal Studies, Canberra, 1971, is the basic reference.

22. For Kenniff, see D. J. Mulvaney and E. B. Joyce, "Archaeological and Geomorphological Investigations on Mt. Moffat Station, Queensland," *Antiquity,* 1964, 38, pp. 263–267.

23. Mulvaney, *Prehistory of Australia,* chap. 5.

24. Ibid., pp. 104–111.

25. The Tasmanians are a fascinating archaeological topic. The principal references are ibid., chap. 5; N. B. Tindale, "Cultural Succession in South-eastern Australia from Late Pleistocene to the Present," *Records of the South Australian Museum,* 1957, 13, pp. 1–47; and his "The Osteology of Aboriginal Man in Tasmania," *Oceania Monographs,* 1965, 12, pp. 1–72.

26. Rhys Jones, "A Speculative Archaeological Sequence for North-west Tasmania," *Records of the Queen Victoria Museum,* Launceston, 1966, 25, pp. 1–25.

27. A. Searcy, *In Australian Tropics,* Macmillan, London, 1909, describes the Trepang trade in progress. See also Mulvaney, *Prehistory of Australia,* p. 66.

28. Quotation from William Thomas (1838) taken from Derek Mulvaney, *The Prehistory of Australia,* Thames and Hudson, London, and Praeger, New York, 1969, p. 66.

11

early americans

1. Anyone interested in the early exploration of North America shouldn't miss Samuel Eliot Morison, *The European Discovery of America,* vol. 1: *The Northern Voyages* A.D. 500 *to 1600,* Oxford University Press, London and New York, 1971. This book is authoritative, entertaining, and crammed with interesting information.

2. A historical survey of New World archaeology is Gordon R. Willey, "A Hundred Years of American Archaeology," *in* J. O. Brew (ed.), *A Hundred Years of Anthropology,* Harvard

University Press, Cambridge, 1968, pp. 29–55. Recent, highly speculative volumes on New World origins are Cyrus H. Gordon, *Before Columbus*, Crown Publishers, New York, 1971, and Betty Bugbee Cusack, *Collectors' Luck: Giant Steps into Prehistory*, G. R. Barnstead Printing Company, Stonehaven, Mass., 1968.

3. Samuel Haven, *Archaeology of the United States*, Smithsonian Institution, Washington, D.C., 1856.

4. J. D. Figgins, "The Antiquity of Man in North America," *Natural History*, 1927, 27, pp. 229–231.

5. On the Bering Land Bridge, see David Hopkins (ed.), *The Bering Land Bridge*, Stanford University Press, Stanford, 1967.

6. Alan Bryan, "Early Man in America and the Late Pleistocene Chronology of Western Canada and Alaska," *Current Anthropology*, 1969, 10, 4, pp. 339–365. See also Karen Wood Workman, *Alaskan Archaeology: A Bibliography*, Alaskan Division of Parks, 1972. For Akmak, see Douglas D. Anderson, "Akmak," *Acta Arctica*, 1970, 15.

7. Gordon R. Willey, *An Introduction to American Archaeology*, vol. 2: *South America*, Prentice-Hall, Englewood Cliffs, N.J., 1971, p. 27. See also Lorena Mirambell, "Excavaciones en un sitio pleistocénico de Tlapacoya, México," *Boletín Instituto Nacional de Antropología e Historia*, 1967, 29, pp. 37–41.

8. Willey's *Introduction to American Archaeology*, vol. 1: *North and Central America*, Prentice-Hall, Englewood Cliffs, N.J., 1967, chap. 2, summarizes the earlier evidence. See also Ruth Gruhn, *The Archaeology of Wilson Butte Cave, South-Central Idaho*, Occasional Papers of the Idaho State Museum no. 6, 1961, and Jesse D. Jennings and Edward Norbeck (eds.), *Prehistoric Man in the New World*, University of Chicago Press, Chicago, 1964, pp. 23–81.

9. Richard S. MacNeish, "Early Man in the Andes," *Scientific American*, 1971, 4, pp. 36–46.

10. Vance Haynes, "Fluted Projectile Points, Their Age and Dispersion," *Science*, 1964, 145, pp. 1408–1413; also H. J. Müller-Beck, "Paleo-Hunters in America: Origins and Diffusion," *Science*, 1966, 152, pp. 1191–1210.

11. A vivid example is Joe Ben Wheat, "A Paleo-Indian Bison Kill," *Scientific American*, 1967, 1, pp. 44–52.

12. The issue of extinction of Pleistocene mammals in North America was discussed by Paul Martin and H. E. Wright, Jr. (eds.), *Pleistocene Extinctions: The Search for a Cause*, Yale University Press, New Haven, 1967.

13. A basic description can be found in Jesse D. Jennings, *The Prehistory of North America*, McGraw-Hill, New York, 1968, chap. 3.

14. For Danger Cave, see Jesse D. Jennings, *Danger Cave*, University of Utah Anthropological Papers no. 27, Salt Lake City, 1957. A summary of this site and of Lovelock and Gypsum caves appears in the same author's *Prehistory*, pp. 139–143. See also Claude Warren and Anthony Ranere, "Outside Danger Cave: A View of Early Men in the Great Basin," in Cynthia Irwin-Williams, *Early Man in Western North America*, Eastern New Mexico University Press, Portales, N.M., 1968, pp. 6–18. Another important site is Humboldt Cave; see Robert F. Heizer and Alex D. Krieger, *The Archaeology of Humboldt Cave, Churchill County, Nevada*, University of California Publications in American Archaeology and Ethnology, Berkeley, 1956, vol. 47, no. 1, pp. 1–190.

15. A number of key references will be found in Robert F. Heizer and Mary A. Whipple's *The California Indians: A Source Book*, University of California Press, Berkeley and London, 1971, especially pp. 186–201, 206–224, 225–261.

16. A good description of the Archaic tradition may be found in Willey, *Introduction to American Archaeology*, vol. 1, pp. 60–64 and chap. 5; see also Jennings, *Prehistory*, chap. 4.

17. The Lake Superior copper trade is described by Tyler J. Bastian, *Prehistoric Copper Mining in Isle Royale National Park, Michigan*, Museum of Anthropology, University of Michigan, Ann Arbor, 1969.

18. For early contact between explores and hunters see Morison's *Northern Voyages*.

19. Willey, *Introduction to American Archaeology*, vol. 2, chap. 2.

20. This is a remarkably strong reaction from such a mild man. Charles Darwin, *The Voyage of the Beagle*, E. P. Dutton, London, 1906, p. 231 (his account was originally published in 1839).

21. W. S. Laughlin and G. H. Marsh, "The Lamellar Flake Manufacturing Site on Anangula Island in the Aleutians," *American Antiquity*, 1954, 20, 1, pp. 27–39. See also Jean S. Aigner, "The Unifacial, Core, and Blade Site on Anangula Island, Aleutians," *Arctic Anthropology*, 1970, 7, 2, pp. 59–88, and Douglas Anderson, "A Stone Age Campsite at the Gateway to America," *Scientific American*, 1968, 218, pp. 24–33.

22. A summary description is in Willey, *Introduction to American Archaeology*, vol. 1, pp. 416–419, which contains references to W. N. Irving's important work on the Arctic Small–Tool Tradition. Iyatayet is described by J. L. Giddings, *The Archaeology of Cape Denbigh*, Brown University Press, Providence, R. I., 1964. The same author's *Ancient Men of the Arctic*, Alfred A. Knopf, New York, 1967, is a popular account. Hans-Georg Bandi, *Eskimo Prehistory*, University of Washington Press, Seattle, 1968, summarizes Arctic archaeology and its complex literature. I found Thomas C. Patterson's *America's Past: A New World Archaeology*, Scott, Foresman and Company, Glenview, Ill., 1973, a useful preliminary guide.

23. H. B. Collins, *The Archaeology of St. Lawrence Island, Alaska*, Smithsonian Miscellaneous Collections, 1937, 96, 1, and J. L. Giddings, "The Archaeology of Bering Strait," *Current Anthropology*, 1960, 1, 2, pp. 121–138. The term Eskimo is thought to have originated from the Indian expression *askimowew:* "he who eats raw."

24. Willey, *Introduction to American Archaeology*, vol. 1, pp. 422–430.

12

the harvest is plenteous

1. Once again, I would commend to you Richard A. Watson and Patty Jo Watson, *Man and Nature: An Anthropological Essay in Human Ecology*, Harcourt, Brace and World, 1969, this time chap. 7. Many points touched in this chapter are covered more thoroughly there.

2. Probably the classic work on the consequences of food production is by V. Gordon Childe, whose popular volumes contain much uncontroversial material on the origins of agriculture. See his *Man Makes Himself*, Watts, London, 1936. It is appropriate to draw attention to a most useful reader on prehistoric agriculture. Many of the papers referred to in this chapter and later ones are to be found in Stuart Struever (ed.), *Prehistoric Agriculture*, Natural History Press, Garden City, N.Y., 1971.

3. William Allan, *The African Husbandman*, Oliver and Boyd, Edinburgh, 1965, is a mine of information on shifting cultivation.

4. This thesis has been expounded in part by Thayer Scudder, *Gathering among African Woodland Savannah Cultivators*, University of Zambia, Institute for African Studies Paper no. 5, Lusaka, 1971. To obtain an idea of the complexity of a subsistence level agricultural economy, try Thayer Scudder, *The Ecology of the Gwembe Tonga*, Manchester University Press, Manchester, 1962. This is an account of a people relying heavily on their environment for supplementary foods.

5. Kent V. Flannery, "Archaeological Systems Theory and Early Mesoamerica," *in* Betty J. Meggers (ed.), *Anthropological Archaeology in the Americas*, Anthropological Society of Washington, Washington, D.C., 1968, pp. 67–87.

6. For a history of research into agricultural origins, see Gary A. Wright, "Origins of Food Production in Southwestern Asia: A Survey of Ideas," *Current Anthropology*, 1971, 12, 4–5, pp. 447–478.

7. Harold L. Roth, "On the Origins of Agriculture," *Journal of the Royal Anthropological Institute*, 1887, 16, pp. 102–136.

8. The dessication theory is well expressed by Childe himself in V. Gordon Childe, *New Light on the Most Ancient East*, 4th ed., Routledge and Kegan Paul, London, 1952. His revolutions are described in detail in his *Man Makes Himself*, Mentor, New York, 1951.

9. Harold Peake and Herbert J. Fleure, *Peasants and Potters*, Oxford University Press, London, 1927.

10. Robert J. Braidwood and Bruce Howe, "Southwestern Asia beyond the Lands of the Mediterranean Littoral," *in* Robert J. Braidwood and Gordon R. Willey (eds.), *Courses*

toward Urban Life, Viking Fund Publications in Anthropology, vol. 32, New York, 1962, pp. 132–146.

11. Carl O. Sauer, *Agricultural Origins and Dispersals,* American Geographical Society, New York, 1952.

12. Robert M. Adams, "The Origins of Agriculture," *in* Sol Tax (ed.), *The Horizons of Anthropology,* Aldine, Chicago, 1964, pp. 120–131.

13. Lewis R. Binford, "Post-Pleistocene Adaptations," *in* Sally R. Binford and Lewis R. Binford (eds.), *New Perspectives in Archaeology,* Aldine, Chicago, 1968, pp. 313–341.

14. See note 1.

15. Kent V. Flannery, "The Ecology of Early Food Production in Mesopotamia," *Science,* 1965, 147, pp. 1247–1256.

16. Frank Hole and Kent V. Flannery, "Excavations at Ali Kosh, Iran, 1961," *Iranica Antiqua,* 1962, 2, pp. 97–148.

17. Eric S. Higgs and Michael R. Jarman, "The Origins of Agriculture: A Reconsideration," *Antiquity,* 1969, 43, pp. 31–41. See also Eric S. Higgs (ed.), *Papers in Economic Prehistory,* Cambridge University Press, Cambridge, 1973.

18. A fundamental reference is R. J. Berry, "The Genetical Implications of Domestication in Animals," *in* Peter J. Ucko and G. W. Dimbleby (eds.), *The Domestication and Exploitation of Plants and Animals,* Duckworth, London, and Aldine, Chicago, 1969, pp. 207–218.

19. It is worth reading Kent V. Flannery, "Origins and Ecological Effects of Early Domestication in Iran and the Near East," *in* ibid., pp. 73–100. But see Higgs and Jarman, "Origins of Agriculture."

20. Dexter Perkins, "The Prehistoric Fauna from Shanidar, Iraq," *Science,* 1964, 144, pp. 1565–1566. Considerable progress has been made in recent years with the measurement of limb bones of domestic and wild animals as a basis for distinguishing tamed and game animals.

21. Jack Harlan has experimented with the harvesting of wild grains, reported in "A Wild Wheat Harvest in Turkey," *Archaeology,* 1967, 20, pp. 197–201.

22. Argued, among others, by Grahame Clarke, *Aspects of Prehistory,* University of California Press, Berkeley, 1970, pp. 91–95.

23. The distribution of wild cereals has been studied by many scientists. A classic work is N. I. Vavilov, "Phytogeographic Basis of Plant Breeding," *Chronica Botanica,* 1951, 13, pp. 14–54. See also his "The Origin, Variation, Immunity, and Breeding of Cultivated Plants," ibid., pp. 1–6. For a survey of early crops in the Near East, see Daniel Zohary, "The Progenitors of Wheat and Barley in Relation to Domestication and Agricultural Dispersal in the Old World," *in* Ucko and Dimbleby, *Domestication and Exploitation,* pp. 47–66.

24. Childe, *Man Makes Himself,* pp. 67–72.

25. The early history of pottery in the Near East is described by James Mellaart, *The Earliest Civilizations of the Near East,* Thames and Hudson, London, and McGraw-Hill, New York, 1965, chap. 4.

26. A. C. Renfrew, J. E. Dixon, and J. R. Cann, "Obsidian and Early Cultural Contact in the Near East," *Proceedings of the Prehistoric Society,* 1966, 32, pp. 1–29, and subsequent articles.

13

the origins of food production: europe and the near east

1. A survey of the relevant research of the past two centuries has been compiled by Gary A. Wright, "The Origins of Food Production in Southwestern Asia: A Survey of Ideas," *Current Anthropology,* 1971, 12, 4–5, pp. 447–478.

2. V. Gordon Childe, *New Light on the Most Ancient East,* 4th ed., Routledge and Kegan Paul, London, 1952.

3. Robert J. Braidwood, "The Agricultural Revolution," *Scientific American,* 1960, 203, p. 134, and Wright, "Origins," pp. 456–457.

4. Lewis R. Binford, "Post-Pleistocene Adaptations," *in* Sally R. Binford and Lewis R.

Binford (eds.), *New Perspectives in Archaeology,* Aldine, Chicago, 1968, pp. 313–341, and Kent V. Flannery, "Origins and Ecological Effects of Early Domestication in Iran and the Near East," *in* Peter J. Ucko and George W. Dimbleby (eds.), *The Domestication and Exploitation of Plants and Animals,* Duckworth, London, and Aldine, Chicago, 1969, pp. 73–100.

5. Such Paleolithic cultures as the Atlitian, Kebaran, and Zarzian belong in this time bracket. For one typical site, Palegawra, see Robert J. Braidwood and Bruce Howe, *Prehistoric Investigations in Kurdistan,* Oriental Institute, University of Chicago, Chicago, 1960.

6. The Natufian was originally described in Dorothy A. E. Garrod and Dorothea M. A. Bate, *The Stone Age of Mt. Carmel,* vol. 1, Oxford University Press, Oxford, 1937. A later review article is D. A. E. Garrod, "The Natufian Culture: The Life and Economy of a Mesolithic People in the Near East," *Proceedings of the British Academy,* 1957, 43, pp. 211–217. For a survey of the literature see Wright, "Origins," pp. 467–468.

7. An introductory survey of Jericho can be found in Kathleen Kenyon, *Archaeology in the Holy Land,* Benn, London, 1961. See also James Mellaart, *The Earliest Civilizations of the Near East,* Thames and Hudson, London, and McGraw-Hill, New York, 1965. Biblical quotation: Joshua 6:20.

8. For Beidha, see Diana Kirkbride, "Beidha: Early Neolithic Village Life South of the Dead Sea," *Antiquity,* 1968, 42, pp. 263–274.

9. Dexter Perkins, "Prehistoric Fauna from Shanidar, Iraq," *Science,* 1964, 144, pp. 1565–1566.

10. For Jarmo, see Braidwood and Howe, *Prehistoric Investigations.* See also Mellaart, *Earliest Civilizations.*

11. Frank Hole, Kent V. Flannery, and James A. Neely, *The Prehistory and Human Ecology of the Deh Luran Plain,* University of Michigan, Museum of Anthropology Memoir no. 1, Ann Arbor, 1969.

12. The domestic animals at Çayönü are described by B. Lawrence, "Evidences of Animal Domestication at Çayönü," *Bulletin of the Turkish Historical Society,* 1969.

13. For Hacilar, see Mellaart, *Earliest Civilizations,* pp. 80 ff. Further references are given there.

14. James Mellaart, *Çatal Hüyük,* Thames and Hudson, London, and Praeger, New York, 1967.

15. V. Gordon Childe, *The Dawn of European Civilization,* Routledge & Kegan Paul, London, 1925.

16. Colin Renfrew, "The Tree-Ring Calibration of Radiocarbon: An Archaeological Evaluation," *Proceedings of the Prehistoric Society,* 1970, 36, pp. 280–311, and Colin Renfrew, "New Configurations in Old World Archaeology," *World Archaeology,* 1970, 2, 2, pp. 199–211. Another useful review is Euan MacKie and others, "Thoughts on Radiocarbon Dating," *Antiquity,* 1971, 45, 179, pp. 197–204. An outline description of the problem and further references are given in Brian M. Fagan, *In the Beginning,* Little, Brown, Boston, 1972, pp. 56–57. See also H. L. Thomas, "Near Eastern, Mediterranean, and European Chronology," *Studies in Mediterranean Archaeology,* 1967.

17. Karl W. Butzer, *Environment and Archeology: An Ecological Approach to Prehistory,* Aldine-Atherton, Chicago, 1971, chap. 33.

18. H. T. Waterbolk, "Food Production in Prehistoric Eruope," *Science,* 1968, 162, pp. 1093–1102.

19. Reiner Protsch and Rainer Berger, "Earliest Radiocarbon Dates for Domesticated Animals," *Science,* 1973, 179, pp. 235–239.

20. Robert J. Rodden, "Excavations at the Early Neolithic Site at Nea Nikomedeia, Greek Macedonia (1961 season)," *Proceedings of the Prehistoric Society,* 1962, 28, pp. 267–288.

21. Ruth Tringham, *Hunters, Fishers, and Farmers of Eastern Europe: 6000–3000 B.C.,* Hutchinson University Library, London, 1971, is an important synthesis of southeast European prehistory.

22. The context of Lepenski Vir is well summarized in ibid., chaps. 2 and 3.

23. The basic summary of European prehistory to refer to throughout the later part of this chapter is Stuart Piggott, *Ancient Europe,* Edinburgh University Press, Edinburgh, and Aldine, Chicago, 1965. For up-to-date references, consult a specialist or specific

notes in this book. For the Danubians, see ibid., pp. 50 ff., and chap. 2, note 53. See also Waterbolk, "Food Production."

24. Literature summarized in Piggott, *Ancient Europe*, p. 57, and chap. 2, note 58.

25. Keller published his finds in five memoirs presented to the Anthropological Society of Zurich. They were subsequently translated into English by J. E. Lee under the title of *The Lake Dwellings of Switzerland and Other Parts of Europe*, Murray, London, 1866. See Glyn Daniel, *A Hundred Years of Archaeology*, Duckworth, London, 1950, pp. 89–93, and Hansjürgen Muller-Beck, "Prehistoric Swiss Lake Dwellings," *Scientific American*, December 1961.

26. The literature on megaliths is enormous. A synthesis is given in Glyn Daniel, *Megaliths in History*, Thames and Hudson, London, 1973. See also Colin Renfrew, "Colonialism and Megalithismus," *Antiquity*, 1967, 4, 41, pp. 276–288 and the same author's "Tree-ring Calibration."

27. J. G. D. Clark, *The Mesolithic Settlement of Northern Europe*, Cambridge University Press, Cambridge, 1938, is a classic description of these cultures.

28. The original experiments were conducted in the late nineteenth century. See Sir John Evans, *Ancient Stone Implements of Great Britain*, Longmans, London, 1897 (2nd ed.), p. 162.

29. A basic description is in J. G. D. Clark, *Prehistoric Europe: The Economic Basis*, Methuen, London, 1952, chap. VII.

14

africa and her prodigies

1. A succinct account of the Nile environment appears in Cyril Aldred, *The Egyptians*, Thames and Hudson, London, and Praeger, New York, 1961, chaps. 2 and 3.

2. In writing this section, I have referred constantly to J. Desmond Clark, "A Re-examination of the Evidence for Agricultural Origins in the Nile Valley," *Proceedings of the Prehistoric Society*, 1971, 37, 2, pp. 34–79.

3. For Qadan, see Fred Wendorf (ed.), *The Prehistory of Nubia*, Southern Methodist University Press, Dallas, 1968, vol. 2, pp. 791–996. The cemetery is described by Fred Wendorf, "A Nubian Final Paleolithic Graveyard near Jebel Sahaba, Sudan," *in* ibid., pp. 954–995.

4. This complicated cultural sequence is described by Philip E. L. Smith, "The Late Paleolithic of North-East Africa in the Light of Recent Research," *American Anthropologist*, 1966, 68, 2, pp. 326–355. For the Kom Ombo environment, see Karl W. Butzer and C. L. Hansen, *Desert and River in Nubia*, Wisconsin University Press, Madison, 1968.

5. G. Caton-Thompson and E. W. Gardner, *The Desert Fayum*, Royal Anthropological Institute, London, 1934, 2 vols.

6. Jacques Vendrier, *Manuel d'archéologie egyptienne*, vol. 1: *Les époques de formation: le préhistoire*, Édition A. et J. Picard, Paris, 1952, is a fundamental source on Merimde and other early sites. See also Bruce G. Trigger, *Beyond History: The Methods of Prehistory*, Holt, Rinehart and Winston, 1968.

7. See Walter B. Emery, *Archaic Egypt*, Penguin Books, London, 1961, and Aldred, *Egyptians*, pp. 66–69.

8. A brief synthesis of Saharan archaeology appears in J. Desmond Clark, *The Prehistory of Africa*, Thames and Hudson, London, and Praeger, New York, 1970, chaps. 4–6.

9. For some discussion of dates, see J. Desmond Clark, "The Problem of Neolithic Culture in Sub-Saharan Africa," *in* W. W. Bishop and J. Desmond Clark (eds.), *Background to Evolution in Africa*, University of Chicago Press, Chicago and London, 1967, pp. 601–628.

10. On the domestication of animals in the Sahara, see Clark, "Re-examination," pp. 52–74.

11. Saharan rock art is vividly described by Henri Lhote, *The Search for the Tassili Frescoes*, Hutchinson, London, 1959.

12. J. Desmond Clark, "The Origins of Food Production in Africa," *Journal of African History*, 1962, 3, 2, pp. 211–228, is a basic synthesis, if a little outdated — a good starting point.

13. On yams, see D. G. Coursey, *Yams in West Africa*, Institute of African Studies, Legon,

Ghana, 1965. See also Clark, "Origins," for a discussion of early agriculture near the forest.

14. Clark, "Problem of Neolithic Culture."
15. An interesting assessment of Africa in prehistory was made by Thurston Shaw in a long review of Grahame Clark's *World Prehistory*, rev. ed., Cambridge University Press, 1969: "Africa in Prehistory: Leader or Laggard?" *Journal of African History*, 1971, 12, 1, pp. 143–154.

15

rice, roots, and ocean voyagers

1. Carl O. Sauer, *Agricultural Origins and Dispersals*, American Geographical Society, New York, 1952.
2. Chester F. Gorman, "Hoabhinian: A Pebble-Tool Complex with Early Plant Associations in Southeast Asia," *Science*, 1969, 163, pp. 671–673. See also Chester F. Gorman, "Hoabhinian and After: Subsistence Patterns in Southeast Asia during the Late Pleistocene and Early Recent Periods," *World Archaeology*, 1971, 2, 3, pp. 300–320.
3. Wilhelm G. Solheim III, "An Earlier Agricultural Revolution," *Scientific American*, 1972, 1, pp. 34–41. This paper summarizes both the Spirit Cave and the Non Nok Tha findings.
4. Matsuo Tsukada, "Vegetation in Subtropical Formosa during the Pleistocene Glaciations and the Holocene," *Palaeogeography, Palaeoclimatology, Palaeoecology*, 1967, 3, pp. 49–64.
5. An important paper is by Kwang-chih Chang, "The Beginnings of Agriculture in the Far East," *Antiquity*, 1970, 44, pp. 175–185. This summarizes both Southeast Asian and Asian finds to 1970.
6. This paragraph relies heavily on Glyn Daniel, *The First Civilizations*, Thames and Hudson, London, 1968, p. 121. The quotation is from Thomas De Quincey.
7. Described by Kwang-chih Chang, *The Archaeology of Ancient China*, rev. ed. Yale University Press, New Haven, 1968, chap. 3.
8. Ping-ti Ho, "Loess and the Origin of Chinese Agriculture," *American Historical Review*, October 1969, pp. 1–36.
9. Chang, *Archaeology of Ancient China*, chap. 3. The reference to early cord-marked pottery is from Chang, "Beginnings of Agriculture," p. 177.
10. Some of the dates are discussed by Chang, both in *Archaeology of Ancient China*, pp. 105–120, and in "Beginnings of Agriculture," pp. 181–184. See also Richard Pearson, "Radiocarbon Dates from China," *Antiquity*, 1973, 47, 186, pp. 141–143, where a date of c. 4400 B.C. is quoted for early irrigation.
11. On Lungshanoid cultures, see Chang, *Archaeology of Ancient China*, chap. 4.
12. Louis de Bougainville, *A Voyage Round the World*, London, 1772.
13. J. C. Beaglehole's work on the diaries of Joseph Banks and James Cook is well known and of the highest quality. Try *The Journals of Captain James Cook on His Voyages of Discovery*, vols. 1 and 2, Hakluyt Society and Cambridge University Press, Cambridge, 1955, 1961. For an introduction to the exploration of the South Seas, try Alan Moorehead's delightful book, *The Fatal Impact*, Hamish Hamilton, London, 1966.
14. Quoted from his journals and Alan Howard, "Polynesian Origins and Migrations," *in* Genevieve A. Highland and others (eds.), *Polynesian Culture History*, Bishop Museum Press, Honolulu, 1967, pp. 45–103.
15. Two fundamental sources on the Pacific are a collection of essays: Highland and others, *Polynesian Culture History*, and a useful reader, Thomas G. Harding and Ben J. Wallace (eds.), *Cultures of the Pacific*, Free Press, New York, 1970.
16. For discussion, see Howard, "Polynesian Origins and Migrations," pp. 61–71.
17. No one should miss Thor Heyerdahl's *Kon-Tiki* George Allen & Unwin, London, 1950. The detailed account of his theories appears in his *American Indians in the Pacific*, George Allen & Unwin, London, 1952.
18. See R. C. Green's review, "The Immediate Origins of the Polynesians," *in* Highland and others, *Polynesian Culture History*, pp. 215–240.

19. Robert C. Suggs, *The Island Civilizations of Polynesia*, Mentor Books, New York, 1960.
20. Andrew Sharp, *Ancient Voyagers in the Pacific*, Penguin Books, London, 1957. See also his "Polynesian Navigation to Distant Islands," *Journal of the Polynesian Society*, 1961, 70, 2, pp. 221–226.
21. The literature is complex, but see Andrew P. Vadya, "Polynesian Cultural Distribution in New Perspective," *American Anthropologist*, 1959, 61, 1, pp. 817–828.
22. Ben R. Finney, "New Perspectives on Polynesian Voyaging," *in* Highland and others, *Polynesian Culture History*, pp. 141–166. I thoroughly enjoyed David Lewis, *The Wake of the Canoes*, Australian National University Press, Canberra, 1972.
23. Some of the data are summarized in Janet Davidson, "Archaeology on Coral Atolls," *in ibid.*, pp. 363–376. Also see R. Groube, "Tonga, Lapita Pottery, and Polynesian Origins," *Journal of the Polynesian Society*, 1971, 80, pp. 278–346.
24. Hawaiian archaeology is scattered in many articles. Fishhook typology is fundamental; see Kenneth Emory, William J. Bonk, and Yoshiko H. Sinoto, *Hawaiian Archaeology: Fishhooks*, Bishop Museum Special Publications, 1959, no. 47.
25. Thomas Gladwin, *East Is a Big Bird: Navigation and Logic on Puluwat Atoll*, Harvard University Press, Cambridge, Mass., 1970.
26. John Mulvaney, "Prehistory from Antipodean Perspectives," *Proceedings of the Prehistoric Society*, 1971, 37, 2, pp. 228–252. This paper is an important statement on the nature and significance of Asian and Pacific archaeology.
27. New Zealand's archaeology is briefly surveyed by Wilfred Shawcross, "Archaeology with a Short, Isolated Time-Scale: New Zealand," *World Archaeology*, 1969, 1, 2, pp. 184–199. This useful paper contains a basic bibliography, and is thoroughly provocative! Moa hunters are described by R. Duff, *The Moa-Hunter Period of Maori Culture*, Government Printer, Wellington, 1956.
28. A fundamental paper on New Zealand agriculture is Kathleen Shawcross, "Fern Root and 18th-Century Maori Food Production in Agricultural Areas," *Journal of the Polynesian Society*, 1967, 76, pp. 330–352. See also L. M. Groube, "The Origin and Development of Earthwork Fortifications in the Pacific," *in* R. C. Green and M. Kelly (eds.), *Studies in Oceanic Culture History*, vol. 1, Pacific Anthropological Records no. 11, 1970, pp. 133–164. Another important paper is Peter L. Bellwood, "Fortifications and Economy in Prehistoric New Zealand," *Proceedings of the Prehistoric Society*, 1971, 37, 1, pp. 56–95.

16

new world agriculture

1. No one should miss George Carter's fascinating essay on pre-Columbian chickens *in* America, which argues that they came from Southeast Asia, *in* Carroll L. Riley, J. Charles Kelley, Campbell W. Pennington, and Robert L. Rands (eds.), *Man across the Sea*, University of Texas Press, Austin, 1971.
2. Carl O. Sauer, *Agricultural Origins and Dispersals*, American Geographical Society, New York, 1952.
3. I have been obliged to neglect Caribbean archaeology in this book. A brief summary appears in Irving Rouse, "The Intermediate Area," *in* Robert J. Braidwood and Gordon R. Willey (eds.), *Courses toward Urban Life*, Viking Fund Publications in Anthropology, no. 32, 1962. See also Gordon R. Willey, *An Introduction to American Archaeology*, vol. 1: *North and Middle America*, Prentice-Hall, Englewood Cliffs, N.J., 1967.
4. The archaeology of Tehuacán is described in a series of monographs: Richard S. MacNeish, *The Prehistory of the Tehuacán Valley*, University of Texas Press, Austin, 1967–.
5. Paul C. Mangelsdorf has written a long series of papers on the origins of maize. One of the best known is Paul C. Mangelsdorf, Richard C. MacNeish, and Walton C. Gallinat, "Domestication of Corn," *Science*, 1964, 143, pp. 538–545. See also MacNeish, *Prehistory of the Tehuacán Valley*, vol. 1.
6. Evidence summarized by Willey, *Introduction to American Archaeology*, vol. 1, chap. 3.
7. In writing this section, I have drawn heavily on *ibid.*, vol. 2: *South America*, Prentice-

Hall, Englewood Cliffs, N.J., 1971, chap. 3; also Edward Lanning, "Early Man in Peru," *Scientific American*, 1965, 213, pp. 68–76, and Thomas C. Patterson, "The Emergence of Food Production in Central Peru," *in* Stuart Struever (ed.), *Prehistoric Agriculture*, Natural History Press, Garden City, N.Y., 1971, pp. 181–207, and L. Kaplan, Thomas F. Lynch, and C. E. Smith, Jr., "Early Cultivated Beans *(Phaseolus vulgaris)* from an Intermontane Peruvian Valley," *Science*, 1973, 179, pp. 76–77.

8. The classic study of the archaeology of a coastal valley is that by Gordon Willey and others of Virú Valley; see Gordon R. Willey, "Prehistoric Settlement Patterns in the Virú Valley, Peru," Smithsonian Institution, Bureau of American Ethnology Bulletin no. 155, Washington, D.C., 1953.

9. For Chilca, see Frederic Engel, *Geografía humana prehistórica y agricultura precolumbina de la Quebrada de Chilca*, vol. 1: *Informe preliminar*, Universidad Agraria, Lima, 1966.

10. For Huaca Prieta, see Junius B. Bird, "Preceramic Cultures in Chicama and Virú," *in* W. C. Bennett (ed.), *A Reappraisal of Peruvian Archaeology*, Society for American Archaeology, Memoir no. 4, Madison, Wisconsin, 1948, pp. 21–28.

11. For Playa Culebras, see Frederic Engel, "Early Sites on the Peruvian Coast," *Southwestern Journal of Anthropology*, 1957, 13, pp. 54–68.

12. Kotosh is summarized in Willey, *Introduction to American Archaeology*, vol. 2, pp. 102–104.

13. The Cochise was documented as long ago as 1941; see Edwin B. Sayles and Ernst Antevs, *The Cochise Culture*, Medallion Papers no. 29, Gila Pueblo, Globe, Arizona, 1941. For subsequent literature, see Jesse D. Jennings, *Prehistory of North America*, McGraw-Hill, New York, 1968, pp. 151–152.

14. Herbert W. Dick, *Bat Cave*, School of American Research Monograph no. 27, Santa Fe, N.M., 1965.

15. Mogollon was first identified by Emil Haury, *The Mogollon Culture of Southwestern New Mexico*, Medallion Papers no. 20, Gila Pueblo, Globe, Arizona, 1936. The subsequent literature is summarized by Jennings, *Prehistory of North America*, pp. 251–258, which I have drawn on here.

16. The most famous Hohokam site is Snaketown; see Harold S. Gladwin, *Excavations at Snaketown*, Medallion Papers no. 25, Gila Pueblo, Globe, Arizona, 1937. See also Emil Haury, *The Stratigraphy and Archaeology of Ventana Cave, Arizona*, University of New Mexico and University of Arizona Presses, Albuquerque and Tucson, 1950. See Jennings, *Prehistory of North America*, p. 264, for further references.

17. Alfred V. Kidder's classic work is *An Introduction to the Study of Southwestern Archaeology*, Papers of the Southwestern Expedition no. 1, Yale University Press, New Haven, 1924.

18. Two important reports by Neil M. Judd describe the Pueblo Bonito site. See Neil M. Judd, *The Material Culture of Pueblo Bonito*, Smithsonian Miscellaneous Collections no. 124, 1954, and *The Architecture of Pueblo Bonito*, Smithsonian Miscellaneous Collections no. 147, 1964, vol. 1. For other references on the Anasazi, see Jennings, *Prehistory of North America*, pp. 264–280. On the general question of carrying capacities, try Ezra Zubrow, "Carrying Capacity and Dynamic Equilibrium in the Prehistoric Southwest," *American Antiquity*, 1971, 36, 2, pp. 127–138.

19. The Woodland tradition is described by Willey, *Introduction to American Archaeology*, vol. 1, chap. 5. See also Stuart Struever, "Woodland Subsistence-Settlement Systems in the Lower Illinois Valley," *in* Sally R. Binford and Lewis R. Binford (eds.), *New Perspectives in Archaeology*, Aldine, Chicago, 1968, pp. 285–312.

20. Adena is described by W. S. Webb and G. E. Snow, *The Adena People*, Reports in Anthropology and Archaeology, vol. 6, University of Kentucky, Lexington, 1945. A second report is W. S. Webb and R. S. Baby, *The Adena People, No. 2*, published for the Ohio Historical Society by the Ohio State University Press, 1957. For the Hopewell, see J. B. Griffin, *The Chronological Position of the Hopewellian Culture in the Eastern United States*, University of Michigan, Museum of Anthropology, Anthropological Papers no. 12, Ann Arbor, 1958.

21. The Mississippian is most ably described by Willey, *Introduction to American Archaeology*, vol. 1, pp. 292–310. Another important reference is Philip Phillips, James A. Ford, and James B. Griffin, *Archaeological Survey in the Lower Mississippi Alluvial Valley, 1940–47*, Peabody Museum Papers, 25, Harvard University, Cambridge, Mass., 1951.

22. Surprisingly little has been published to date on Cahokia. See W. K. Moorhead, *The

Cahokia Mounds, Bulletin, University of Illinois, Urbana, 1928, vol. 26, no. 4. Also see Melville L. Fowler (ed.), "Explorations into Cahokian Archaeology," *Illinois Archaeological Survey Bulletin,* no. 7, 1969.

23. See John R. Swanton's translation of Le Page du Pratz, *Histoire de la Louisiane,* Paris, 1758. Printed in Smithsonian Institution, *Bureau of American Ethnology Bulletin no. 43,* Washington, D.C., 1911, pp. 144–149. This important account has been reprinted in Jesse D. Jennings and E. Adamson Hoebel (eds.), *Readings in Anthropology,* 2nd ed., McGraw-Hill, New York, 1966.

17

civilization: the problem of causes

1. V. Gordon Childe, *The Prehistory of European Society,* Pelican Books, Harmondsworth, 1956, p. 78, and his *Man Makes Himself,* Watts, London, 1936.
2. In writing this essay, I owe a great deal to Colin Renfrew's *The Emergence of Civilization,* Methuen, London, 1972, chaps. 1–3.
3. Robert M. Adams, *The Evolution of Urban Society,* Aldine, Chicago, 1966, p. 119.
4. Karl A. Wittfogel, *Oriental Despotism: A Comparative Study of Total Power,* Yale University Press, New Haven, 1957. See also the contributions by Wittfogel and Julian Steward to Julian Steward and others (eds.), *Irrigation Civilizations: A Comparative Study,* Pan American Union, Washington, D.C., 1955.
5. Robert M. Adams, "Early Civilizations, Subsistence, and Environment," *in* Carl H. Kraeling and Robert M. Adams (eds.), *City Invincible,* Oriental Institute, University of Chicago, 1960, pp. 269–295.
6. Robert M. Adams, "Developmental Stages in Ancient Mesopotamia," *in* Steward and others, *Irrigation Civilizations.*
7. Clyde Kluckhohn, "The Moral Order in the Expanding Society," *in* Kraeling and Adams, *City Invincible.*
8. Colin Renfrew, *The Emergence of Civilization,* Methuen, London, 1972, chaps. 1–3, forms the background for this section. A massive and wide-ranging volume of essays on urban life is Peter J. Ucko, Ruth Tringham, and G. W. Dimbleby (eds.), *Man, Settlement and Urbanism,* Duckworth, London, 1972.
9. Henri Frankfort, *The Birth of Civilization in the Near East,* Doubleday, New York, 1951, p. 16.
10. Renfrew, *The Emergence of Civilization,* p. 73.
11. Kent V. Flannery, "Archaeological Systems Theory and Early Mesoamerica," *in* Betty J. Meggers (ed.), *Anthropological Archaeology in the Americas,* Anthropological Society of Washington, Washington D.C., 1968, pp. 67–87.

18

mesopotamia and the first cities

1. A tell is an Arabic word meaning "small hill." Their formation is described in Brian M. Fagan, *In the Beginning,* Little, Brown, Boston, 1972, pp. 122–123. See also Seton Lloyd, *Mounds of the Near East,* Edinburgh University Press, Edinburgh, and Aldine, Chicago, 1963.
2. An outline account of early Mesopotamian excavations is given in Glyn Daniel, *The First Civilizations,* Thames and Hudson, London, 1968, chap. 2. Austen Henry Layard has been the subject of an admirable biography: Gordon Waterfield, *Layard of Nineveh,* Murray, London, 1963.
3. The Halafian is described by James Mellaart, *The Earliest Civilizations of the Near East,* Thames and Hudson, London, and McGraw-Hill, New York, 1965, chap. 4.
4. For Ubaid culture, see Mellaart, *Earliest Civilizations,* chap. 5.
5. Our description of the delta and its economy is based on numerous sources. Excellent basic syntheses are given in ibid. and by Max E. L. Mallowan, *Early Mesopotamia and Iran,* Thames and Hudson, London, and McGraw-Hill, New York, 1965.

6. Ibid., chaps. 1–3.
7. For Warka, see E. Heinrich (ed.), *Vörlaufiger Bericht über Uruk-Warka,* vols. 1–14, Berlin, 1929–1959.
8. For copper in antiquity, see R. F. Tylecote, *Metallurgy in Archaeology,* Edward Arnold, London, 1962, chap. 2.
9. The Sumerian civilization is vividly described by Samuel N. Kramer, *The Sumerians,* University of Chicago Press, Chicago and London, 1963; Sir Leonard Woolley, *Ur Excavations,* vol. 2: *The Royal Cemetery,* Publications of the Joint Expedition of the British Museum and of the Museum of the University of Pennsylvania to Mesopotamia, British Museum, London, 1934, pp. 33–38, 41–44.
10. For a general discussion, see Karl W. Butzer, *Environment and Archeology, An Ecological Approach to Prehistory,* 2nd ed., Aldine-Atherton, Chicago, 1971; also Robert M. Adams, *The Evolution of Urban Society,* Aldine-Atherton, Chicago, 1966.

19

pharaohs, chiefs, and indus merchants

1. See Chapter 1; also Grafton Elliot Smith, *The Migrations of Early Culture,* Murray, London, 1915.
2. J. Desmond Clark, *The Prehistory of Africa,* Thames and Hudson, London, and Praeger, New York, 1970, chap. 6.
3. Cyril Aldred, *The Egyptians,* Thames and Hudson, London, and Praeger, New York, 1961, chap. 4.
4. Henri Frankfort, *The Birth of Civilization in the Near East,* Williams and Norgate, London, 1951, chap. 4 and Appendix.
5. David Diringer, *Writing,* Thames and Hudson, London and Praeger, New York, 1962, pp. 46–53, contains an admirable summary of hieroglyphics. See also Michael Pope's *Decipherment,* Thames and Hudson, London, 1973. The word "hieroglyphic" is a partial transliteration of three Greek words: *hierós,* "holy"; *glypheîn,* "to carve"; and *grámmata,* "letters" — which together mean "sacred carved letters."
6. The arguments are summarized by Frankfort, *Birth of Civilization,* and by Glyn Daniel, *The First Civilizations,* Thames and Hudson, London, chap. 4.
7. Aldred, *Egyptians,* pp. 74–75.
8. Ibid., chaps. 9 and 10, summarizes Ancient Egyptian life very clearly.
9. The archives of Thebes are a massive source of information on Egyptian workmen. Try also George Steindorff and Keith C. Seele, *When Egypt Ruled the East,* 2nd ed., University of Chicago Press, Chicago and London, 1957.
10. The tomb of Tutankhamun is of course the most famous archaeological discovery of all time. See Howard Carter et al., *The Tomb of Tut-ankh-Amun,* Macmillan, London, 1923, 1927, 1933.
11. For the later history of the Nile Valley, see Roland Oliver and John D. Fage, *A Short History of Africa,* Pelican Books, Harmondsworth, 1962.
12. Peter Shinnie, *Meroe,* Thames and Hudson, London, and Praeger, New York, 1967.
13. The kingdom of Axum is described by Oliver and Fage, *Short History of Africa,* pp. 50–52.
14. Donald Harden, *The Phoenicians,* Thames and Hudson, London, and Praeger, New York, 1962.
15. A vivid account of the Saharan trade in the nineteenth century has been written by E. W. Bovill, *The Golden Trade of the Moors,* Oxford University Press, London, 1958. Many of its descriptive details are perhaps applicable to earlier trade.
16. Oliver and Fage, *Short History of Africa,* chap. 6.
17. For early ironworking in Africa, see Clark, *Prehistory of Africa,* pp. 214–223.
18. A comprehensive discussion of Bantu origins is given in Roland Oliver and Brian M. Fagan, "The Emergence of Bantu Africa," *in* John D. Fage (ed.), *The Cambridge History of Africa,* vol. 2, Cambridge University Press, Cambridge, 1974, chap. 2, in press.
19. See David W. Phillipson, "Early Iron-Using Peoples of Southern Africa," *in* Leonard

Thompson (ed.), *African Societies in Southern Africa*, Heinemann, London, 1969, pp. 24–49.

20. An attractive, illustrated account of African history is Basil Davidson, *Africa: History of a Continent*, Weidenfeld & Nicholson, London, 1966.

21. On Ghana, see Nehemia Levtzion, *Ancient Ghana and Mali*, Methuen, London, 1973.

22. The kingdom of Mali is covered not only by Levtzion, ibid., but also by Charles Monteil, "Les Empires du Mali: Etude d'histoire et de sociologie soudanais," *Bulletin de Commission d'Etudes Historiques et Scientifiques*, A.O.F., Paris, 1929, pp. 291–447.

23. John D. Hunwick, "Songhay, Bornu and Hausaland in the sixteenth century," *in* Jacob F. A. Ajayi and Michael Crowder (eds.), *History of West Africa*, vol. 1, Longmans, 1971, pp. 120–157.

24. The most widely available account of the Karanga kingdom is in Brian M. Fagan, *Southern Africa during the Iron Age*, Thames and Hudson, London, and Praeger, New York, 1965, chaps. 8 and 9.

25. Peter L. Garlake, "Rhodesian Ruins — a Preliminary Assessment of Their Styles and Chronology," *Journal of African History*, 1970, 9, 4, pp. 495–514, is an admirable summary of the site. See also the same author's *Great Zimbabwe*, Thames and Hudson, London, 1973.

26. A basic sourcebook is James Duffy, *Portuguese Africa*, Harvard University Press, Cambridge, and Oxford University Press; London, 1951. This volume is a little out of date — consult a specialist.

27. The writings of the explorers make fascinating reading. An admirable biography offers a starting point: Fawn Brodie, *The Devil Drives: A Life of Sir Richard Burton*, Eyre and Spottiswoode, London, 1957.

28. For discussion, see Sir Mortimer Wheeler, *Early India and Pakistan*, rev. ed., Thames and Hudson, London, and Praeger, New York, 1968, and references in note 29 below. For a recent collection of essays, see Norman Hammond (ed.), *South Asian Archaeology*, Noyes Press, Park Ridge, N.J., 1973.

29. The Indus civilization is described in ibid., chap. 5; Sir Mortimer Wheeler, *The Indus Civilization*, 3rd ed., Cambridge University Press, Cambridge, 1968; D. H. Gordon, *The Prehistoric Background of Indian Culture*, Bhulabhai Memorial Institute, Bombay, 1958; and Walter A. Fairservis, *The Roots of Ancient India: The Archaeology of Early Indian Civilization*, Macmillan, New York, 1971.

30. Robert L. Raikes, *Water, Weather, and Prehistory*, John Baker, London, 1967. For a lively account, see George F. Dales, "The Decline of the Harappans," *Scientific American*, May 1966. A more technical account is Robert L. Raikes, "The End of the Ancient Cities of the Indus," *American Anthropologist*, 1964, 66, 2, pp. 284–299.

20

european society in transition

1. V. Gordon Childe, *The Dawn of European Civilization*, Routledge & Kegan Paul, London, 1925. The impact of the new chronologies is discussed by Colin Renfrew, "New Configurations in Old World Archaeology," *World Archaeology*, 1970, 2, 2, pp. 199–211.

2. Seton Lloyd, *Early Highland Peoples of Anatolia*, Thames and Hudson, London, and McGraw-Hill, New York, 1967.

3. Described and illustrated in ibid., pp. 54–55.

4. On the Hittites, see O. R. Gurney, *The Hittites*, Pelican Books, Harmondsworth, 1961. An account of the geography of the Hittite empire is J. Garstang and O. R. Gurney, *The Geography of the Hittite Empire*, British Institute of Archaeology at Ankara, Occasional Paper no. 5, London, 1959.

5. A description of King Alcinous's palace in the Odyssey. One of the best translations is by E. V. Rieu, Homer, *The Odyssey*, Penguin Books, Harmondsworth, 1945. Quotation from p. 114.

6. For Heinrich Schliemann, see Glyn Daniel, *A Hundred Years of Archaeology*, Duckworth, London, 1950, pp. 136–141.

7. Sir Arthur Evans's life has been vividly told by his half-sister, Joan Evans, *Time and Chance*, Longmans, London, 1943.

8. For the earliest settlement of Knossos, see John Evans, "Neolithic Knossos: The Growth of a Settlement," *Proceedings of the Prehistoric Society*, 1972, 37, 2, pp. 81–117.

9. Sinclair Hood's, *The Minoans*, Thames and Hudson, London, and Praeger, New York, 1971, is an up-to-date, brief account of the Minoans. The same author's *Home of the Heroes: The Aegean before the Greeks*, Thames and Hudson, London, and McGraw-Hill, New York, 1967, is also invaluable.

10. Colin Renfrew, *The Emergence of Civilization*, Methuen, London, 1972, is a fundamental source on Aegean prehistory and contains the full arguments for this point of view.

11. Arthur J. Evans, *The Palace of Minos at Knossos*, vols. 1–4, is the classical account.

12. One of the best descriptions of Knossos was written by J. D. S. Pendlebury, *The Archaeology of Crete*, Faber and Faber, London, 1939 (reprinted, 1963).

13. Mary Renault, *The King Must Die*, Random House, New York, 1963, is her most famous book.

14. The archaeology of Thera: a vivid reconstruction of the eruption appears in Spyridon Marinatos, "Have Excavations on the Island of Thera Solved the Riddle of the Minoans?" *National Geographic*, May 1972.

15. Stuart Piggott's *Ancient Europe*, Edinburgh University Press, Edinburgh, and Aldine, Chicago, 1965, chap. 3, contains a useful description of the amber trade. I have used this reference extensively throughout this chapter. For the Mycenaeans see Lord William Taylour, *The Mycenaeans*, Thames and Hudson, London, and Praeger, New York, 1964; also L. R. Palmer, *Mycenaeans and Minoans*, 2nd ed., Faber and Faber, London, 1965.

16. David Diringer, *Writing*, Thames and Hudson, London, and Praeger, New York, 1962, pp. 54–63, and John Chadwick, *The Decipherment of Linear B*, Cambridge University Press, Cambridge, 1958.

17. Colin Renfrew, "The Autonomy of the South-East European Copper Age," *Proceedings of the Prehistoric Society*, 1969, 35, pp. 12–47; see also Ruth Tringham, *Hunters, Fishers and Farmers of Eastern Europe*, Hutchinson University Library, London, 1971, chap. 4.

18. The Wessex culture is described in a rather outdated account by John F. S. Stone, *Wessex*, Thames and Hudson, London, and Praeger, New York, 1958. Stonehenge has been the subject of much literature, eccentric and otherwise. Two basic accounts are Richard J. C. Atkinson, *Stonehenge*, Pelican Books, Harmondsworth, 1960, and George Hawkins, *Stonehenge Decoded*, Souvenir Press, New York, 1965. No one should miss Stuart Piggott's, *The Druids*, Thames and Hudson, London, and Praeger, New York, 1968.

19. J. G. D. Clark, *Prehistoric Europe: The Economic Basis*, Methuen, London, 1952, chap. 7.

20. Christopher F. C. Hawkes, *The Prehistoric Foundations of Europe to the Mycenaean Age*, Methuen, London, 1940.

21. Hugh Hencken, *Tarquinia and the Etruscans*, Thames and Hudson, London, and Praeger, New York, 1971.

22. Ralph Rowlett, "The Iron Age North of the Alps," *Science*, 1967, 161, pp. 123–134.

23. P. Jacobsthal, *Early Celtic Art*, Oxford University Press, Oxford, 1944, is still the classic work on La Tène art.

24. Herodotus, *The Histories*, bk. 4, chap. 65.

25. Sergei I. Rudenko, *Frozen Tombs of Siberia: The Pazyryk Burials of Iron Age Horsemen*, trans. M. W. Thompson, University of California Press, Berkeley, 1970. This is also a basic reference on Scythian art. See also M. I. Artamonov, "Frozen Tombs of the Scythians," *Scientific American*, May 1965.

26. Two fundamental books on Ancient Greece are: M. I. Kinley, *The Ancient Greeks*, Chatto and Windus, London, 1963, and H. D. F. Kitto, *The Greeks*, Pelican Books, Harmondsworth, 1955.

27. Thucydides, *History of the Peloponnesian War*. A good translation is that by Sir R. Livingstone, Oxford University Press, Oxford, 1943.

28. Donald Harden, *The Phoenicians*, Thames and Hudson, London, and Praeger, New York, 1962.

29. Diringer, *Writing*.
30. Piggott, *Ancient Europe*, p. 192.
31. The Etruscans are described by R. Bloch, *The Origins of Rome*, Thames and Hudson, London, and Praeger, New York, 1960. See also Alain Hus, *The Etruscans*, Evergreen, New York, 1961.
32. Apart from Bloch, *Origins of Rome*, try Michael Grant, *The Romans*, Weidenfeld & Nicholson, London, 1960. The best Roman source is Titus Livy (59 B.C.–A.D. 17), *Early History of Rome*, bks. 1–4, trans. Aubrey de Selincourt, Penguin Books, Harmondsworth, 1966.
33. B. H. Warnington, *Carthage*, Hale, London, 1960.
34. For early Christianity and the Roman Empire, see A. H. M. Jones, *Constantine and the Conversion of Europe*, Hodder, London, 1968.
35. On Islam, see Francesco Gabrieli, *Muhammed and the Conquests of Islam*, Weidenfeld & Nicholson, London, 1968.
36. A beautiful account of Christopher Columbus, his voyages, and his times is Björn Landström, *Columbus*, Allen & Unwin, London, 1967.

21

the cities of asia

1. Quoted from Kwang-chih Chang, *The Archaeology of Ancient China*, Yale University Press, New Haven, 1968, 2nd ed., p. 192. I have drawn heavily on this admirable synthesis while writing this chapter.
2. The theories are discussed by Glyn Daniel, *The First Civilizations*, Thames and Hudson, London, 1968, pp. 131–134.
3. Chang, *Archaeology of Ancient China*, chap. 4.
4. Lung-shan cultures are described in detail in Chang, ibid., pp. 150–160. C14 date quoted by Richard Pearson, "Radiocarbon Dates from China," *Antiquity*, 1973, 47, 186, pp. 141–143.
5. Scapulimancy has long been a feature of Chinese culture. Animal shoulder blades (scapulae) were used to predict the future and tell omens. A heated metal point was applied to one side of a shoulder blade. The heat produced cracks on the other side of the bone. The shapes of these cracks formed a pattern that determined the answers to the question posed to the priests. See ibid., pp. 135–137 and 153–167.
6. Chinese writing is well described by David Diringer, *Writing*, Thames and Hudson, London, and Praeger, New York, 1962, chap. 3.
7. Noel Barnard, *Bronze Casting and Bronze Alloys in Ancient China*, Australian National University and Monumenta Serica, Tokyo, 1901, p. 108.
8. For a summary of different theories, see Chang, *Archaeology of Ancient China*, pp. 238–239.
9. Here I have adopted the framework and chronology given by Kwang-chih Chang; see ibid., pp. 228–240.
10. Quoted from Paul Wheatley, "Archaeology and the Chinese City," *World Archaeology*, 1970, 2, 2, pp. 159–185. I have drawn on this paper extensively here. No one seriously interested in the archaeology of Chinese cities should miss the same author's monumental volume, *A Pivot of the Four Quarters: A Preliminary Inquiry into the Origins and Character of the Ancient Chinese City*, Edinburgh University Press, Edinburgh, and Aldine, Chicago, 1971.
11. Described both by Wheatley, "Archaeology," and Chang, *Archaeology of Ancient China*, pp. 209–218.
12. The Shang royal graves are described by Chang, *Archaeology of Ancient China*, pp. 218–226. See also Chêng Tê-k'un, *Archaeology in China*, vol. 2: *Shang China*, Heffers, Cambridge, 1960.
13. Chang, *Archaeology of Ancient China*, p. 241. Another fundamental reference is Li Chi, *The Beginnings of Chinese Civilization*, Washington University Press, Seattle, 1957.
14. For details, see Chang, *Archaeology of Ancient China*, chaps. 7–9.

22
maya, aztec, and inca:
early civilizations in the new world

1. Anyone interested in the Spanish conquest of Mexico should begin with Hernando Cortes, *Five Letters of Cortes to the Emperor, 1519–26,* trans. J. Bayard Morris, rev. ed., Norton, New York, 1962. For pre-Columbian contacts, an authoritative and up-to-date summary of the issues is Carol L. Riley, J. Charles Kelley, Campbell W. Pennington, and Robert L. Rands (eds.), *Man across the Sea,* University of Texas Press, Austin, 1971. For a review of recent literature, see Glyn Daniel, "The Second American," *Antiquity,* 1972, 46, 184, pp. 288–292.
2. Muriel Porter Weaver, *The Aztecs, Maya, and Their Predecessors,* Seminar Press, New York, 1972, is one basic source for this chapter. She includes some discussion of environmental topics. Another source is William T. Sanders and Barbara J. Price, *Mesoamerica: The Evolution of a Civilization,* Random House, New York, 1968.
3. I have used the chronology and terminology employed by Gordon R. Willey, *An Introduction to American Archaeology,* vol. 1: *North and Middle America,* Prentice-Hall, Englewood Cliffs, N.J., 1966, chap. 3. This volume is a basic source on Mesoamerican archaeology.
4. Tehuacán is well described in the monographs on the valley: R. E. MacNeish and others, *The Prehistory of the Tehuacán Valley,* University of Texas, Austin, 1967–.
5. Willey, *Introduction to American Archaeology,* vol. 1, p. 98.
6. Ignacio Bernal, *The Olmec World,* University of California Press, Berkeley, 1969, and Michael D. Coe, *The Jaguar's Children,* Museum of Primitive Art, New York, 1965. Elizabeth Benson's edited volume, *Dumbarton Oaks Conference on the Olmec,* Dumbarton Oaks Research Library and Collection, Washington, D.C., 1968, includes important contributions to the subject. Michael D. Coe's *America's First Civilization: Discovering the Olmec,* American Heritage, New York, 1968, is a good starting point on the Olmec.
7. On La Venta, see Phillip Drucker, *La Venta, Tabasco: A Study of Olmec Ceramics and Art,* Smithsonian Institution, Bureau of American Ethnology Bulletin no. 170, Washington, D.C., 1959.
8. The "Long Count" is summarized by Willey, *Introduction,* vol. 1, pp. 135–138.
9. On Teotihuacán, Michael Coe's, *Mexico* (Thames and Hudson, London, and Praeger, New York, 1962) has a good description and many basic references. For the latest work at the site, see René Millon, "Teotihuacán: Completion of Map of Giant Ancient City in the Valley of Mexico," *Science,* 1970, 164, pp. 1077–1082. René Millon and others have described the Pyramid of the Sun in "The Pyramid of the Sun at Teotihuacán: 1959 Investigations," *Transactions of the American Philosophical Society,* 1965, 55, no. 6.
10. See Millon and others, "The Pyramid of the Sun." A fascinating account of trade at Teotihuacán has been written by Lee Parsons and Barbara Price, "Mesoamerican Trade and Its Role in the Emergence of Civilization," *Contributions of the University of California Archaeological Research Facility,* Berkeley, 1971, pp. 169–195.
11. M. D. Coe, *The Maya,* Thames and Hudson, London, and Praeger, New York, 1966, is a fundamental reference for this civilization. See also J. E. S. Thompson, *The Rise and Fall of Maya Civilization,* University of Oklahoma Press, Norman, 1966. See also William L. Rathje, "The Origin and Development of Lowland Classic Maya Civilization," *American Antiquity,* 1971, 36, 3, pp. 275–285.
12. Mayan script was described by J. E. S. Thompson, *Maya Hieroglyphic Writing: Introduction,* Carnegie Institution of Washington, Washington, D.C., and University of Oklahoma Press, Norman, 1950.
13. Willey, *Introduction to American Archaeology,* vol. 1, p. 136.
14. The collapse of the Maya has been discussed, among others, by Gordon R. Willey and Dimitri Shimkin, "The Collapse of Classic Maya Civilization in the Southern

Lowlands: A Symposium Summary Statement," *Southwestern Journal of Anthropology*, 1971, 27, 1, pp. 1–18. On the rise and fall of states, see Robert Carneiro, "A Theory of the Origin of the State," *Science*, 1970, 169, 2947, pp. 733–738.

15. On Toltecs and Tula, see Beatrice P. Dutton, "Tula of the Toltecs," *El Palacio*, 1955, 62, 7–8, pp. 195–251; also Eric Wolfe, *Sons of the Shaking Earth*, University of Chicago Press, Chicago, 1959.

16. The Aztecs are well described by Bernard Diaz del Castillo, *The True History of the Conquest of New Spain*, trans. A. P. Maudslay, Hakluyt Society, London, 1908–1916. For archaeology, see Willey, *Introduction to American Archaeology*, vol. 1, pp. 156–161; for social and economic structure, see Friedrich Kats, *Situación social y Económica de los Aztecas durante los siglos XV y XVI*, Universidad Nacional Antónoma de México, Mexico City, 1966.

17. Tenochtitlán is best visited in company with Hernando Cortés himself; see note 1. Also see Edward Calnek, "Settlement Patterns and Chinampa Agriculture at Tenochtitlán," *American Antiquity*, 1972, 37, 1, pp. 104–115.

18. The archaeology of Peru has been ably summarized by G. H. S. Bushnell, *Peru*, rev. ed., Thames and Hudson, London, and Praeger, New York, 1963. In writing this account, I have drawn both on this reference and on Willey, *Introduction to American Archaeology*, vol. 2: *South America*, Prentice-Hall, Englewood Cliffs, N.J., 1971. Throughout this part of the chapter, I have adopted Willey's terminology and dating. The reader can identify dating controversies by consulting the notes to Willey's chap. 3. See also J. J. Rowe and Dorothy Menzel (eds.), *Peruvian Archaeology: Selected Readings*, Peek, Palo Alto, 1967.

19. A good analysis and description of the Chavín art style is John H. Rowe, *Chavín Art: An Inquiry into Its Form and Meaning*, Museum of Primitive Art, New York, 1962. In the interests of clarity I have omitted discussion of the Paracas culture of southern Peru (Willey, *Introduction to American Archaeology*, vol. 1, pp. 127 ff.).

20. For Gallinazo, see Gordon R. Willey, *Prehistoric Settlement Patterns in the Virú Valley, Peru*, Smithsonian Institution, Bureau of American Ethnology Bulletin no. 155, Washington, D.C., 1953.

21. Mochica is described by G. H. S. Bushnell, *Peru*, Thames and Hudson, London, and Praeger, New York, rev. ed., 1963. See also Rafael Larco Hoyle, "A Culture Sequence for the North Coast of Peru," in Julian H. Steward (ed.), *Handbook of South American Indians*, Smithsonian Institution, Bureau of American Ethnology Bulletin no. 143, Washington, D.C., 1946, vol. 2, pp. 149–175.

22. Summarized briefly by Willey, *Introduction*, vol. 2, pp. 142–148.

23. For Huari, see John H. Rowe, Donald Collier, and Gordon R. Willey, "Reconnaissance Notes on the Site of Huari, near Ayacucho, Peru," *American Antiquity*, 1950, 16, 2, pp. 120–137. A highly complex study of the Huari problem is Dorothy Menzel, "Style and Time in the Middle Horizon," *Nawpa Pacha*, 1964, 2, pp. 1–106.

24. The Tiahuanaco site is described by E. P. Lanning, *Peru before the Incas*, Prentice-Hall, Englewood Cliffs., N.J., 1967, chap. 9. He also describes Huari.

25. Lanning, *Peru before the Incas*, chap. 10. A recent, vivid, popular account: Michael E. Moseley and Carol Mackey, "Chan Chan, Peru's Ancient City of Kings," *National Geographic*, March 1973, pp. 319–345.

26. Garcilaso de la Vega (el Inca), *The First Part of the Royal Commentaries of the Incas*, trans. Clements R. Markham, Hakluyt Society, London, 1869–1871.

27. Chincha and Ica are discussed in Dorothy Menzel, "The Pottery of Chincha," *Nawpa Pacha*, 1966, 4, pp. 63–76.

28. The classic source on the Inca empire is W. H. Prescott, *History of the Conquest of Peru*, Everyman's Library, no. 301, London and New York, 1908. For archaeology, see John H. Rowe, "An Introduction to the Archaeology of Cuzco," *Peabody Museum Papers*, Harvard University, Cambridge, 1944, vol. 27, no. 2. The same author's *Inca Culture at the Time of the Spanish Conquest*, Smithsonian Institution, Bureau of American Ethnology Bulletin no. 143, Washington D.C., 1946, vol. 2, pp. 183–331, is a key source, while the literature is summarized by Gordon R. Willey, *Introduction to American Archaeology*, vol. 2, pp. 175–183.

23
epilogue

1. J. H. Plumb, *The Death of the Past*, Macmillan, London, 1969.
2. Richard A. Watson and Patty Jo Watson, *Man and Nature*, Harcourt, Brace and World, New York, 1969.
3. A thoughtful and provocative essay discusses Atomic Man in ibid., chap. 10.

glossary

The terms are divided into cultural and settlement units. Insofar as possible, the definitions below have been followed for this book. Archaeological terminology holds perils for both layman and expert, and interested readers should consult a specialist for further information.

cultural units

The following terms are used in both New World and Old World archaeology.
artifact: any object altered or manufactured by man.
industry: all the artifacts of one kind found at a site.
assemblage: all the industries found together at one site.
culture: "an archaeological culture is an assemblage of artifacts that recurs repeatedly associated together in dwellings of the same kind and with burials of the same rite. The arbitrary peculiarities of all cultural traits are assumed to be concrete associations of the common social traditions that bind together a culture. Artifacts hang together in assemblages, not only because they were used in the same age, but also because they were used by the same people, made or executed in accordance with techniques, rites or styles prescribed by a social tradition, handed on by precept and example and modifiable in the same way."[1] *Note: this term is most commonly used in this way in Old World archaeology, but can occur in the New.*
culture trait: an item, element, or feature in an archaeological (or anthropological) culture.
The following terms are more frequently used in the New World:
horizon: "a primarily spatial community represented by cultural traits and assemblages whose nature and mode of occurrence permit the assumption of a broad and rapid spread."[2]

---

[1] V. Gordon Childe, "Neolithic House Types in Temperate Europe," *Proceedings of the Prehistoric Society,* 1949, 15, pp. 49–60.
[2] Gordon R. Willey and Philip Phillips, *Method and Theory in American Archaeology,* University of Chicago Press, Chicago, 1958, p. 33.

phase: "an archaeological unit possessing traits sufficiently characteristic to distinguish it from all other units similarly conceived, whether of the same or other cultures or civilizations, spatially limited to the order of magnitude of a locality or region and chronologically limited to a relatively brief period of time."[3]

tradition: in archaeological terms: "a primarily temporal continuity represented by persistent configurations in simple technologies or other systems of related forms."[4]

settlement units

We have arbitrarily adopted the following definitions proposed by Edward Lanning and John Rowe, two experts on Peruvian archaeology, and subsequently modified by Gordon R. Willey.[5]

a camp: a dwelling spot of a temporary or semipermanent nature, presumably only occupied seasonally. Its population is estimated at less than 100 people. Often an independent settlement, it could also be a satellite of a larger community.

a village: a permanent living site housing between 100 and 1,000 people, which is either self-contained or a satellite of a larger political or economic unit, such as a city or a ceremonial center.

a town: a medium-sized permanent settlement, housing between 1,000 and 5,000 persons, which is either self-sufficient or could fulfill a larger function as a governmental or a religious center supported by, but holding sway over, small satellite communities.

a city: a large, permanent, concentrated settlement of more than 5,000 people. Cities show a magnification of the function of some towns.

a ceremonial center: the site of ritualized functions of religion, government, military power, and probably trade. This site may occur unaccompanied by densely settled populations. The term relates to the phenomenon of such a center, rather than to its precise location either in, or away from, a city or town.

    The population limits associated with each settlement type are, of course, quite arbitrary, but they should help in visualizing the size of different settlements favored by prehistoric man.

[3] Ibid., p. 22.
[4] Ibid., p. 37.
[5] John H. Rowe, "Urban Settlements in Ancient Peru," *Nawpa Pacha* 1, 1, pp. 1–27, Institute of Andean Studies, Berkeley, 1963; Edward P. Lanning, *Peru before the Incas*, Prentice-Hall, Englewood Cliffs, N.J., 1967; and Gordon R. Willey, *An Introduction to American Archaeology*, vol. 2: *South America*, Prentice-Hall, Englewood Cliffs, N.J., 1971.

index